PRACTICE FOR THE ARMED FORCES TEST

★ **NEW REVISED EDITION** ★

PRACTICE FOR THE ARMED FORCES TEST

E.P. STEINBERG, M.A.

FOREWORD BY HARRY D. WILFONG, Ph.D.

Technical Advisor, Testing Directorate,
Department of Defense,
U.S. Military Enlistment Processing Command

ARCO PUBLISHING, INC.
NEW YORK

Eleventh Edition, Third Printing, 1982

Published by Arco Publishing, Inc.
219 Park Avenue South, New York, N.Y. 10003

Library of Congress Cataloging in Publication Data

Steinberg, Eve P.
  Practice for the Armed Forces test.

  Revision of: Practice for the Armed Forces test / D. R.
Turner.
  1. United States—Armed Forces—Examinations.
I. Turner, David Reuben, 1915–   . Practice for the
Armed Forces test.   II. Title.
U408.5.S74   1981   153.9′4355   88-10799
ISBN 0-668-05303-8 (Paper Edition)   AACR2
ISBN 0-668-05558-8 (Library Edition)

Printed in the United States of America

CONTENTS

FOREWORD: HOW THE ARMED SERVICES VOCATIONAL APTITUDE BATTERY CAN HELP YOU

The types of jobs required to run, operate and maintain the sophisticated weapons system and technology of today's military are quite different from those required during World War II. In fact, almost eighty percent of all military occupations have their counterparts in the civilian business and industrial community. For example, the combination of jobs required to run and operate a modern-day aircraft carrier is the same combination of jobs necessary to operate a medium sized U.S. city—electrician, plumber-steamfitter, chef, firefighter, forklift operator, electronic equipment repair technician, clerk, personnel specialist, accountant, computer operator, communications specialist—plus a variety of highly technical jobs that you will not find in your average American city but which you will find in highly specialized industries.

It is precisely these types of jobs that the Department of Labor projects will be in great demand between now and 1990. Even though you may not be considering the military as a career, you owe it to yourself to at least become acquainted with the range of skills required by jobs in the skilled trades, vocational and technical career areas. After all, that is where most of our jobs exist. As the nation's largest employer of young men and women, the military is also the nation's largest trainer of young men and women for the important and available careers of the future.

Enlistees in the military will be assigned to training programs in those areas for which they are best suited. These areas are identified by ASVAB. The years spent in the military are years of service to one's country, years to accumulate money, years to gain maturity, and years in which to learn skills that can be applied in the civilian working world.

Of course, the military services hope that enlistees will recognize the challenge and advancement opportunities in the armed services and that they will stay on and make the military their careers. With our all-volunteer military, this is the ideal. However, the enlistee is under no obligation to remain in the service once the original commitment has been fulfilled. The valuable training gained in the service is a bonus that you take with you when you go out into the modern industrialized civilian world.

ASVAB is the first step. ASVAB provides you with one means of exploring your own interests and your own acquired skills in mechanical, electronic, shop, automotive and other trade technical areas. ASVAB results can point out to you the best direction in which to head your talents, can identify the best training path and career for you. Take advantage of the advice and assistance it has to offer.

Harry D. Wilfong, Ph.D.
Technical Advisor
Testing Directorate
United States Military
Enlistment Processing Command

HOW TO USE THIS BOOK

You will get the most benefit from this book if you use it with respect. By this we mean treat it seriously, follow instructions, observe time limits and do not cheat. We also mean that you should read every chapter and answer every question.

Find yourself a quiet spot with good light and a clear work space. Eliminate as many distractions as possible. Set aside specified periods of at least an hour at a time for your test preparation. If possible, try to set aside a couple of three-hour periods so that you can try working straight through one or two exams, just as you will on exam day.

Start at the beginning of the book. Read through each chapter carefully so that you can appreciate what you are studying, how to use the book and how to take the exam. Refer back to these chapters as needed. Be sure to reread the chapter on test-taking shortly before exam day.

Begin your active preparation by taking the first model exam. Sharpen two or three number 2 pencils with erasers and bring them to your work area along with a few pieces of scratch paper. If you have a portable kitchen timer, bring it to your work area, too. If you have no timer, put a clock or watch in an easily visible spot. Tear out the answer sheet. Then read the directions for part one and answer the practice questions. Carefully read the explained answers. Be sure that you understand the directions before you turn the page to the first question and set the timer. Use the full time allowed for each part. If you finish working before the time is up, check over your work. If time runs out before you have finished, stop and mark the place where time ran out. Later on you will want to go back and answer the remaining questions just for the practice. When the time allowed for a part is up, turn the page to the directions, practice questions and explained answers for the next part. When you are sure that you understand what to do, turn the page, set the timer and answer the questions for that part. Continue in this way through the model exam.

When you have completed all ten parts, check your answers against the correct answers which follow the exam. Look back at the questions to see where and why you went wrong. Fill out the score sheet so that you can compare your performance on the various parts of the exam.

Proceed through the entire book. Study the chapters that teach you how to answer the questions. Give extra time to those chapters dealing with the types of questions on which you showed weakness.

Work with a dictionary. Look up *every* unfamiliar word in this book. If you run across a word you do not know while doing the exams, circle the word and look it up later. Look up words you find in the reading passages, new words from among answer choices, words you find in the explanations, words you meet in the study chapters. You are far more likely to remember a word which you have looked up for yourself than a word you have attempted to memorize from a list. If you can understand every word used in this book, you have a broad-based vocabulary and are fully prepared for the verbal requirements of the exam.

Try another model exam. After checking your answers, return to the study chapters that deal with the areas in which you still need help.

Even if you feel that you have improved to the maximum of your ability, even if you are certain that you are ready, complete the book and read all the chapters. Any additional practice will add to your confidence and improve your scores.

ALL ABOUT THE EXAM

WHAT IS ASVAB?

ASVAB is the Armed Services Vocational Aptitude Battery. ASVAB is the exam given to all prospective members of the army, navy, air force, marine corps, army and air reserves, and army national guard.

The ASVAB is a series of ten parts or tests, each yielding a separate score. One combination of scores on the ASVAB serves as the AFQT or Armed Forces Qualifying Test. This is the score that determines whether or not a candidate will be accepted in a particular branch of the armed services. The AFQT score is derived from a composite of a candidate's scores on the Word Knowledge, Arithmetic Reasoning, Paragraph Comprehension and Numerical Operations sections of ASVAB. The passing AFQT score varies from service to service and according to previous education. The passing AFQT is lowest for a high school graduate entering the army and highest for a non high school graduate entering the air force. Candidates with a GED diploma must score much higher for acceptance into the army or the air force than candidates with a regular high school diploma. The reserves, navy and marine corps treat all high school diplomas equally. On the other hand, a woman high school graduate who wishes to be a marine must earn an AFQT score more than twice as high as that of her male counterparts.

Besides the AFQT, a number of other composite scores are derived from the ASVAB. These composite scores serve to identify the areas in which you show greatest aptitude. In other words, the composite scores are used to predict your success in various training programs and vocational areas. If you score above a certain grade on the appropriate combination of tests, you may be guaranteed admission to the training school of the specialty to which that combination applies.

For the **ARMY**, the crucial scores for the various training areas are as follows:

Combat—Arithmetic Reasoning, Coding Speed, Automotive/Shop, Mechanical Comprehension

Field Artillery—Arithmetic Reasoning, Coding Speed, Mathematics Knowledge, Mechanical Comprehension

Electronics Repair—General Science, Arithmetic Reasoning, Mathematics Knowledge, Electronics Information

Operators and Food Handlers—Numerical Operations, Automotive/Shop, Mechanical Comprehension and Verbal (combined Word Knowledge and Paragraph Comprehension)

5

Surveillance/Communications—Numerical Operations, Coding Speed, Automotive/Shop, Verbal

Mechanical Maintenance—Numerical Operations, Automotive/Shop, Mechanical Comprehension, Electronics Information

General Maintenance—General Science, Automotive/Shop, Mathematics Knowledge, Electronics Information

Clerical—Numerical Operations, Coding Speed, Verbal

Skilled Technical—General Science, Mathematics Knowledge, Mechanical Comprehension, Verbal

General Technical—Arithmetic Reasoning, Verbal

For the **MARINE CORPS** the crucial scores are:

General Technical—Arithmetic Reasoning and Verbal

General Maintenance—General Science, Automotive/Shop, Mathematics Knowledge, Electronics Information

Electronics Repair—General Science, Automotive/Shop, Mathematics Knowledge, Electronics Information

Clerical—Numerical Operations, Coding Speed, Verbal

Mechanical Maintenance—Arithmetic Reasoning, Automotive/Shop, Mechanical Comprehension, Electronics Information

Combat—Numerical Operations, Automotive/Shop, Verbal

Field Artillery—Arithmetic Reasoning, Automotive/Shop, Verbal

For the **AIR FORCE** the crucial scores are:

Mechanical—General Science, 2 × Automotive/Shop, Mechanical Comprehension (Automotive/Shop is so important that it counts twice in calculating your score.)

Administrative—Numerical Operations, Coding Speed, Verbal

General—Arithmetic Reasoning, Verbal

Electronics—General Science, Arithmetic Reasoning, Mathematics Knowledge, Electronics Information

The **NAVY, RESERVES,** and **NATIONAL GUARD** have similar requirements. Obviously, if you have your eye on a specific training school, you will want to prepare yourself very thoroughly so that you can earn a high composite score in the field of your choice.

WHO TAKES ASVAB?

Everyone who wishes to serve in the armed forces of the United States takes ASVAB. The AFQT serves as a screening test. It eliminates those who are not qualified to serve. The combined test scores help the services to assign high school graduates and non-graduates to the training schools for which they are best suited. College graduates who wish to apply for officer's candidate training must then submit to further testing. There may be additional testing for various specialties, but ASVAB is the first step for everyone.

ASVAB 5 is unlike the regular ASVAB described up to now in that ASVAB 5 may be taken by persons who are unsure as to whether or not they wish to join the armed services or even by persons who are sure they do not want to enlist. ASVAB 5 is given only in high schools to high school students. It is a very worthwhile tool in the hands of the high school counselor. In the same way that ASVAB guides the armed services in placement of recruits, ASVAB 5 guides the school counselor as he or she advises students about their further training and career goals. If a high school student who has taken ASVAB 5 decides to join the armed forces, the student or graduate need not retake ASVAB. Where there are differences between the two exams, the forms are comparable and scores can be converted to yield all the same composites. On the other hand, the student who has taken ASVAB 5 is not stuck with the scores earned. Any recruit may take the ASVAB at enlistment.

WHEN AND WHERE IT IS GIVEN

Shortly after you have indicated your sincere intent to join the armed forces, your recruiter will show you a few sample ASVAB questions. On the basis of how you handle these few questions, your recruiter will either discourage you from attempting to enlist in the particular service or will tell you where and when to report for testing. The exam is not given by recruiters at recruiting offices. There are established examination centers at convenient locations throughout the country at which trained administrators administer the exam almost every day.

FORMAT OF THE EXAMINATION

The ASVAB is divided into ten parts or tests. Each part has its own instructions. Each part is timed and scored separately. Along with the instructions for each part, there are a few practice questions. At the examination, you will be given a chance to answer the practice questions before you take the timed test. The test administrator will go over the answers to the practice questions with you to make certain you understand exactly what to do. You may ask questions during the instructional period.

The ASVAB is a multiple-choice examination. For each question you are offered four answer choices. (Part 6, Coding Speed, has five answer choices.) Only one answer choice is absolutely correct. You must choose what you think is the BEST answer and mark the letter of that answer on your separate answer sheet.

Your ASVAB score is based upon the number of questions you answer correctly. There is no penalty for wrong answers. A wrong answer simply is not a right answer, so you get no credit for it. Since wrong answers do not count against you, there is no harm in guessing. With the exception of the two highly speeded parts (Numerical Operations and Coding Speed) you should try to answer every question. The model exams in this book will give you the experience you need so that you can pace yourself to answer all questions.

The chart that follows describes the ASVAB. At this time there are three different forms of the ASVAB in use. Each form has the same ten parts in the same order. Each form has the same number of questions in each test and is timed the same. All the questions are of equal difficulty; only the actual questions are different. The use of different forms helps to discourage cheating. Your friend may have questions that are different from yours, but his exam is otherwise equal to yours in every way.

Part	Number of Questions	Working Time in Minutes
1. General Science	25	11
2. Arithmetic Reasoning	30	36
3. Word Knowledge	35	11
4. Paragraph Comprehension	15	13
5. Numerical Operations	50	3
6. Coding Speed	84	7
7. Auto & Shop Information	25	11
8. Mathematics Knowledge	25	24
9. Mechanical Comprehension	25	19
10. Electronics Information	20	9

NATURE OF THE QUESTIONS

The questions on the following pages are typical of those which you may expect on this exam. Each part begins with directions very much like those on the actual exam. The answer to each question is explained so that you may understand the kind of thinking that is involved in finding the answer.

PART 1

GENERAL SCIENCE

The general science part of your examination asks questions based upon the science you learned in high school. For each question there are four possible answers. Only one answer is correct. Choose the answer which you think is correct and mark the corresponding space on your answer sheet. Try these questions.

1. Of the following, the process which will result in water that is the most nearly chemically pure is

   1-A aeration
   1-B distillation
   1-C chlorination
   1-D filtration

   1. Ⓐ Ⓑ Ⓒ Ⓓ

1-B DISTILLATION is the correct answer. Aeration (A) adds air to the water, but does nothing to purify it. Chlorination (B) may make water safe to drink, but it does so by adding chemicals, not by purifying the water. Filtration (D) removes solid matter from water, but does not make it chemically pure. Distilled water is made by evaporating water and collecting the water vapor. The vapor is then allowed to cool so that it becomes liquid again. Since the chemicals in water do not evaporate, they remain in the original container and the "new" water is chemically pure.

2. Of the following, the one which is *not* characteristic of poison ivy is that it has

   2-A milky juice
   2-B three leaflet clusters
   2-C shiny leaves
   2-D white berries

   2. Ⓐ Ⓑ Ⓒ Ⓓ

3-A MILKY JUICE is the correct answer. Poison ivy has shiny leaves (C) in three leaflet clusters (B) and may have white berries (D). If you see such a plant, do *not* try to break a stem to check for milky juice. Poison ivy does not have milky juice, but if you handle poison ivy you are likely to get a painful rash.

3. At one time milk was called "the perfect food" because it contained so many nutrients vital to growth and health. Milk is no longer called "the perfect food" because

   3-A the formula has changed
   3-B pasteurization destroys its value
   3-C calcium has been determined to be harmful
   3-D it lacks iron

   3. Ⓐ Ⓑ Ⓒ Ⓓ

3-D IT LACKS IRON is the correct answer. Infants do not require iron, so milk is still a "perfect food" for them. Children and adults must have iron in their diets to insure against anemia and to maintain their strength and health. Cows have not changed the formula by which they make milk (A); pasteurization (B) destroys bacteria, not food value; calcium (C) is vital to the formation and strength of bones and teeth.

4. Of the following, the physical property *least* frequently used in determining the nature of an unknown chemical is

   4-A taste
   4-B odor
   4-C solubility
   4-D state

   4. Ⓐ Ⓑ Ⓒ Ⓓ

4-A TASTE is the correct answer. An unknown substance might well be poisonous, hence it is dangerous to routinely use a taste test. Odor (B), solubility (C) and state (solid, liquid, gaseous) (D) are all less hazardous measures for use in the chemical laboratory.

PART 2

ARITHMETIC REASONING

The arithmetic reasoning questions require careful thinking as well as arithmetic calculation. Some problems require more than one step for their solutions. You must decide exactly what the question asks; then you must determine the best method for finding the answer; finally, you must work out the problem on your scratch paper. Be sure to mark the letter of the correct answer on your answer sheet. Try these questions.

1. Six girls sold the following number of boxes of cookies: 42, 35, 28, 30, 24, 27. What was the average number of boxes sold by each girl?

1-A 26
1-B 29
1-C 30
1-D 31

1. Ⓐ Ⓑ Ⓒ Ⓓ

1-D To find the average, add all the numbers and divide the sum by the number of terms. 42 + 35 + 28 + 30 + 24 + 27 = 186 ÷ 6 = 31

2. The cost of sending a telegram is 52 cents for the first ten words and $2\frac{1}{2}$ cents for each additional word. The cost of sending a 14-word telegram is

2-A 62 cents
2-B 63 cents
2-C 69 cents
2-D 87 cents

2. Ⓐ Ⓑ Ⓒ Ⓓ

2-A 14 words = 10 words + 4 words
10 words cost 52 cents
4 words @ 2.5 cents = 4 × 2.5 = 10 cents
52 cents + 10 cents = 62 cents

3. A stock clerk has on hand the following items:

500 pads worth four cents each
130 pencils worth three cents each
50 dozen rubber bands worth two cents per dozen

If, from this stock, he issues 125 pads, 45 pencils, and 48 rubber bands, the value of the remaining stock would be

3-A $6.43
3-B $8.95
3-C $17.63
3-D $18.47

3. Ⓐ Ⓑ Ⓒ Ⓓ

3-D 500 − 125 = 375 pads @ $.04 = $15.00
130 − 45 = 85 pencils @ $.03 = $ 2.55
50 dozen − 4 dozen = 46 dozen rubber bands @ $.02 = $.92
$15 + $2.55 + $.92 = $18.47

4. As an employee at a clothing store, you are entitled to a 10% discount on all purchases. When the store has a sale, employees are also entitled to the 20% discount offered to all customers. What would you have to pay for a $60 jacket bought on a sale day?

4-A $6
4-B $10.80
4-C $36
4-D $43.20

4. Ⓐ Ⓑ Ⓒ Ⓓ

4-D $60 × .10 = $6 (employee discount)
$60 − $6 = $54
$54 × .20 = $10.80 (sale discount)
$54 − $10.80 = $43.20

5. How many square yards of linoleum are needed to cover a floor having an area of 270 square feet?

5-A   24
5-B   28
5-C   30
5-D   33

5. Ⓐ Ⓑ Ⓒ Ⓓ

5-C 9 square feet = 1 square yard
270 sq. ft. ÷ 9 = 30 sq. yds.

6. If a pie is divided into 40 parts, what percent is one part of the whole pie?

6-A   .4
6-B   2.5
6-C   4.0
6-D   25

6. Ⓐ Ⓑ Ⓒ Ⓓ

6-B The whole pie is 100%. Each part is $\frac{1}{40}$
100 ÷ 40 = 2.5%

PART 3

WORD KNOWLEDGE

The questions in this part test how well you understand the meanings of words. Each question has an underlined word. Read all four possible answers and decide which one has a meaning closest to the meaning of the underlined word. On your answer sheet mark the letter of the answer you choose. Try these questions.

1. Speak most nearly means

  1-A tell
  1-B talk
  1-C explain
  1-D question

  1. Ⓐ Ⓑ Ⓒ Ⓓ

1-B TALK is the correct answer. When one *speaks* or *talks* one may *tell* (A), *explain* (C) or *question* (D). Since both *speak* and *talk* include all the other choices, they are most nearly alike in meaning.

2. They discovered the missing boxes in the morning.

  2-A sought
  2-B opened
  2-C found
  2-D noticed

  2. Ⓐ Ⓑ Ⓒ Ⓓ

2-C FOUND is the best answer. *Noticed* (D) could be a correct answer, but, since the boxes were missing, a search is suggested and *found* is the best meaning for *discovered*. (A) *sought* and (B) *opened* are wrong.

3. Entirely most nearly means

  3-A almost
  3-B largely
  3-C publicly
  3-D completely

3. Ⓐ Ⓑ Ⓒ Ⓓ

3-D COMPLETELY is the correct answer. *Almost* (A) and *largely* (B) are incorrect because they both mean *less than entirely*. *Publicly* (C) is totally unrelated in meaning.

4. Penalty most nearly means

  4-A foul
  4-B mistake
  4-C punishment
  4-D fine

  4. Ⓐ Ⓑ Ⓒ Ⓓ

4-C PUNISHMENT is the correct answer. A *penalty* may be imposed upon someone who commits a *foul* (A) in a sports contest or upon someone who makes a *mistake* (B). A *fine* (D) is only one kind of *penalty*.

5. The retiring teacher had taught for thirty-two years.

  5-A starting over
  5-B leaving
  5-C shy
  5-D promoted

  5. Ⓐ Ⓑ Ⓒ Ⓓ

5-B LEAVING is the best answer. *Retiring* can also mean *shy* (C), but in this sentence it makes more sense to conclude that after thirty-two years of teaching the teacher is ready to *leave*. (A) *starting over* and (D) *promoted* are not meanings of *retiring*.

PART 4

PARAGRAPH COMPREHENSION

The paragraph comprehension part of your test battery requires concentration and attention to detail. First you must read and understand the paragraph. Then you must read and understand each of the answer choices, noticing the differences of meaning or emphasis that are imparted by little words. There is one question based upon each paragraph. You must answer that question on the basis of what is stated or implied in the passage, even if you know a better answer and even if you know the information in the paragraph to be false. In some cases more than one answer might be correct, but you must choose the BEST answer and mark its letter on your answer sheet. Try these questions.

1. There has been a slump in first-aid training in the industries, and yet one should not fall into the error of thinking there is less interest in first aid in industry. The falling off has been in the number of new employees needing such training. It appears that in industries interested in first-aid training there is now actually a higher percentage so trained than there ever was before.

The paragraph implies that first-aid training is

1-A a means of avoiding the more serious effects of accidents
1-B being abandoned because of expense
1-C of great importance to employees
1-D sometimes given new workers in industry

1. Ⓐ Ⓑ Ⓒ Ⓓ

1-D Since the paragraph discusses the fact that fewer new employees require first-aid training, obviously some of them do. Presumably this training is given to those needing it. The passage does not discuss the usefulness of this training.

2. Taxes are deducted each pay period from the amount of salaries or wages, including payments for overtime and night differential, paid to employees of the postal service in excess of the withholding exemptions allowed under the Internal Revenue Act. The amount of tax to be withheld from each payment of wages to any employee, except fourth-class postmasters, will be determined from the current official table of pay and withholding exemptions published by the Post Office Department.

The salaries of most postal employees

2-A are paid in amounts depending upon the exemptions fixed by the Department
2-B do not include overtime or night differential payments
2-C are determined by provisions of the Internal Revenue Act
2-D are subject to tax deductions

2. Ⓐ Ⓑ Ⓒ Ⓓ

2-D The paragraph states that the Post Office complies with IRS regulations in withholding taxes from salaries and wages. The IRS determines the tax, not the salaries, as suggested in choice C.

3. In a lightning-like military advance, similar to that used by the Germans, the use of persistent chemicals is unnecessary. It might even be a considerable detriment to a force advancing over a broad front.

The paragraph best supports the statement that

3-A chemicals should not be used by a defending army

3-B the Germans advanced in a narrow area

3-C an advancing army may harm itself through the use of chemicals

3-D chemical warfare is only effective if used by an advancing army

3. Ⓐ Ⓑ Ⓒ Ⓓ

3-C In stating that the use of chemicals might be a detriment to an advancing force, the paragraph means that an advancing army might cause harm to itself with its own chemicals.

4. Of the 300 cars owned in 1895, only four were manufactured in this country. Of the 100 million registered in 1973, most were manufactured in America.

Cars registered in this country in 1973

4-A were far in excess of those manufactured abroad in 1895

4-B were manufactured in the United States

4-C increased considerably over the preceding decade

4-D were largely of domestic construction

4. Ⓐ Ⓑ Ⓒ Ⓓ

4-D The main point of the paragraph is that by 1973 most cars in the U.S. were American-made cars. While choice A is also true, it misses the meaning of the paragraph. Choice B implies that *all* the cars were made in America, while the passage states that *most* cars were. Choice C is irrelevant.

PART 5

NUMERICAL OPERATIONS

The numerical operations part of your test battery consists of fifty very simple arithmetic questions which must be answered in only three minutes. Obviously, speed is a very important factor. You should not attempt to compute these answers using pencil and scratch paper. Instead, solve each problem in your head, then choose the correct answer from among the four choices and mark the letter of the correct answer on your answer sheet. If you are not sure of an answer, guess and go on to the next question. Do not skip any questions. You will most certainly not have time to go back to fill in. Since a wrong answer will not count against you, it cannot hurt to guess. Many people cannot complete all fifty questions in the three minutes allowed. Do not be upset if you cannot finish. Just answer as many questions as you can. Try these questions.

1. $4 + 6 =$

   1-A 8
   1-B 2
   1-C 10
   1-D 12

   1. Ⓐ Ⓑ Ⓒ Ⓓ

1-C $4 + 6 = 10$

2. $12 \div 2 =$

   2-A 4
   2-B 6
   2-C 8
   2-D 10

   2. Ⓐ Ⓑ Ⓒ Ⓓ

2-B $12 \div 2 = 6$

3. $6 + 6 =$

   3-A 0
   3-B 1
   3-C 12
   3-D 36

   3. Ⓐ Ⓑ Ⓒ Ⓓ

3-C $6 + 6 = 12$

4. $8 - 5 =$

   4-A 3
   4-B 13
   4-C 17
   4-D 4

   4. Ⓐ Ⓑ Ⓒ Ⓓ

4-A $8 - 5 = 3$

5. $1 + 1 =$

   5-A 0
   5-B 11
   5-C 1
   5-D 2

   5. Ⓐ Ⓑ Ⓒ Ⓓ

5-D $1 + 1 = 2$

6. $4 \times 3 =$

   6-A 9
   6-B 18
   6-C 12
   6-D 7

   6. Ⓐ Ⓑ Ⓒ Ⓓ

6-C $4 \times 3 = 12$

7. $6 \times 3 =$

   7-A 9
   7-B 21
   7-C 18
   7-D 24

  7. Ⓐ Ⓑ Ⓒ Ⓓ

7-C $6 \times 3 = 18$

8. $9 \div 3 =$

   8-A 6
   8-B 3
   8-C 13
   8-D 15

  8. Ⓐ Ⓑ Ⓒ Ⓓ

8-B $9 \div 3 = 3$

9. $30 \div 6 =$

   9-A 4
   9-B 5
   9-C 6
   9-D 12

  9. Ⓐ Ⓑ Ⓒ Ⓓ

9-B $30 \div 6 = 5$

10. $9 - 8 =$

   10-A 7
   10-B 1
   10-C 17
   10-D 5

  10 Ⓐ Ⓑ Ⓒ Ⓓ

10-B $9 - 8 = 1$

PART 6

CODING SPEED

The coding part of your exam is different from all other parts of the exam. Nothing that you have learned enters into your answering of these questions. Coding is a test of your memory, your eye-hand coordination and your working speed.

Before each set of questions you will find a "key." The key consists of ten words listed in alphabetical order. Each word has a four-digit code number assigned to it.

In the set of questions you will find the same ten words, scrambled and sometimes repeated. Following each word in the test are *five* answer choices in columns labelled "A" to "E." Each answer choice is a four-digit number. The answer choices are in ascending order; that is, the lowest number is always in column A, the next higher number is in column B, and so on to the highest number in column E. You must look at the word, find the correct code number among the choices and mark on your answer sheet the letter of the column in which you found the correct code number.

On the actual examination you must work very quickly. You have only seven minutes in which to try to answer eighty-four questions. Use the sample questions that follow to develop a system that works for you—memorization, some sort of word-number association, a mathematical formula or any private method that helps you work up speed and accuracy. Many people cannot finish this part in the time allowed. Do not be upset if you cannot finish. Just do your best. Try these questions.

Key

band 2241	dog 1715	nail 4462
branch 5016	gravy 3230	orange 7096
castle 8317	hot 2046	wife 9812
	mare 6735	

Answers

		A	B	C	D	E	
1.	castle	2046	4462	6735	8317	9812	1. Ⓐ Ⓑ Ⓒ Ⓓ Ⓔ
2.	hot	2046	2241	5016	6735	8317	2. Ⓐ Ⓑ Ⓒ Ⓓ Ⓔ
3.	mare	1715	3230	6735	7096	9812	3. Ⓐ Ⓑ Ⓒ Ⓓ Ⓔ
4.	gravy	2241	3230	4462	6735	8317	4. Ⓐ Ⓑ Ⓒ Ⓓ Ⓔ
5.	orange	1715	5016	6735	7096	9812	5. Ⓐ Ⓑ Ⓒ Ⓓ Ⓔ
6.	branch	2241	4462	5016	6735	7096	6. Ⓐ Ⓑ Ⓒ Ⓓ Ⓔ
7.	wife	3230	5016	7096	8317	9812	7. Ⓐ Ⓑ Ⓒ Ⓓ Ⓔ
8.	band	2241	4462	5016	6735	8317	8. Ⓐ Ⓑ Ⓒ Ⓓ Ⓔ
9.	dog	1715	2046	2241	5016	7096	9. Ⓐ Ⓑ Ⓒ Ⓓ Ⓔ
10.	nail	2046	4462	6735	8317	9812	10. Ⓐ Ⓑ Ⓒ Ⓓ Ⓔ
11.	orange	3230	5016	6735	7096	8317	11. Ⓐ Ⓑ Ⓒ Ⓓ Ⓔ
12.	branch	2046	2241	3230	4462	5016	12. Ⓐ Ⓑ Ⓒ Ⓓ Ⓔ

The correct answers are:

1-D	4-B	7-E	10-B
2-A	5-D	8-A	11-D
3-C	6-C	9-A	12-E

Key

bug 8076	grass 7601	star 2790
cow 6306	pencil 5015	uncle 9876
exit 4273	post 1119	water 4799
	rope 3838	

Answers

	A	B	C	D	E	
13. pencil	2790	3838	4273	5015	7601	13. Ⓐ Ⓑ Ⓒ Ⓓ Ⓔ
14. cow	4273	6306	7601	8076	9876	14. Ⓐ Ⓑ Ⓒ Ⓓ Ⓔ
15. exit	1119	2790	4273	5015	6306	15. Ⓐ Ⓑ Ⓒ Ⓓ Ⓔ
16. uncle	4273	4799	7601	8076	9876	16. Ⓐ Ⓑ Ⓒ Ⓓ Ⓔ
17. rope	3838	4273	5015	7601	8076	17. Ⓐ Ⓑ Ⓒ Ⓓ Ⓔ
18. bug	1119	2790	3838	8076	9876	18. Ⓐ Ⓑ Ⓒ Ⓓ Ⓔ
19. grass	2790	4273	6306	7601	8076	19. Ⓐ Ⓑ Ⓒ Ⓓ Ⓔ
20. post	1119	3838	5015	7601	9876	20. Ⓐ Ⓑ Ⓒ Ⓓ Ⓔ
21. water	2790	4273	4799	5015	6306	21. Ⓐ Ⓑ Ⓒ Ⓓ Ⓔ
22. cow	4273	4799	5015	6306	8076	22. Ⓐ Ⓑ Ⓒ Ⓓ Ⓔ
23. star	2790	3838	4799	6306	7601	23. Ⓐ Ⓑ Ⓒ Ⓓ Ⓔ
24. grass	4273	4799	7601	8076	9876	24. Ⓐ Ⓑ Ⓒ Ⓓ Ⓔ

The correct answers are:

13-D	16-E	19-D	22-D
14-B	17-A	20-A	23-A
15-C	18-D	21-C	24-C

PART 7

AUTO & SHOP INFORMATION

The auto and shop information questions test your knowledge and understanding of automobiles and of tools and shop practices. The answers to many questions come straight from your life experience. However, if this is not your area of interest, there will be questions to which you do not know the answer. Make the most sensible guess. Answer all questions. Mark the letter of your choice on your answer sheet. Try these questions.

1. A green puddle under the front end of a car means that the car is losing

    1-A power steering fluid
    1-B antifreeze
    1-C transmission fluid
    1-D crankcase oil

1. Ⓐ Ⓑ Ⓒ Ⓓ

1-B ANTIFREEZE is green. Power steering fluid (A) and transmission fluid (C) are pink. Crankcase oil (D) is brown.

2. Shock absorbers are part of the

    2-A engine
    2-B upholstery
    2-C suspension
    2-D exhaust system

2. Ⓐ Ⓑ Ⓒ Ⓓ

2-C Shock absorbers are the heavy duty springs in the SUSPENSION. The rear shock absorbers are very near the exhaust system (D), but they are not part of that system. While springs in the upholstery (B) may indeed absorb shocks, they are not called *shock absorbers*.

3.

STEEL POCKET RULE
1 2 3 4 5 6

It would be most appropriate to use the tool above to

    3-A measure a living room for carpeting
    3-B pry open a tight can of paint
    3-C measure the distance between exposed terminals on a live switchboard
    3-D draw straight lines on a poster

3. Ⓐ Ⓑ Ⓒ Ⓓ

3-D The short straight edge would be fine for drawing straight lines on cardboard or paper. The measurements of a room (A), if taken with a six inch rule, would be highly inaccurate. A pocket rule is not sturdy enough to pry open a paint can (B) and the ruler would be damaged besides. Using a steel ruler when working with electricity (C) is very dangerous.

4. Wood screws properly used as compared to nails properly used

    4-A are easier to install
    4-B generally hold better
    4-C are easier to drive flush with surface
    4-D are more likely to split the wood

4. Ⓐ Ⓑ Ⓒ Ⓓ

4-B Wood screws are usually *more* difficult to install than are nails, but they are often preferable because they generally HOLD BETTER and are *less* likely to split the wood.

5. Worn universal joints make themselves known by

    5-A a "clunk" when the car is first started and put into driving gear
    5-B steam rising from the hood of the car
    5-C difficulty in starting the engine in cold weather
    5-D sticking doors

5. Ⓐ Ⓑ Ⓒ Ⓓ

5-A The "clunk" of the universals is a very distinctive noise. Steam rising from the hood (B)

most likely is caused by a broken water hose. The universals have nothing to do with the engine (C) and sticking doors (D) may need to have their hinges oiled.

6. Thermopane is made of two sheets of glass separated by

    6-A a sheet of celluloid
    6-B wire mesh

6-C an air space
6-D mica

6. Ⓐ Ⓑ Ⓒ Ⓓ

6-C Thermopane is clear, unobstructed glass with an insulating layer of air between the two sheets. While it is more expensive than regular glass, thermopane's insulating ability makes it an energy saver.

PART 8

MATHEMATICS KNOWLEDGE

To solve the problems in this part, you must draw upon your knowledge of high school mathematics. The problems require you to use simple algebra and geometry along with arithmetic skills and reasoning power. Some questions can be answered in your head. Others will require the use of scratch paper. If you use scratch paper for your calculations, be sure to mark the letter of the correct answer on your answer sheet. Try these questions.

1. A square measures 8 inches on one side. By how much will the area be increased if its length is increased by 4 inches and its width decreased by 2 inches?

   1-A 14 sq. in.
   1-B 12 sq. in.
   1-C 10 sq. in.
   1-D 8 sq. in.

1. Ⓐ Ⓑ Ⓒ Ⓓ

1-D Area = length × width
    Area of square = 8 × 8 = 64 sq. in.
    Area of rectangle = (8 + 4) (8 − 2) =
    12 × 6 = 72 sq. in.
    72 − 64 = 8 sq. in.

2. $100 - x = 5^2$ What is the value of x?

   2-A 75
   2-B 25
   2-C 5
   2-D 50

2. Ⓐ Ⓑ Ⓒ Ⓓ

2-A To square a number multiply it by itself.
     $100 - x = 5^2$
     $100 - x = 5 \times 5$
     $100 - x = 25$
     $100 - 25 = x$
          $x = 75$

3. 42 divided by .06 =

   3-A 7
   3-B 70
   3-C 700
   3-D .7

3. Ⓐ Ⓑ Ⓒ Ⓓ

3-C To divide by a decimal, convert the divisor to a whole number by moving the decimal point to the right. Move the decimal point of the dividend the same number of spaces to the right. Place the decimal point of the quotient directly above the new location of the decimal point of the dividend.

$$.06\overline{)42.00} = 700.$$

4. Aluminum bronze consists of copper and aluminum, usually in the ratio of 10:1 by weight. If an object made of this alloy weighs 77 pounds, how many pounds of aluminum does it contain?

   4-A 7.7
   4-B 7.0
   4-C 70.0
   4-D 10

4. Ⓐ Ⓑ Ⓒ Ⓓ

4-B Copper and aluminum in the ratio of 10:1 means 10 parts copper to 1 part aluminum.

    Let x = weight of aluminum
  Then 10 x = weight of copper
    $10x + x = 77$
        $11x = 77$
         $x = 7$

5. After spending two-thirds of her money, a girl has $1.50 left. The amount she had at first was

   5-A $1.00
   5-B $3.00

5-C $3.50

5-D $4.50

5. Ⓐ Ⓑ Ⓒ Ⓓ

5-D Let x = amount of money the girl started with

$$x - \frac{2}{3}x = \frac{1}{3}x$$

$$\frac{1}{3}x = \$1.50$$

$$x = \$1.50 \times 3$$

$$x = \$4.50$$

6.

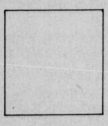

The length of each side of the square shown is $\frac{2x}{3} + 1$. The perimeter of the square is

6-A $\dfrac{8x + 4}{3}$

6-B $\dfrac{2x}{3} + 4$

6-C $\dfrac{8x + 12}{3}$

6-D $\dfrac{2x}{3} + 16$

6. Ⓐ Ⓑ Ⓒ Ⓓ

6-C Since the perimeter of a square is four times the length of a side, it is

$$4\left(\frac{2x}{3} + 1\right), \text{ or } \frac{8x + 12}{3}$$

PART 9

MECHANICAL COMPREHENSION

Part 9 consists of questions about your understanding of general mechanical and physical principles. Your understanding of these principles will come from your own observations, from experience in working with mechanical devices and from your reading and school courses. Answer all the questions as best you can, marking the letter of your choice on your answer sheet. Try these questions.

1.

The figure above represents an enclosed water chamber, partially filled with water. The number 1 indicates air in the chamber and 2 indicates a pipe by which water enters the chamber. If the water pressure in the pipe, 2, increases then the

1-A water pressure in the chamber will be decreased
1-B water level in the chamber will fall
1-C air in the chamber will be compressed
1-D air in the chamber will expand

1. Ⓐ Ⓑ Ⓒ Ⓓ

1-C If water pressure in the pipe is increased, more water will flow into the water chamber. Since the chamber is enclosed, the air will be unable to escape. As more water enters the chamber, the existing air must be compressed into a smaller space.

2.

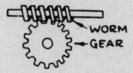

The figure here shows a worm and a gear. If the worm rotates slowly on its shaft, the gear will

2-A not turn
2-B turn very slowly
2-C turn rapidly
2-D oscillate

2. Ⓐ Ⓑ Ⓒ Ⓓ

2-B Since the teeth of the gear are meshed with the worm, the movement of one demands the movement of the other. If the worm were to rotate very rapidly, the gear would spin rapidly. Since the worm is rotating slowly, the gear will turn slowly.

3.

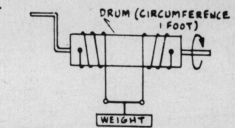

One complete revolution of the windlass drum shown above will move the weight up

3-A ½ foot
3-B 1½ feet
3-C 1 foot
3-D 2 feet

3. Ⓐ Ⓑ Ⓒ Ⓓ

3-C Since the circumference of the drum is one foot, one complete revolution of the drum will take

23

up one foot of each rope. As each of the separate ropes supporting the weight is shortened by one foot, the weight will move up one foot.

4.

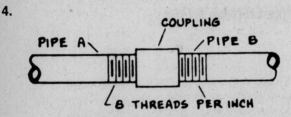

PIPE A

COUPLING

PIPE B

8 THREADS PER INCH

If pipe A is held in a vise and pipe B is turned ten revolutions with a wrench, the overall length of the pipes and coupling will decrease

4-A $\frac{5}{8}$ inch
4-B $2\frac{1}{2}$ inches
4-C $1\frac{1}{4}$ inches
4-D $3\frac{3}{4}$ inches

4. Ⓐ Ⓑ Ⓒ Ⓓ

4-C The overall length of pipes and coupling could decrease or increase, depending upon the direction in which pipe B is turned. However, as stated in this question, pipe B is turned so as to disappear into the coupling. Since there are 8 threads to the inch, eight complete revolutions of the pipe would shorten the pipes and coupling by one inch. An additional two turns, for a total of ten, would shorten the pipes and coupling by an additional two-eighths or one-fourth of an inch.

PART 10

ELECTRONICS INFORMATION

The questions in this part test your knowledge and understanding of electricity, radio and electronics. To answer some of the questions all you need is common sense. Other questions can be answered on the basis of experience, courses and reading. Answer all the questions. Mark the letter of your answer on the answer sheet. Try these questions.

1. The fuse of a certain circuit has blown and is replaced with a fuse of the same rating which also blows when the switch is closed. In this case

1-A a fuse of higher current rating should be used

1-B a fuse of higher voltage rating should be used

1-C the fuse should be temporarily replaced by a heavy piece of wire

1-D the circuit should be checked

1. Ⓐ Ⓑ Ⓒ Ⓓ

1-D The purpose of a fuse is to protect a circuit from overheating through overloading or through the action of a malfunctioning appliance on that circuit. When a fuse burns out, the first test is to try a fresh fuse. It is always possible that the first fuse simply burned out from old age. If the second fuse blows immediately, assuming the fuses were of current rating for that circuit, a heavier, higher rated fuse should NEVER be substituted, nor should the circuit be closed with wire or a penny. The blowing of the fuse is a warning of trouble on the circuit. The circuit must be carefully checked for overload, appliances in poor condition and frayed wires.

2. A copper wire with twice the diameter of another copper wire has a current carrying capacity

2-A four times as great

2-B twice as great

2-C half as great

2-D three times as great

2. Ⓐ Ⓑ Ⓒ Ⓓ

2-A A copper wire with twice the diameter of another copper wire is four times as heavy and therefore can carry four times as much current. You can prove this to yourself by substituting some simple figures in the formula for the area of a circle, $A = \pi r^2$.

If the diameter of a wire is 6cm., then its radius is 3cm.

$$\pi \times 3^2 = 3.14 \times 9 = 28.26 \text{ sq. cm.}$$

If the diameter of wire is 12cm, then its radius is 6cm.

$$\pi \times 6^2 = 3.14 \times 36 = 113.04 \text{ sq. cm.,}$$ which is four times 28.26 sq. cm.

3. A completely short circuited heater resistance will be

3-A hotter than normal

3-B cooler than normal

3-C inoperative

3-D white hot

3. Ⓐ Ⓑ Ⓒ Ⓓ

3-C A complete short circuit means no circuit at all. If there is no circuit then the heater resistance will be inoperative.

4. A megawatt is

4-A ten watts

4-B one hundred watts

4-C one thousand watts

4-D one million watts

4. Ⓐ Ⓑ Ⓒ Ⓓ

4-D *Mega*, from the Greek, means a million or multiplied by a million.

5. The inert gas present in an incandescent lamp is primarily intended to

   5-A increase the luminous output
   5-B decrease filament evaporation
   5-C activate the surface of the filament
   5-D reduce the hazards when the glass is shattered

   5. Ⓐ Ⓑ Ⓒ Ⓓ

5-B Early light bulbs burned out very quickly because the air inside the bulb promoted evaporation of the filament. The inert gas which is now pumped into light bulbs does not promote evaporation of the filament, and it displaces the air which would otherwise be in the bulb. The gas serves no other purpose.

6. One disadvantage of porcelain as an insulator is that it is

   6-A only good for low voltage
   6-B not satisfactory on a.c. circuits
   6-C a brittle material
   6-D difficult to clean

   6. Ⓐ Ⓑ Ⓒ Ⓓ

6-C Porcelain is an excellent insulator at all voltages and on all types of circuits, but it is extremely breakable, so its use must be limited.

TEST-TAKING TECHNIQUES

Your last minute preparations for any exam are based strictly on common sense. They include getting a good night's sleep and leaving home early enough so that you do not need to rush or worry. It is a good idea to wear a watch to your exam so that you can keep track of your own time and pace yourself. There are no other materials you need bring to the exam. Pencils and scratch paper will be issued to you.

Once all examinees are seated in the examination room, the test administrator will hand out forms and will give instructions for filling them out. Listen carefully and follow all instructions. Ask questions if necessary. The administrator will tell you of the procedure that will be followed when the exam begins. He or she will tell you how to recognize the *start* and *stop* signals, what to do if all your pencils break or if a page seems to be missing from your test booklet. The instructions should be step-by-step and should be very clear, but if you are uncertain about anything, do not hesitate to ask. No one keeps a record of who asks questions, even questions that seem to be foolish.

Before each part of the exam, there is a page of directions and practice questions. You will get a chance to read the page and answer the questions before timing begins on that part. The test administrator will go over the practice questions with the group and will explain the correct answers. This is your chance to ask questions. You must understand what you are to do before timing begins on a part. You cannot ask questions once testing is under way. Each part of your exam will be timed separately. You will have a chance to read instructions, answer practice questions and discuss both instructions and answers to the practice questions before actually taking each part.

When you do begin each part of the exam, we urge you to READ every word of every question. Be alert for exclusionary words that might affect your answer—words like "not," "most," "all," "every," "except."

READ all four choices before you mark your answer. It is statistically true that most errors are made when the correct answer is (D). Too many people mark the first answer that seems correct, without reading through all the choices to find out which answer is *best*.

The following list consists of important suggestions for taking this exam. Read the suggestions now before you attempt the model exams in this book. Read them again right before you take the exam. You will find them all useful.

1. Mark your answers by completely blackening the answer space of your choice.
2. Mark only ONE answer for each question, even if you think that more than

one answer is correct. You must choose only one. If you mark more than one answer, the scoring machine will consider you wrong.

3. If you change your mind, erase completely. Leave no doubt as to which answer you mean.

4. If you use scratch paper, be certain to mark the answer on the answer sheet.

5. Check often to be sure that the question number matches the answer space, that you have not skipped a space by mistake.

6. Try to answer every question. If you are unsure of an answer you mark, put a check next to the question in the question booklet. Then, if you have time, you can quickly spot those questions to which you would like to give some extra thought.

7. Guess if you must. If you do not know the answer to a question, eliminate the answers that you know are wrong and guess from among those remaining. If you have no idea whatsoever of the answer to a question, guess anyway. There is no penalty for a wrong answer, so even a wild guess gives you a 25% chance to be right. If you leave the space blank, you have no chance at all to be correct.

8. If you notice that time is about to run out and you have not completed all the questions, mark all the remaining questions with the same answer. Some will probably be correct. In doing this, choose an answer other than (A). (A) is generally the correct answer less often than the other choices.*

9. Stay alert. Be careful not to mark a wrong answer because you were not concentrating. An example of this type of error might be: The correct answer to a Mathematics question is choice (B), which is the letter "d," and you mark (D) instead of (B).

10. Do not panic. If you do not finish any part before time is up, do not worry. If you are accurate, you can do well without finishing. At any rate, do not let your performance on any one part affect your performance on any other part.

11. Check and recheck. If you finish any part before time is up, do not daydream. Check to be sure that each question is answered in the right space and that there is only one answer for each question. Return to the difficult questions and rethink them.

Good luck!

---

*Do not rush to complete Part 5, Numerical Operations, or Part 6, Coding Speed, in the manner described above. Use every second of those two parts to answer the questions according to the directions. You are not expected to finish those two tests, and accuracy is important.

FIRST MODEL EXAM

ANSWER SHEET—FIRST MODEL EXAM

PART 1—GENERAL SCIENCE

1 Ⓐ Ⓑ Ⓒ Ⓓ   6 Ⓐ Ⓑ Ⓒ Ⓓ   11 Ⓐ Ⓑ Ⓒ Ⓓ   16 Ⓐ Ⓑ Ⓒ Ⓓ   21 Ⓐ Ⓑ Ⓒ Ⓓ
2 Ⓐ Ⓑ Ⓒ Ⓓ   7 Ⓐ Ⓑ Ⓒ Ⓓ   12 Ⓐ Ⓑ Ⓒ Ⓓ   17 Ⓐ Ⓑ Ⓒ Ⓓ   22 Ⓐ Ⓑ Ⓒ Ⓓ
3 Ⓐ Ⓑ Ⓒ Ⓓ   8 Ⓐ Ⓑ Ⓒ Ⓓ   13 Ⓐ Ⓑ Ⓒ Ⓓ   18 Ⓐ Ⓑ Ⓒ Ⓓ   23 Ⓐ Ⓑ Ⓒ Ⓓ
4 Ⓐ Ⓑ Ⓒ Ⓓ   9 Ⓐ Ⓑ Ⓒ Ⓓ   14 Ⓐ Ⓑ Ⓒ Ⓓ   19 Ⓐ Ⓑ Ⓒ Ⓓ   24 Ⓐ Ⓑ Ⓒ Ⓓ
5 Ⓐ Ⓑ Ⓒ Ⓓ   10 Ⓐ Ⓑ Ⓒ Ⓓ   15 Ⓐ Ⓑ Ⓒ Ⓓ   20 Ⓐ Ⓑ Ⓒ Ⓓ   25 Ⓐ Ⓑ Ⓒ Ⓓ

PART 2—ARITHMETIC REASONING

1 Ⓐ Ⓑ Ⓒ Ⓓ   7 Ⓐ Ⓑ Ⓒ Ⓓ   13 Ⓐ Ⓑ Ⓒ Ⓓ   19 Ⓐ Ⓑ Ⓒ Ⓓ   25 Ⓐ Ⓑ Ⓒ Ⓓ
2 Ⓐ Ⓑ Ⓒ Ⓓ   8 Ⓐ Ⓑ Ⓒ Ⓓ   14 Ⓐ Ⓑ Ⓒ Ⓓ   20 Ⓐ Ⓑ Ⓒ Ⓓ   26 Ⓐ Ⓑ Ⓒ Ⓓ
3 Ⓐ Ⓑ Ⓒ Ⓓ   9 Ⓐ Ⓑ Ⓒ Ⓓ   15 Ⓐ Ⓑ Ⓒ Ⓓ   21 Ⓐ Ⓑ Ⓒ Ⓓ   27 Ⓐ Ⓑ Ⓒ Ⓓ
4 Ⓐ Ⓑ Ⓒ Ⓓ   10 Ⓐ Ⓑ Ⓒ Ⓓ   16 Ⓐ Ⓑ Ⓒ Ⓓ   22 Ⓐ Ⓑ Ⓒ Ⓓ   28 Ⓐ Ⓑ Ⓒ Ⓓ
5 Ⓐ Ⓑ Ⓒ Ⓓ   11 Ⓐ Ⓑ Ⓒ Ⓓ   17 Ⓐ Ⓑ Ⓒ Ⓓ   23 Ⓐ Ⓑ Ⓒ Ⓓ   29 Ⓐ Ⓑ Ⓒ Ⓓ
6 Ⓐ Ⓑ Ⓒ Ⓓ   12 Ⓐ Ⓑ Ⓒ Ⓓ   18 Ⓐ Ⓑ Ⓒ Ⓓ   24 Ⓐ Ⓑ Ⓒ Ⓓ   30 Ⓐ Ⓑ Ⓒ Ⓓ

PART 3—WORD KNOWLEDGE

1 Ⓐ Ⓑ Ⓒ Ⓓ   8 Ⓐ Ⓑ Ⓒ Ⓓ   15 Ⓐ Ⓑ Ⓒ Ⓓ   22 Ⓐ Ⓑ Ⓒ Ⓓ   29 Ⓐ Ⓑ Ⓒ Ⓓ
2 Ⓐ Ⓑ Ⓒ Ⓓ   9 Ⓐ Ⓑ Ⓒ Ⓓ   16 Ⓐ Ⓑ Ⓒ Ⓓ   23 Ⓐ Ⓑ Ⓒ Ⓓ   30 Ⓐ Ⓑ Ⓒ Ⓓ
3 Ⓐ Ⓑ Ⓒ Ⓓ   10 Ⓐ Ⓑ Ⓒ Ⓓ   17 Ⓐ Ⓑ Ⓒ Ⓓ   24 Ⓐ Ⓑ Ⓒ Ⓓ   31 Ⓐ Ⓑ Ⓒ Ⓓ
4 Ⓐ Ⓑ Ⓒ Ⓓ   11 Ⓐ Ⓑ Ⓒ Ⓓ   18 Ⓐ Ⓑ Ⓒ Ⓓ   25 Ⓐ Ⓑ Ⓒ Ⓓ   32 Ⓐ Ⓑ Ⓒ Ⓓ
5 Ⓐ Ⓑ Ⓒ Ⓓ   12 Ⓐ Ⓑ Ⓒ Ⓓ   19 Ⓐ Ⓑ Ⓒ Ⓓ   26 Ⓐ Ⓑ Ⓒ Ⓓ   33 Ⓐ Ⓑ Ⓒ Ⓓ
6 Ⓐ Ⓑ Ⓒ Ⓓ   13 Ⓐ Ⓑ Ⓒ Ⓓ   20 Ⓐ Ⓑ Ⓒ Ⓓ   27 Ⓐ Ⓑ Ⓒ Ⓓ   34 Ⓐ Ⓑ Ⓒ Ⓓ
7 Ⓐ Ⓑ Ⓒ Ⓓ   14 Ⓐ Ⓑ Ⓒ Ⓓ   21 Ⓐ Ⓑ Ⓒ Ⓓ   28 Ⓐ Ⓑ Ⓒ Ⓓ   35 Ⓐ Ⓑ Ⓒ Ⓓ

PART 4—PARAGRAPH COMPREHENSION

1 Ⓐ Ⓑ Ⓒ Ⓓ   5 Ⓐ Ⓑ Ⓒ Ⓓ   9 Ⓐ Ⓑ Ⓒ Ⓓ   13 Ⓐ Ⓑ Ⓒ Ⓓ
2 Ⓐ Ⓑ Ⓒ Ⓓ   6 Ⓐ Ⓑ Ⓒ Ⓓ   10 Ⓐ Ⓑ Ⓒ Ⓓ   14 Ⓐ Ⓑ Ⓒ Ⓓ
3 Ⓐ Ⓑ Ⓒ Ⓓ   7 Ⓐ Ⓑ Ⓒ Ⓓ   11 Ⓐ Ⓑ Ⓒ Ⓓ   15 Ⓐ Ⓑ Ⓒ Ⓓ
4 Ⓐ Ⓑ Ⓒ Ⓓ   8 Ⓐ Ⓑ Ⓒ Ⓓ   12 Ⓐ Ⓑ Ⓒ Ⓓ

PART 5–NUMERICAL OPERATIONS

1 Ⓐ Ⓑ Ⓒ Ⓓ	11 Ⓐ Ⓑ Ⓒ Ⓓ	21 Ⓐ Ⓑ Ⓒ Ⓓ	31 Ⓐ Ⓑ Ⓒ Ⓓ	41 Ⓐ Ⓑ Ⓒ Ⓓ
2 Ⓐ Ⓑ Ⓒ Ⓓ	12 Ⓐ Ⓑ Ⓒ Ⓓ	22 Ⓐ Ⓑ Ⓒ Ⓓ	32 Ⓐ Ⓑ Ⓒ Ⓓ	42 Ⓐ Ⓑ Ⓒ Ⓓ
3 Ⓐ Ⓑ Ⓒ Ⓓ	13 Ⓐ Ⓑ Ⓒ Ⓓ	23 Ⓐ Ⓑ Ⓒ Ⓓ	33 Ⓐ Ⓑ Ⓒ Ⓓ	43 Ⓐ Ⓑ Ⓒ Ⓓ
4 Ⓐ Ⓑ Ⓒ Ⓓ	14 Ⓐ Ⓑ Ⓒ Ⓓ	24 Ⓐ Ⓑ Ⓒ Ⓓ	34 Ⓐ Ⓑ Ⓒ Ⓓ	44 Ⓐ Ⓑ Ⓒ Ⓓ
5 Ⓐ Ⓑ Ⓒ Ⓓ	15 Ⓐ Ⓑ Ⓒ Ⓓ	25 Ⓐ Ⓑ Ⓒ Ⓓ	35 Ⓐ Ⓑ Ⓒ Ⓓ	45 Ⓐ Ⓑ Ⓒ Ⓓ
6 Ⓐ Ⓑ Ⓒ Ⓓ	16 Ⓐ Ⓑ Ⓒ Ⓓ	26 Ⓐ Ⓑ Ⓒ Ⓓ	36 Ⓐ Ⓑ Ⓒ Ⓓ	46 Ⓐ Ⓑ Ⓒ Ⓓ
7 Ⓐ Ⓑ Ⓒ Ⓓ	17 Ⓐ Ⓑ Ⓒ Ⓓ	27 Ⓐ Ⓑ Ⓒ Ⓓ	37 Ⓐ Ⓑ Ⓒ Ⓓ	47 Ⓐ Ⓑ Ⓒ Ⓓ
8 Ⓐ Ⓑ Ⓒ Ⓓ	18 Ⓐ Ⓑ Ⓒ Ⓓ	28 Ⓐ Ⓑ Ⓒ Ⓓ	38 Ⓐ Ⓑ Ⓒ Ⓓ	48 Ⓐ Ⓑ Ⓒ Ⓓ
9 Ⓐ Ⓑ Ⓒ Ⓓ	19 Ⓐ Ⓑ Ⓒ Ⓓ	29 Ⓐ Ⓑ Ⓒ Ⓓ	39 Ⓐ Ⓑ Ⓒ Ⓓ	49 Ⓐ Ⓑ Ⓒ Ⓓ
10 Ⓐ Ⓑ Ⓒ Ⓓ	20 Ⓐ Ⓑ Ⓒ Ⓓ	30 Ⓐ Ⓑ Ⓒ Ⓓ	40 Ⓐ Ⓑ Ⓒ Ⓓ	50 Ⓐ Ⓑ Ⓒ Ⓓ

PART 6—CODING SPEED

1 Ⓐ Ⓑ Ⓒ Ⓓ Ⓔ	15 Ⓐ Ⓑ Ⓒ Ⓓ Ⓔ	29 Ⓐ Ⓑ Ⓒ Ⓓ Ⓔ	43 Ⓐ Ⓑ Ⓒ Ⓓ Ⓔ	57 Ⓐ Ⓑ Ⓒ Ⓓ Ⓔ	71 Ⓐ Ⓑ Ⓒ Ⓓ Ⓔ
2 Ⓐ Ⓑ Ⓒ Ⓓ Ⓔ	16 Ⓐ Ⓑ Ⓒ Ⓓ Ⓔ	30 Ⓐ Ⓑ Ⓒ Ⓓ Ⓔ	44 Ⓐ Ⓑ Ⓒ Ⓓ Ⓔ	58 Ⓐ Ⓑ Ⓒ Ⓓ Ⓔ	72 Ⓐ Ⓑ Ⓒ Ⓓ Ⓔ
3 Ⓐ Ⓑ Ⓒ Ⓓ Ⓔ	17 Ⓐ Ⓑ Ⓒ Ⓓ Ⓔ	31 Ⓐ Ⓑ Ⓒ Ⓓ Ⓔ	45 Ⓐ Ⓑ Ⓒ Ⓓ Ⓔ	59 Ⓐ Ⓑ Ⓒ Ⓓ Ⓔ	73 Ⓐ Ⓑ Ⓒ Ⓓ Ⓔ
4 Ⓐ Ⓑ Ⓒ Ⓓ Ⓔ	18 Ⓐ Ⓑ Ⓒ Ⓓ Ⓔ	32 Ⓐ Ⓑ Ⓒ Ⓓ Ⓔ	46 Ⓐ Ⓑ Ⓒ Ⓓ Ⓔ	60 Ⓐ Ⓑ Ⓒ Ⓓ Ⓔ	74 Ⓐ Ⓑ Ⓒ Ⓓ Ⓔ
5 Ⓐ Ⓑ Ⓒ Ⓓ Ⓔ	19 Ⓐ Ⓑ Ⓒ Ⓓ Ⓔ	33 Ⓐ Ⓑ Ⓒ Ⓓ Ⓔ	47 Ⓐ Ⓑ Ⓒ Ⓓ Ⓔ	61 Ⓐ Ⓑ Ⓒ Ⓓ Ⓔ	75 Ⓐ Ⓑ Ⓒ Ⓓ Ⓔ
6 Ⓐ Ⓑ Ⓒ Ⓓ Ⓔ	20 Ⓐ Ⓑ Ⓒ Ⓓ Ⓔ	34 Ⓐ Ⓑ Ⓒ Ⓓ Ⓔ	48 Ⓐ Ⓑ Ⓒ Ⓓ Ⓔ	62 Ⓐ Ⓑ Ⓒ Ⓓ Ⓔ	76 Ⓐ Ⓑ Ⓒ Ⓓ Ⓔ
7 Ⓐ Ⓑ Ⓒ Ⓓ Ⓔ	21 Ⓐ Ⓑ Ⓒ Ⓓ Ⓔ	35 Ⓐ Ⓑ Ⓒ Ⓓ Ⓔ	49 Ⓐ Ⓑ Ⓒ Ⓓ Ⓔ	63 Ⓐ Ⓑ Ⓒ Ⓓ Ⓔ	77 Ⓐ Ⓑ Ⓒ Ⓓ Ⓔ
8 Ⓐ Ⓑ Ⓒ Ⓓ Ⓔ	22 Ⓐ Ⓑ Ⓒ Ⓓ Ⓔ	36 Ⓐ Ⓑ Ⓒ Ⓓ Ⓔ	50 Ⓐ Ⓑ Ⓒ Ⓓ Ⓔ	64 Ⓐ Ⓑ Ⓒ Ⓓ Ⓔ	78 Ⓐ Ⓑ Ⓒ Ⓓ Ⓔ
9 Ⓐ Ⓑ Ⓒ Ⓓ Ⓔ	23 Ⓐ Ⓑ Ⓒ Ⓓ Ⓔ	37 Ⓐ Ⓑ Ⓒ Ⓓ Ⓔ	51 Ⓐ Ⓑ Ⓒ Ⓓ Ⓔ	65 Ⓐ Ⓑ Ⓒ Ⓓ Ⓔ	79 Ⓐ Ⓑ Ⓒ Ⓓ Ⓔ
10 Ⓐ Ⓑ Ⓒ Ⓓ Ⓔ	24 Ⓐ Ⓑ Ⓒ Ⓓ Ⓔ	38 Ⓐ Ⓑ Ⓒ Ⓓ Ⓔ	52 Ⓐ Ⓑ Ⓒ Ⓓ Ⓔ	66 Ⓐ Ⓑ Ⓒ Ⓓ Ⓔ	80 Ⓐ Ⓑ Ⓒ Ⓓ Ⓔ
11 Ⓐ Ⓑ Ⓒ Ⓓ Ⓔ	25 Ⓐ Ⓑ Ⓒ Ⓓ Ⓔ	39 Ⓐ Ⓑ Ⓒ Ⓓ Ⓔ	53 Ⓐ Ⓑ Ⓒ Ⓓ Ⓔ	67 Ⓐ Ⓑ Ⓒ Ⓓ Ⓔ	81 Ⓐ Ⓑ Ⓒ Ⓓ Ⓔ
12 Ⓐ Ⓑ Ⓒ Ⓓ Ⓔ	26 Ⓐ Ⓑ Ⓒ Ⓓ Ⓔ	40 Ⓐ Ⓑ Ⓒ Ⓓ Ⓔ	54 Ⓐ Ⓑ Ⓒ Ⓓ Ⓔ	68 Ⓐ Ⓑ Ⓒ Ⓓ Ⓔ	82 Ⓐ Ⓑ Ⓒ Ⓓ Ⓔ
13 Ⓐ Ⓑ Ⓒ Ⓓ Ⓔ	27 Ⓐ Ⓑ Ⓒ Ⓓ Ⓔ	41 Ⓐ Ⓑ Ⓒ Ⓓ Ⓔ	55 Ⓐ Ⓑ Ⓒ Ⓓ Ⓔ	69 Ⓐ Ⓑ Ⓒ Ⓓ Ⓔ	83 Ⓐ Ⓑ Ⓒ Ⓓ Ⓔ
14 Ⓐ Ⓑ Ⓒ Ⓓ Ⓔ	28 Ⓐ Ⓑ Ⓒ Ⓓ Ⓔ	42 Ⓐ Ⓑ Ⓒ Ⓓ Ⓔ	56 Ⓐ Ⓑ Ⓒ Ⓓ Ⓔ	70 Ⓐ Ⓑ Ⓒ Ⓓ Ⓔ	84 Ⓐ Ⓑ Ⓒ Ⓓ Ⓔ

PART 7—AUTO & SHOP INFORMATION

1 Ⓐ Ⓑ Ⓒ Ⓓ	6 Ⓐ Ⓑ Ⓒ Ⓓ	11 Ⓐ Ⓑ Ⓒ Ⓓ	16 Ⓐ Ⓑ Ⓒ Ⓓ	21 Ⓐ Ⓑ Ⓒ Ⓓ
2 Ⓐ Ⓑ Ⓒ Ⓓ	7 Ⓐ Ⓑ Ⓒ Ⓓ	12 Ⓐ Ⓑ Ⓒ Ⓓ	17 Ⓐ Ⓑ Ⓒ Ⓓ	22 Ⓐ Ⓑ Ⓒ Ⓓ
3 Ⓐ Ⓑ Ⓒ Ⓓ	8 Ⓐ Ⓑ Ⓒ Ⓓ	13 Ⓐ Ⓑ Ⓒ Ⓓ	18 Ⓐ Ⓑ Ⓒ Ⓓ	23 Ⓐ Ⓑ Ⓒ Ⓓ
4 Ⓐ Ⓑ Ⓒ Ⓓ	9 Ⓐ Ⓑ Ⓒ Ⓓ	14 Ⓐ Ⓑ Ⓒ Ⓓ	19 Ⓐ Ⓑ Ⓒ Ⓓ	24 Ⓐ Ⓑ Ⓒ Ⓓ
5 Ⓐ Ⓑ Ⓒ Ⓓ	10 Ⓐ Ⓑ Ⓒ Ⓓ	15 Ⓐ Ⓑ Ⓒ Ⓓ	20 Ⓐ Ⓑ Ⓒ Ⓓ	25 Ⓐ Ⓑ Ⓒ Ⓓ

PART 8—MATHEMATICS KNOWLEDGE

1 Ⓐ Ⓑ Ⓒ Ⓓ	6 Ⓐ Ⓑ Ⓒ Ⓓ	11 Ⓐ Ⓑ Ⓒ Ⓓ	16 Ⓐ Ⓑ Ⓒ Ⓓ	21 Ⓐ Ⓑ Ⓒ Ⓓ
2 Ⓐ Ⓑ Ⓒ Ⓓ	7 Ⓐ Ⓑ Ⓒ Ⓓ	12 Ⓐ Ⓑ Ⓒ Ⓓ	17 Ⓐ Ⓑ Ⓒ Ⓓ	22 Ⓐ Ⓑ Ⓒ Ⓓ
3 Ⓐ Ⓑ Ⓒ Ⓓ	8 Ⓐ Ⓑ Ⓒ Ⓓ	13 Ⓐ Ⓑ Ⓒ Ⓓ	18 Ⓐ Ⓑ Ⓒ Ⓓ	23 Ⓐ Ⓑ Ⓒ Ⓓ
4 Ⓐ Ⓑ Ⓒ Ⓓ	9 Ⓐ Ⓑ Ⓒ Ⓓ	14 Ⓐ Ⓑ Ⓒ Ⓓ	19 Ⓐ Ⓑ Ⓒ Ⓓ	24 Ⓐ Ⓑ Ⓒ Ⓓ
5 Ⓐ Ⓑ Ⓒ Ⓓ	10 Ⓐ Ⓑ Ⓒ Ⓓ	15 Ⓐ Ⓑ Ⓒ Ⓓ	20 Ⓐ Ⓑ Ⓒ Ⓓ	25 Ⓐ Ⓑ Ⓒ Ⓓ

PART 9—MECHANICAL COMPREHENSION

1 Ⓐ Ⓑ Ⓒ Ⓓ	6 Ⓐ Ⓑ Ⓒ Ⓓ	11 Ⓐ Ⓑ Ⓒ Ⓓ	16 Ⓐ Ⓑ Ⓒ Ⓓ	21 Ⓐ Ⓑ Ⓒ Ⓓ
2 Ⓐ Ⓑ Ⓒ Ⓓ	7 Ⓐ Ⓑ Ⓒ Ⓓ	12 Ⓐ Ⓑ Ⓒ Ⓓ	17 Ⓐ Ⓑ Ⓒ Ⓓ	22 Ⓐ Ⓑ Ⓒ Ⓓ
3 Ⓐ Ⓑ Ⓒ Ⓓ	8 Ⓐ Ⓑ Ⓒ Ⓓ	13 Ⓐ Ⓑ Ⓒ Ⓓ	18 Ⓐ Ⓑ Ⓒ Ⓓ	23 Ⓐ Ⓑ Ⓒ Ⓓ
4 Ⓐ Ⓑ Ⓒ Ⓓ	9 Ⓐ Ⓑ Ⓒ Ⓓ	14 Ⓐ Ⓑ Ⓒ Ⓓ	19 Ⓐ Ⓑ Ⓒ Ⓓ	24 Ⓐ Ⓑ Ⓒ Ⓓ
5 Ⓐ Ⓑ Ⓒ Ⓓ	10 Ⓐ Ⓑ Ⓒ Ⓓ	15 Ⓐ Ⓑ Ⓒ Ⓓ	20 Ⓐ Ⓑ Ⓒ Ⓓ	25 Ⓐ Ⓑ Ⓒ Ⓓ

PART 10—ELECTRONICS INFORMATION

1 Ⓐ Ⓑ Ⓒ Ⓓ	6 Ⓐ Ⓑ Ⓒ Ⓓ	11 Ⓐ Ⓑ Ⓒ Ⓓ	16 Ⓐ Ⓑ Ⓒ Ⓓ
2 Ⓐ Ⓑ Ⓒ Ⓓ	7 Ⓐ Ⓑ Ⓒ Ⓓ	12 Ⓐ Ⓑ Ⓒ Ⓓ	17 Ⓐ Ⓑ Ⓒ Ⓓ
3 Ⓐ Ⓑ Ⓒ Ⓓ	8 Ⓐ Ⓑ Ⓒ Ⓓ	13 Ⓐ Ⓑ Ⓒ Ⓓ	18 Ⓐ Ⓑ Ⓒ Ⓓ
4 Ⓐ Ⓑ Ⓒ Ⓓ	9 Ⓐ Ⓑ Ⓒ Ⓓ	14 Ⓐ Ⓑ Ⓒ Ⓓ	19 Ⓐ Ⓑ Ⓒ Ⓓ
5 Ⓐ Ⓑ Ⓒ Ⓓ	10 Ⓐ Ⓑ Ⓒ Ⓓ	15 Ⓐ Ⓑ Ⓒ Ⓓ	20 Ⓐ Ⓑ Ⓒ Ⓓ

PART 1

GENERAL SCIENCE

The general science part of your examination asks questions based upon the science you learned in high school. For each question there are four possible answers. Only one answer is correct. Choose the answer which you think is correct and mark the corresponding space on your answer sheet. Try these questions.

1. The functions of plant roots may normally include all of the following *except*

1-A photosynthesis
1-B absorption
1-C food storage
1-D support

1. Ⓐ Ⓑ Ⓒ Ⓓ

1-A PHOTOSYNTHESIS is the correct answer. Photosynthesis is the process by which the leaves of a plant manufacture food for that plant. Since light is required for photosynthesis, the roots of the plant are not involved with the process. The roots do help store the food (C), absorb water (B) and support the plant (D).

2. Of the following, the one that expands when it freezes is:

2-A carbon dioxide
2-B iron
2-C glass
2-D water

2. Ⓐ Ⓑ Ⓒ Ⓓ

2-D WATER is the correct answer. Water expands its volume when it freezes. If a glass jar is filled with water, tightly capped and frozen, it will crack and burst. The glass (C) does not expand along with the water. Carbon dioxide (A) and iron (B) do not expand when frozen.

3. A child with extremely thin arms and legs and with a large, distended (swollen) belly is probably suffering from

3-A tuberculosis
3-B child abuse
3-C malnutrition
3-D measles

3. Ⓐ Ⓑ Ⓒ Ⓓ

3-C MALNUTRITION is the correct answer. The symptoms described are commonly seen in the children of war-torn nations which have experienced crop failures. An undernourished child is likely to be more susceptible to disease (A) and (D), but need not have a disease to display the symptoms. Child abuse (B) only occasionally takes the form of starving the child.

4. Cloud-seeding is of limited usefulness in drought management because

4-A dry ice is very expensive
4-B a special type of airplane is required
4-C the water from seeded clouds is not as wet as natural rain water
4-D sufficient quantity of the right kind of clouds must be present in the right place

4. Ⓐ Ⓑ Ⓒ Ⓓ

4-D There *must* be enough clouds in the drought-stricken area if cloud-seeding is to be of any use. Unfortunately, this is not usually the case. Many kinds of airplanes (B) can be used to drop the pellets of dry ice (A) which are relatively cheap. The water produced by this method (C) is just as acceptable as natural rain water, but there is not enough of it.

DO NOT TURN THE PAGE UNTIL YOU ARE TOLD TO DO SO

GENERAL SCIENCE

TIME: 11 Minutes—25 Questions

1. Under natural conditions large quantities of organic matter decay after each year's plant growth has been completed. As a result of such conditions

    1-A   many animals are deprived of adequate food supplies
    1-B   soil erosion is accelerated
    1-C   soils maintain their fertility
    1-D   earthworms are added to the soil

2. Which of the following does *not* belong with the others?

    2-A   bat
    2-B   whale
    2-C   horse
    2-D   alligator

3. The most likely reason why dinosaurs became extinct was that they

    3-A   were killed by erupting volcanoes
    3-B   were eaten as adults by the advancing mammalian groups
    3-C   failed to adapt to a changing environment
    3-D   killed each other in combat

4. Which of the following is a chemical change?

    4-A   magnetizing a rod of iron
    4-B   burning one pound of coal
    4-C   mixing flake graphite with oil
    4-D   vaporizing one gram of mercury in a vacuum

5. A person with high blood-pressure should

    5-A   take frequent naps
    5-B   avoid salt
    5-C   eat only iodized salt
    5-D   exercise vigorously

6. One-celled animals belong to the group of living things known as

    6-A   protozoa
    6-B   annelida
    6-C   porifera
    6-D   arthropoda

7. Spiders can be distinguished from insects by the fact that spiders have

    7-A   hard outer coverings
    7-B   large abdomens
    7-C   four pairs of legs
    7-D   biting mouth parts

8. An important ore of uranium is called

    8-A   hematite
    8-B   chalcopyrite
    8-C   bauxite
    8-D   pitchblende

9. Of the following, the lightest element known on earth is

    9-A   hydrogen
    9-B   oxygen
    9-C   helium
    9-D   air

10. Of the following gases in the air, the most plentiful is

    10-A   argon
    10-B   oxygen
    10-C   nitrogen
    10-D   carbon dioxide

11. The time it takes for light from the sun to reach the earth is approximately

    11-A   four years
    11-B   eight minutes
    11-C   four months
    11-D   sixteen years

12. Of the following types of clouds, the ones which occur at the greatest height are called

12-A cirrus
12-B nimbus
12-C cumulus
12-D stratus

13. A new drug for treatment of tuberculosis was being tested in a hospital. Patients in Group A actually received doses of the new drug; those in Group B were given only sugar pills. Group B represents

13-A a scientific experiment
13-B a scientific method
13-C an experimental error
13-D an experimental control

14. The statement that carrots help one to see in the dark is

14-A ridiculous
14-B reasonable because orange is a reflective color
14-C reasonable because carrots are high in Vitamin A
14-D reasonable because rabbits see very well at night

15. Radium is stored in lead containers because

15-A the lead absorbs the harmful radiations
15-B radium is a heavy substance
15-C lead prevents the disintegration of the radium
15-D lead is cheap

16. A boy examining his finger under a microscope could see no epidermal cells because

16-A these cells are located under the skin
16-B the nail blocked his view
16-C each single cell is larger than the area of the microscope field
16-D a finger is about one-half-inch thick

17. Limes were eaten by British sailors in order to

17-A justify their nickname, "Limeys"
17-B pucker their mouths to resist the wind
17-C satisfy their craving for something acid
17-D prevent scurvy

18. The time that it takes for the earth to rotate 45° is

18-A one hour
18-B four hours
18-C three hours
18-D ten hours

19. Of the following glands, the one which regulates the metabolic rate is the

19-A adrenal
19-B thyroid
19-C salivary
19-D thymus

20. All of the following are Amphibia *except* the

20-A salamander
20-B frog
20-C lizard
20-D toad

21. Of the following planets, the one which has the shortest revolutionary period around the sun is

21-A Earth
21-B Jupiter
21-C Mercury
21-D Venus

22. A popular shrub that produces bell-shaped, yellow flowers in early spring is the

22-A tulip
22-B forsythia
22-C azalea
22-D flowering dogwood

23. A circuit breaker is used in many homes instead of a

23-A switch
23-B fire extinguisher
23-C fuse
23-D meter box

24. What is the name of the negative particle which circles the nucleus of the atom?

    24-A neutron
    24-B meson
    24-C proton
    24-D electron

25. Which of the following rocks can be dissolved with a weak acid?

    25-A sandstone
    25-B gneiss
    25-C granite
    25-D limestone

STOP

IF YOU FINISH THIS PART BEFORE THE TIME IS UP, CHECK OVER YOUR WORK ON THIS PART ONLY. DO NOT GO ON UNTIL YOU ARE TOLD TO DO SO.

ARITHMETIC REASONING

The arithmetic reasoning questions require careful thinking as well as arithmetic calculation. Some problems require more than one step for their solutions. You must decide exactly what the question asks; then you must determine the best method for finding the answer; finally, you must work out the problem on your scratch paper. Be sure to mark the letter of the correct answer on your answer sheet. Try these questions.

1. A recipe for 6 quarts of punch calls for $\frac{3}{4}$ cups of sugar. How much sugar is needed for 9 quarts of punch?

   1-A five-eighths of a cup
   1-B seven-eighths of a cup
   1-C $1\frac{1}{8}$ cups
   1-D $2\frac{1}{4}$ cups

   1. Ⓐ Ⓑ Ⓒ Ⓓ

1-C First find out how much sugar is needed for one quart of punch.

$$\frac{3}{4}\text{ cups} \div 6 = \frac{3}{4} \times \frac{1}{6} = \frac{\overset{1}{\cancel{3}}}{4} \times \frac{1}{\underset{2}{\cancel{6}}} = \frac{1}{8}$$

For 9 quarts of punch: $9 \times \frac{1}{8} = \frac{9}{8} = 1\frac{1}{8}$

2. How many yards of ribbon will it take to make 45 badges if each badge uses 4 inches of ribbon?

   2-A 5
   2-B 9
   2-C 11
   2-D 15

   2. Ⓐ Ⓑ Ⓒ Ⓓ

2-A 45 badges × 4 inches each = 180 inches needed
There are 36 inches in one yard.
180 inches ÷ 36 = 5 yards of ribbon needed

3. A clerk can add 40 columns of figures an hour by using an adding machine and 20 columns of figures an hour without using an adding machine. What is the total number of hours it will take the clerk to add 200 columns of figures if $\frac{3}{5}$ of the work is done by machine and the rest without the machine?

   3-A 6 hours
   3-B 7 hours
   3-C 8 hours
   3-D 9 hours

   3. Ⓐ Ⓑ Ⓒ Ⓓ

3-B $\frac{3}{5}$ of 200 = 120 columns by machine @ 40 columns per hour = 3 hours
200 − 120 = 80 columns without machine @ 20 columns per hour = 4 hours
3 hours + 4 hours = 7 hours to complete the job.

4. Oil once sold at $42\frac{1}{2}$ cents a quart. The cost of 4 gallons of oil was

   4-A $6.50
   4-B $6.60
   4-C $6.70
   4-D $6.80

   4. Ⓐ Ⓑ Ⓒ Ⓓ

4-D One gallon = four quarts
4 gals. = 16 qts.
16 qts. × $42\frac{1}{2}$ = 16 × $.425 = $6.80

DO NOT TURN THE PAGE UNTIL YOU ARE TOLD TO DO SO

ARITHMETIC REASONING

TIME: 36 Minutes—30 Questions

1. If a man invests $1,000 at an annual rate of 5%, how much interest will the man have after one year?

   1-A $20
   1-B $50
   1-C $100
   1-D $120

2. If a load of snow contains 3 tons, it will weigh how many lbs.?

   2-A 3,000 lbs.
   2-B 1,500 lbs.
   2-C 12,000 lbs.
   2-D 6,000 lbs.

3. A pint of milk is what part of half a gallon?

   3-A $\frac{1}{8}$
   3-B $\frac{1}{4}$
   3-C $\frac{1}{2}$
   3-D $\frac{1}{16}$

4. At the rate of four peaches for a quarter, 20 peaches will cost

   4-A 80¢
   4-B $1.00
   4-C $1.20
   4-D $1.25

5. A boy deposited in his savings account the money he had saved during the summer. Find the amount of his deposit if he had 10 one-dollar bills, 9 half dollars, 8 quarters, 16 dimes, and 25 nickels.

   5-A $16.20
   5-B $17.42
   5-C $18.60
   5-D $19.35

6. How many minutes are there in 1 day?

   6-A 60
   6-B 1440
   6-C 24
   6-D 1440 × 60

7. One year the postage rate for sending 1 ounce of mail first class was increased from 3 cents to 4 cents. What was the percent of increase in the postage rate?

   7-A $12\frac{1}{2}$%
   7-B 15%
   7-C $33\frac{1}{3}$
   7-D 40%

8. On a scale drawing, a line $\frac{1}{4}$ inch long represents a length of 1 foot. On the same drawing, what length represents 4 feet?

   8-A 1 inch
   8-B 2 inches
   8-C 3 inches
   8-D 4 inches

9. What is the greatest number of half-pint bottles that can be filled from a 10-gallon can of milk?

   9-A 160
   9-B 170
   9-C 16
   9-D 17

10. If six girls can paint a fence in two days, how many girls, working at the same uniform rate, can finish it in one day?

    10-A 2
    10-B 3
    10-C 12
    10-D 4

11. If 3 apples cost 24¢, how many dozen apples can be bought for $1.92?

    11-A $1\frac{1}{2}$
    11-B 1
    11-C 2
    11-D $5\frac{1}{3}$

12. How much time is there between 8:30 a.m. today and 3:15 a.m. tomorrow?

12-A $17\frac{3}{4}$ hrs.
12-B $18\frac{2}{3}$ hrs.
12-C $18\frac{1}{2}$ hrs.
12-D $18\frac{3}{4}$ hrs.

13. A clerk is requested to file 800 cards. If he can file cards at the rate of 80 cards an hour, the number of cards remaining to be filed after 7 hours of work is

13-A   140
13-B   240
13-C   250
13-D   260

14. A man's weekly salary is increased from $350 to $380. The percent of increase is, most nearly,

14-A   6 percent
14-B $8\frac{1}{2}$ percent
14-C   10 percent
14-D $12\frac{1}{2}$ percent

15. A truck going at a rate of 20 miles an hour will reach a town 40 miles away in how many hours?

15-A   3 hrs.
15-B   4 hrs.
15-C   1 hr.
15-D   2 hrs.

16. If a barrel has a capacity of 100 gallons, it will contain how many gallons when it is two-fifths full?

16-A   20 gal.
16-B   40 gal.
16-C   60 gal.
16-D   80 gal.

17. If a salary of $20,000 is subject to a 20 percent deduction, the net salary is

17-A $14,000
17-B $15,500
17-C $16,000
17-D $18,000

18. If $1000 is the cost of repairing 100 square yards of pavement, the cost of repairing one square yard is

18-A $10
18-B $100
18-C $150
18-D $300

19. If a man's base pay is $23,000 and it is increased by a bonus of $500 and a seniority increment of $1,350, his total salary is

19-A $24,850
19-B $23,500
19-C $25,850
19-D $24,500

20. If an annual salary of $21,600 is increased by a bonus of $720 and by a service increment of $1200, the total pay rate is

20-A $22,320
20-B $22,800
20-C $23,320
20-D $23,520

21. A man takes out a $5,000 life insurance policy at a yearly rate of $29.62 per $1,000. What is the yearly premium?

21-A $ 90.10
21-B $100.10
21-C $126.10
21-D $148.10

22. On her maiden voyage the *S.S. United States* made the trip from New York to England in 3 days, 10 hours and 40 minutes, beating the record set by the *R.M.S. Queen Mary* in 1938 by 10 hours and 2 minutes. How long did it take the *Queen Mary* to make the trip?

22-A   3 days 20 hrs. 42 mins.
22-B   3 days 15 hrs. 38 mins.
22-C   3 days 12 hrs. 2 mins.
22-D   3 days 8 hrs. 12 mins.

23. Gary bought a shirt for $18.95. He gave the clerk $20.00. How much change did Gary get?

23-A $2.05
23-B $1.95

23-C $1.05
23-D $ .05

24. John bought 20 party favors for $66.00. What was the cost of each one?

24-A $3.35
24-B $3.30
24-C $2.45
24-D $3.50

25. An inch on a map represents 200 miles. On the same map a distance of 375 miles is represented by

25-A $1\frac{1}{2}$ inches
25-B $1\frac{7}{8}$ inches
25-C $2\frac{1}{4}$ inches
25-D $2\frac{3}{4}$ inches

26. The number of half-pound packages of tea that can be made up from a box which holds $10\frac{1}{4}$ pounds of tea is

26-A 5
26-B $10\frac{1}{2}$
26-C 20
26-D $20\frac{1}{2}$

27. A pile of magazines is 4 feet high. If each magazine is $\frac{3}{4}$ of an inch thick, the number of magazines is

27-A 36
27-B 48
27-C 64
27-D 96

28. Walnuts are selling at $2.19 for a 5-pound bag. The cost for 10 pounds is

28-A $2.19 × 10
28-B $2.19 × 2
28-C $2.19 × 50
28-D $2.19 × 5 ÷ 10

29. Five girls each ate 3 cookies from a box containing 2 dozen. What part of a dozen was left?

29-A $\frac{1}{8}$
29-B $\frac{1}{4}$
29-C $\frac{3}{4}$
29-D $\frac{7}{8}$

30. A folding chair regularly sells for $29.50. How much money is saved if the chair is bought at a 20% discount?

30-A $4.80
30-B $5.90
30-C $6.20
30-D $7.40

END OF PART 2

IF YOU FINISH BEFORE THE TIME IS UP, CHECK TO BE CERTAIN THAT YOU HAVE MARKED ALL OF YOUR ANSWERS ON THE ANSWER SHEET. THEN CHECK OVER YOUR WORK ON THIS PART ONLY. DO NOT RETURN TO PART ONE. DO NOT GO ON TO THE NEXT PART UNTIL YOU ARE TOLD TO DO SO.

PART 3

WORD KNOWLEDGE

The questions in this part test how well you understand the meanings of words. Each question has an underlined word. Read all four possible answers and decide which one has a meaning closest to the meaning of the underlined word. On your answer sheet mark the letter of the answer you choose. Try these questions.

1. Mended most nearly means

  1-A repaired
  1-B torn
  1-C clean
  1-D tied

  1. Ⓐ Ⓑ Ⓒ Ⓓ

1-A REPAIRED is the correct answer. *Mended* means *fixed* or *repaired*. *Torn* (B) might be the state of an object before it is mended. The repair might be made by *tying* (D), but not necessarily. *Clean* (C) is wrong.

2. His conduct was becoming of an officer.

  2-A happening to
  2-B turning into
  2-C improving as
  2-D proper for

  2. Ⓐ Ⓑ Ⓒ Ⓓ

2-D PROPER FOR is the correct answer. The underlined word *of* is given to you in a sentence because *becoming* may have more than one meaning. If you try to substitute each answer choice in the sentence, you will find that only (D) makes sense.

3. The pitcher missed nearly the whole season because of chronic arm trouble.

  3-A painful
  3-B frequent
  3-C imaginary
  3-D dangerous

3. Ⓐ Ⓑ Ⓒ Ⓓ

3-B FREQUENT is the correct answer. The condition of the pitcher's arm may or may not have been *dangerous* (D) and it most certainly was *painful* (A), but it was its *frequency*, its *chronic nature*, that made him miss so much of the season. *Imaginary* (C) is not the meaning of *chronic*.

4. Oral most nearly means

  4-A spoken
  4-B loud
  4-C secret
  4-D by heart

  4. Ⓐ Ⓑ Ⓒ Ⓓ

4-A SPOKEN is the correct answer. Something *oral* is always *spoken,* whether *loudly* (B) or in *secret* (C) or *from memory* (D).

5. Calculated most nearly means

  5-A multiplied
  5-B added
  5-C answered
  5-D figured out

  5. Ⓐ Ⓑ Ⓒ Ⓓ

5-D FIGURED OUT is the best answer. *Calculating* may well include *multiplying* (A) or *adding* (B) in order to arrive at the *answer* (C), but not all *calculations* need be mathematical. Since the word *calculated* was not given to you in a sentence, the most general definition is the best answer.

DO NOT TURN THE PAGE UNTIL YOU ARE TOLD TO DO SO

WORD KNOWLEDGE

TIME: 11 Minutes—35 Questions

1. Double most nearly means

  1-A almost
  1-B half
  1-C twice
  1-D more than

2. Purchase most nearly means

  2-A charge
  2-B supply
  2-C order
  2-D buy

3. Hollow most nearly means

  3-A empty
  3-B brittle
  3-C rough
  3-D smooth

4. The packages were kept in a secure place.

  4-A distant
  4-B safe
  4-C convenient
  4-D secret

5. Customary most nearly means

  5-A curious
  5-B necessary
  5-C difficult
  5-D common

6. The carpenter was criticized for his slipshod work.

  6-A slow
  6-B careful
  6-C careless
  6-D original

7. Captive most nearly means

  7-A savage
  7-B jailer
  7-C spy
  7-D prisoner

8. Vegetation most nearly means

  8-A food
  8-B plant life
  8-C moisture
  8-D bird life

9. Fictitious most nearly means

  9-A imaginary
  9-B well-known
  9-C odd
  9-D easy to remember

10. The policeman consoled the weeping child.

  10-A found
  10-B scolded
  10-C carried home
  10-D comforted

11. The preface of the book was very interesting.

  11-A title page
  11-B introduction
  11-C table of contents
  11-D appendix

12. To penetrate most nearly means

  12-A to enter into
  12-B to bounce off
  12-C to dent
  12-D to weaken

13. Villainous most nearly means

  13-A untidy
  13-B dignified
  13-C homely
  13-D wicked

14. It is my <u>conviction</u> that you are wrong.

    14-A guilt
    14-B imagination
    14-C firm belief
    14-D fault

15. <u>Punctual</u> most nearly means

    15-A polite
    15-B thoughtful
    15-C proper
    15-D prompt

16. <u>Juvenile</u> most nearly means

    16-A delinquent
    16-B lovesick
    16-C youthful
    16-D humorous

17. <u>Concisely</u> most nearly means

    17-A accurately
    17-B briefly
    17-C fully
    17-D officially

18. <u>Unite</u> most nearly means

    18-A improve
    18-B serve
    18-C uphold
    18-D combine

19. The principal <u>defended</u> the striking teachers.

    19-A delayed
    19-B shot at
    19-C protected
    19-D informed on

20. The <u>aim</u> of the enlistee was to join the Navy.

    20-A bullseye
    20-B goal
    20-C duty
    20-D promise

21. <u>Assemble</u> most nearly means

    21-A bring together
    21-B examine carefully
    21-C locate
    21-D fill

22. <u>Merchants</u> most nearly means

    22-A producers
    22-B advertisers
    22-C bankers
    22-D storekeepers

23. <u>Compel</u> most nearly means

    23-A tempt
    23-B persuade
    23-C force
    23-D disable

24. The eagle has a <u>keen</u> eye.

    24-A bright
    24-B shiny
    24-C sharp
    24-D tiny

25. <u>Startled</u> most nearly means

    25-A surprised
    25-B chased
    25-C punished
    25-D arrested

26. <u>Forthcoming</u> events are listed on the bulletin board.

    26-A weekly
    26-B interesting
    26-C social
    26-D approaching

27. <u>Verdict</u> most nearly means

    27-A approval
    27-B decision
    27-C sentence
    27-D arrival

28. <u>Self-sufficient</u> most nearly means

    28-A independent
    28-B conceited
    28-C stubborn
    28-D clever

29. In his hand the hiker carried a sturdy <u>staff</u>.

    29-A pack
    29-B stick
    29-C loaf
    29-D musical instrument

30. <u>Insignificant</u> most nearly means

    30-A unimportant
    30-B unpleasant
    30-C secret
    30-D thrilling

31. <u>Acquired</u> most nearly means

    31-A sold
    31-B plowed
    31-C desired
    31-D obtained

32. <u>Exhaustion</u> most nearly means

    32-A fear
    32-B overconfidence
    32-C extreme tiredness
    32-D unsteadiness

33. The door was left <u>ajar</u>.

    33-A blocked
    33-B locked
    33-C unlocked
    33-D open

34. <u>Inferior</u> most nearly means

    34-A noticeable
    34-B second-rate
    34-C lasting
    34-D excellent

35. The hikers noticed several <u>crevices</u> in the rocks.

    35-A plants
    35-B uneven spots
    35-C cracks
    35-D puddles

END OF PART 3

IF YOU FINISH BEFORE TIME IS UP, CHECK YOUR WORK ON THIS PART ONLY. DO NOT GO BACK TO EITHER PREVIOUS PART. DO NOT GO ON TO THE NEXT PART UNTIL YOU ARE TOLD TO DO SO.

PART 4

PARAGRAPH COMPREHENSION

The paragraph comprehension part of your test battery requires concentration and attention to detail. First you must read and understand the paragraph. Then you must read and understand each of the answer choices, noticing the differences of meaning or emphasis which are imparted by little words. There is one question based upon each paragraph. You must answer that question on the basis of what is stated or implied in the passage, even if you know a better answer and even if you know the information in the paragraph to be false. In some cases more than one answer might be correct, but you must choose the BEST answer and mark its letter on your answer sheet. Try these questions.

1. Life is too short for one person to do very many things well. The person who determines fairly early what he can do that he likes to do, and who goes at it hard and stays with it, is likely to do the best work and find the most peace of mind.

The reason the average man does not master many different jobs is that he

1-A desires peace of mind
1-B seldom has more than a few interests
1-C is unable to organize his ideas
1-D lacks the necessary time

1. Ⓐ Ⓑ Ⓒ Ⓓ

1-D The first sentence answers the question. It says that life is too short for one person to do many things well, which means the same thing as "there just isn't enough time."

2. For the United States, Canada has become the most important country in the world, yet there are few countries about which Americans know less. Canada is the third largest country in the world; only Russia and China are larger. The area of Canada is more than a quarter of the whole British Empire.

The paragraph best supports the statement that

2-A the British Empire is smaller than Russia or China
2-B the territory of China is greater than that of Canada
2-C Americans know more about Canada than about China or Russia
2-D the United States is the most important nation in the world as far as Canada is concerned

2. Ⓐ Ⓑ Ⓒ Ⓓ

2-B The paragraph states that Russia and China are larger than Canada. No other answer to this question is correct. Choices C and D make statements in direct contradiction of the paragraph. Choice A is wrong because the paragraph compares the size of *Canada* with that of Russia and China, not the size of the *British Empire* with Russia and China.

DO NOT TURN THE PAGE UNTIL YOU ARE TOLD TO DO SO

PARAGRAPH COMPREHENSION

TIME: 13 Minutes—15 Questions

1. Television reached in 20 years the goal toward which print had been working for 500; to extend its audience to include the entire population. By 1973 in the United States, nine out of ten families watched 45 million sets going an average of five hours a day.

   The paragraph best supports the statement that

   1-A the entire nation has TV sets
   1-B nine out of ten individuals watch an average of five hours a day
   1-C the TV viewing public grew much more rapidly than did the reading public
   1-D there are more TV sets in the United States than in other countries

2. Formerly it was only unskilled labor that was shifted from place to place in the wake of industrial booms. Since so many business concerns have become nationwide in the fields they cover, the white-collar workers have been in a similar state of motion.

   The growth of big business has resulted in

   2-A a shifting supply of unskilled labor
   2-B an increased tendency toward movement of workers
   2-C an increased proportion of white-collar jobs
   2-D the stabilization of industrial booms

3. There exists a false but popular idea that a clue is a mysterious fact that most people overlook but which some very keen investigator easily discovers and recognizes as having, in itself, a remarkable meaning. The clue is most often an ordinary fact that an observant person picks up—something that gains its significance when, after a long series of careful investigations, it is connected with a network of other clues.

   To be of value clues must be

   3-A discovered by skilled investigators
   3-B found under mysterious circumstances
   3-C connected with other facts
   3-D discovered soon after the crime

4. It was formerly thought that whole wheat and graham breads were far superior to white bread made from highly refined wheat flour. However, it is now believed that the general use of milk solids in white bread significantly narrows the nutritional gap between the two types of bread. About the only dietary advantages now claimed for whole wheat bread are higher content of iron and vitamin B, both easily obtainable in many other common foods.

   The paragraph best supports the statement that

   4-A white bread is fattening because of its milk content
   4-B whole wheat bread is not much more nutritious than white bread
   4-C whole wheat bread contains roughage
   4-D white bread contains neither iron nor vitamin B

5. It is wise to choose a duplicating machine that will do the work required with the greatest efficiency and at the least cost. Users with a large volume of business need speedy machines that cost little to operate and are well made.

   The paragraph best supports the statement that

   5-A most users of duplicating machines prefer low operating cost to efficiency
   5-B a well-built machine will outlast a cheap one

5-C a duplicating machine is not efficient unless it is sturdy

5-D a duplicating machine should be both efficient and economical

6. The location of a railway line is necessarily a compromise between the desire to build the line with as little expense as possible and the desire to construct it so that its route will cover that over which trade and commerce are likely to flow.

The route selected for a railway line

6-A should be the one over which the line can be built most cheaply

6-B determines the location of commercial centers

6-C should always cover the shortest possible distance between its terminals

6-D cannot always be the one involving the lowest construction costs

7. A survey to determine the subjects that have helped students most in their jobs shows that typewriting leads all other subjects in the business group. It also leads among the subjects college students consider most valuable and would take again if they were to return to high school.

The paragraph best supports the statement that

7-A the ability to type is an asset in business and in school

7-B students who return to night school take typing

7-C students with a knowledge of typing do superior work in college

7-D success in business is assured those who can type

8. Direct lighting is the least satisfactory lighting arrangement. The desk or ceiling light with a reflector which diffuses all the rays downward is sure to cause glare on the working surface.

Direct lighting is least satisfactory as a method of lighting chiefly because

8-A the light is diffused causing eye strain

8-B the shade on the individual desk lamp is not constructed along scientific lines

8-C the working surface is usually obscured by the glare

8-D direct lighting is injurious to the eyes

9. It is a common assumption that city directories are prepared and published by the cities concerned. However, the directory business is as much a private business as is the publishing of dictionaries and encyclopedias. The companies financing the publication make their profits through the sales of the directories themselves and through the advertising in them.

The paragraph best supports the statement that

9-A the publication of a city directory is a commercial enterprise

9-B the size of a city directory limits the space devoted to advertising

9-C many city directories are published by dictionary and encyclopedia concerns

9-D city directories are sold at cost to local residents and businessmen

10. The view is widely held that butter is more digestible and better absorbed than other fats because of its low melting point. There is little scientific authority for such a view. As margarine is made today, its melting point is close to that of butter, and tests show only the slightest degree of difference in digestibility of fats of equally low melting points.

The paragraph best supports the statement that

10-A butter is more easily digested than margarine

10-B there is not much difference in the digestibility of butter and margarine

10-C most people prefer butter to margarine

10-D it sometimes becomes necessary to use a substitute for butter

11. The problem in adult education seems to be not the piling up of facts but practice in thinking.

The paragraph best supports the statement that

11-A educational methods for adults and young people should differ

11-B adults do not seem to retain new facts

11-C a well-educated adult is one who thinks but does not have a store of information

11-D adult education should stress ability to think

12. The coloration of textile fabrics composed of cotton and wool generally requires two processes, as the process used in dyeing wool is seldom capable of fixing the color upon cotton. The usual method is to immerse the fabric in the requisite baths to dye the wool and then to test the partially dyed material in the manner found suitable for cotton.

The dyeing of textile fabrics composed of cotton and wool

12-A is more successful when the material contains more cotton than wool

12-B is not satisfactory when solid colors are desired

12-C is restricted to two colors for any one fabric

12-D is based upon the methods required for dyeing the different materials

13. Both the high school and the college should take the responsibility for preparing the student to get a job. Since the ability to write a good application letter is one of the first steps toward this goal, every teacher should be willing to do what he can to help the student learn to write such letters.

The paragraph best supports the statement that

13-A inability to write a good letter often reduces one's job prospects

13-B the major responsibility of the school is to obtain jobs for its students

13-C success is largely a matter of the kind of work the student applies for first

13-D every teacher should teach a course in the writing of application letters

14. "White collar" is a term used to describe one of the largest groups of workers in American industry and trade. It distinguishes those who work with the pencil and the mind from those who depend on their hands and the machine. It suggests occupations in which physical exertion and handling of materials are not primary features of the job.

"White collar" workers are

14-A not so strong physically as those who work with their hands

14-B those who supervise workers handling materials

14-C all whose work is entirely indoors

14-D not likely to use machines so much as are other groups of workers

15. Any business not provided with capable substitutes to fill all important positions is a weak business. Therefore, a foreman should train each man not only to perform his own particular duties but also to do those of two or three positions.

The paragraph best supports the statement that

15-A dependence on substitutes is a sign of a weak organization

15-B training will improve the strongest organization

15-C the foreman should be the most expert at any particular job under him

15-D vacancies in vital positions should be provided for in advance

END OF PART 4

IF YOU FINISH BEFORE TIME IS UP, CHECK OVER YOUR WORK ON THIS PART ONLY. DO NOT GO BACK TO ANY PREVIOUS PART. DO NOT GO ON UNTIL YOU ARE TOLD TO DO SO.

PART 5

NUMERICAL OPERATIONS

The numerical operations part of your test battery consists of fifty very simple arithmetic questions which must be answered in only three minutes. Obviously, speed is a very important factor. You should not attempt to compute these answers using pencil and scratch paper. Instead, solve each problem in your head, then choose the correct answer from among the four choices and mark the letter of the correct answer on your answer sheet. If you are not sure of an answer, guess and go on to the next question. Do not skip any questions. You will most certainly not have time to go back to fill in. Since a wrong answer will not count against you, it cannot hurt to guess. Many people cannot complete all fifty questions in the three minutes allowed. Do not be upset if you cannot finish. Just answer as many questions as you can. Try these questions.

1. 3 − 1 =

1-A 2
1-B 3
1-C 4
1-D 1

1. Ⓐ Ⓑ Ⓒ Ⓓ

1-A 3 − 1 = 2

2. 8 × 2 =

2-A 6
2-B 16
2-C 12
2-D 10

2. Ⓐ Ⓑ Ⓒ Ⓓ

2-B 8 × 2 = 16

3. 4 + 1 =

3-A 2
3-B 3
3-C 4
3-D 5

3. Ⓐ Ⓑ Ⓒ Ⓓ

3-D 4 + 1 = 5

4. 7 × 6 =

4-A 11
4-B 13
4-C 24
4-D 42

4. Ⓐ Ⓑ Ⓒ Ⓓ

4-D 7 × 6 = 42

5. 10 − 3 =

5-A 7
5-B 13
5-C 8
5-D 6

5. Ⓐ Ⓑ Ⓒ Ⓓ

5-A 10 − 3 = 7

6. 1 + 7 =

6-A 6
6-B 7
6-C 8
6-D 9

6. Ⓐ Ⓑ Ⓒ Ⓓ

6-C 1 + 7 = 8

DO NOT TURN THE PAGE UNTIL YOU ARE TOLD TO DO SO

NUMERICAL OPERATIONS

TIME: 3 Minutes—50 Questions

1. $5 + 3 =$

1-A 2
1-B 6
1-C 8
1-D 11

2. $8 - 6 =$

2-A 7
2-B 2
2-C 12
2-D 14

3. $12 \div 2 =$

3-A 10
3-B 3
3-C 4
3-D 6

4. $4 + 6 =$

4-A 12
4-B 10
4-C 3
4-D 2

5. $6 \times 3 =$

5-A 3
5-B 9
5-C 12
5-D 18

6. $9 + 5 =$

6-A 14
6-B 4
6-C 13
6-D 16

7. $10 \div 5 =$

7-A 5
7-B 15
7-C 2
7-D 25

8. $2 \times 9 =$

8-A 18
8-B 36
8-C 16
8-D 15

9. $8 + 3 =$

9-A 13
9-B 12
9-C 11
9-D 15

10. $1 + 6 =$

10-A 5
10-B 6
10-C 7
10-D 9

11. $7 - 2 =$

11-A 5
11-B 9
11-C 14
11-D 7

12. $5 - 0 =$

12-A 0
12-B 1
12-C 5
12-D 10

13. $6 \times 7 =$

13-A 13
13-B 24
13-C 27
13-D 42

14. $7 + 6 =$

14-A 11
14-B 13
14-C 14
14-D 21

15. 8 − 5 =

15-A   13
15-B   11
15-C   4
15-D   3

16. 6 + 8 =

16-A   2
16-B   10
16-C   12
16-D   14

17. 4 × 6 =

17-A   12
17-B   16
17-C   24
17-D   28

18. 3 + 3 =

18-A   3
18-B   6
18-C   0
18-D   9

19. 2 − 1 =

19-A   2
19-B   3
19-C   0
19-D   1

20. 4 × 0 =

20-A   4
20-B   1
20-C   16
20-D   0

21. 9 × 1 =

21-A   10
21-B   11
21-C   9
21-D   8

22. 4 + 8 =

22-A   32
22-B   24
22-C   12
22-D   4

23. 5 − 1 =

23-A   4
23-B   5
23-C   6
23-D   15

24. 9 + 3 =

24-A   3
24-B   6
24-C   12
24-D   15

25. 4 × 6 =

25-A   21
25-B   24
25-C   26
25-D   28

26. 7 + 2 =

26-A   3
26-B   5
26-C   9
26-D   14

27. 8 + 8 =

27-A   0
27-B   1
27-C   8
27-D   16

28. 15 ÷ 3 =

28-A   5
28-B   3
28-C   12
28-D   45

29. 2 × 8 =

29-A   6
29-B   16
29-C   18
29-D   36

30. 1 + 6 =

30-A   16
30-B   12
30-C   7
30-D   6

31. 40 ÷ 8 =

31-A   4
31-B   5
31-C   6
31-D   8

32. 7 × 6 =

32-A   24
32-B   36
32-C   42
32-D   48

33. 4 + 5 =

33-A   9
33-B   7
33-C   11
33-D   1

34. 6 × 2 =

34-A   8
34-B   4
34-C   36
34-D   12

35. 10 − 8 =

35-A   80
35-B   18
35-C   12
35-D   2

36. 7 ÷ 1 =

36-A   1
36-B   7
36-C   0
36-D   8

37. 9 + 4 =

37-A   11
37-B   13
37-C   15
37-D   17

38. 3 × 8 =

38-A   24
38-B   32
38-C   36
38-D   42

39. 1 + 7 =

39-A   6
39-B   7
39-C   8
39-D   5

40. 6 × 6 =

40-A   12
40-B   18
40-C   36
40-D   66

41. 8 + 9 =

41-A   15
41-B   17
41-C   19
41-D   21

42. 1 + 3 =

42-A   1
42-B   2
42-C   3
42-D   4

43. 2 × 7 =

43-A   5
43-B   9
43-C   12
43-D   14

44. 35 ÷ 7 =

44-A   12
44-B   7
44-C   6
44-D   5

45. 10 − 9 =

45-A   11
45-B   19
45-C   1
45-D   0

46. 3 + 4 =

   46-A 9
   46-B 7
   46-C 5
   46-D 1

47. 8 − 6 =

   47-A   2
   47-B   4
   47-C 12
   47-D 14

48. 8 ÷ 2 =

   48-A   6
   48-B 16

48-C 10
48-D   4

49. 6 + 7 =

   49-A 11
   49-B 13
   49-C 15
   49-D   9

50. 9 + 1 =

   50-A   8
   50-B   9
   50-C 10
   50-D 11

END OF PART 5

IF YOU FINISH THIS PART BEFORE THE TIME IS UP, CHECK OVER YOUR WORK ON THIS PART ONLY. DO NOT GO ON UNTIL YOU ARE TOLD TO DO SO.

PART 6

CODING SPEED

The coding part of your exam is different from all other parts of the exam. Nothing that you have learned enters into your answering of these questions. Coding is a test of your memory, your eye-hand coordination and your working speed.

Before each set of questions you will find a "key." The key consists of ten words listed in alphabetical order. Each word has a four-digit code number assigned to it.

In the set of questions you will find the same ten words, scrambled and sometimes repeated. Following each word in the test are *five* answer choices in columns labelled A to E. Each answer choice is a four-digit number. The answer choices are in ascending order; that is, the lowest number is always in column A, the next higher number is in column B and so on to the highest number in column E. You must look at the word, find the correct code number among the choices and mark on your answer sheet the letter of the column in which you found the correct code number.

On the actual examination you must work very quickly. You have only seven minutes in which to try to answer eighty-four questions. Use the sample questions that follow to develop a system that works for you—memorization, some sort of word-number association, a mathematical formula or any private method that helps you work up speed and accuracy. Many people cannot finish the coding test in the time allowed. Do not be upset if you cannot finish. Just do your best. Try these questions.

Key

bee	8176	fish	5921	moon	3672
cattle	4238	gloves	4970	nose	6482
diet	1910	lake	2286	rail	7657
		ledge	1152		

Answers

		A	B	C	D	E	
1.	diet	1910	2286	4970	6482	7657	1. Ⓐ Ⓑ Ⓒ Ⓓ Ⓔ
2.	rail	2286	5921	6482	7657	8176	2. Ⓐ Ⓑ Ⓒ Ⓓ Ⓔ
3.	fish	1152	1910	4238	5921	6482	3. Ⓐ Ⓑ Ⓒ Ⓓ Ⓔ
4.	nose	2286	4238	4970	5921	6482	4. Ⓐ Ⓑ Ⓒ Ⓓ Ⓔ
5.	gloves	4238	4970	5921	7657	8176	5. Ⓐ Ⓑ Ⓒ Ⓓ Ⓔ
6.	lake	2286	3672	4970	6482	7657	6. Ⓐ Ⓑ Ⓒ Ⓓ Ⓔ
7.	bee	1910	4238	6482	7657	8176	7. Ⓐ Ⓑ Ⓒ Ⓓ Ⓔ
8.	ledge	1152	2286	3672	4238	5921	8. Ⓐ Ⓑ Ⓒ Ⓓ Ⓔ
9.	cattle	1152	1910	3672	4238	6482	9. Ⓐ Ⓑ Ⓒ Ⓓ Ⓔ
10.	gloves	1910	4970	5921	6482	8176	10. Ⓐ Ⓑ Ⓒ Ⓓ Ⓔ
11.	moon	2286	3672	4238	4970	6482	11. Ⓐ Ⓑ Ⓒ Ⓓ Ⓔ
12.	fish	1152	1910	3672	4238	5921	12. Ⓐ Ⓑ Ⓒ Ⓓ Ⓔ

The correct answers are:

1-A	**4**-E	**7**-E	**10**-B
2-D	**5**-B	**8**-A	**11**-B
3-D	**6**-A	**9**-D	**12**-E

Key

cat 3382	empty 3571	oil 8513
cough 5842	fudge 4002	spoon 7975
dime 9186	game 8934	white 6300
	heart 1010	

Answers

		A	B	C	D	E	
13.	fudge	1010	3382	4002	8934	9186	**13.** Ⓐ Ⓑ Ⓒ Ⓓ Ⓔ
14.	cough	3571	5842	6300	7975	8513	**14.** Ⓐ Ⓑ Ⓒ Ⓓ Ⓔ
15.	white	4002	5842	6300	8513	9186	**15.** Ⓐ Ⓑ Ⓒ Ⓓ Ⓔ
16.	spoon	3382	3571	5842	6300	7975	**16.** Ⓐ Ⓑ Ⓒ Ⓓ Ⓔ
17.	cat	1010	3382	4002	5842	9186	**17.** Ⓐ Ⓑ Ⓒ Ⓓ Ⓔ
18.	oil	3571	7975	8513	8934	9186	**18.** Ⓐ Ⓑ Ⓒ Ⓓ Ⓔ
19.	heart	1010	3382	3571	7975	8934	**19.** Ⓐ Ⓑ Ⓒ Ⓓ Ⓔ
20.	dime	3382	3571	4002	8513	9186	**20.** Ⓐ Ⓑ Ⓒ Ⓓ Ⓔ
21.	empty	3571	5842	6300	8513	8934	**21.** Ⓐ Ⓑ Ⓒ Ⓓ Ⓔ
22.	game	3382	4002	5842	8934	9186	**22.** Ⓐ Ⓑ Ⓒ Ⓓ Ⓔ
23.	cough	1010	4002	5842	6300	7975	**23.** Ⓐ Ⓑ Ⓒ Ⓓ Ⓔ
24.	empty	1010	3382	3571	5842	8513	**24.** Ⓐ Ⓑ Ⓒ Ⓓ Ⓔ

The correct answers are:

13-C	**16**-E	**19**-A	**22**-D
14-B	**17**-B	**20**-E	**23**-C
15-C	**18**-C	**21**-A	**24**-C

DO NOT TURN THE PAGE UNTIL YOU ARE TOLD TO DO SO

CODING SPEED

TIME: 7 Minutes—84 Questions

Key

bird 7011	ghost 9212	rat 4643
car 6300	jury 2912	stump 8956
egg 1237	maroon 5873	window 6766
	pump 3061	

Answers

		A	B	C	D	E
1.	maroon	4643	5873	6766	8956	9212
2.	window	1237	2912	4643	6766	8956
3.	jury	2912	3061	5873	6300	7011
4.	rat	1237	3061	4643	6300	6766
5.	ghost	2912	4643	5873	8956	9212
6.	bird	3061	4643	6300	6766	7011
7.	stump	5873	6300	6766	7011	8956
8.	car	1237	3061	6300	6766	9212
9.	egg	1237	2912	3061	5873	8956
10.	pump	2912	3061	4643	6300	6766
11.	window	3061	6300	6766	7011	9212
12.	rat	3061	4643	5873	6766	8956

Key

blue 5913	food 1238	roast 4650
clown 3761	hat 8884	toe 7277
dust 9009	lamp 2212	wish 6702
	money 8648	

Answers

		A	B	C	D	E
13.	clown	1238	2212	3761	8884	9009
14.	wish	3761	4650	5913	6702	7277
15.	roast	2212	4650	6702	8648	8884
16.	blue	1238	2212	3761	4650	5913
17.	roast	1238	3761	4650	7277	8884
18.	dust	3761	5913	6702	8648	9009
19.	food	1238	2212	4650	6702	8648
20.	toe	4650	5913	6702	7277	8884
21.	lamp	2212	3761	6702	8648	8884
22.	money	4650	5913	8648	8884	9009
23.	clown	3761	4650	6702	7277	9009
24.	hat	1238	2212	5913	8648	8884

Key

ant 4848	fog 6848	queen 7512
bus 9735	house 2345	tree 8864
drama 1981	laugh 5005	zoo 4584
	note 3689	

Answers

		A	B	C	D	E
25.	laugh	2345	4584	4848	5005	8864
26.	queen	1981	2345	3689	6848	7512
27.	ant	2345	4584	4848	6848	8864
28.	drama	1981	2345	3689	7512	9735
29.	note	1981	3689	4584	8864	9735
30.	fog	3689	4584	4848	6848	8864
31.	tree	4584	4848	6848	8864	9735
32.	bus	1981	2345	3689	7512	9735
33.	house	2345	3689	4584	5005	7512
34.	zoo	2345	4584	4848	6848	8864
35.	note	3689	4848	5005	7512	9735
36.	laugh	2345	3689	5005	6848	7512

Key

art 1066	flower 4003	silence 6969
clue 3682	hood 7877	spoon 9060
down 5974	ice 8880	taxi 1001
	pants 2468	

Answers

		A	B	C	D	E
37.	silence	3682	4003	6969	8880	9060
38.	hood	1066	4003	5974	7877	9060
39.	pants	1001	2468	3682	4003	6969
40.	clue	3682	4003	6969	8880	9060
41.	art	1001	1066	4003	7877	8880
42.	down	2468	4003	5974	6969	7877
43.	ice	1001	1066	4003	8880	9060
44.	flower	4003	5974	6969	7877	8880
45.	spoon	2468	3682	6969	8880	9060
46.	down	1066	3682	4003	5974	6969
47.	hood	1001	2468	6969	7877	9060
48.	taxi	1001	1066	4003	8880	9060

Key

angel 7717	flood 5846	llama 2573
brick 1492	gown 3232	nut 9089
eye 6943	ink 4921	red 5487
	joke 8614	

Answers

	A	B	C	D	E
49. flood	1492	4921	5487	5846	6943
50. gown	2573	3232	6943	8614	9089
51. joke	1492	4921	5846	7717	8614
52. nut	1492	2573	3232	8614	9089
53. angel	2573	4921	6943	7717	8614
54. ink	1492	4921	6943	7715	8614
55. red	1492	4912	5487	5846	6943
56. eye	4921	6943	7717	8614	9089
57. brick	1492	4912	5846	6943	8614
58. llama	2573	3232	4921	6943	9089
59. eye	1492	2573	3232	5846	6943
60. ink	2573	3232	4921	7717	8614

Key

apple 6080	devil 4598	roof 7503
bud 2722	drum 5489	shoe 9890
cone 1787	ear 3343	train 4672
	frown 8932	

Answers

	A	B	C	D	E
61. devil	4598	4672	5489	8932	9890
62. ear	1787	2722	3343	5489	6080
63. frown	2722	4598	5489	7503	8932
64. drum	3343	4598	4672	5489	9890
65. bud	1787	2722	4672	6080	7503
66. roof	1787	2722	5489	7503	8932
67. train	4598	4672	5489	6080	8932
68. cone	1787	3343	4598	5489	9890
69. apple	2722	5489	6080	7503	9890
70. bud	1787	2722	3343	4598	8932
71. drum	2722	4598	5489	6080	7503
72. frown	1787	3343	5489	8932	9890

Key

arch 2641	dress 5959	mud 7777
battle 1686	fuzz 4769	puzzle 8724
coin 9559	green 3480	stew 4162
	hair 6931	

Answers

	A	B	C	D	E
73. puzzle	1686	4769	6931	8724	9559
74. fuzz	2641	3480	4162	4769	5959
75. stew	2641	4162	6931	7777	8724
76. battle	1686	2641	4162	6931	8724
77. mud	3480	4769	5959	7777	9559
78. green	1686	3480	4162	6931	8724
79. coin	2641	4162	5959	7777	9559
80. arch	2641	4162	4769	6931	8724
81. dress	1686	4769	5959	8724	9559
82. hair	4162	4769	5959	6931	7777
83. puzzle	1686	4162	6931	7777	8724
84. dress	2641	3480	4162	4769	5959

END OF PART 6

IF YOU FINISH BEFORE TIME IS UP, MAKE SURE YOU HAVE AN-SWERED ALL THE QUESTIONS. DO NOT GO BACK TO ANY PREVIOUS PART. DO NOT TURN THE PAGE UNTIL YOU ARE TOLD TO DO SO.

PART 7

AUTO & SHOP INFORMATION

The auto and shop information questions test your knowledge and understanding of automobiles and of tools and shop practices. The answers to many questions come straight from your life experience. However, if this is not your area of interest, there will be questions to which you do not know the answer. Make the most sensible guess. Answer all questions. Mark the letter of your choice on your answer sheet. Try these questions.

1. The muffler on a car serves to

   1-A   filter the exhaust fumes
   1-B   keep the car warm
   1-C   reduce exhaust sounds
   1-D   protect against body damage

   1. Ⓐ Ⓑ Ⓒ Ⓓ

1-C The muffler is, in effect, a silencer. It cuts down exhaust noise. While the muffler is part of the exhaust system, it has no effect on the fumes (A).

2. The probable reason why a moving car with power steering might suddenly become hard to steer is that

   2-A   the emergency brake is on
   2-B   the wheels are out of alignment
   2-C   transmission belts are stretched
   2-D   the engine has stalled

   2. Ⓐ Ⓑ Ⓒ Ⓓ

2-D Power steering is powered by the car's engine. If the engine STALLS, the power assistance vanishes and the car becomes very difficult to steer. The car might be hard to steer if the emergency brake was on (A), but this would be noticed at the outset of a trip, not suddenly after the car had been moving, Out of alignment wheels (B) also affect steering, but the effect is constant, not

sudden. Transmission (C) has nothing to do with steering.

3.

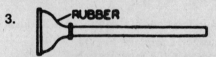

The tool above is most likely to be used by a

   3-A   stonemason
   3-B   plumber
   3-C   carpenter
   3-D   machinist

   3. Ⓐ Ⓑ Ⓒ Ⓓ

3-B The tool is a plunger. It is used by a PLUMBER to dislodge material that is clogging drains.

4. The frequency of oiling and greasing of bearings and other moving parts of machinery depends mainly on the

   4-A   size of the parts requiring lubrication
   4-B   speed at which the parts move
   4-C   ability of the operator
   4-D   amount of use of the equipment

   4. Ⓐ Ⓑ Ⓒ Ⓓ

4-D Lubrication of machinery is scheduled according to time elapsed and amount of use. All the other reasons offered are irrelevant.

DO NOT TURN THE PAGE UNTIL YOU ARE TOLD TO DO SO

AUTO & SHOP INFORMATION

TIME: 11 Minutes—25 Questions

1. Most automobile engines run according to the

    1-A rotary cycle
    1-B intake-exhaust cycle
    1-C four-stroke cycle
    1-D two-stroke cycle

2. The most important rule for a driver to remember in the care of an automobile battery is to

    2-A make certain that the points are properly adjusted in the spark plugs
    2-B burn the headlights or play the radio, occasionally, while the ignition is turned on
    2-C have the battery discharged at regular intervals, weekly in the winter, bi-weekly in the summer
    2-D keep the level of the liquid above the plates

3. The function of the rotor is to

    3-A open and close the distributor points
    3-B rotate the distributor cam
    3-C distribute electricity to the spark plugs
    3-D rotate the distributor shaft

4. A governor is used on an automobile primarily to limit its

    4-A rate of acceleration
    4-B maximum speed
    4-C fuel consumption
    4-D stopping distance

5. The headlights to automobiles are found to be connected ordinarily in

    5-A parallel
    5-B series
    5-C diagonal
    5-D perpendicular

6. A wood screw that can be tightened by a wrench is known as a

    6-A lag screw
    6-B carriage screw
    6-C Philips screw
    6-D monkey screw

7. The reason that a lubricant prevents rubbing surfaces from becoming hot is that the oil

    7-A is cold and cools off the rubbing metal surfaces
    7-B is sticky, preventing the surfaces from moving over each other too rapidly
    7-C forms a smooth layer between the two surfaces, preventing their coming into contact
    7-D makes the surfaces smooth so that they move easily over each other

8.

The tool shown above is used to

    8-A set nails
    8-B set lead anchors
    8-C drill holes in concrete
    8-D centerpunch for holes

9. An expansion bolt is used to

    9-A enlarge a hole
    9-B fasten into hollow tile
    9-C allow for expansion and contraction
    9-D fasten into solid masonry

10. The length of a 10-penny nail is, in inches

    10-A $2\frac{1}{2}$
    10-B 3
    10-C $3\frac{1}{2}$
    10-D 4

11. Glazier's points are used to

   11-A hold glass in wooden window sash
   11-B scratch glass so that it can be broken to size
   11-C force putty into narrow spaces between glass and sash
   11-D remove broken glass from a pane

12. The tool that is best suited for use with a wood chisel is

12-A

12-B

12-C

12-D

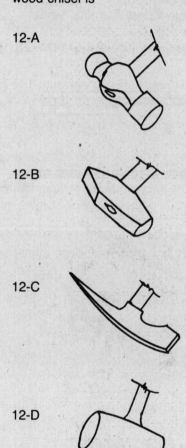

13. The set in the teeth of a hand saw primarily

   13-A prevents the saw from binding
   13-B makes the saw cut true
   13-C gives the saw a sharper edge
   13-D removes the sawdust

14. A fuel injection system on an automobile engine eliminates the necessity for

   14-A a manifold
   14-B a carburetor
   14-C spark plugs
   14-D a distributor

15. When reference is made to the "Compression Ratio" of an automotive gasoline engine, this is best described to be the

   15-A volume above the piston at top dead center
   15-B displacement volume as the piston moves down to bottom dead center
   15-C total volume of a cylinder divided by its clearance volume
   15-D displacement volume of a cylinder divided by its clearance volume

16. Reverse flushing of a clogged gasoline engine block and radiator cooling system is done properly by

   16-A not removing the thermostat out of the engine block
   16-B connecting the flushing gun at the bottom of the engine block
   16-C using air and water
   16-D using low pressure steam

17. A mechanic sets the proper electrode gap on a sparkplug most accurately if he uses a

   17-A dial gauge
   17-B round wire feeler gauge
   17-C square wire feeler gauge
   17-D conventional flat feeler gauge

18. Water in the cooling system should be

   18-A alkaline
   18-B acid
   18-C salty
   18-D neutral

19. Wood ladders should not be painted because

   19-A paint will wear off rapidly due to the conditions under which ladders are used
   19-B ladders are slippery when painted

19-C it is more effective to store the ladder in a dry place

19-D paint will hide defects in the ladder

20.

The tool shown above is used to measure

20-A clearances
20-B wire thickness
20-C inside slots
20-D screw pitch

21. A lathe would normally be used in making which of the following items?

21-A a hockey stick
21-B a picture frame
21-C a bookcase
21-D a baseball bat

22. The term "whipping" when applied to rope means

22-A binding the ends with cord to prevent unraveling
22-B coiling the rope in as tight a ball as possible
22-C lubricating the strands with tallow
22-D wetting the rope with water to cure it

23. Alcohol is put into the radiator of an automobile in cold weather because it

23-A lowers the boiling point of the mixture
23-B lowers the freezing point of the mixture

23-C raises the boiling point of the mixture
23-D raises the freezing point of the mixture

24. Lacquer thinner would most likely be used to

24-A clean oil paint from a brush immediately after use
24-B rinse a new paint brush before using it
24-C clean a paint brush upon which paint has hardened
24-D remove paint from the hands

25. The tool used to measure the depth of a hole is

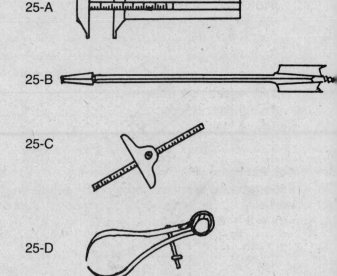

END OF PART 7

IF YOU FINISH BEFORE TIME IS UP, CHECK OVER YOUR WORK ON THIS PART ONLY. DO NOT RETURN TO ANY PREVIOUS PART. DO NOT TURN THE PAGE UNTIL YOU ARE TOLD TO DO SO.

MATHEMATICS KNOWLEDGE

To solve the problems in this part, you must draw upon your knowledge of high school mathematics. The problems require you to use simple algebra and geometry along with arithmetic skills and reasoning power. Some questions can be answered in your head. Others will require the use of scratch paper. If you use scratch paper for your calculations, be sure to mark the letter of the correct answer on your answer sheet. Try these questions.

1. Two rectangular boards each measuring 5 feet by 3 feet are placed together to make one large board. How much shorter will the perimeter be if the two long sides are placed together than if the two short sides are placed together?

   1-A   2 feet
   1-B   4 feet
   1-C   6 feet
   1-D   8 feet

1. Ⓐ Ⓑ Ⓒ Ⓓ

1-B Perimeter = 2 l + 2 w
If the two long sides are together the perimeter will be

   5 + 3 + 3 + 5 + 3 + 3 = 22

If the two short sides are together, the perimeter will be

   3 + 5 + 5 + 3 + 5 + 5 = 26

26 − 22 = 4 feet shorter

2. 1% of 8 =

   2-A   8
   2-B   .8
   2-C   .08
   2-D   .008

2. Ⓐ Ⓑ Ⓒ Ⓓ

2-C To remove a % sign, divide the number by 100.
Thus, 1% = 1/100 = .01.
1% of 8 is the same as 1% times 8 = .01 × 8 = .08

3. When 81.3 is divided by 10 the quotient is

   3-A   0.0813
   3-B   0.813
   3-C   8.13
   3-D   813

3. Ⓐ Ⓑ Ⓒ Ⓓ

3-C

```
        8.13
  10)81.30
     80
      1 3
      1 0
        30
        30
```

4. +1 −1 +1 −1 +1 . . . and so on where the last number is +1, has a sum of

   4-A   0
   4-B   −1
   4-C   +1
   4-D   2

4. Ⓐ Ⓑ Ⓒ Ⓓ

4-C Each minus 1 cancels out the plus 1 before it. Since the final term is +1, which is not cancelled out by a −1, the sum is +1.

DO NOT TURN THE PAGE UNTIL YOU ARE TOLD TO DO SO

MATHEMATICS KNOWLEDGE

TIME: 24 Minutes—25 Questions

1. If 30 is divided by .06, the result is

   1-A 5
   1-B 50
   1-C 500
   1-D 5000

2. 36 yards and 12 feet divided by 3 =

   2-A 40 ft.
   2-B 124 ft.
   2-C $12\frac{1}{4}$ yds.
   2-D 12 yds.

3. 150 is what percent of 30?

   3-A 50
   3-B 150
   3-C 180
   3-D 500

4. In the formula I = p + prt, what does I equal when p = 500, r = 20%, t = 2?

   4-A 10,000
   4-B 700
   4-C 8,000
   4-D 12,000

5. If 5 pints of water are needed to water each square foot of lawn, the minimum gallons of water needed for a lawn 8′ by 12′ is

   5-A 5
   5-B 20
   5-C 40
   5-D 60

6.

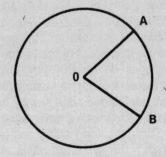

In the figure above, ∠AOB = 60°. If O is the center of the circle, then minor arc AB is what part of the circumference of the circle?

   6-A $\frac{1}{2}$
   6-B $\frac{1}{3}$
   6-C $\frac{1}{6}$
   6-D $\frac{1}{8}$

7. In a bag there are red, green, black, and white marbles. If there are 6 red, 8 green, 4 black, and 12 white, and one marble is to be selected at random, what is the probability it will be white?

   7-A $\frac{1}{5}$
   7-B $\frac{2}{5}$
   7-C $\frac{4}{15}$
   7-D $\frac{2}{15}$

8. A man has T dollars to invest; after he invests $1,000 how much money does he have remaining?

   8-A T + 1000
   8-B T − 1000
   8-C 1000 − T
   8-D 1000T

9. 25.726 × .04 =

9-A 102.904
9-B 10.2904
9-C .0102904
9-D 1.02904

10. 5 is what percent of 25?

10-A 5
10-B 50
10-C 500
10-D 20

11. A rectangular field is 900 yds. by 240 yds. What is the largest number of rectangular lots 120 yds. by 60 yds. that it can be divided into?

11-A 20
11-B 60
11-C 30
11-D 40

12. $\sqrt{\frac{9}{64} + \frac{16}{64}}$ =

12-A $\frac{5}{8}$
12-B $\frac{7}{64}$
12-C $\frac{5}{64}$
12-D $\frac{25}{64}$

13. If $\frac{3}{4}$ of a class is absent and $\frac{2}{3}$ of those present leave the room, what fraction of the original class remains in the room?

13-A $\frac{1}{24}$
13-B $\frac{1}{4}$
13-C $\frac{1}{12}$
13-D $\frac{1}{8}$

14. If a = 3, then $a^a \cdot a$ =

14-A 9
14-B 51
14-C 18
14-D 81

15. A group left on a trip at 8:50 A.M. and reached their destination at 3:30 P.M. How long, in hours and minutes, did the trip take?

15-A 3 hours 10 minutes
15-B 4 hours 40 minutes
15-C 5 hours 10 minutes
15-D 6 hours 40 minutes

16. If .04y = 1, then y =

16-A .025
16-B 25
16-C .25
16-D 250

17. (3 + 2)(6 − 2)(7 + 1) = (4 + 4)(x). What is the value of x?

17-A 13 + 2
17-B 14 + 4
17-C 4 + 15
17-D 8 + 12

18. In the diagram below, chord TU =

18-A $(TY + UY)^2$

18-B $\sqrt{TY} + TU$

18-C $\sqrt{TY^2 + UY^2}$

18-D $\dfrac{TY \times UY}{2}$

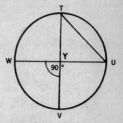

19. From a temperature of 15°, a drop of 21° would result in a temperature of

19-A −36°
19-B 36°
19-C −6°
19-D −30°

20. A certain highway intersection has had A accidents over a ten-year period, resulting in B deaths. What is the yearly average death rate for the intersection?

20-A A + B − 10

20-B $\dfrac{B}{10}$

20-C $10 - \dfrac{A}{B}$

20-D $\dfrac{A}{10}$

21. 10 to the fifth power may correctly be expressed as

    21-A 10×5
    21-B 5^{10}
    21-C $5\sqrt{10}$
    21-D $10 \times 10 \times 10 \times 10 \times 10$

22. $2.2 \times .00001 =$

    22-A .0022
    22-B .00022
    22-C .000022
    22-D .0000022

23. The figure on the right is a

    23-A hexagon
    23-B octagon
    23-C pentagon
    23-D decahedron

24. $8! = 8 \times 7 \times 6 \times 5 \times 4 \times 3 \times 2 \times 1$
    $4! =$

    24-A 4^4
    24-B 32
    24-C 4^2
    24-D 24

25. If T tons of snow fall in 1 second, how many tons fall in M minutes?

    25-A 60 MT
    25-B MT + 60
    25-C MT
    25-D $\dfrac{60\,M}{T}$

END OF PART 8

IF YOU COMPLETE YOUR WORK BEFORE TIME IS UP, CHECK TO BE SURE THAT YOU HAVE MARKED ALL THE ANSWERS ON YOUR ANSWER SHEET. THEN CHECK OVER YOUR WORK ON THIS PART ONLY. DO NOT GO BACK TO ANY PREVIOUS PART. DO NOT GO ON TO THE NEXT PAGE UNTIL YOU ARE TOLD TO DO SO.

MECHANICAL COMPREHENSION

Part 9 consists of questions about your understanding of general mechanical and physical principles. Your understanding of these principles will come from your own observations, from experience in working with mechanical devices and from your reading and school courses. Answer all the questions as best you can, marking the letter of your choice on your answer sheet. Try these questions.

1.

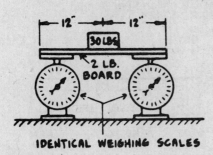

IDENTICAL WEIGHING SCALES

The weight held by the board and placed on the two identical scales will cause *each* scale to read

1-A　8 lbs.
1-B　16 lbs.
1-C　15 lbs.
1-D　32 lbs.

1. Ⓐ Ⓑ Ⓒ Ⓓ

1-B Since the 32 total pounds (30-lb. weight plus 2-lb. board) are exactly evenly distributed between the two scales, each scale is supporting exactly one half of the weight. Hence, each scale will read 16 pounds.

2.

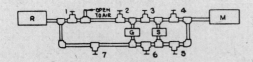

In the figure above, assume that all valves are closed. For air to flow from R, through G, then through S to M open

2-A　valves 1, 2, 6 and 4

2-B　valves 7, 3 and 4
2-C　valves 7, 6 and 4
2-D　valves 7, 3 and 5

2. Ⓐ Ⓑ Ⓒ Ⓓ

2-D The air from R must follow a route down through valve 7, up through G, then through valve 3, down through S, to the right through 5, then up and over to M. The air could not pass through valves 1 and 2 to G because it would escape through the opening between valves 1 and 2. If either valve 4 or valve 6 were to be opened, the air would be diverted from the appointed route.

3.

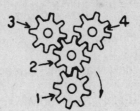

The figure above shows four gears. If gear 1 turns as shown, then the gears turning in the same direction are

3-A　2, 3 and 4
3-B　2 and 4
3-C　2 and 3
3-D　3 and 4

3. Ⓐ Ⓑ Ⓒ Ⓓ

3-D A turning gear always turns the gear with which it interlocks in the opposite direction. If gear 1 turns clockwise, then gear 2 must turn counterclockwise. In turn, gears 3 and 4, since they are both turned by gear 2, must both turn clockwise.

DO NOT TURN THE PAGE UNTIL YOU ARE TOLD TO DO SO

MECHANICAL COMPREHENSION

TIME: 19 Minutes—25 Questions

1.

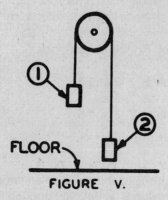

FLOOR

FIGURE V.

The figure above represents a pulley, with practically no friction, from which two ten-pound weights are suspended as indicated. If a downward force is applied to weight 1, it is most likely that weight 1 will

1-A come to rest at the present level of weight 2

1-B move downward until it is level with weight 2

1-C move downward until it reaches the floor

1-D pass weight 2 in its downward motion and then return to its present position

2.

INLET

OPEN TANK

1-INCH DIAMETER OUTLET

2-INCH DIAMETER OUTLET

Eight gallons of water per minute are flowing at a given time from the one-inch outlet in the tank shown. What is the amount of water flowing at that time from the two-inch outlet?

2-A 64 gallons per minute

2-B 32 gallons per minute

2-C 16 gallons per minute

2-D 2 gallons per minute

3.

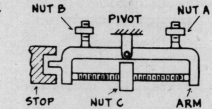

NUT B   PIVOT   NUT A

STOP   NUT C   ARM

The arm in the figure above is exactly balanced as shown. If nut "A" is removed entirely then, in order to rebalance the arm, it will be necessary to turn

3-A nut "C" toward the right

3-B nut "C" toward the left

3-C nut "B" up

3-D nut "B" down

4. The purpose of an air valve in a heating system is to

4-A prevent pressure from building up in a room due to the heated air

4-B relieve the air from steam radiators

4-C allow excessive steam pressure in the boiler to escape to the atmosphere

4-D control the temperature in the room

5.

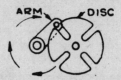

ARM   DISC

The figure above shows a slotted disc turned

by a pin on a rotating arm. One revolution of the arm turns the disc

5-A 1/4 turn
5-B 1/2 turn
5-C 3/4 turn
5-D one complete turn

6.

The figure above shows a brass and an iron strip continuously riveted together. High temperatures would probably

6-A have no effect at all
6-B bend the strips
6-C separate the strips
6-D shorten the strips

7.

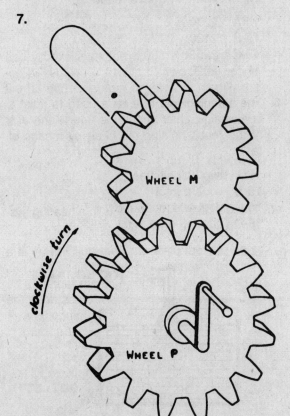

Study the gear wheels in the figure above,

then determine which of the following statements is true.

7-A If you turn wheel M clockwise by means of the handle, wheel P will also turn clockwise.
7-B It will take the same time for a tooth of wheel P to make a full turn as it will for a tooth of wheel M.
7-C It will take less time for a tooth of wheel P to make a full turn than it will take a tooth of wheel M.
7-D It will take more time for a tooth of wheel P to make a full turn than it will for a tooth of wheel M.

8. Condensation on cold water pipes is frequently prevented by

8-A insulating the pipe
8-B keeping the temperature of cold water at least 10° above the freezing point
8-C keeping the cold water lines near the hot water lines
8-D oiling or greasing the outside of the pipe

9.

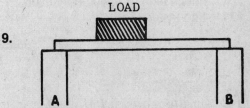

In the figure above, which upright supports the greater part of the load?

9-A upright A
9-B upright B
9-C they support it equally
9-D it cannot be determined

10.

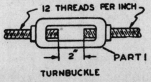

For the turnbuckle shown, the number of complete turns of Part 1, required to make the ends of the threaded rods meet is

10-A 6
10-B 18

10-C   12
10-D   24

11. With the same water pressure, the amount of water that can be carried by a 2-inch pipe as compared with a 1-inch pipe is

11-A   twice as much
11-B   3 times as much
11-C $3\frac{1}{2}$ times as much
11-D   4 times as much

12.

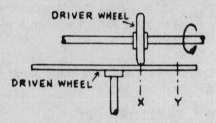

When the driver wheel is moved from location X to location Y, the driven wheel will

12-A   reverse its direction of rotation
12-B   turn slower
12-C   not change its speed of rotation
12-D   turn faster

13.

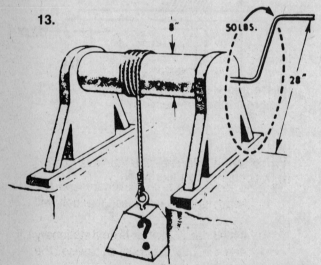

In the diagram above, the axle eight inches in diameter has attached a handle 28 inches in diameter. If a force of 50 lb. is applied to the handle, the axle will lift a weight of

13-A   224 lb.
13-B   175 lb.

13-C   200 lb.
13-D   88 lb.

14. The main purpose of expansion joints in steam lines is to

14-A   provide for changes in length of heated pipe
14-B   allow for connection of additional radiators
14-C   provide locations for valves
14-D   reduce breakage of pipe due to minor movement of the building frame

15.

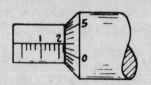

The micrometer above reads

15-A   .2270
15-B   .2120
15-C   .2252
15-D   .2020

16. The standing end of a rope used to hoist a boatswain's chair should be tied to the eye of the ropes holding the chair by means of (a)

16-A   two half hitches
16-B   square knot
16-C   double sheet bend
16-D   bowline on a bight

17.

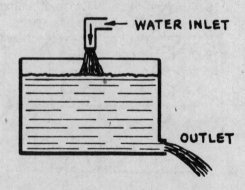

If water is flowing into the tank at the rate of 120 gallons per hour and flowing out of the

tank at a constant rate of one gallon per minute, the water level in the tank will

17-A rise 1 gallon per minute
17-B rise 2 gallons per minute
17-C fall 2 gallons per minute
17-D fall 1 gallon per minute

18.

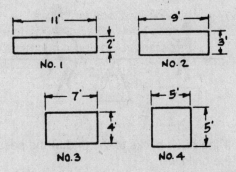

No. 1 No. 2 No. 3 No. 4

Shown are the bottoms of four bins for storing materials. If the bins are all capable of holding the same amount of any particular material, then you would expect the bin with the least height of sides to be the one whose bottom is shown as

18-A No. 1
18-B No. 3
18-C No. 2
18-D No. 4

19. If the flush tank of a water-closet fixture overflows, the fault is likely to be

19-A failure of the ball to seat properly
19-B excessive water pressure
19-C defective trap in the toilet bowl
19-D water-logged float

20.

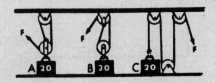

Which pulley arrangement requires the least force at F in order to lift the weight?

20-A A
20-B B
20-C C
20-D All three require the same force

21. At atmospheric pressure, water changes to steam at _____ degrees F.

21-A 100
21-B 183
21-C 212
21-D 237

22.

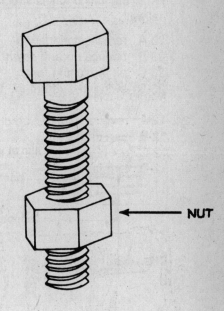

NUT

Which of the following statements is true?

22-A If the nut is held stationary and the head turned clockwise, the bolt will move up.
22-B If the head of the bolt is held stationary and the nut is turned clockwise, the nut will move down.
22-C If the head of the bolt is held stationary and the nut is turned clockwise, the nut will move up.
22-D If the nut is held stationary and the bolt is turned counterclockwise, the nut will move up.

23.

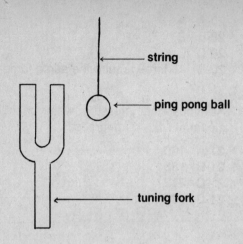

string

ping pong ball

tuning fork

When the tuning fork is struck, the ping pong ball will

23-A   remain stationary
23-B   bounce up and down
23-C   hit the tuning fork
23-D   swing away from the tuning fork

24.

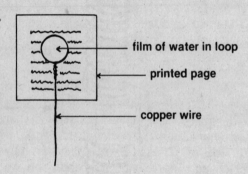

film of water in loop

printed page

copper wire

The print looked at through the film of water will

24-A   be too blurred to read
24-B   look the same as the surrounding print
24-C   be enlarged
24-D   appear smaller

25.

If the adult backs to the end of the seesaw, the child will

25-A   remain stationary
25-B   fly into the air
25-C   hit the ground hard
25-D   slide to its end of the seesaw

END OF PART 9

IF YOU FINISH BEFORE TIME IS UP, CHECK OVER YOUR WORK ON THIS PART ONLY. DO NOT RETURN TO ANY PREVIOUS PART. DO NOT GO ON UNTIL YOU ARE TOLD TO DO SO.

PART 10

ELECTRONICS INFORMATION

The questions in this part test your knowledge and understanding of electricity, radio and electronics. To answer some of the questions all you need is common sense. Other questions can be answered on the basis of experience, courses and reading. Answer all the questions. Mark the letter of your answer on the answer sheet. Try these questions.

1. The plug of a portable tool should be removed from the convenience outlet by grasping the plug and not by pulling on the cord because

   1-A the plug is easier to grip than the cord
   1-B pulling on the cord may allow the plug to fall on the floor and break
   1-C pulling on the cord may break the wires off the plug terminals
   1-D the plug is generally better insulated than the cord

   1. Ⓐ Ⓑ Ⓒ Ⓓ

1-C Yanking at an electric cord can cause hidden damage inside the plug. The force can cause terminals to loosen or bits of wire to break off and fray. Frayed wires can in turn come into contact with the opposite pole, causing fire or short circuit in the plug at some later date.

2. The one of the following which could *not* be correctly used in describing a toggle switch is

   2-A single-hole mounting
   2-B slow-acting
   2-C three-way
   2-D double-pole

   2. Ⓐ Ⓑ Ⓒ Ⓓ

2-B A toggle switch is an ordinary light switch, like the ones you find on your walls at home. The method of mounting a toggle switch depends upon the manufacture of the switch and upon the number of switches in the unit. Toggle switches come in great variety, some controlling auxiliary outlets like those in bathroom fixtures, some sharing control of the same fixture with another switch in another location. The one characteristic which IS TRUE of all toggle switches is that they are *fast* acting. There is no time lag. You flip the switch, and the light is on.

3. Asbestos is commonly used as the covering of electric wires in locations where there is likely to be high

   3-A voltage
   3-B humidity
   3-C temperature
   3-D current

   3. Ⓐ Ⓑ Ⓒ Ⓓ

3-C Asbestos is an excellent insulator against heat. If electric wires are to be used under conditions where they are exposed to very high, possibly damaging, heat, the wires are covered with asbestos for their own protection.

DO NOT TURN THE PAGE UNTIL YOU ARE TOLD TO DO SO

ELECTRONICS INFORMATION

TIME: 9 Minutes—20 Questions

1. The core of an electro-magnet is usually

   1-A aluminum
   1-B lead
   1-C brass
   1-D iron

2. An electrician should consider all electrical equipment "alive" unless he definitely knows otherwise. The main reason for this practice is to avoid

   2-A doing unnecessary work
   2-B energizing the wrong circuit
   2-C personal injury
   2-D de-energizing a live circuit

3. If the radio tubes of a certain receiver are to be operated with their filaments (or heaters) in series, it is most important that their ratings be the same with respect to filament or heater

   3-A voltage
   3-B current
   3-C power
   3-D temperature

4. The device used to change a.c. to d.c. is a

   4-A frequency changer
   4-B regulator
   4-C transformer
   4-D rectifier

5.

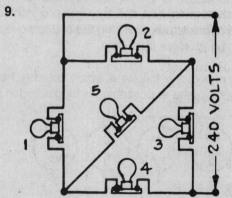

The reading of the kilowatt-hour meter is

5-A 9672
5-B 1779
5-C 2770
5-D 0762

6. The standard colors of the outer coverings of wires used in series lighting circuits are

   6-A Positive—black; Negative—white; Series—red
   6-B Positive—black; Negative—red; Series—white
   6-C Positive—white; Negative—black; Series—red
   6-D Positive—red; Negative—white; Series—black

7. Electrical contacts are opened or closed when the electrical current energizes the coils of a device called a

   7-A reactor
   7-B transtat
   7-C relay
   7-D thermostat

8. To determine directly whether all finished wire installations possess resistance between conductors, and between conductors and ground, use

   8-A clamps
   8-B set screws
   8-C shields
   8-D megger

9.

The five lamps shown are each rated at 120-volts, 60-watts. If all are good lamps, lamp no. 5 will be

9-A much brighter than normal
9-B about its normal brightness
9-C much dimmer than normal
9-D completely dark

10. When connecting a lamp bank or portable tool to a live 600-volt d.c. circuit, the best procedure is to make the negative or ground connection first and then the positive connection. The reason for this procedure is that

10-A electricity flows from positive to negative
10-B there is less danger of accidental shock
10-C the reverse procedure may blow the fuse
10-D less arcing will occur when the connection is made

11. The three elements of a transistor are

11-A collector, base, emitter
11-B collector, grid, cathode
11-C plate, grid, emitter
11-D plate, base, cathode

12. Is it proper procedure to ground the frame of a portable motor?

12-A No
12-B No, if it is A.C.
12-C Yes, unless the tool is specifically designed for use without a ground
12-D Yes, if the operation takes place at less than 150 volts

13. In comparing Nos. 00, 8, 12 and 6 A.W.G. wires, the smallest of the group is

13-A No. 00
13-B No. 8
13-C No. 12
13-D No. 6

14.

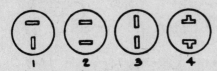

The convenience outlet that is known as a *polarized* outlet is number

14-A 1
14-B 2
14-C 3
14-D 4

15. In a house bell circuit, the push button for ringing the bell is generally connected in the secondary of the transformer feeding the bell. One reason for doing this is to

15-A save power
15-B keep line voltage out of the push button circuit
15-C prevent the bell from burning out
15-D prevent arcing of the vibrator contact points in the bell

16.

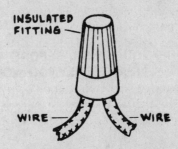

INSULATED FITTING

WIRE — — WIRE

Wires are often spliced by the use of a fitting like the one shown above. The use of this fitting does away with the need for

16-A skinning
16-B cleaning
16-C twisting
16-D soldering

17. In order to control a lamp from two different positions it is necessary to use

17-A two single pole switches
17-B one single pole switch and one four way switch
17-C two three-way switches
17-D one single pole switch and two four way switches

18. The *least* likely result of a severe electric shock is

18-A unconsciousness
18-B a burn

18-C   clenched muscles
18-D   heavy breathing

19.

The sketch shows a head-on view of a three-pronged plug used with portable electrical power tools. Considering the danger of shock when using such tools, it is evident that the function of the U-shaped prong is to

19-A   insure that the other two prongs enter the outlet with the proper polarity
19-B   provide a half-voltage connection when doing light work
19-C   prevent accidental pulling of the plug from the outlet
19-D   connect the metallic shell of the tool motor to ground

20. A compound motor usually has

20-A   only a shunt field
20-B   both a shunt and a series field
20-C   only a series field
20-D   no brushes

END OF EXAMINATION

IF YOU FINISH BEFORE TIME IS UP, CHECK YOUR WORK ON THIS PART ONLY. DO NOT GO BACK TO ANY PREVIOUS PART.

CORRECT ANSWERS—FIRST MODEL EXAM

PART 1—GENERAL SCIENCE

1. C	5. B	8. D	11. B	14. C	17. D	20. C	23. C
2. D	6. A	9. A	12. A	15. A	18. C	21. C	24. D
3. C	7. C	10. C	13. D	16. D	19. B	22. B	25. D
4. B							

PART 2—ARITHMETIC REASONING

1. B	5. D	9. A	13. B	17. C	21. D	25. B	28. B
2. D	6. B	10. C	14. B	18. A	22. A	26. D	29. C
3. B	7. C	11. C	15. D	19. A	23. C	27. C	30. B
4. D	8. A	12. D	16. B	20. D	24. B		

PART 3—WORD KNOWLEDGE

1. C	6. C	11. B	16. C	20. B	24. C	28. A	32. C
2. D	7. D	12. A	17. B	21. A	25. A	29. B	33. D
3. A	8. B	13. D	18. D	22. D	26. D	30. A	34. B
4. B	9. A	14. C	19. C	23. C	27. B	31. D	35. C
5. D	10. D	15. D					

PART 4—PARAGRAPH COMPREHENSION

1. C	3. C	5. D	7. A	9. A	11. D	13. A	15. D
2. B	4. B	6. D	8. C	10. C	12. D	14. D	

PART 5—NUMERICAL OPERATIONS

1. C	8. A	15. D	21. C	27. D	33. A	39. C	45. C
2. B	9. C	16. D	22. C	28. A	34. D	40. C	46. B
3. D	10. C	17. C	23. A	29. B	35. D	41. B	47. A
4. B	11. A	18. B	24. C	30. C	36. B	42. D	48. D
5. D	12. C	19. D	25. B	31. B	37. B	43. D	49. B
6. A	13. D	20. D	26. C	32. C	38. A	44. D	50. C
7. C	14. B						

PART 6—CODING SPEED

1. B	12. B	23. A	34. B	45. E	55. C	65. B	75. B
2. D	13. C	24. E	35. A	46. D	56. B	66. D	76. A
3. A	14. D	25. D	36. C	47. D	57. A	67. B	77. D
4. C	15. B	26. E	37. C	48. A	58. A	68. A	78. B
5. E	16. E	27. C	38. D	49. D	59. E	69. C	79. E
6. E	17. C	28. A	39. B	50. B	60. C	70. B	80. A
7. E	18. E	29. B	40. A	51. E	61. A	71. C	81. C
8. C	19. A	30. D	41. B	52. E	62. C	72. D	82. D
9. A	20. D	31. D	42. C	53. D	63. E	73. D	83. E
10. B	21. A	32. E	43. D	54. B	64. D	74. D	84. E
11. C	22. C	33. A	44. A				

PART 7—AUTO & SHOP INFORMATION

1. C	5. A	8. B	11. A	14. B	17. B	20. D	23. B
2. D	6. A	9. D	12. D	15. C	18. D	21. D	24. C
3. C	7. C	10. B	13. A	16. C	19. D	22. A	25. C
4. B							

PART 8—MATHEMATICS KNOWLEDGE

1. C	5. D	8. B	11. C	14. D	17. D	20. B	23. B
2. A	6. C	9. D	12. A	15. D	18. C	21. D	24. D
3. D	7. B	10. D	13. C	16. B	19. C	22. C	25. A
4. B							

PART 9—MECHANICAL COMPREHENSION

1. C	5. A	8. A	11. D	14. A	17. A	20. A	23. D
2. B	6. B	9. A	12. B	15. A	18. B	21. C	24. C
3. A	7. D	10. C	13. B	16. C	19. D	22. B	25. B
4. B							

PART 10—ELECTRONICS INFORMATION

1. D	4. D	7. C	10. B	13. C	15. B	17. C	19. D
2. C	5. A	8. D	11. A	14. A	16. D	18. D	20. B
3. B	6. A	9. D	12. C				

SCORE SHEET—FIRST MODEL EXAM

Now that you have taken and corrected your first exam, you will want to figure out your score on each part and on the exam as a whole. By converting each score into a percent, you can immediately see where your strengths lie and where you may want to do extra work to bring up your score. And, after you complete the book, you will be able to see the progress you have made after experience with all these questions.

The scores you convert to percents will be very useful to you. The actual exam, however, is *not* scored in percents. The ASVAB raw scores (number right) are converted to standard scores expressed within a rough range of 20 to 70. The formula by which the scores are converted is not available, nor would it be very useful to you. You should, however, be aware that the combined scores required for guaranteed admission to the training school of your choice are neither combined raw scores nor combined percents. The services combine standard scores when they determine your eligibility for each area.

PART	NUMBER CORRECT	NUMBER OF QUESTIONS	
GENERAL SCIENCE	_____ ÷ 25 =	_____ × 100 =	_____%
ARITHMETIC REASONING	_____ ÷ 30 =	_____ × 100 =	_____%
WORD KNOWLEDGE	_____ ÷ 35 =	_____ × 100 =	_____%
PARAGRAPH COMPREHENSION	_____ ÷ 15 =	_____ × 100 =	_____%
NUMERICAL OPERATIONS	_____ ÷ 50 =	_____ × 100 =	_____%
CODING SPEED	_____ ÷ 84 =	_____ × 100 =	_____%
AUTO & SHOP INFORMATION	_____ ÷ 25 =	_____ × 100 =	_____%
MATHEMATICS KNOWLEDGE	_____ ÷ 25 =	_____ × 100 =	_____%
MECHANICAL COMPREHENSION	_____ ÷ 25 =	_____ × 100 =	_____%
ELECTRONICS INFORMATION	_____ ÷ 20 =	_____ × 100 =	_____%
TOTAL	_____ ÷ 334 =	_____ × 100 =	_____%

STEPS TO TAKE AFTER THE FIRST MODEL EXAM

You have taken the first model exam. You have scored yourself and have before you your score on each part of the exam. Now you want to know what you can do to improve, to raise your marks and to qualify for the training program of your choice.

To a large extent, your learning experiences of the last eighteen or so years are the determining factors in how you perform on this exam. If you have been a "reader," then you probably have an extensive vocabulary and probably do well when you must answer questions based upon reading passages. If your favorite activities have taken place in a "shop," then chances are you will earn your best scores in "Auto and Shop Information," "Mechanical Comprehension" and "Electronics Information." If science has always fascinated you, then you are more likely to have gathered more information in that area and will have a high mark in "General Science." And if you have always liked math and done well in it, you probably will do well in "Arithmetic Reasoning," "Numerical Operations" and "Mathematics Knowledge."

Some parts of the exam really do not lend themselves to any further instruction at this time. Improvement on the two heavily speeded parts can be gained only through practice. If you have time after you have completed this book, go back and do over the "Numerical Operations" and "Coding Speed" parts of all the exams. Your answer sheets will be filled, but you can get good practice writing your letter answers on a blank piece of paper. You are unlikely to remember any of these answers, so doing the tests again will give you valuable practice and will help your speed. You will find some helpful hints for "Numerical Operations" in the math refresher course which follows, but for the most part, repeating the questions will do you the most good.

If it has been a few years since you last took math in school, you may well have forgotten some basic rules, formulas and methods. A brush-up can be very helpful to you, especially for the "Arithmetic Reasoning" and "Mathematics Knowledge" parts of your exam. The next chapter should *not,* however, be considered a comprehensive mathematics course. Many topics have been omitted altogether. We have purposefully kept the math refresher course short and have limited it to formulas, concepts and procedures which you are most likely to need most often. The course is short enough so that you can master it before you take your exam.

Another chapter which you should find helpful is the one that deals with the verbal parts of the exam—"Word Knowledge" and "Paragraph Comprehension."

This chapter gives you help in preparing for these parts of the exam and valuable suggestions for answering verbal questions.

"General Science" is a vast field. There is so much information included under the heading "general science" that it would be impossible to give you a cram course at this time. Where your knowledge is lacking, you must rely on common sense and calculated guesses. Similarly, there is little that can be taught on an "instant" basis in the area of "Shop Information."

While the examination combines the areas of "Automotive and Shop Information," our instructional chapters on the workings of the automobile combine information on mechanical principles with the automotive information. The automobile is a complex machine; all of its components are dependent on mechanical principles. You should find these chapters very helpful with the "Mechanical Comprehension" part of the exam as well as with the "Auto & Shop Information" part. The short chapter on "Electrical Theory and Work" will, in four brief pages, fill you in on some basic definitions and facts to supplement your knowledge and common sense in answering "Electronics Information" questions.

MATHEMATICS REFRESHER COURSE

Before we begin a systematic discussion of mathematics necessary to Arithmetic Reasoning and Mathematics Knowledge, let us quickly list a few basic rules which must be mastered for speed and accuracy in performing Numerical Operations. You should memorize these rules:

Any number multiplied by 0 = 0.
    $5 \times 0 = 0$.
Any number divided by 0 = 0.
    $2 \div 0 = 0$
If 0 is added to any number, the number does not change.
    $7 + 0 = 7$
If 0 is subtracted from any number, that number does not change.
    $4 - 0 = 4$
If a number is multiplied by 1, that number does not change.
    $3 \times 1 = 3$
If a number is divided by 1, that number does not change.
    $6 \div 1 = 6$
A number added to itself is doubled.
    $4 + 4 = 8$
If a number is subtracted from itself, the answer is 0.
    $9 - 9 = 0$
If a number is divided by itself, the answer is 1.
    $8 \div 8 = 1$

If you have memorized these rules, you should be able to write the answers to the questions in the following exercise as fast as you can read the questions.

Exercise 1. Answers appear on page 97.

1. $1 - 1 =$		**7.** $5 + 0 =$
2. $3 \div 1 =$		**8.** $4 - 0 =$
3. $6 \times 0 =$		**9.** $2 \div 1 =$
4. $6 - 0 =$		**10.** $7 - 7 =$
5. $8 \div 0 =$		**11.** $8 \times 0 =$
6. $9 \times 1 =$		**12.** $4 \div 0 =$

13. $1 + 0 =$ **17.** $6 + 6 =$
14. $3 - 0 =$ **18.** $4 - 4 =$
15. $5 \times 1 =$ **19.** $5 \div 5 =$
16. $9 \div 1 =$ **20.** $6 \times 1 =$

The more rules, procedures and formulas you are able to memorize, the easier it will be to solve mathematical problems on your exam and throughout life. Become thoroughly familiar with the following rules and try to commit to memory as many as possible.

When multiplying a number by 10, 100, 1000, etc., move the decimal point to the right a number of spaces equal to the number of zeros in the multiplier. If the number being multiplied is a whole number, push the decimal point to the *right by* inserting the appropriate number of zeros.

$$.36 \times 100 = 36.$$
$$1.2 \times 10 = 12.$$
$$5. \times 10 = 50.$$
$$60.423 \times 100 = 6042.3$$

When dividing a number by 10, 100, 1000, etc., again count the zeros, but this time move the decimal point to the *left*.

$$123. \div 100 = 1.23$$
$$352.8 \div 10 = 35.28$$
$$16. \div 100 = .16$$
$$7. \div 1000 = .007$$

Exercise 2.

1. $18 \times 10 =$ **6.** $.12 \div 100 =$
2. $5 \div 100 =$ **7.** $4.5 \times 10 =$
3. $1.3 \times 1000 =$ **8.** $83.28 \div 1000 =$
4. $3.62 \times 10 =$ **9.** $761 \times 100 =$
5. $9.86 \div 10 =$ **10.** $68.86 \div 10 =$

When adding or subtracting decimals, it is most important to keep the decimal points in line. Once the decimal points are aligned, proceed with the problem in exactly the same way as with whole numbers, simply maintaining the location of the decimal point.

36.08	If you find it easier,	036.0800
745.	you may fill in the	745.0000
+ 4.362	spaces with zeros.	+ 004.3620
58.6	The answer will be	058.6000
.0061	unchanged.	000.0061
844.0481		844.0481

$$\begin{array}{r} 82.1 \\ - \quad 7.928 \\ \hline 74.172 \end{array} \qquad \begin{array}{r} 82.100 \\ - \quad 7.928 \\ \hline 74.172 \end{array}$$

Exercise 3.

1. 1.52 + .389 + 42.9 =
2. .6831 + .01 + 4.26 + 98 =
3. 84 − 1.9 =
4. 3.25 + 5.66 + 9.1 =
5. 17 − 12.81 =

6. 46.33 − 12.1 =
7. 51 + 7.86 + 42.003 =
8. 35.4 − 18.21 =
9. .85 − .16 =
10. 7.6 + .32 + 830 =

When multiplying decimals, you can ignore the decimal points until you reach the product. Then the placement of the decimal point is dependent upon the sum of the places to the right of the decimal point in both the multiplier and number being multiplied.

$$\begin{array}{r} 1.482 \\ \times \quad .16 \\ \hline 8892 \\ 14820 \\ \hline .23712 \end{array}$$

    1.482   (3 places to right of decimal point)
  × .16   (2 places to right of decimal point)
  .23712   (5 places to right of decimal point)

You cannot divide by a decimal. If the divisor is a decimal, you must move the decimal point to the right until the divisor becomes a whole number, an integer. Count the number of spaces by which you moved the decimal point to the right and move the decimal point in the dividend (the number being divided) the same number of spaces to the right. The decimal point in the answer should be directly above the decimal point in the dividend.

$$.06\overline{)4.2\,1.2} \quad\quad 7\,0.2$$

      7 0.2   Decimal point moves two spaces
.06.)4.2 1.2   to the right.

Exercise 4.

1. 3.62 × 5.6 =
2. 92 × .11 =
3. 18 ÷ .3 =
4. 1.5 × .9 =
5. 7.55 ÷ 5 =

6. 6.42 ÷ 2.14 =
7. 12.01 × 3 =
8. 24.82 ÷ 7.3 =
9. .486 ÷ .2 =
10. .21 × 12 =

When fractions are to be added or subtracted they must have the same denominator, a *common denominator*. The common denominator is a number into which the denominators of all the fractions in the problem can be divided without a remainder. The common denominator of $\frac{3}{8}$, $\frac{5}{6}$, $\frac{1}{4}$, and $\frac{2}{3}$ is 24. If you want to add these fractions, they must all be converted to fractions with the denominator 24. Convert each fraction by dividing 24 by the denominator and multiplying the numerator by the quotient.

$$\frac{3}{8} = \frac{(24 \div 8) \times 3}{24} = \frac{3 \times 3}{24} = \frac{9}{24}$$

$$\frac{5}{6} = \frac{(24 \div 6) \times 5}{24} = \frac{4 \times 5}{24} = \frac{20}{24}$$

$$\frac{1}{4} = \frac{(24 \div 4) \times 1}{24} = \frac{6 \times 1}{24} = \frac{6}{24}$$

$$\frac{2}{3} = \frac{(24 \div 3) \times 2}{24} = \frac{8 \times 2}{24} = \frac{16}{24}$$

Now you can add the fractions:

$$\frac{3}{8} = \frac{9}{24}$$

$$\frac{5}{6} = \frac{20}{24}$$

$$\frac{1}{4} = \frac{6}{24}$$

$$\frac{2}{3} = \frac{16}{24}$$

$$\overline{\frac{51}{24}}$$

The answer, $\frac{51}{24}$, is an improper fraction; that is, its numerator is greater than its denominator. To convert the answer to a mixed number, divide the numerator by the denominator and express the remainder as a fraction.

$$\frac{51}{24} = 51 \div 24 = 2\frac{3}{24} = 2\frac{1}{8}$$

Exercise 5. Express your answers as simple mixed numbers.

1. $\frac{2}{4} + \frac{3}{5} + \frac{1}{2} =$

2. $\frac{6}{8} - \frac{2}{4} =$

3. $\frac{1}{3} + \frac{1}{2} =$

4. $\frac{4}{5} - \frac{3}{5} =$

5. $\frac{7}{8} + \frac{3}{4} + \frac{1}{3} =$

6. $\frac{1}{2} + \frac{1}{4} + \frac{2}{3} =$

7. $\frac{5}{6} - \frac{1}{2} =$

8. $\frac{5}{8} - \frac{1}{3} =$

9. $\frac{5}{12} + \frac{3}{4} =$

10. $\frac{8}{9} - \frac{2}{3} =$

When multiplying fractions, multiply numerators by numerators and denominators by denominators.

$$\frac{3}{5} \cdot \frac{4}{7} \cdot \frac{1}{5} = \frac{3 \times 4 \times 1}{5 \times 7 \times 5} = \frac{12}{175}$$

In multiplying fractions, try to work with numbers that are as small as possible. You can make numbers smaller by *cancelling*. Cancel by dividing the numerator of any one fraction and the denominator of any one fraction by the same number.

$$\frac{\overset{1}{\cancel{3}}}{\underset{2}{\cancel{4}}} \cdot \frac{\overset{1}{\cancel{2}}}{\underset{3}{\cancel{9}}} = \frac{1 \times 1}{2 \times 3} = \frac{1}{6}$$

In this case the numerator of the first fraction and the denominator of the other fraction were divided by 3, while the denominator of the first fraction and the numerator of the other fraction were divided by 2.

To divide by a fraction, invert the fraction following the division sign and multiply.

$$\frac{3}{16} \div \frac{1}{8} = \frac{3}{\underset{2}{\cancel{16}}} \times \frac{\overset{1}{\cancel{8}}}{1} = \frac{3}{2} = 1\tfrac{1}{2}$$

Exercise 6. Cancel wherever possible and express your answer in the simplest terms possible.

1. $\dfrac{4}{5} \cdot \dfrac{3}{6} =$

2. $\dfrac{2}{4} \cdot \dfrac{8}{12} \cdot \dfrac{7}{1} =$

3. $\dfrac{3}{4} \div \dfrac{3}{8} =$

4. $\dfrac{5}{2} \div \dfrac{3}{6} =$

5. $\dfrac{8}{9} \cdot \dfrac{3}{4} \cdot \dfrac{1}{2} =$

6. $\dfrac{7}{8} \div \dfrac{2}{3} =$

7. $\dfrac{4}{6} \cdot \dfrac{8}{12} \cdot \dfrac{10}{3} =$

8. $\dfrac{1}{6} \cdot \dfrac{7}{6} \cdot \dfrac{12}{3} =$

9. $\dfrac{3}{7} \div \dfrac{9}{4} =$

10. $\dfrac{2}{3} \div \dfrac{2}{3} =$

The line in a fraction means "divided by." To change a fraction to a decimal follow through on the division.

$$\tfrac{4}{5} = 4 \div 5 = .8$$

To change a decimal to a percent, move the decimal point two places to the right and add a percent sign.

.8 = 80%

Exercise 7. Change each fraction first to a decimal to three places and then to a percent.

1. $\dfrac{2}{4}$

2. $\dfrac{7}{8}$

3. $\dfrac{5}{6}$

4. $\dfrac{6}{8}$

5. $\dfrac{3}{4}$

6. $\dfrac{2}{3}$

7. $\dfrac{3}{5}$

8. $\dfrac{4}{10}$

9. $\dfrac{1}{4}$

10. $\dfrac{2}{5}$

To find a percent of a number, change the percent to a decimal and multiply the number by it.

5% of 80 = 80 × .05 = 4

To find out what a number is when a percent of it is given, change the percent to a decimal and divide the given number by it.

5 is 10% of what number?

5 ÷ .10 = 50

To find what percent one number is of another number, create a fraction by putting the part over the whole. Reduce the fraction if possible, then convert it to a decimal (remember: the line means *divided by,* so divide the numerator by the denominator) and change to a percent by multiplying by 100, moving the decimal point two places to the right.

4 is what percent of 80?

$$\frac{4}{80} = \frac{1}{20} = .05 = 5\%$$

Exercise 8.

1. 10% of 32 =
2. 8 is 25% of what number?

3. 12 is what percent of 24?
4. 20% of 360 is

5. 5 is what percent of 60?

6. 12 is 8% of what number?

7. 6% of 36 =

8. 25 is 5% of what number?

9. 70 is what percent of 140?

10. What percent of 100 is 19?

An equation is an equality. The values on either side of the equal sign in an equation must be equal. In order to learn the value of an unknown in an equation, do the same thing to both sides of the equation so as to leave the unknown on one side of the equal sign and its value on the other side.

$$X - 2 = 8$$

Add 2 to both sides of the equation.

$$X - 2 + 2 = 8 + 2; X = 10$$

$$5X = 25$$

Divide both sides of the equation by 5.

$$\frac{\overset{1}{\cancel{5}}X}{\underset{1}{\cancel{5}}} = \frac{25}{5}; X = 5$$

$$Y + 9 = 15$$

Subtract 9 from both sides of the equation.

$$Y + 9 - 9 = 15 - 9; Y = 6$$

$$A \div 4 = 48$$

Multiply both sides of the equation by 4.

$$\frac{\overset{1}{\cancel{4}}A}{\underset{1}{\cancel{4}}} = 48 \times 4; A = 192$$

Sometimes more than one step is required to solve an equation.

$$6A \div 4 = 48$$

First, multiply both sides of the equation by 4.

$$\frac{6A}{\underset{1}{\cancel{4}}} \times \frac{\overset{1}{\cancel{4}}}{1} = 48 \times 4; 6A = 192$$

Then divide both sides of the equation by 6.

$$\frac{\overset{1}{\cancel{6}}A}{\underset{1}{\cancel{6}}} = \frac{192}{6}; A = 32$$

Exercise 9. Solve for X.

1. X + 13 = 25

2. 4X = 84

3. X − 5 = 28

4. X ÷ 9 = 4

5. 3X + 2 = 14

6. $\frac{X}{4}$ − 2 = 4

7. 10X − 27 = 73

8. 2X ÷ 4 = 13

9. 8X + 9 = 81

10. 2X ÷ 11 = 6

Area is the space enclosed by a plane (flat) figure. A rectangle is a plane figure with four right angles. Opposite sides of a rectangle are of equal length and are parallel to each other. To find the area of a rectangle, multiply the length of the base of the rectangle by the length of its height. Area is *always* expressed in square units.

A = bh
A = 9 ft. × 3 ft.
A = 27 sq. ft.

A square is a rectangle in which all four sides are the same length. The area of a rectangle is found by squaring the length of one side, which is exactly the same as multiplying the square's length by its width.

A = s^2
A = 4 in. × 4 in.
A = 16 sq. in.

A triangle is a three-sided plane figure. The area of a triangle is found by multiplying the base by the altitude (height) and dividing by two.

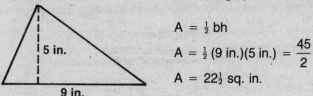

A = $\frac{1}{2}$ bh

A = $\frac{1}{2}$ (9 in.)(5 in.) = $\frac{45}{2}$

A = $22\frac{1}{2}$ sq. in.

A circle is a perfectly round plane figure. The distance from the center of a circle to its rim is its radius. The distance from one edge to the other through the center is its diameter. The diameter is twice the length of the radius.

Pi (π) is a mathematical value equal to approximately 3.14 or $\frac{22}{7}$. Pi is frequently used in calculations involving circles. The area of a circle is found by squaring the radius and multiplying it by π.

A = πr^2
A = $\pi(4 \text{ cm.})^2$
A = 16π sq. cm.
You may leave the area in terms of pi unless you are told what value to assign π.

Exercise 10. Find the area.

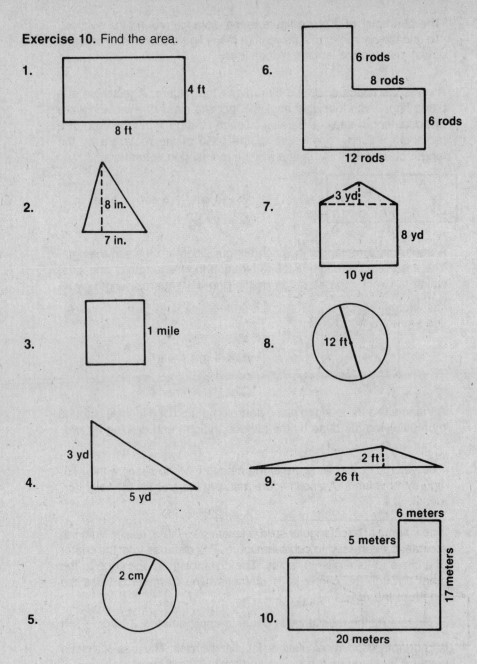

1. 4 ft / 8 ft

2. 8 in. / 7 in.

3. 1 mile

4. 3 yd / 5 yd

5. 2 cm

6. 6 rods / 8 rods / 6 rods / 12 rods

7. 3 yd / 8 yd / 10 yd

8. 12 ft

9. 2 ft / 26 ft

10. 6 meters / 5 meters / 17 meters / 20 meters

The perimeter of a plane figure is the distance around the outside. To find the perimeter of a polygon (a plane figure bounded by straight lines) just add the lengths of the sides.

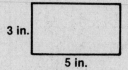

P = 3 in. + 5 in. + 3 in. + 5 in.
  = 16 in.

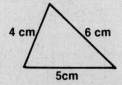

P = 4 cm. + 6 cm. + 5 cm.
  = 15 cm.

The perimeter of a circle is called the *circumference*. The formula for the circumference of a circle is πd or $2\pi r$, which are both, of course, the same thing.

$$C = 2 \cdot 3 \cdot \pi = 6\pi$$

The volume of a solid figure is the measure of the space within. To figure the volume of a solid figure, multiply the area by the height or depth.

The volume of a rectangular solid is length × width × height. Volume is always expressed in cubic units.

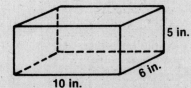

V = lwh

V = (10 in.)(6 in.)(5 in.)

V = 300 cu. in.

The volume of a cube is the cube of one side.

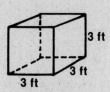

$V = s^3$

$V = (3 \text{ ft.})^3$

V = 27 cu. ft.

The volume of a cylinder is π times the square of the radius of the base times the height.

$V = \pi r^2 h$

$V = \pi \, (4 \text{ in.})^2 \, (5 \text{ in.})$

$V = \pi \, (16)(5) = 80\pi \text{ cu. in.}$

Exercise 11.

1. Find the perimeter.

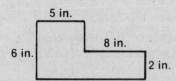

2. Find the volume.

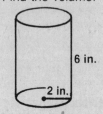

3. Find the circumference.

4. Find the volume.

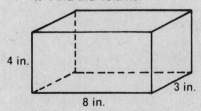

5. Find the volume.

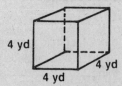

6. Find the perimeter.

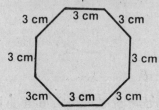

7. Find the perimeter.

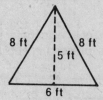

8. Find the perimeter.

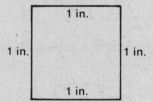

The sum of the angles of a straight line is 180°.

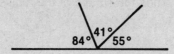

The sum of the angles of a triangle is 180°.

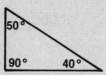

The sum of the angles of a rectangle is 360°.

The sum of the angles of a circle is 360°.

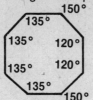

The sum of the angles of a polygon of n sides is (n − 2)180°.

$$(8 - 2)(180°)$$
$$6 \cdot 180° = 1080°$$

Exercise 12. What is the size of the unlabelled angle?

1.

3.

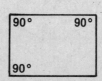

2.

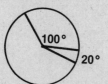

4.

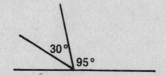

5.

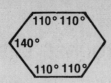

7.

6.

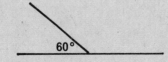

8.

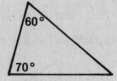

ANSWERS TO MATH REFRESHER COURSE EXERCISES

Exercise 1.

1. 0
2. 3
3. 0
4. 6
5. 0
6. 9
7. 5
8. 4
9. 2
10. 0

11. 0
12. 0
13. 1
14. 3
15. 5
16. 9
17. 12
18. 0
19. 1
20. 6

Exercise 2.

1. 180
2. .05
3. 1300
4. 36.2
5. .986

6. .0012
7. 45
8. .08328
9. 76100
10. 6.886

Exercise 3.

1. 44.809
2. 102.9531
3. 82.1
4. 18.01
5. 4.19

6. 34.23
7. 100.863
8. 17.19
9. .69
10. 837.92

Exercise 4.

1. 20.272
2. 10.12
3. 60
4. 1.35
5. 1.51

6. 3
7. 36.03
8. 3.4
9. 2.43
10. 2.52

Exercise 5.

1. $\dfrac{32}{20} = 1\dfrac{12}{20} = 1\dfrac{3}{5}$

2. $\dfrac{2}{8} = \dfrac{1}{4}$

3. $\dfrac{5}{6}$

4. $\dfrac{1}{5}$

5. $\frac{47}{24} = 1\frac{23}{24}$

6. $\frac{17}{12} = 1\frac{5}{12}$

7. $\frac{2}{6} = \frac{1}{3}$

8. $\frac{7}{24}$

9. $\frac{14}{12} = 1\frac{2}{12} = 1\frac{1}{6}$

10. $\frac{2}{9}$

Exercise 6.

1. $\frac{2}{5}$

2. $2\frac{1}{3}$

3. 2

4. $\frac{15}{3} = 5$

5. $\frac{1}{3}$

6. $\frac{21}{16} = 1\frac{5}{16}$

7. $1\frac{13}{27}$

8. $\frac{7}{9}$

9. $\frac{4}{21}$

10. 1

Exercise 7.

1. $.50 = 50\%$

2. $.875 = 87\frac{1}{2}\%$

3. $.833 = 83\frac{1}{3}\%$

4. $.75 = 75\%$

5. $.75 = 75\%$

6. $.666 = 66\frac{2}{3}\%$

7. $.60 = 60\%$

8. $.40 = 40\%$

9. $.25 = 25\%$

10. $.40 = 40\%$

Exercise 8.

1. $32 \times .10 = 3.2$

2. $8 \div .25 = 32$

3. $\frac{12}{24} = \frac{1}{2} = .50 = 50\%$

4. $360 \times .20 = 72$

5. $\frac{5}{60} = \frac{1}{12} = .0833 = 8\frac{1}{3}\%$

6. $12 \div .08 = 150$

7. $36 \times .06 = 2.16$

8. $25 \div .05 = 500$

9. $\frac{70}{140} = \frac{1}{2} = .50 = 50\%$

10. $\frac{19}{100} = .19 = 19\%$

Exercise 9.

1. $X = 12$

2. $X = 21$

3. $X = 33$

4. $X = 36$

5. $X = 4$

6. $X = 24$

7. $X = 10$

8. $X = 26$

9. $X = 9$

10. $X = 33$

Exercise 10

1. $A = bh$
   $A = 8 \times 4 = 32$ sq. ft.
2. $A = \frac{1}{2}bh$
   $A = \frac{1}{2}(7 \times 8)$
   $A = \frac{1}{2}(56) = 28$ sq. in.
3. $A = s^2$
   $A = 1^2 = 1$ sq. mile
4. $A = \frac{1}{2}bh$
   $A = \frac{1}{2}(5 \times 3)$
   $A = \frac{1}{2}(15) = 7\frac{1}{2}$ sq. yds.
5. $A = \pi r^2$
   $A = \pi 2^2$
   $A = 4\pi$ sq. cm.
6. $A = bh$
   $A = 12 \times 6 + (12 - 8) \times 6$
   $A = 12 \times 6 + 4 \times 6$
   $A = 72 + 24 = 96$ sq. rd.

7. $A = bh$
   $A = 10 \times 8 = 80$ sq. yds.

   $A = \frac{1}{2}bh$
   $A = \frac{1}{2}(10 \times 3) = \frac{1}{2}(30)$
   $A = 15$ sq. yds.

   $80 + 15 = 95$ sq. yds.
8. $A = \pi r^2$
   $A = \pi 6^2$
   $A = 36\pi$ sq. ft.
9. $A = \frac{1}{2}bh$
   $A = \frac{1}{2}(26 \times 2) = \frac{1}{2}(52)$
   $A = 26$ sq. ft.
10. $A = bh$
    $A = 6 \times 5 + 20 \times (17 - 5)$
    $A = 6 \times 5 + 20 \times 12$
    $A = 30 + 240 = 270$ sq. meters

Exercise 11.

1. $P = 6 + 5 + (6 - 2) + 8 + 2 + (8 + 5) = 38$ in.
2. $V = \pi r^2 h$
   $V = \pi \times 2^2 \times 6$
   $V = \pi \times 4 \times 6$
   $V = 24\pi$ cu. in.
3. $C = 2\pi r$
   $C = 2 \times \pi \times 7$
   $C = 14\pi$ cm.
4. $V = lwh$
   $V = 8 \times 3 \times 4$
   $V = 96$ cu. in.

5. $V = s^3$
   $V = 4^3 = 4 \times 4 \times 4$
   $V = 64$ cu. yd.
6. $P = 3 + 3 + 3 + 3 + 3 + 3 + 3 + 3$
   $P = 24$ cm.
7. $P = 8 + 8 + 6 = 22$ ft.
8. $P = 1 + 1 + 1 + 1 = 4$ in.

Exercise 12.

1. $80°$
2. $240°$
3. $90°$
4. $55°$

5. $140°$
6. $120°$
7. $180°$
8. $50°$

HELP WITH THE VERBAL QUESTIONS

The Verbal questions of your exam are found in two parts, Word Knowledge and Paragraph Comprehension.

WORD KNOWLEDGE

The "Word Knowledge" questions test your understanding of words. In these questions, you are given a word and asked to choose another word which has the same meaning or most nearly the same meaning as the given word. This is a test of synonyms.

Sometimes the given word is presented in a sentence. If the given word is in a sentence, you should always try substituting the choices in the place of the underlined word. This procedure may help you to find the answer. Consider:

The surface of the <u>placid</u> lake was as smooth as glass.

A cold
B muddy
C deep
D calm

Any one of the choices might be substituted for the word *placid,* and the sentence would still be entirely sensible. However, if the surface of the lake was as smooth as glass, the water would have had to be very *calm.* Thus, while a cold, muddy or deep lake could have a smooth surface, it is most reasonable to assume, on the basis of the sentence, that *placid* means *calm.*

Or, consider the following question:

The camel is sometimes called the ship of the <u>desert</u>.

A abandon
B ice cream
C sandy wasteland
D leave

Here the sentence is absolutely necessary to the definition of the word. Without the sentence, you would not know whether the word *desert* is to be pronounced *de·sert'*, which means *to leave* or *to abandon,* or *de'sert,* which means a *sandy wasteland.* If you are not sure of your spelling, the sentence can also spare you the confusion of *desert* with *dessert,* which is the last course of a meal.

On the other hand, the sentence may be of no use at all:

The robbery suspect had a <u>sallow</u> complexion.

  A ruddy
  B pale
  C pock-marked
  D freckled

The sentence shows you a use of the word *sallow,* that it is used to describe a complexion, but it gives no clue that *sallow* means *pale.* You either know the meaning of the word or you must guess.

If the given word is not part of a sentence, or if the sentence is of no use in defining the word, you must rely on other clues. Perhaps you have seen the word used but were never sure what it meant. Look carefully. Can you see any part of a word of which you do know the meaning? An example:

<u>Remedial</u> most nearly means

  A reading
  B slow
  C corrective
  D special

Your association is probably "remedial reading." Be careful. *Remedial* does not mean *reading. Remedial* is an adjective, *reading* the noun it modifies. Slow readers may receive remedial reading instruction in special classes. The *remedial* reading classes are intended to *correct* bad reading practices. Do you see the word *remedy* in *remedial*? You know that a *remedy* is a *cure* or a *correction* for an ailment. If you combine all the information you now have, you can choose *corrective* as the word which most nearly means *remedial.*

Sometimes you can figure the meaning of a word by combining your knowledge with elimination of wrong answers. For instance:

<u>Infamous</u> most nearly means

  A well-known
  B poor
  C disgraceful
  D young

The first word you see when you look at *infamous* is *famous. Famous,* of course, means *well-known.* Since the prefix *in* often means *not,* you will eliminate (A) as the answer. A person who is not well-known might be poor, but not necessarily. *Poor* should not be eliminated as a possible answer, but you should carefully consider the other choices before choosing *poor.* Since *in* meaning *not* is a negative prefix, you should be looking for a negative word as the meaning of *infamous.*

There is no choice meaning *not famous,* so you must look for negative fame. *Disgrace* is a negative kind of *fame.* A person who behaves *disgracefully* is well-known for his bad behavior; he is *infamous.* If you had chosen *young* as your answer, you would have mistakenly seen *infant* in *infamous.* You must be careful and thorough when figuring out the meanings of words.

In the past few paragraphs we have given you suggestions for figuring out the meanings of words when there is any possibility for doing so. Many "Word Knowledge" questions give you no such possibility. Often, you simply must know the meaning of the word. Since this is so often the case, we will here repeat the advice we gave you in Chapter 1, How To Use This Book.

Work with a dictionary. Look up words you meet in anything you read. Look up *every* unfamiliar word in this book. If you run across a word you do not know while doing the exams, circle the word and look it up later. Look up words you find in the reading passages, new words from among answer choices, words you find in the explanations, words you meet in the study chapters. Looking up words for yourself is the best way to learn them. If you understand every word used in this book, you are well on your way toward a broad-based vocabulary and should be able to handle Word Knowledge and Paragraph Comprehension.

PARAGRAPH COMPREHENSION

"Paragraph Comprehension" questions test not only how well you understand what you read, but also how well you can interpret the meaning of the passage and the intent of the author. Reading speed is vital for success with "Paragraph Comprehension" questions. You cannot even attempt to answer questions based upon a paragraph if you have not had time to read it.

The best way to increase your reading speed is to read. Read everything in sight between now and the exam. Newspaper reading is an especially good way to improve your reading skills. Don't be satisfied with just the opening paragraph of each article. Push yourself to read the whole story and give it your full attention as you read. If your mind wanders, you will not comprehend what you read.

To read with understanding your eyes must fixate (stop). Most people fixate on each word because that is the way reading is taught in the early grades. For adults, this method wastes a great deal of time. The key to increasing your reading speed is to take in more words each time your eyes stop. If a line has ten words in it and you are able to read the line by stopping only twice instead of ten times, you would be reading five times as fast as you do now. Try to train yourself.

Don't *subvocalize.* If you can hear every word you read, you are subvocalizing. No matter how fast you can talk, you can read faster if you stop subvocalizing. Some people have found that putting pebbles in their mouths or chewing on pencils helps them to stop subvocalizing. For others, awareness of the possibility is enough to help them to correct this bad habit.

In building up reading speed try using your hand. When you read, move your hand or pencil underneath the line you are reading. Because your eyes tend to move as quickly as your pencil, you will not stop on every word, you will not regress (look back) and you probably will not subvocalize. However, what you may do is concentrate on your pencil and not on the reading passage. This is why you must practice this technique before using it on your test. Start your hand or your pencil at the second or third word in the line and stop it before the last word in the line. Your peripheral vision (what you see at the edges) will pick up the first and last words in the lines and you will save time by not having to focus on them.

Become more aware of words. "Word Knowledge" and "Paragraph Comprehension" are tied together to yield a "Verbal" score because they are so closely interrelated. You cannot have a large vocabulary without reading. You cannot understand what you read without an understanding of the words. When you look up words, study the roots, prefixes and suffixes so that you can apply all that you know whenever you meet unfamiliar words.

HOW TO ANSWER READING COMPREHENSION QUESTIONS

1. Skim the paragraph to get a general idea of the subject matter and of the point that is being made.
2. Reread the paragraph, giving attention to details and point of view. Be alert for the author's hints as to what he or she thinks is important. Phrases such as "Note that . . .", "Of importance is . . ." and "Do not overlook . . ." give clues to what the writer is stressing.
3. If the author has quoted material from another source, be sure that you understand the purpose of the quote. Does the author agree or disagree?
4. Carefully read the question or incomplete statement. Determine exactly what is being asked. Watch for negatives or all-inclusive words, such as "always," "never," "all," "only," "every," "absolutely," "completely," "none," "entirely," "no." These words can affect your choice of answer.
5. Read all four answer choices. Do not rush to choose the first answer that might be correct. Eliminate those choices that are obviously incorrect. Reread the remaining choices and refer to the paragraph, if necessary, to determine the *best* answer.
6. Avoid inserting your own judgments into your answers. Even if you disagree with the author or even if you spot a factual error in the paragraph, you must answer on the basis of what is stated or implied in the paragraph.
7. Do not allow yourself to spend too much time on any one question. If looking back at the paragraph does not help you to find or figure out the answer, choose from among the answers remaining after you eliminate the obviously wrong answers, and go on to the next paragraph.

WHAT MAKES AUTOS RUN

Fundamentally the automobile is a compartment mounted on wheels with some self-contained means for propelling it over the ground.

Of course, today's automobiles consist of a great deal more than that. Easy-riding suspension systems, soft comfortable seats, headlights for night-driving, windshield wipers, rear-view mirrors and many other driver conveniences and safety features. If these were lacking, we would feel that the car was quite incomplete. Yet the fundamentals are still there, and there was a time when many of these "extras" were unknown to the builders of automobiles.

One of the fundamentals is without doubt the wheel. When the wheel was first discovered—probably in the form of a log or a section of a log—the world took a long step forward. For thousands of years, the wheel has made transportation easier.

But for most of that time the wheel served only as a support for the vehicle, to make it easier for something to pull it or push it. A separate motive power propelled the vehicle—slaves, animals, or even the wind.

Finally came the time when the motive power was made a part of the vehicle, driving the wheels which in turn propelled the whole thing—engine, carriage, passengers and all. Then the internal combustion engine, with

its light weight and comparatively high efficiency, made the automobile a practical mechanism for transporting people from where they were to where they wanted to be. This was the beginning of the automobile we know today.

It is easy to see that the very least we need to make an automobile go is an engine and some means of connecting the engine to the wheels. It might look something like the illustration. The engine turns the shaft, which runs back toward the rear wheels.

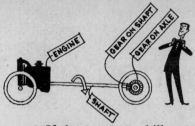

It has a gear on the end which meshes with a gear on the axle connecting the rear wheels together. As the first shaft turns, it rotates the axle and the wheels propel the car.

If there were no hills around, and we didn't want to go very fast and didn't want to turn any corners, this arrangement might work. But in an actual automobile, we have some more parts between the engine and the wheels. All we show now is where they are and their names. From here on in this book we're going to take them up one by one and try to explain what they are and what they do and How the Wheels Revolve.

ENGINE

THE POWER of an automobile engine comes from the burning of a mixture of gasoline and air in a small, enclosed space. When this mixture burns it expands greatly, and pushes out in all directions. It happens so quickly that we sometimes call it an explosion. This push or pressure can be used to move a part of the engine, and the movement of this part is eventually transmitted back to the wheels to drive the car.

Looking at an engine under the hood of an automobile, it seems to be a complicated sort of thing with hundreds of pieces and attachments and what-nots. But we can forget about most of these for the present, and consider only the basic parts.

First we must have a cylinder. This is something like a tall metal can, or a pipe closed at one end. In fact some of the early automobiles used cast iron pipe for cylinders.

Inside the cylinder we have a piston. This is a plug which is close-fitting but which can slide up and down easily. It is the part of the engine mentioned above which is moved by the expanding gases, being driven down on each power impulse or explosion.

Now we must find some way to change that up-and-down motion to rotary motion to propel the car. For this we have a connecting rod and crankshaft. The crankshaft is a shaft with an off-set portion, the crank, which describes a circle as the shaft rotates. The top end of the connecting rod is fastened to the piston, so it goes up and down in a straight line. The bottom end is fastened to the crank, so that end has to go around in a circle as the piston moves up and down.

This is the most common way of changing straight line motion to rotary motion. Familiar examples of it are a kitchen meat grinder or a bicycle. In the latter the foot pedal is the crank and our leg the connecting rod. Our knee moves up and down in a straight line while our foot goes round in a circle.

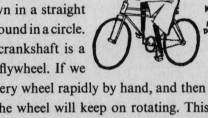

On one end of the crankshaft is a heavy wheel called the flywheel. If we turn a grindstone or emery wheel rapidly by hand, and then let go, the wheel will keep on rotating. This is the same action as the flywheel. It keeps the engine turning between power impulses.

These are the basic parts of an engine; but what we have shown here would make only a single-cylinder engine. All automobile engines today have four or more cylinders. They can be arranged in one straight row, which we call an in-line engine, or in two rows set at an angle, descriptively called a V-type engine. In either case we have only one crankshaft, but it has a number of cranks instead of only one. With a number of cylinders the flywheel does not have such a big job to do because the power impulses occur more often and thus keep the crankshaft turning.

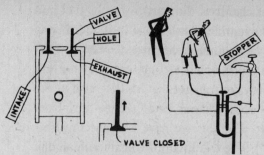

This basic engine we have put together so far has no way of getting the fuel-air mixture into it or burned gases out of it. We need some "doors," which in this case we call valves. Two holes are cut in the top of the cylinder, one for intake and one for exhaust. Metal discs are arranged to fit tightly over the holes to close them, but when pushed down they open the holes to allow passage of the gases through them. They work very much like the familiar stopper in a washbowl, but turned upside down.

The valves are controlled by rocker arms and rods which are moved by a camshaft. This is a shaft with cams or bumps on it— one bump for each valve—which

push up on the rods to open the valves. The camshaft is driven by the crankshaft, at one-half speed. The cams are accurately shaped and located, and the shaft rotates at just the proper speed, as the valves must open and close at exactly the right moment.

In order to produce power, the engine needs a supply of gasoline and air mixed in the proper proportions. The carburetor does the mixing job. Gasoline is pumped from the tank to the carburetor by the fuel pump. This operates in much the same manner as the old-fashioned water pump, each stroke pushing a little fuel on to the carburetor where it goes first to the float chamber.

Air enters the carburetor through the air cleaner, being pulled in by the pumping action of the engine pistons

working in the cylinders. The air flows through a venturi (a reduced passage in the carburetor) at high speed, then past the end of a tube leading from the float chamber. This sucks out the fuel into the air stream, breaking the liquid up into a fine mist and mixing it thoroughly with the air. An atomizer or garden sprayer works in a similar manner. Then the fuel and air mixture goes on into the engine, the amount being controlled by a throttle valve at the base of the carburetor, which is opened or closed by movement of the accelerator pedal.

A good mixture for burning in an engine is about 15 pounds of air to 1 pound of gasoline. Air being so much lighter than gasoline, this means that for every gallon of gasoline we burn, we use enough air to fill a room 10 feet square and more than 10 feet high. We call them gasoline engines, but it is easy to see that in some ways air plays the more important part.

Now we have everything we need to make an engine run except something to start the mixture burning in the cylinder. Any kind of a spark will do it. In a cigarette lighter we make a spark by friction against a special metal. In an engine we do it electrically.

A spark plug is inserted in the top of each cylinder, and a spark is created by electricity jumping across the gap between the two electrodes of the plug.

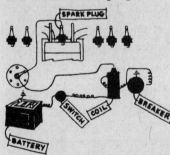

A battery furnishes the electricity, but several additional pieces of equipment are necessary for a complete ignition system. The coil and the breaker cooperate to develop a very high voltage, and the distributor is responsible for getting the high voltage electricity to the right spark plug at the right time.

All of this must take place very rapidly. In an eight-cylinder engine driving a car 55 miles per hour, the ignition system would have to furnish about 7,350 sparks per minute, or 123 each second. And it must do this at exactly the right time and without a miss.

8 SPARK PLUGS-55 MILES PER HOUR—
123 SPARKS PER SECOND

The reason the valve mechanism and ignition system must perform their duties at just the right time is that an engine operates with a certain definite cycle of events—over and over again, at a high rate of speed. Now that we have all the necessary parts of an engine, we can see how it actually works.

Most automobile engines are four-cycle engines. This means they operate on a four-

stroke cycle, taking four strokes of the piston— down, up, down, up—for one complete cycle of events.

INTAKE STROKE

On the first stroke the intake valve is open and the piston moves down, pulling in the fuel-air mixture until the cylinder is full. This is the *intake stroke*.

Then the intake valve closes and the piston starts up on the *compression stroke*. It squeezes the mixture into a small space at the top of the cylinder which increases the pressure in the cylinder to almost 200 pounds per square inch.

COMPRESSION STROKE

IGNITION

Between the second and third strokes, ignition or firing takes place. The spark, jumping the gap of the spark plug, ignites the mixture of fuel and air squeezed at the top of the cylinder. In burning, the mixture of course gets very hot and tries to expand in all directions. The pressure rises to about 600 or 700 pounds per square inch. The piston is the only thing that can move, so the expanding gases push it down to the

POWER STROKE

bottom of the cylinder. This is the *power stroke*.

The fuel is burned and the energy in the gases has been used up in pushing the piston downward. Now it is necessary to clear these burned gases out of the cyl-

EXHAUST STROKE

inder to make room for a new charge. On the *exhaust stroke*, the exhaust valve opens and the piston pushes the gases out through the opening.

So the cycle is completed and we are ready to start over again with the intake stroke of the next cycle. Intake—Compression—Power—Exhaust. Over and over again through the same series of actions. The crankshaft is going around continuously while the piston is going up and down, but we should note that it is only on the power stroke that the piston is driving it around. On the other three strokes, the crankshaft is driving the piston. There is one power stroke to every two revolutions of the crankshaft. This is for each cylinder, of course; with an eight-cylinder engine there are 4 power strokes for each revolution.

MORE SQUEEZE... MORE POWER

PISTON MOVING UP SQUEEZES MIXTURE OF AIR AND FUEL

We described what happens on the compression stroke, but we did not go into detail as to its importance. We hear talk of "compression ratio" and "high compression engines," all of which has to do with how much we squeeze the mixture in the cylinder before igniting it. It is a fundamental fact of internal combustion engines that the more we compress the mixture—the harder we squeeze it—the more power we get from it.

Compression ratio is a measure of how much we squeeze the mixture. If the cylinder holds 100 cubic inches when the piston is all the way down in its lowest position, and 10 cubic inches when the piston is up as far as it can go, we say the compression ratio is 10 to 1. The mixture has been compressed into a space 1/10 as large as it originally occupied. Fifty years ago 4 to 1 was a common figure for the compression ratio of automobile engines. This has increased over the years, and today compression ratios range upward of 8 to 1.

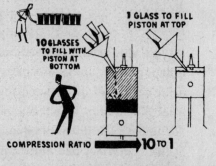

1 GLASS TO FILL PISTON AT TOP

10 GLASSES TO FILL WITH PISTON AT BOTTOM

COMPRESSION RATIO ➤ 10 TO 1

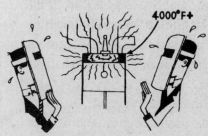

4000°F+

Thus far we have put together the main parts of an automobile engine. Such an engine would run —but it would not run very long. When the mixture of fuel and air burns in the cylinder, it creates a temperature of 4000 to 4500 degrees Fahrenheit. This is almost twice the temperature at which iron melts. So it is easy to see that if we did not have a cooling system our engine would not last very long.

The usual way of cooling the engine is to put water jackets around the hottest parts. Water is constantly circulated through these by a small pump. The heat of the cylinder makes the water hot, and it then goes to the radiator where it is cooled by the outside air passing through. Then it starts back to the engine again to do more cooling. It is actually very much like a steam or hot water heating system in a home. The engine is our boiler which heats up the water which then goes to a radiator where it gives up its heat to the air.

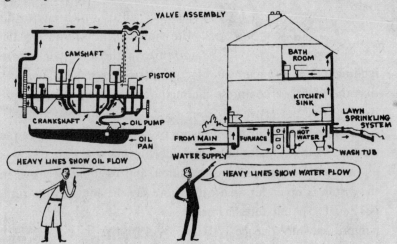

We also need a lubrication system for our engine. If all the rotating and reciprocating parts were running metal against metal, with no film of oil between them, they would soon heat up and stick. The friction would also make it harder for the parts to turn. So we have a reservoir of oil in the crankcase, where a pump forces it to the bearings and more critical points in the engine. Some of it flows through tubes and some through passages drilled in the crankshaft and connecting rods. The lubrication system might be compared to the water system in a house. The liquid is forced from one central place through pipes to many different locations where it is needed.

We must have some way of starting the engine. It has to be turning over before it can run under its own power, and we give it this initial start by means of an electric motor. This is somewhat similar to the motor in our vacuum cleaner or washing machine. It runs on electricity from the battery, and the starter switch is similar to the electric wall switch which turns on the lights in our home.

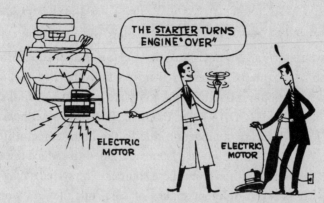

There is one more important piece of electrical equipment. This is the alternator. It looks something like the starter motor, but

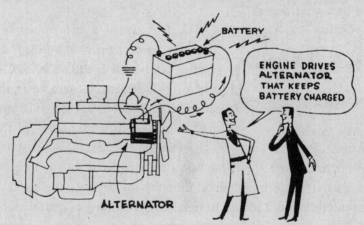

its job is just the opposite. Instead of taking electricity from the battery to start the engine, the alternator is driven by the engine and generates electric current which feeds back into the battery to keep it charged for starting. The alternator also supplies power for the ignition system, lights, radio, and other electrical units.

We have put together a complete automobile engine—at least enough parts of one so that it will start and keep on running. But before we talk about how power from the engine is sent back to the rear wheels to drive the car, let's look briefly at something that is found on all cars produced today—the systems that are used to control the emission of pollutants to the atmosphere.

There are three major pollutants that are emitted from automobiles into the atmosphere—hydrocarbons, carbon monoxide, and oxides of nitrogen. Hydrocarbons, which we can think of as

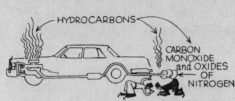

essentially unburned gasoline, come from the exhaust pipe and the engine's crankcase as a result of the combustion process. They also enter the atmosphere from the carburetor and the fuel tank through an evaporation process. Carbon monoxide (CO) results from partially burned fuel when rich fuel/air mixtures do not allow complete combustion all the way to carbon dioxide (CO_2). Oxides of nitrogen, on the other hand, are gases formed during combustion due to the high temperatures.

Today's cars have built-in systems designed to reduce the three major pollutants emitted from these sources. The systems may vary somewhat between different makes of cars, but they all work to perform the same job—reducing emissions of hydrocarbons, carbon monoxide, and oxides of nitrogen. Let's see what the systems are and what they do.

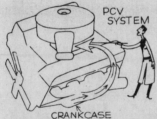

The first emission control applied to automobile engines was called the positive crankcase ventilation (PCV) system. This system, introduced in the early 1960's, is still in use today. During the "compression strokes" of the pistons, small amounts of gasoline vapors are forced past the piston rings from the combustion chamber and into the engine crankcase. These infinitesimal amounts of vapors expelled each engine cycle would add up to significant quantities of hydrocarbon (HC) emissions if they were allowed to enter the atmosphere. They don't, however, because the PCV system directs these vapors back to the intake system so that they are burned in the combustion chambers.

There is another system—Air Injection—that helps control hydrocarbon and carbon monoxide (CO) emissions in the exhaust. Air is injected by a pump into the engine's exhaust ports to cause further burning of the hot gasoline vapors before they pass out the exhaust pipe.

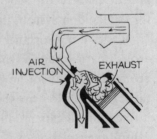

As government emission standards became more strict, engineers and scientists had to find new ways to achieve the required control. At the same time, they had to come up with a system that would provide good fuel economy and not affect the smooth operation of an automobile.

The result was the development of a device called a *catalytic converter*, which was first introduced on most 1975-model cars made in the U.S. This emission control system oxidizes HC and CO into harmless water vapor and carbon dioxide as the exhaust gases pass through a canister containing pellets which are coated with a catalyst material. A catalyst promotes chemical reactions, allowing them to take place at much lower than normal temperatures and more rapidly than a chemical reaction ordinarily would proceed. In the case of the catalytic converter emission control system, this means that catalysts allow more nearly complete oxidation of hydrocarbons and carbon monoxide at a much lower temperature than ordinary "burning."

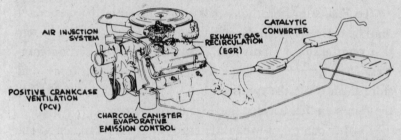

The catalytic converter has played a major role in reducing the emission of hydrocarbons and carbon monoxide from exhaust pipes into the atmosphere. It has also promoted improved fuel economy and has helped engineers "tune" the engine for a more pleasant car to drive.

Although the present catalytic converter, an oxidizing converter, does an excellent job in controlling HC and CO emissions, it isn't effective in controlling oxides of nitrogen (NOx), the third type of pollutant in exhaust gases. Oxides of nitrogen are different than HC and CO because they will not burn to harmless combustion products. Instead, control of NOx in the engine exhaust usually requires measures to prevent its formation.

Oxides of nitrogen are formed anytime you have very high temperatures in the oxidation process (usually above 3000°F or 1090°C) when air is used to provide the oxygen. Air contains 79% nitrogen and 21% oxygen, so you could say the air burns.

The formation of NOx in an engine is minimized by diluting the fuel/air mixture entering the combustion chamber. This helps reduce the peak combustion temperature. One system being used to control NOx emission is called Exhaust Gas Recirculation (EGR). With this system, small quantities of exhaust gases are recirculated back into the intake system of the engine to dilute the fuel/air mixture. Engineers are also looking at a "Three-Way Catalyst Closed Loop System" in which all three pollutants can be removed from the exhaust gases by a single catalytic converter. Such a system has been used already in a limited number of production cars.

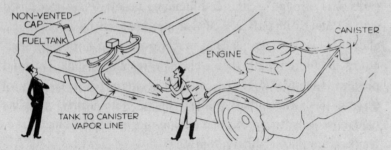

To reduce hydrocarbons that evaporate from the carburetor and the fuel tank when the engine is not running, there's a system that vents gasoline vapors into a canister filled with carbon granules. These granules act like a sponge and soak up the fumes and store them while the car is parked. When the engine starts up, the fumes are fed back to the engine and burned.

Further control of exhaust emissions has been brought about within the engine by changing the shape of the combustion chambers, using a leaner air-fuel ratio (more air in the mixture that goes to the cylinders for combustion), regulating the temperature of the air entering the carburetor, increasing the speed at which the engine idles, and modifying spark timing for stop and go driving. These changes to the engine all combine to help achieve more complete combustion and decrease exhaust emissions.

DRIVE SYSTEM

THE FIRST THING needed in the drive system is a device that will completely disconnect the engine from the rear wheels and the rest of the power transmission system. This will allow the engine to run when the car is standing still.

Suppose we mount two ordinary pie tins, each on a shaft, as

shown. As long as they are not touching each other, we can spin one as fast as we want to without affecting the other at all. But

if we move them together when one of them is spinning, the other will begin to turn and almost immediately both shafts will be turning together as one unit. This is the general principle of operation of the disc, or friction, clutch used in automobiles having manual shift transmissions. The discs are forced together by strong springs, and are separated by pushing down on the clutch pedal in the driver's compartment.

Cars equipped with automatic transmissions do not have a friction clutch or clutch pedal. We will discuss those shortly but, first we will cover the manual shift type transmission and drive system.

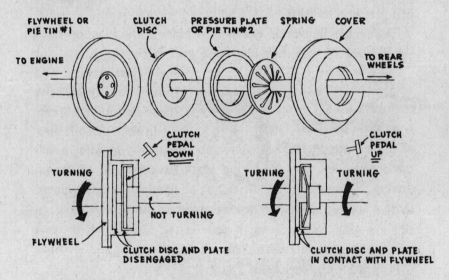

A transmission is used in automobiles to enable us to change the speed of the engine in relation to the speed of the rear wheels. When a car is starting up or in heavy going at low speed, we need more twisting force on the rear wheels to make it go than we need cruising along a good highway at constant speed. The transmission gives us this increased twisting force, and also allows the engine to run faster.

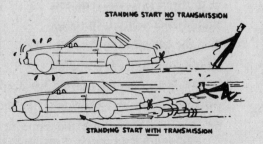

The latter is important because an internal combustion engine does not develop very much power at low speed. When the car has picked up speed, the transmission is shifted to change the speed ratio between the engine and the wheels, and eventually is shifted into its highest gear.

The transmission is a system of gears. Suppose we have a small gear with 12 teeth driving a larger gear with 24 teeth. When the first gear has made one complete revolution, we might say that

it has gone around a distance equivalent to 12 teeth. The second one has gone around the same distance—12 teeth—but this means only one-half a revolution for the larger gear. So this second gear, and the shaft it is fastened to, always turn at one-half the speed of the first gear and its shaft.

A familiar household example of gears is the hand-operated egg beater. We can turn the large gear fairly slowly and the small gears meshing with it turn rapidly to drive the beaters at high speed.

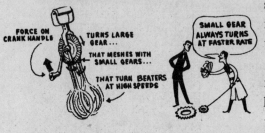

In a manual shift automobile transmission we have several combinations of gears arranged so that we can select the one we want to use at any moment. For low gear, or first, a small gear on the engine shaft drives a large gear on another shaft. This reduces the speed and increases the twisting force. Then a small gear on the second shaft drives a large gear on the drive shaft which goes to the rear axle. This reduces the speed and increases the twist still more, giving a ratio of about 3 to 1 for starting up or heavy pulling.

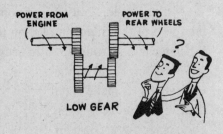

When the car has started we need less twisting force to turn the rear wheels and we would like more speed. For intermediate or second gear, we use the same first pair of gears as in low.

We disconnect the second pair, however, and drive through two other gears. These are arranged with the larger one driving the smaller, so there is less overall speed reduction than in first gear, about 1⅔ to 1.

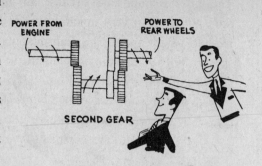

Most of the time while we are driving we need no reduction at all in the transmission. This is third, or high gear, and the engine shaft is connected directly to the drive shaft. They both revolve at the same speed, that is a 1 to 1 ratio.

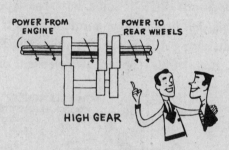

One very important requirement of a transmission is to provide means to make a car back up. Reverse gear is very much like first, giving about the same ratio and using the same four gears. It also uses a fifth gear, however, which causes the drive-shaft to turn in the opposite direction.

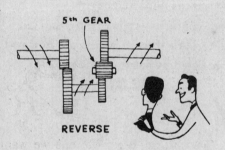

This makes a complete manual shift transmission of the conventional type, with three speeds forward and one reverse. The gears are mounted in a metal case filled with oil to lubricate the gears and bearings. The various speeds are selected by moving a gearshift in the driver's compartment.

Many manual transmissions today have four or five speeds, sometimes called overdrive. In these higher gear ratios, the engine is actually turning slower than the drive shaft and rear axle. With the high gear ratios and lower engine speeds, fuel economy can be significantly improved.

STATOR

LIKE A DOUGHNUT CUT IN HALF WITH A PLATE IN BETWEEN

TURBINE BLADES PUMP

Most cars built today have some form of automatic transmission, which eliminates the clutch and the need to shift gears manually to obtain the right gear ratios. There are various types, but most of them are similar in the way they affect the driving of the car.

They usually have a hydraulic drive of some sort. The type that is in wide use today is the three-element torque converter. Imagine taking a doughnut, slicing it in two, and putting blades on the inside of each half. Both halves represent two elements of the torque converter—the pump, or driving element, and the turbine, or driven element. Now, between these two halves place a plate that also has blades. This is the third element of the converter called the stator.

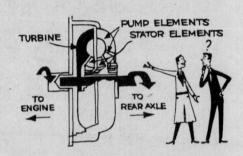

TURBINE

PUMP ELEMENTS
STATOR ELEMENTS
?

TO ENGINE

TO REAR AXLE

All three elements are in a casing filled with oil, which is circulated by means of the blades. Let's see what happens when we place the automatic transmission selector in the Drive position.

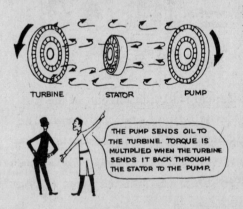

TURBINE STATOR PUMP

THE PUMP SENDS OIL TO THE TURBINE. TORQUE IS MULTIPLIED WHEN THE TURBINE SENDS IT BACK THROUGH THE STATOR TO THE PUMP.

The pump is mechanically connected to the engine's crankshaft, so it always rotates when the engine runs. When the engine is started, the pump begins rotating and sends oil, spinning in a clockwise direction, against the blades of the turbine to start it turning. The spinning oil has energy which the turbine absorbs and converts into torque, or twisting force, which then is sent to the rear wheels. When the oil leaves the turbine it spins in a counterclockwise direction, and if it went back to the pump spinning in this direction it would slow it down. We would lose any torque that had been gained. To make sure this doesn't happen, we use the blades of the stator which does not rotate (not just yet, anyway) to change the direction of the oil flow so it spins again in a clockwise direction. When the oil now enters the pump it adds to the torque the pump receives from the engine, the pump starts to turn faster, and

we start to obtain torque multiplication. The cycle of oil going from the pump to the turbine, then through the stator, and back to the pump is repeated over and over until the

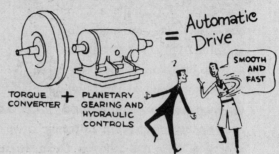

car reaches a speed where torque multiplication is no longer needed. When this happens, the stator starts to turn freely (it's fixed to rotate only clockwise). The pump and turbine then rotate at nearly the same speed and act like a fluid coupling, or clutch. We now have a situation similar to high gear in a manual shift

transmission where the engine crankshaft is connected directly to the driveshaft and both revolve at nearly the same speed. The stator stops rotating when torque multiplication is needed.

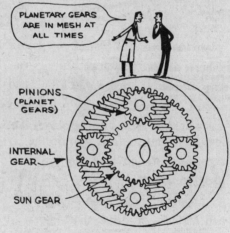

The turbine is connected by a shaft to a gear transmission located behind the converter. The

transmission usually used contains planetary gear sets and provides the desired number of forward speed gear ratios automatically. These gear ratios may also be selected manually for greater engine braking or exceptionally hard pulling. A reverse gear and neutral are also provided. The planetary type of gear

transmission has its gears in mesh at all times. Gear ratios for different driving conditions are obtained using hydraulic controls that cause friction bands and clutches to grab and hold certain gears of the set stationary while the others rotate.

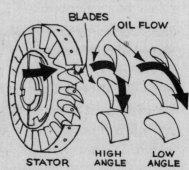

Hydraulic torque converters

can have variations in the design of their basic components. Some elements may have their blades set at a fixed angle to the flow of oil. Others may have blades that are hydraulically operated to pro-

vide varying blade angles automatically. For example, a stator could have a low angle for maximum efficiency during the average operating range of the transmission and a high angle for increased acceleration and performance (when more torque is needed at the rear wheels). There also are variations in the way the components are arranged in hydraulic torque converters. Some have two stators, others have multiple sets of pump and turbine blades. Differences can exist, too, in the way the planetary gears are combined with the pump, turbine, and stator elements.

Under ordinary circumstances, however, these variations will not make a great deal of difference to the driver of the car. He still will find no clutch pedal and will have no shifting to do, except when he wants to back up. And for forward driving, all he has to do is step on the accelerator to go and the brake pedal to stop.

From the transmission the propeller shaft, or drive shaft, goes back to the rear axle. This is simply a solid or tubular steel shaft. The universal joint allows the rear axle to move up or down in relation to the transmission without bending or breaking the shaft. It is something like the gimbals of a compass on a boat, which allows the compass to remain level at all times no matter how the boat rolls or pitches.

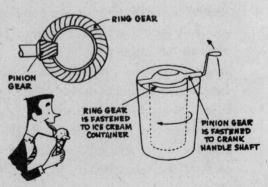

In the rear axle we have two sets of gears. The first—ring gear and pinion—is simply to transmit the power around a corner. It

enables the propeller shaft to drive the axle shafts which are at right angles to it. The old-fashioned ice cream freezer has a set of gears to do the same thing.

If we didn't ever have to turn a corner that is all the gearing we would need at the rear axle. But when we turn a corner the outside wheel has to travel farther than the inside wheel, and so it has to go faster during that time. It is like a squad of soldiers making a turn; the outside man has to march much faster than the one on the inside. We have a set of gears called the differential to take care of this.

The differential consists of two small bevel gears on the ends of the axle shafts meshed with two bevel gears (for simplicity we show only one) mounted in the differential frame. This frame is fastened solidly to the ring gear. When

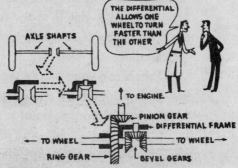

the car is going straight ahead, the frame and the gears all rotate as a unit, with no motion between one another. But when the car is turning, one wheel wants to go faster than the other, so the gears on the axle shafts rotate relative to the other

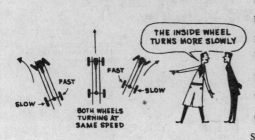

small gear. If the ring gear were stationary, one axle would turn frontward and the other one backward. But inasmuch as the ring gear is turning the whole unit, it means that one axle is turning faster than the ring gear and the other is turning slower by the

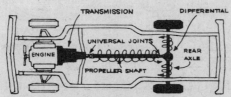

COMPLETE POWER PATH—ENGINE TO REAR WHEELS

same amount. This can be carried to the point where one wheel is stationary and the other one is turning at twice ring gear speed, which is the situation we sometimes get when one wheel is on a slippery spot and the other isn't. Some cars, however, can be equipped with a limited slip differential, a type of differential that allows the major driving force to go to the wheel having greater traction.

The axle shafts, of course, drive the wheels and make the car move, which is the point we have been getting to all this time. We now have a complete rear wheel drive system, just as outlined at the beginning. Power starts at the engine and eventually gets to the rear wheels, after passing through various mechanisms so that it will arrive there in the proper form.

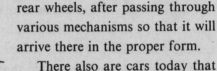

There also are cars today that have front wheel drive. The same basic components are used as for the rear wheel drive system, but all the components are arranged up front of the driver. The power flow from the engine is to the front wheel axle shafts. Instead of the rear wheels pushing the car forward, the front wheels pull the car along.

There is one more part of the car we should mention before we are through. We have shown how we get the car to move, but another very important point is to be able to stop it.

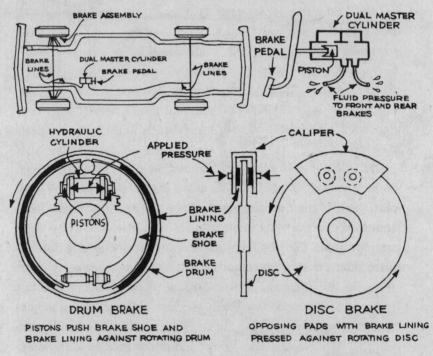

Brakes are provided for this purpose. There is one in each of the four wheels, and they are simply a method of applying friction to the rotating wheels to stop them. It is like rubbing a stick against the rim of a child's wagon wheels.

Two types of brake systems can be found on today's cars—the drum brake or the disc brake. In the drum brake system, two stationary brake shoes covered with a special friction material, called brake lining, are forced outward by hydraulic pressure against the inside of a metal drum that rotates with the wheel. A system of steel tubes filled with a special hydraulic brake fluid runs from a master cylinder to each brake. When the driver steps on the brake pedal, pressure is built up in the master cylinder and this pressure is transmitted through the tubes, called brake lines, to pistons located inside a hydraulic cylinder in each wheel. The pistons move outward and push the shoes against the brake drum. As a safety feature, today's cars have a dual master cylinder which provides two independent hydraulic systems, one for the front wheels and one for the rear.

In the disc brake system, the brake lining is bonded to brake shoes positioned on each side of a rotating disc located in the wheel. When the brake pedal is applied, hydraulic pressure transmitted from the dual master cylinder causes a caliper to clamp the opposing shoes against the disc (it's like taking your thumb and forefinger and squeezing them together against a rotating plate).

The brake is a friction device that converts work into heat, and the amount of heat created by the brakes during a fast stop from high speed is amazing. Because of this, proper cooling of the brakes is an important consideration during their design.

So now we have everything we need to make a car go and to make it stop. It is not a complete car of course. There are other parts which are necessary, and many others which have been added over the years in the interest of safety, comfort, dependability and so forth. The research people—engineers and scientists of many sorts—have been constantly improving the automobile until it is a far cry from the horseless carriage of its early days. And this improvement goes on year after year, and will continue as long as men are free to experiment and develop new things under a system of individual enterprise and competition.

When we look at the cars going by on the street, we don't see any of these parts we have been talking about—except the tires. And when we look inside the car, even then we don't see all those parts of the engine and the power transmission system. But when we get in the driver's seat and drive down the road, then it is different. We certainly know that something is there.

We hope this booklet has given you a better idea of what that "something" is—those unseen parts that make an automobile an automobile and not just a stationary room with comfortable seats.

We hope that it will help you take care of those parts better and to control them properly when driving. Mechanically it is easy to drive a car. A touch on the accelerator pedal and away we go. We press on the brake and come to an easy stop. Fast or slow . . . up hill and down . . . stop, go, stop . . . about all it takes is a movement of the foot.

But it takes more than a movement of the foot to drive *safely*. It takes a brain to decide what to do and when to do it. Just like anything else, when we have power over something we have a responsibility for it too. All the safety is built into the car that the manufacturer knows how to put in, but he can't build the driver to specifications. The driver has a powerful mechanism at his command, and it is up to him to use it properly.

(Courtesy: General Motors Corporation.)

MECHANICAL PRINCIPLES AND THE AUTOMOBILE

"What makes an automobile go?"

"Why, the engine, of course," is the reply.

"No," someone objects. "The wheels turning around make it go."

Such an argument is ridiculous because it is easy to see that we need both. We must have a source of power, an engine, and we must have something which actually furnishes the push or pull that moves the vehicle.

Many people, however, forget about the second part of this chain of power. Everybody talks of gasoline engines or Diesel engines, and they take it for

granted that if the engine runs there is nothing else to think about. The curious person who does try to find out what happens beyond the engine immediately runs into complicated equations, talk of involute curves, compound gears, and so forth. And he decides that here is a place for engineers, not for him.

In this section we will explain what happens to the power after it leaves the engine — particularly the power from *internal combustion* engines used in automobiles. The engine's crankshaft rotates at a certain speed and with a certain force. But what happens between the place where power is developed (the engine) and where it finally is used (the wheels)? This

is what we will be concerned with here.

Not too many years ago about the only method of transmitting power to a vehicle was a shaft or straps to fasten it behind an animal. The wheels were only to make it easier to pull—they did not make it move. One of the earliest and simplest examples of a vehicle carrying its own engine, which turns a wheel to make it go, is the bicycle. The engine, of course, is the rider. He makes the front sprocket, or gear, go around, which drives the chain, which makes the rear sprocket go around. Since this is fastened solidly to the wheel, the wheel goes around, rolls along the ground, and moves the bicycle and rider with it. Here we have

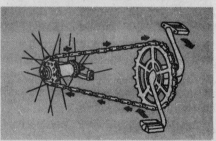

a familiar mechanism which is a definite example of generating power in one place and using it in another place.

But when the internal combustion engine came along, it brought some

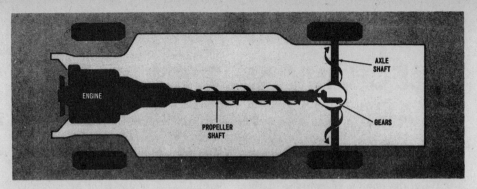

new problems in transmitting power. The internal combustion engine has certain fundamental characteristics which require rather complicated gearing to make an automobile do the things we want it to do. Power can be transmitted in various ways. But as it comes from the crankshaft of an engine, it is in the form of twist. The engine acts like a powerful giant turning a crank handle which exerts this twisting force on the shafts and gears which connect the engine to the driving wheels.

Let us see how this would work in a very simplified form of an automobile power transmission system. This system would not be very satisfactory for starting the car, turning corners, or climbing hills, but for just driving along on a straight, level road it would be all right. There is a long shaft, called the propeller shaft, with one end fastened to the rear of the engine crankshaft, and on its other end, between the rear wheels, is a gear. Running from the center of one rear wheel to the other—fastened solidly to each —is the axle shaft. And at the center of this axle is fastened a circular gear with gear teeth on one side. The two gears fit together, so that as the propeller shaft turns, or twists, the axle also turns and causes the wheels to go around. Since the wheels rest solidly on the ground, we might say that they try to push the ground backward when they begin to turn. But the ground does not move—so in order to turn, the wheels must roll forward. They necessarily move the car forward with

them, which is what we have been trying to do all the time.

As we said, this is a very simplified arrangement. In fact about all we are doing is to make our path of power turn a corner. Or to be more accurate, perhaps we should say that our path splits and each half goes off at a right angle. Our only object is to get that twisting force of the crankshaft back to the rear of the vehicle and facing in a direction where it can twist the wheels. All we have been trying to do is get power from one place to another.

But that is only a part of most power transmission systems. And in many cases the least important part. We often use gears—or wheels, pulleys, etc.—for other purposes.

First, there is the question of speed. Suppose there is an engine running at one speed, but we have a machine we want to drive at half that speed. We can do this with gears. If we want the machine to run twice as fast as the engine, we can do that also—with different gears. We will see how a little later.

Second, there is torque. Webster says torque is "that which produces or tends to produce rotation or torsion." In everyday words, it is a force which tries to make something rotate. It is a twist. We usually can put the word "twist" in the place of "torque" and the meaning will be exactly the same but engineers prefer "torque."

We use gears to increase or reduce torque. We might have an engine connected directly to a machine by a solid

Torque is twist

chines. There are six of these machines —the lever, pulley, wheel and axle, inclined plane, wedge, and screw. Let us look at them briefly, with particular attention to one or two which we are going to hear more about later.

We are all familiar with the *lever,* an example of which is the teeter totter. If a child is on one end and his father on the other, the child will go up and

the heavier person down. But if his father moves closer to the center of the board, nearer and nearer the pivot point, there will come a time when the small weight of the child will raise the heavier person on the other side. If the father weighs twice as much as the child, they will just balance when the father is half as far from the pivot as the child is. That is leverage, or mechanical advantage—a weight in one place lifts a heavier weight in another place, or a force applied at one point of the lever produces a greater force at another point.

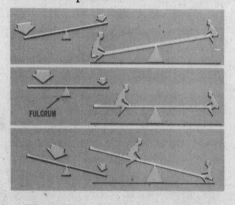

shaft, and the engine could not produce enough torque, or twist, to turn that shaft and run the machine. By putting the right size and kind of gears between the engine and machine, we could increase the twisting force enough to run the machine.

Speed changes and torque changes are related. Gear systems which change one will almost always change the other. But before we get into the why's and wherefore's of that, we are going to discuss briefly some fundamentals of mechanics. These may be old and familiar, but they will help explain a lot that follows.

Machines

There are a number of ways a man can increase the force he can apply with his own muscles. Some get to be rather complicated, but they are all made up of one or more simple ma-

The point of support, or the pivot point, is called the *fulcrum.* This may

be between the two forces, as shown, or at one end. And the forces or weights may be arranged in different ways.

We have examples of levers all around us. A pair of pliers pinches something with much more force than we apply with our fingers. With a crowbar we can lift more than we can lift directly. A nut cracker and a wheelbarrow are other levers in common use.

There are also examples of levers in which the force is decreased. We simply turn things the other way

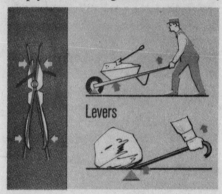

Levers

around. Fire tongs do not hold the chunk of coal as tightly as we are squeezing the handles. The fish end of a fishing pole does not have the same force that we are supplying near the other end. Our own forearm is a good example of this type of lever. The muscle pulls at a point very close to the fulcrum, and the weight we are lifting is way out at the end.

One thing should be noticed in all of these cases. When the force is in-

creased, it does not move as far. We may move the handles of a pair of pliers an inch to get a movement of an eighth of an inch at the jaws. The long end of the crowbar moves several feet to move the weight a few inches. Looking at the other side of it, we can jerk a fish out of ten feet of water by moving our hands less than a foot. Whatever we gain in force, we sacrifice in distance, and vice versa.

There are many arrangements of *pulleys*. With the simple one shown here we can hold 100 pounds with a force of 50 pounds. Each rope supports 50 pounds. By arrangements of more pulleys and thus more supporting ropes, we can get a greater mechanical advantage than the 2 to 1 shown. However, we have the same condition

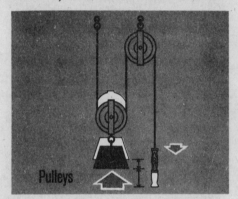

Pulleys

we mentioned with the lever. If our 50 pound force moves 1 foot, it will raise the 100 pound weight only ½ foot.

The *wheel and axle* is usually just a wheel fastened to a rod, like the steering wheel of an automobile. A

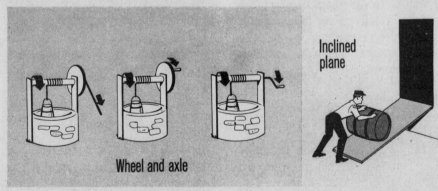

Wheel and axle

Inclined plane

force applied to the outside of the big wheel produces a greater twisting force on the small rod than if we twisted the rod itself. Sometimes we use a handle instead of a wheel, a crank, but this does not change the principle. Take a crank and a rod with a rope around it and we have a windlass. The hand will move several feet in turning the crank around once. This will turn the rod around once which will wind the rope up only a few inches. But it will lift a much greater weight than we could lift by pulling directly on the rope.

If a truck driver wants to get a barrel onto his truck, he lays a plank from the ground to the edge of the truck platform and rolls the barrel up. This plank is an *inclined plane*. He has to move the barrel a greater distance than he would by lifting it straight up, but it is a lot easier. He can get a barrel on the truck this way that he could not possibly lift.

The *wedge* is just a form of inclined plane. We push it under or between the objects to be moved instead of moving the object up the incline.

The *screw* is also a member of the the same family. It is an inclined plane wrapped around a rod. As we follow the thread around the outside of the rod, we are continually going up hill. One complete turn of the screw moves the nut only the short distance between two threads. This distance is called the *pitch* of the screw. With a wood screw the action is just the same. Each turn of the screw moves it into the wood a distance equal to the pitch. The metal nut must have threads on the inside which will fit exactly the threads on the outside of the screw, but the wood screw cuts its own threads in the wood as it moves inward.

These few devices we have named often are combined in more complicated mechanisms, and sometimes it is difficult to recognize them as these same simple things. But if we take them

apart and look them over carefully, we will find the familiar characteristics of the lever, the screw, or one of the others.

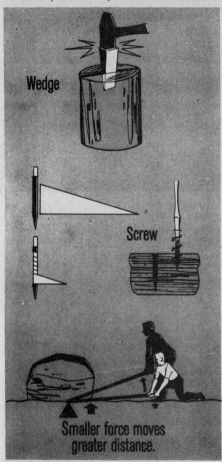

Smaller force moves greater distance.

We shall find also that all these devices work on the same principle. That principle is that if we increase a force by means of one of these machines, that force cannot move as far as the original smaller force moves. As we have pointed out in each case, when we increase the force, we sacrifice distance. In textbooks, the formula says that *work equals force times distance*. And we cannot increase work by means of a lever. If we could, we would have perpetual motion. So the work remains the same, and if force increases, distance decreases, and vice versa.

The action of gears—the principle on which they work—is exactly the same as this. But before we get into that, let us see what a gear is, and what different kinds there are.

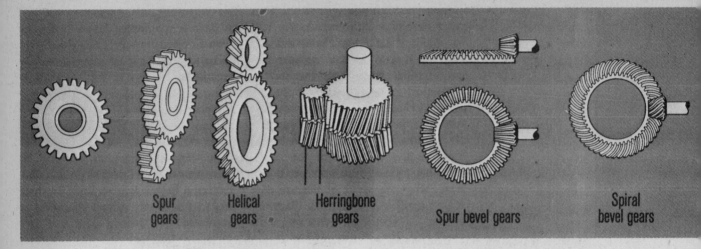

Spur gears Helical gears Herringbone gears Spur bevel gears Spiral bevel gears

What is a Gear?

A gear is a wheel with projections on it called *teeth*. These teeth may be on the edge, on the side, or halfway between. A gear usually is fastened to a shaft. Sometimes it turns and applies a twisting force to the shaft, and sometimes the shaft is turning and turns the gear with it.

The simplest type of gear is the *spur* gear. This has its teeth cut straight across the edge. For years it was almost universal, but other types have become more common in the transportation field. We will use it a lot in this book, however, even in places where it is not ordinarily used. It is easier to see and understand its motions, and the principle is exactly the same.

Another type is the *helical gear*. This is the same as the spur gear, but its teeth are cut at an angle. The teeth of the gear it meshes with must be cut at the same angle. It is usually quieter than the ordinary spur gear, and for that reason is preferred for many uses. For the same reason we sometimes use *herringbone* gears. This is like two helical gears fastened together tightly side by side.

When our power must turn a corner, we ordinarily use a *bevel* gear. The teeth of this gear are not cut on the edge. They are cut, we might say, across the corner. Sometimes it is a spur bevel gear, with straight teeth, but it is more likely to be a *spiral bevel* gear. This is somewhat like a helical gear, except that the teeth, in addition to being cut at an angle, also are curved.

We are going to leave out all the technical terms we can, but there is one we should explain. *Pitch diameter* is the diameter of the *pitch circle*. The

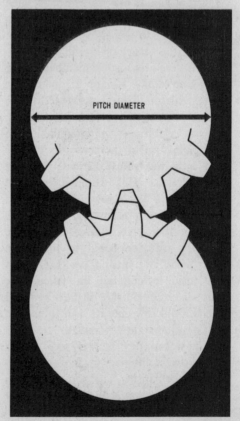

PITCH DIAMETER

pitch circle is a purely imaginary line running through the gear teeth at a point usually a little outside the half way point of the tooth. The easiest way to define it is to suppose we have two smooth rollers running together instead of toothed gears. They are of such a size that they run at exactly the same speeds as the gears. In such a case the pitch diameter of a gear would be the same as the diameter of the corresponding roller. From now on in this book, when we speak of the size of a gear we will mean the pitch diameter, as that is what really determines its speed and other characteristics.

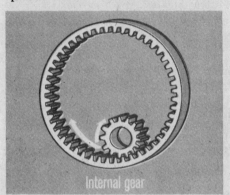

Internal gear

There is still another way of classifying gears. They can be external or internal. To the ordinary person the word "gear" will always bring to mind a picture of an external gear, and he usually will be right. But internal gears do play an important part in some mechanisms, as we will see later. An internal gear is simply a ring with teeth cut on the inside instead of the outside. To mesh with it we must have an external gear of smaller size.

What Does a Gear Do?

A gear is a spinning lever. It can increase or decrease torque in exactly the same way that a lever increases or decreases force. If you are interested in the explanation of this, more details are given on bottom. But these details are not necessary to understand what gears do and why we use them. The main thing to remember is that if we have a small gear fastened on one shaft driving a bigger gear on another shaft, the torque of the second shaft will be increased. The second shaft will have more twisting force than the first shaft.

A GEAR IS A SPINNING LEVER

Take an ordinary lever, 20 inches long, pivoted on a fulcrum.

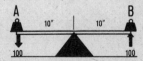

A 100 pound force down at A exerts a 100 pound force up at B.
$$100 \times 10 = 100 \times 10$$

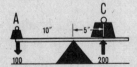

A 100 pound force down at A exerts a 200 pound force up at C.
$$100 \times 10 = 200 \times 5$$

Now change the fulcrum into a shaft, fastened solidly to the lever. If a force pushes down on one end of the lever, this applies a twist, or torque, to the shaft.

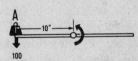

A force of 100 pounds at A causes a torque of 1000 pound-inches on the shaft.
$$100 \times 10 = 1000$$

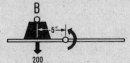

A force of 200 pounds at B also causes a torque of 1000 pound-inches on the shaft.
$$200 \times 5 = 1000$$

What happens if we turn things around the other way, and have the shaft try to turn the lever? If the shaft exerts a torque of 1000 pound-inches, it will create a force of 100 pounds at A, or 200 pounds at B.

* * *

Now let us take two of these levers, one 10 inches long and the other 20 inches long. Arrange them so one end of the short one is resting on one end of the long one. A torque of 500 pound-inches is applied to the shaft of the shorter one. The shafts are at the mid-point of each lever.

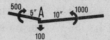

There will be a force of 100 pounds down at A, the end of the short lever. (100 x 5 = 500)

This will exert the same force, 100 pounds, down at the end of the long lever. This force will create a torque on the second shaft of 1000 pound-inches. (100 x 10 = 1000)

Our input torque was 500 pound-inches, and our output torque is now 1000 pound-inches, because the lever is longer.

But these two levers would not move the shaft very far. So we add another pair of levers, and then another.

When we have added enough of these to fill the circle, we have a set of gears.

The driving gear is 10 inches in diameter; the driven gear 20 inches. The input torque is 500 pound-inches; the output torque 1000 pound-inches. Thus the torque is multiplied in the same ratio as the size of the gears.

The torque will be increased.

If we have an engine driving the small gear, our system now will be able to turn something—say a machine of some sort—that the engine could not turn when they were connected directly together.

The amount of torque increase de-pends on the relative size of the gears. If the pitch diameter of the second gear is twice the diameter of the first gear, the torque will be doubled. If the second gear is three times as big the torque will be three times as much. But, if the *driving* gear is twice as big as the *driven* gear, the output torque will be cut down to ½ the input torque.

We can also think of a gear as another class of simple machine — the wheel and axle. A force applied at the outside edge of a gear, that is, where the teeth are, will exert a twist on the shaft. And the bigger the gear is, the greater will be this twist. With equal forces on the teeth of two gears, the shaft of the larger gear will have the greater torque. This is what we have when two gears are in mesh and one is driving the other.

In all this we have to remember one thing. We do not obtain this increased torque for nothing. We are not discoverers of perpetual motion and claim that we obtain more power out of the engine because we have added some gears to the system. We are still dealing with levers and they still follow the same rules. With levers we said that

whatever we gain in force we lose in distance. When talking about gears and shafts we say *whatever we gain in torque we lose in speed*. The two statements are not exactly the same, but we can think of them that way for the moment.

The best way to show this is to count the number of teeth on two gears. The teeth must all be the same size to fit together properly. Therefore, if the diameter of one gear is twice the diameter of the other, the big one must have twice as many teeth as the small one. Let us say 24 and 12 teeth respectively. As the small one, the driving gear, goes all the way around once, its 12 teeth have meshed with 12 teeth of the larger gear. That means the large one has turned around only halfway. The small one has to go around again before the large one completes one revolution. So, for every two revolutions of the small driving gear the large driven gear revolves once. And for every 1,000 revolutions of the small one the large one has made 500 revolutions. So, if an engine driving the small gear is running at a speed of 1,000 revolutions per minute (rpm) the machine driven by the large gear is turning over only 500 rpm. We have doubled the torque furnished by the engine. We have increased the twist on the second shaft so now it can turn the machine when perhaps it could not before. But the machine turns only half as fast as it would if it were connected directly to the engine.

Counting the number of teeth on gears is usually easier than measuring the pitch diameter. And as we have just shown it will give us the same information concerning the gear ratio—that is, the amount of change in torque and speed. If the driving gear has 10 teeth and the driven gear 30 teeth, it will take 3 revolutions of the first to get the second all the way around through one revolution. Thus the speed of the driven gear will be ⅓ the speed of the

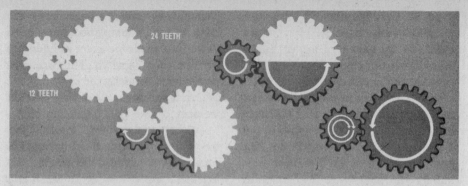

driving gear, and we know from this that the torque will be multiplied by 3. We would say that the gear ratio was 30/10 or 3 to 1. This applies equally as well if we have an odd combination of numbers, such as 39 and 19, only it is not so easy to do the mathematics in our head. The gear ratio would be 39/19, or a little over 2 to 1.

The gear with the greater number of teeth will always turn slower and will produce the greater torque.

Sometimes we are glad to have this reduction in speed along with the torque increase. In fact the main purpose of gears in some mechanisms is to act as speed reducers. In other cases we need both more torque and less speed, so we gain both ways. On the other hand, sometimes we may wish to increase the speed. Maybe we have a machine that has to run at 2,000 rpm and an engine running at 1,000 rpm. In that case we use a gear ratio of 2 to 1 again, but we have to put the large gear on the engine shaft and the small one on the machine shaft. The torque

will be cut in half, but if the engine has enough power to drive the machine under those conditions, the machine will run at the required speed of 2,000 rpm. But we cannot eat our cake and have it too. If we need both more torque and more speed, there is nothing we can do about it—except get more power from the engine.

What we have been saying is really the same thing as is expressed by the formula found in text books — that *power equals torque times speed*. The gears cannot change the power; that stays the same. Therefore, if the torque increases, the speed must decrease; if the speed goes up, the torque must go down.

In some mechanisms we have more than two gears between the input and output. A clock or watch—one of the very early users of gears—is a good example of multiple gears in series.

But suppose we look at something simpler to begin with. We will use our same two gears with 12 and 24 teeth and call them *A* and *B*. To these we

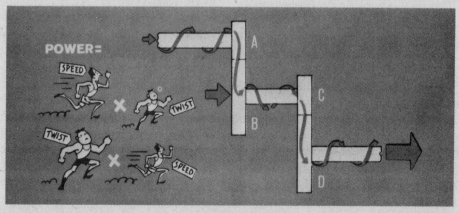

add another pair of gears *C* and *D* which also have 12 and 24 teeth respectively. The small gear *C* is fastened on the same shaft as large gear *B*. Now let us follow the path of the power flowing through this gear train. The engine is connected to the top shaft and is still running at 1,000 rpm. We already know what happens with the first two gears. The speed is cut in half and the torque doubled. So our second shaft is turning only 500 rpm which means that gear *C* is turning at that same speed. Now we can forget about the first two gears and consider only *C* and *D*. We know what happens there, too, because they are just the same gears with a ratio of 2 to 1. Our speed will be halved again and the torque doubled once more. So our last shaft, which is driving the machine, is turning at only 250 rpm, but it is applying to the machine a torque or twist 4 times as much as that delivered by the engine. The over-all ratio of the whole system is 4 to 1.

In any simple case such as this we can get the same effect by using only two gears of the proper ratio. Sometimes, however, there is too great a difference to be efficient, and sometimes it is a matter of convenience or space saving. In actual practice we ordinarily would not arrange the gears as we have here. We would save room by moving the third shaft up above the second. The result would be exactly the same, and we would have the added advantage that the first and third shafts would be directly in line. What we really have here now is a simplified arrangement of a manual shift automobile transmission. The third shaft would extend back to the rear axle to drive the wheels. But we will get into that a little later.

There is another feature in using four gears here instead of two which is sometimes an advantage. And this brings up a characteristic of gears which has probably been self-evident but which we have not mentioned. It has to do with direction of rotation. Looking at a pair of gears it is easy to see that if one shaft rotates clockwise, the other must go counterclockwise. This may be a nuisance in some installations, and in some others it may be just what we want. Sometimes gears are used to reverse the direction of rotation and for no other reason. But if we want the output shaft to run the same way as the input shaft, we must use at least three gears. Or, we can use a combination of more gears such as we have just been discussing. To find out which way the final shaft runs in any complicated

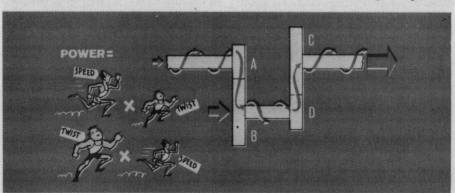

system of gearing, the best procedure is to go through the whole system and figure out which way each gear turns. And do not forget the exception to the above—when an ordinary external gear is driving an internal gear, both shafts will rotate in the same direction.

We should point out one more thing before we leave this subject. If we consider the gear system of any wheeled vehicle, we must consider the wheels themselves. The size of the wheels has just as much to do with the overall drive ratio as do the gears. It is the backward force the wheel exerts on the ground which makes the vehicle go, and if we have a certain torque or twist on the wheel shaft, this force at the ground depends on the size of the wheel. The larger the wheel, the less the force.

As an example, let us look at the bicycle as it was back in the early 1890's—that great high front wheel with the rider perched on top. The size of the front wheel was a matter of much pride and argument in those days. A 56-inch wheel was fairly good.

But a long-legged person who could straddle a 60-inch wheel really had something to brag about.

Why was the wheel made so big? It is very simple. They used a big wheel instead of using gears. The pedals were connected directly to the hub of the wheel, so every time the rider's feet went around once the wheel went around once. With a wheel of the size used today that would mean that the bicycle would move forward about 7 feet. But one revolution of that big wheel would roll it forward about 15 feet. This meant that pedalling at the same speed would make the high-wheeler go twice as fast. It might be harder to get started and tough-going on hills, but speed was what counted.

Eventually, the driving wheel was reduced to about half its former size and gears were used to give the rider the same effect he had before. Let us say we have 20 teeth on the front sprocket (gear) and 10 teeth on the rear sprocket. Disregard the chain because all it does is allow us to separate the gears. As far as the ratio is concerned we can think of the gears as meshing together directly. So we have a ratio of 1 to 2. The back gear will revolve twice as fast as the front gear, and thus the wheel will go around twice each time the pedals go around once. This gives us exactly the same result as if the wheel were twice as big and the pedals connected directly to it. The gears have cut the torque in half, but the driving wheel is only half the size of the big wheel, so the force between

Pedals go around once, wheel goes around once.

Pedals go around once, wheel goes around twice.

the wheel and the ground is the same in both cases.

Friction

Thus far we have neglected to mention friction, which always enters into the transmission of power. Friction has its good points and its bad points. We would have difficulty doing a great many things if there were no friction.

Try walking without it, for example. The only reason an automobile moves is because of the friction between the tires and the road. Also, an automobile clutch depends entirely on friction.

But in transmitting power, most of the effects of friction that we think about and talk about are the troublesome ones. That is probably because they are the ones we have to do something about. Whenever two gears run together, there is friction. This means that some of the power is used up—wasted—in overcoming that friction. A shaft running in a bearing creates friction, which means more wasted power. If there is too much of this friction in any one place, it means that the part will get very hot. This may result in swelling and sticking and all sorts of damage.

So we have to do the same things that are done in almost every moving mechanism. We have to use bearings to cut down the friction of all rotating shafts, and we have to furnish lubrication to these bearings and to the gears.

A little oil makes all the difference in the world in the amount of friction. A thin film of oil—no matter how thin —permits two metal surfaces of the right kind to rub against each other for very long periods with little wear and no damage. There are various ways to get this lubricant to the right place. Sometimes a pump forces oil under pressure to the points needing it; it circulates all the time the mechanism is running. Many parts are oiled by the mist and spray splashed up by gears churning the oil in the bottom of the case. Other points are packed permanently with grease, or have means to force grease into them every so often.

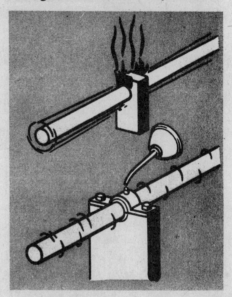

Plain bearings are used in many places—that is, bearings in which a metal shaft runs inside a metal ring of special bearing material. But in power transmission systems we use a number of anti-friction bearings. These are ball bearings, roller bearings, or needle bearings. They let us do things which without them would be difficult and complicated, if not impossible. They have a lot to do with the high speeds at which shafts and gears now run.

In all our discussion and figures so far we have not taken friction into account. All our mechanisms were perfect machines, with no losses due to friction. We are going to continue to do that to a large extent in the rest of this booklet. Friction is a variable factor and hard to pin down. Bearings

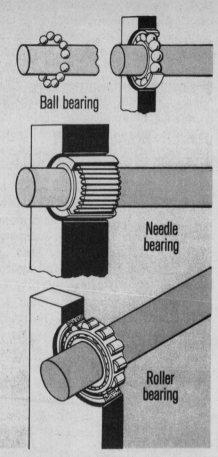

Ball bearing

Needle bearing

Roller bearing

and lubrication are a very important subject, but too large a subject to cover here. So in most of the examples we will show, we will just assume that the mechanism has proper bearings and is well lubricated in some way or other.

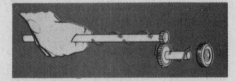

Why a Transmission?

The question might be asked, "Why use a transmission anyway? If any gain in torque is at the expense of speed, and vice versa, why not just put in an engine of the proper size and use only the gears necessary to get the power to where we need it?"

This argument might hold good for certain conditions. But in the cases we are going to consider in this book, where we have an internal combustion engine driving a vehicle, there are two things against it. First, the car needs different amounts of power to make it go properly under different conditions. Second, the power provided by the engine also can change greatly, depending on the operating conditions.

When we are considering an automobile, quite a lot of force is needed to start it moving. Less force is needed to keep it moving at a moderate speed. A lot of force is needed again to move it at very high speeds, and of course we have hills to contend with. So it is easy to see that we never know from one moment to the next just what force is going to be required at the wheels.

If we consider the characteristics of the engine, it is easy to see that we do not always get the power from it when we want it. We just said we needed a

We gain in two ways.

lot of force to get started, when the vehicle is standing still or moving very slowly. And that is just the time that the engine does not furnish very much power. One of the characteristics of an internal combustion engine is that it must run fairly fast before it can produce much power. Its shaft does not twist very hard when it turns over slowly.

But if we use the right size and kind of gears we can let the engine run at high speed while the wheels are turning slowly, and at the same time they themselves increase the torque being delivered by the engine. Thus the transmission is responsible for more twist on the propeller shaft because it lets the engine run faster and deliver more power. It increases that twist still more by its multiplication of torque. So for starting, this arrangement is fine. But it is not so good for higher speeds, and that is why automobiles have some means for changing the gear ratio, depending on the load and speed of the car and the judgment of the driver.

It is possible to drive a car without ever shifting gears if we are careful to stay on hard level roads and if we do not object to other cars going by us and leaving us behind at traffic signals.

POWER TRANSMISSION SYSTEM IN AN AUTOMOBILE

In an automobile there are a lot of things between the engine and the drive wheels. Some kinds of cars have more, others have less. Some have one thing, others have something else. They all have more than the simplified system shown in the early part of this booklet. As we said, that might be all right for driving straight ahead on a level road, but there would be a lot of places where it would not be all right. So we will start out here with a complete power transmission system of a typical automobile. We will explain briefly what each part does, without much attention to how it does it, and we may take liberties with what it looks like. Later on we will take up the more important parts individually and go into greater detail.

Clutch

Starting from the engine, the first thing we come to is the clutch. Its job is to disconnect the engine from the power transmission system when the driver so desires. When it is disengaged, the driving and driven plates are separated.

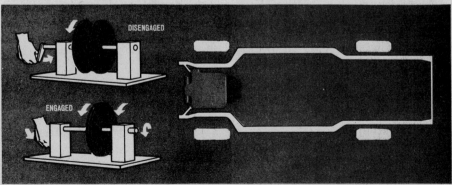

DISENGAGED

ENGAGED

What the engine does has no effect on the rest of the drive system and what the wheels are doing has no effect on the engine. There are several reasons why we want to be able to do that at certain times and under certain conditions.

Transmission

After the clutch comes the transmission. The reason for calling it this is not too clear. "Torque converter" or the English expression "gear set" gives us a better idea of what it is and what it does. But everyone still calls it "transmission." Its purpose is to let us change the ratio of speed between the engine and the rear wheels. When the car is starting we can run the engine fast and drive the wheels slowly, increasing the torque or driving force at the same time. When we are going faster we can change the ratio, so that the wheels are turning at more nearly

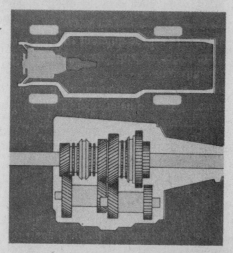

the same speed as the engine. Finally, in direct drive, the shaft behind the transmission is connected directly to the shaft from the clutch, and it is just as if the transmission were not there at all. There is also a reverse gear in the transmission, so that we can make the car go backward, and a neutral position, in which no movement or power is transmitted.

Propeller Shaft, Universal Joints

Back of the transmission is the propeller shaft which runs to the rear of the car. This is a hollow or solid steel shaft, sometimes enclosed in an outer tube, sometimes left open. At the front end is a universal joint, and in many cars there is another universal joint at the rear end of the shaft. These usually are made up of two U-shaped pieces at right angles to each other and fastened together by a cross having arms of equal length. The U-shaped yokes

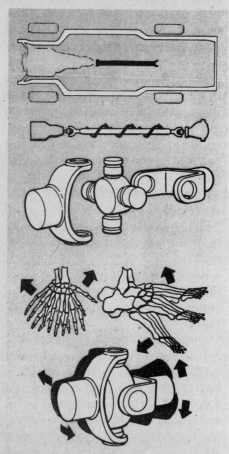

pivot on the arms of the cross. Since there are two of these pivots, the two shafts can be at an angle to one another and can still turn around and transmit power. They do not have to be in a straight line. This is very important, because even if we could design the car to have them in a straight line to begin with, every time we went over a bump they would get out of line. The rear axle moves with the wheels, up and down with every bump, while the transmission does not move so much, being fastened to the frame. So the universal joint lets the propeller shaft keep on turning even though its two ends are moving around relative to each other.

Final Drive

At the rear end of the propeller shaft is fastened a short shaft carrying a gear on the end. This is a bevel gear and is called the *pinion*. It meshes with the *ring gear* which is mounted on the rear axle. The job of the pinion and ring gear combination, or *final drive* as it often is called, is to take the torque provided by the propeller shaft, increase it, and turn it at right angles so it can twist the wheels and drive the car.

For many years these rear axle gears were of the spiral bevel type. But now most cars use what are called *hypoid* gears. They are about the same as spiral bevel gears, except that the pinion does not meet the ring gear at its centerline. It meets it at a lower point, which means that the shape of the teeth must be different. This allows the propeller shaft to be lowered and, in turn, the overall car height.

Since the pinion is much smaller than the ring gear, we know immediately that there is a speed reduction here, and an increase in torque. In today's passenger cars the rear axle ratios generally average about 3 to 1. The axles and wheels are turning only about one third as fast as the propeller shaft. It should be noted that this speed

reduction and torque increase are always there and always stay the same. Even when we say that we are in direct drive we are referring only to the transmission, and this rear axle ratio is still effective. And if the transmission is in low gear, say a ratio of 3 to 1 (it is actually less than this in most of today's cars), the overall ratio between the engine and rear wheels will be 3 × 3, or 9 to 1.

Differential

In the simplified automobile drive system which we showed in the first part of this booklet, the ring gear was fastened directly to a solid axle which ran from one wheel to the other. This would be all right for going straight.

But when the car turns a corner, the wheel on the outside of the turn must travel farther than the inside wheel. It is like a horse race. The jockeys all try to get the inside position on the curves because the inside horse does not have to run as far as those on the outside. In an automobile we use a differential to take care of this. The differential is meant for just one thing—to let the wheels turn at different speeds while still driving the car. It transmits equal torque to both wheels even when one is going faster than the other. If it was not necessary to have this differ-

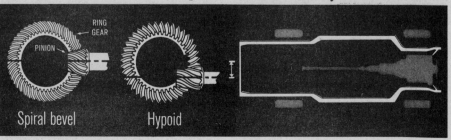

Spiral bevel   Hypoid

RING GEAR

PINION

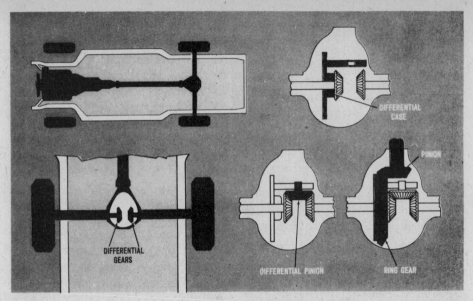

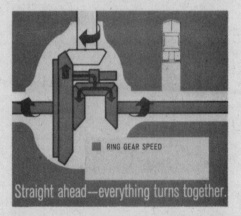

Straight ahead—everything turns together.

RING GEAR SPEED

ence in speed, we could do without the differential and have a much simpler rear axle and drive system.

A differential is one of those mechanisms whose action is easy to see when it is working right in front of you, but it is not so easy to describe. We will build it up piece by piece, however, and try to show how simple it really is.

First we have the two axles, each with a wheel on one end and a gear on the other end. These are small spur bevel gears, and are called *differential gears* or *side gears*. Then we add what is called the differential case, which we show as just a crooked bar fastened around one of the axles. It is loose on the axle, however, so it can turn around on it. In this case we mount another gear, the *differential pinion*. This is a small bevel gear which fits in between the two side gears and meshes with both of them. There we have all the necessary parts for a differential—just three gears and a case.

We will add one more part, however, to make it easier to tell the story. That is the ring gear mentioned before. It is fastened solidly to the differential case. Thus the case rotates all the time, at the same speed as the ring gear. This should be noted carefully, as we

are likely to think of a "case" as something stationary, just an enclosure

for the working parts. But here it is the driving member of the differential. As long as the ring gear rotates the case goes around, too, at the same speed. It carries the differential pinion around with it, but otherwise it knows nothing about what is going on in the differential. It just keeps rotating.

When we go straight ahead on a smooth road, the wheels turn at the same speed. Engine power drives the ring gear, so the differential case goes around, carrying the pinion with it. This turns the two side gears, and the whole mechanism revolves as one solid unit. The gears are not turning on one another. The pinion is simply connecting the two side gears together; they

RING GEAR SPEED
LESS THAN RING GEAR SPEED
MORE THAN RING GEAR SPEED

One wheel slower, one wheel faster.

could just as well be bolted together solidly. They are turning at the same speed as the differential case. It is the same as if we had no differential at all, because our wheels are traveling together and we do not need one.

Now let us take the other extreme and hold one wheel so it cannot turn. What happens in the differential? The case turns as before, carrying the pinion with it. But one axle is held, so its side gear cannot go around.

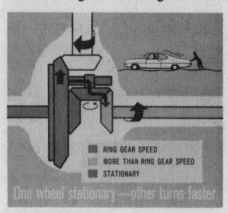

RING GEAR SPEED
MORE THAN RING GEAR SPEED
STATIONARY

One wheel stationary—other turns faster

Therefore, the pinion must turn. The pinion is being carried around by the case, but at the same time is revolving around its own short shaft. It must in order to stay meshed with the stationary side gear. It is running around the stationary gear.

But what is happening to the other side gear while this is going on? It is meshed with the pinion too, but it is free to turn. It is being turned just the same as it was in the first case, but *in addition* it is being turned more by

the revolving of the pinion on its own shaft. The pinion is revolving in the right direction so that its motion is added to the movement of the differential case. So the second side gear is turning faster than before. In fact this axle and wheel are turning exactly twice as fast as when the two wheels were running at the same speed.

Now let us take a situation in between these two extremes. Both wheels are turning, but one is going faster than the other. This is the case we ordinarily have in an automobile turning a corner. The inside wheel travels a shorter distance than the outside wheel; therefore it must turn around more slowly.

The inside wheel—and thus the differential gear on its axle shaft—is revolving more slowly than the differential case. The differential gear is turning more slowly than the pinion is being carried around. So we have the same general effect as when it was held tight—the pinion must turn on its own shaft. It will not turn as fast as before but it will turn. And it again turns in a direction to add to the speed of the opposite differential gear. It adds to it exactly the amount taken away from the slower gear and wheel. That is the way a differential must work—what is subtracted from one side must be added to the other. The ring gear speed always splits the difference between the two.

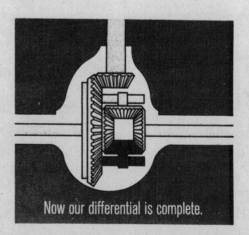

Now our differential is complete.

To make our mechanism look more like the real thing, we will add a little to it. This does not change its operation in any way however. We will complete the case, and add another pinion to the bottom. This pinion simply does exactly the same thing as the first one, and helps it do the job we have just described.

Limited Slip Differential

The differential is a very necessary thing. It acts as a sort of balance between the rear wheels. But it can be a nuisance at times. This is usually when we have a situation giving us the result we mentioned earlier—one wheel standing still, the other going twice as fast as usual. It is easy to do this. All we have to do is stop the car so one rear wheel is on dry pavement or road, and the other is on a slick patch of ice. The differential will drive the wheel which is the easier to turn. So the wheel on the ice will just spin, the other one will stand still, and— which is usually more important—the car will stand still. We get the same effect when one wheel is stuck in deep sand or mud, and the other one is comparatively free to turn. To avoid this trouble, limited slip differentials have been developed which permit the major part of the driving force to go to the wheel having the most traction.

Axles, Wheels

The axles are comparatively slender steel shafts. They have a flange at the outer end to which the wheel and brake drum are bolted. Around the axle is the axle housing. This holds the parts of the brake which do not turn with the wheel, and supports the bearing in which the outer end of the axle shaft runs.

The wheel itself is essentially a metal disc with a rim around the outside into which the tire fits. It is the outside surface of the tire which pushes on the ground and really makes the car move. But the engine furnishes the force, and all the other things we have just mentioned have a certain part of the job to do in getting that force from one place to the other.

This completes a general discussion of the main components of an automotive power transmission system. We will now go into more detail about the kinds of power transmission systems found in today's cars, show how they operate, and discuss some of their more important parts. We will begin with the manual shift transmission, then talk about automatic transmissions. Finally, we will mention some of the different arrangements found in power transmission systems today, such as front wheel drive.

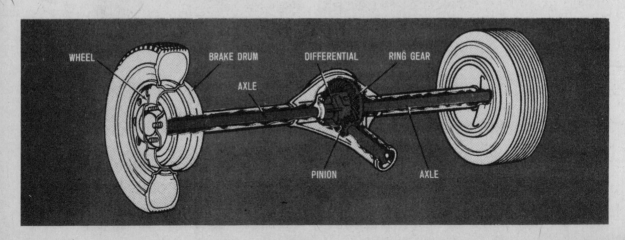

WHEEL   BRAKE DRUM   DIFFERENTIAL   RING GEAR   AXLE   PINION   AXLE

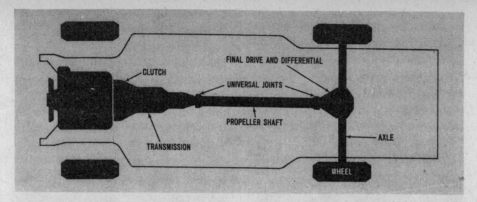

FINAL DRIVE AND DIFFERENTIAL

CLUTCH

UNIVERSAL JOINTS

PROPELLER SHAFT

TRANSMISSION

AXLE

WHEEL

MANUAL SHIFT TRANSMISSION

A manual shift transmission allows the driver control over the speed at which the gear ratios are to be changed to provide power at the driving wheels. Most of the manual shift transmissions used in today's cars have three forward gear ratios, or "speeds", although four-speed transmissions also are available. In any case, before the gears can be shifted, the clutch must be disconnected from the engine. This was touched on briefly before but now we'll explain in more detail just how this is accomplished.

Clutch

It is sometimes said that a good clutch *must slip* while being engaged and *must not slip* when it is engaged. This is almost a definition of a clutch. It is easy to see why when we consider what a clutch is for and what we want it to do.

First, we need something to disconnect the engine from the wheels, so that the engine can run while the car is standing still. Otherwise we would have to stop the engine every time we came to a traffic light. And it would be a problem to start the engine while it was connected to the drive system. Also, with manual shift transmissions, we have to disconnect it from the engine to shift gears easily.

There are various ways in which we could take care of these things, but we need something else. We need something which will take hold *gradually,* which will not jump abruptly from no connection at all to a direct, solid connection. When we want to start a car, we have to speed the engine up to get enough power to move it. At the same time the wheels are standing still. We cannot, in one moment, bring the speed of the wheels up to the speed of the engine; there would be a terrible jerk. And when we shift gears after the car is moving, we have almost the same situation—the wheels and propeller shaft are not turning at the same speed as the engine. So we want something which will slip a little, which will take hold gently at first and gradually grab harder and harder. Thus the rear wheels can start to move slowly and gradually pick up speed, until finally everything is turning at the same rate and the clutch is solidly engaged. From then on, of course, we do not want any slipping, because that is just wasting power and heating things up.

The kind of clutch we are talking about depends on friction for transmitting power. In fact, its full name is "friction clutch," as there are other types of devices commonly called clutches. In most automobiles the clutch consists of one plate squeezed tightly between two other plates. The one in the middle is the *driven member;* it is connected to the shaft leading back into the transmission. The other two are the *driving members;* they are connected directly to the

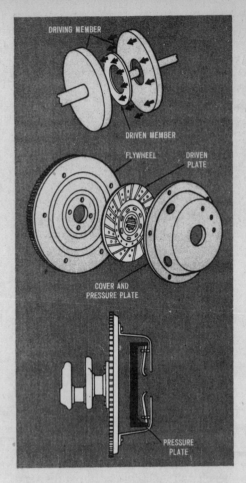

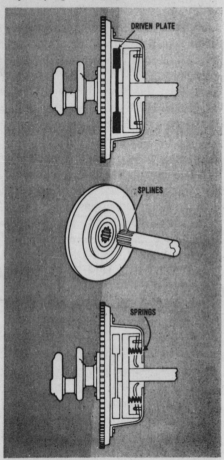

but the plate can slide forward and backward on the shaft.

A series of coil springs, or sometimes one large flat spring, act between the clutch cover and the pressure plate. They push the pressure plate toward the flywheel, squeezing the driven plate between the two. The springs are always trying to engage the clutch, and they are strong enough to keep it from slipping under any ordinary conditions. To disengage the clutch, the driver pushes on the pedal. This works through levers to pull back the pressure plate against the force of the springs. This loosens the driven plate and disconnects the transmission shaft from the engine crankshaft.

There have been many different designs of clutches in the past and the present ones do not all look just like what we have shown. Sometimes more than one driven plate is used, with a

engine. A strong spring, or springs, forces the two driving members together. This tightens their grip on the middle plate until they are all turning together as one unit.

The engine flywheel is used for the first driving member. Its surface is made very smooth where the driven plate pushes up against it.

The other driving member is called the *pressure plate*. It is a fairly heavy ring of cast iron, smooth on one side. It is fastened to the cover, which is bolted to the flywheel, so they all turn together. It is fastened in such a way that it can slide back and forth.

The *driven plate* is a flat disc of steel with friction facing fastened on each side. The plate is fastened by *splines* to a shaft going to the transmission. This means it fits into grooves on the shaft so that they must turn together

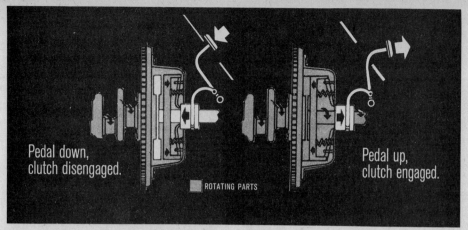

Pedal down, clutch disengaged.

Pedal up, clutch engaged.

■ ROTATING PARTS

corresponding increase in the number of driving plates. And there are other differences. But they all work on the same principle.

Transmission Gearing

The transmission is a case full of gears located behind the clutch. The case is usually fastened to the clutch housing, so the whole thing looks like an extension of the engine. The purpose of the transmission, as mentioned, is to vary the speed and torque of the rear axle in relation to the speed and torque of the engine.

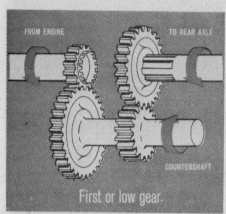

FROM ENGINE   TO REAR AXLE

COUNTERSHAFT

First or low gear.

Most passenger cars in this country have three ratios or "speeds" in the transmission for forward driving, and what we say here will apply to the simple, three-speed manual shift.

First speed, or *low gear,* is used for starting and for steep hills or heavy going in sand or mud. It lets the engine run fast while the car runs slowly. The engine runs 2½ to 3 times as fast as the propeller shaft. The exact figure varies in different cars. This means, of course, that the torque of the propeller shaft is increased just as much as its speed is cut down. Thus we have a lot of twist on the rear wheels to get the car started from a stand-still, or for use any other time we need it.

This is done with four gears and three shafts. A small gear on the shaft from the clutch drives a larger gear fastened to the transmission *countershaft.* Another smaller gear fastened on the countershaft drives a large gear on the third shaft. This last shaft goes to a universal joint on the front end of the propeller shaft. Thus we have the same arrangement shown earlier. There is a certain speed reduction in the first two gears, and then some more reduction in the second set of two gears. The countershaft is running at a speed between the speeds of the other two shafts. And the third shaft of course is running most slowly and with the greatest torque.

Second, or *intermediate gear,* works about the same way. The first two gears are the same as we used in low gear. The next pair are different, however. They are almost the same size, and sometimes the countershaft gear may be the larger. Thus the countershaft runs at the same speed as before, but there is little if any additional reduction from that to the third shaft.

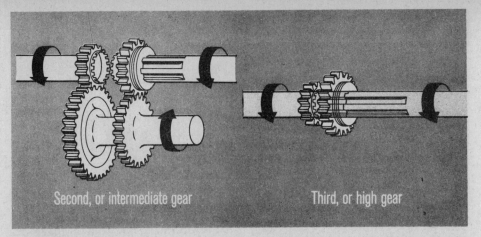

Second, or intermediate gear   Third, or high gear

So the wheels will run faster for the same engine speed than they did in low gear. The usual ratio in second speed is around 1⅔ to 1. This means that the propeller shaft will run at 1,000 rpm when the engine is running 1,670.

Third, or *high speed,* is direct drive. The transmission does not do anything. We simply connect the first and third shafts together, and they turn as one. The propeller shaft turns at the same speed as the engine, and delivers engine torque. Sticking to figures, we would say the ratio is 1 to 1.

Besides the three forward speeds, there are two other combinations we can get in a transmission. There is *neutral,* in which the transmission shaft is entirely disconnected from the clutch shaft, and the engine cannot drive the propeller shaft or anything beyond the transmission. It has about the same effect as disengaging the clutch. And there is *reverse.* It is a complicated matter to make an internal combustion engine run backwards, so we run it in one direction all the time and use gears to reverse the direction of rotation. We put an extra gear between the countershaft and the final drive shaft. It is called the *reverse idler.* We drive the countershaft in the same way as before, it drives this reverse idler which in turn drives the low speed gear on the final drive shaft. The system is just like low gear except for this extra gear. This changes the direction

of rotation, and we can see that the final shaft is turning opposite to what it was in all the previous cases. The ratio of reverse is about the same as low gear, or even lower. This is logical, because we may want to pull hard in reverse but we never want to back up very fast.

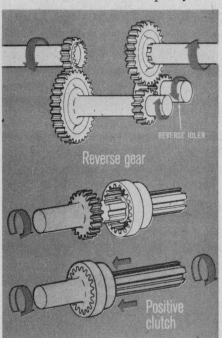

REVERSE IDLER

Reverse gear

Positive clutch

We have shown all the combinations found in a typical three-speed transmission. These can be put together in various ways to make a complete transmission, but we cannot show them all here. They first used to slide the gears back and forth on the shafts to get them into mesh and out of mesh. This can be done by using a square shaft or a splined, or grooved, shaft. In this way a gear is fastened solidly to its shaft as far as revolving is concerned, but it can slide along it.

Now we commonly use the so-called *constant mesh* transmission. Some of the gears still slide, but some are constantly in mesh with each other and rotate all the time. But these gears do not necessarily drive the shaft. They are free to rotate on it until they are connected to it by a clutch. We should explain that this is not a friction clutch. It is a *positive clutch*—more like a gear —having teeth that fit into similar teeth on the gear. It is called a clutch because its only job is to connect or disconnect the gear and the shaft.

Let us look at a complete constant mesh transmission, and note briefly what gears and shafts there are. There is the clutch shaft with gear *A* fastened solidly to it. There is the countershaft with all three gears, *B, C,* and *D,* fastened solidly to it. *A* and *B* are constant mesh gears, so whenever the engine is running and the clutch engaged, the countershaft and its three gears are turning. Then there is the transmission main shaft, with the two gears *E* and *F.* Gear *E* is in constant mesh with *C,* but is free to rotate on its own shaft except when connected to it by a clutch arrangement. Gear *F* is splined to the main shaft, so it turns with it but can slide back and forth. Finally we have the reverse idler, which is now a short shaft with the two gears *G* and *H* solidly fastened to it. *G* is always in mesh with *D*.

This may look rather complicated, but there is not really a great deal to it. And with this arrangement it is very simple to get any speed or gear we want. We can see that even in neutral the countershaft gears, gear *E,* and the reverse idler gears all revolve. But the main shaft stands still. Now suppose we slide gear *F* along the shaft. If we slide it in one direction it meshes with *D* and we have low gear. If we slide it the other way it meshes with *H* and we have reverse. We are using two gears on the reverse idler now, but as they are both fastened solidly on the same shaft and rotate in the same direction, the principle has not changed from that in our first example.

The path the power takes through the transmission in the various speeds is shown more clearly on page 153.

The other speeds we need are second and high. We get these by means of a positive clutch arrangement which slides between gears *A* and *E.* When it slides to the right it connects *E* to its shaft and we have second speed. When it slides to the left it connects the main shaft to the clutch shaft and we have direct drive.

We should mention one thing here. For the sake of convenience, we have shown spur gears being used in the transmission. In passenger cars, the usual practice is to use helical gears because of their quieter operation. Spur gears are used sometimes in truck transmissions.

How do we shift these gears and clutches to get the different speeds? We

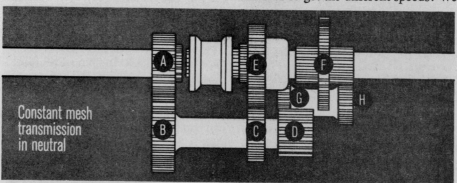

Constant mesh transmission in neutral

have seen that we only have to move two things—the low speed gear and the double clutch. These both have grooves

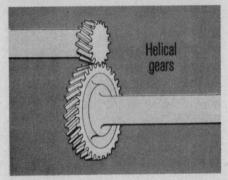

Helical gears

in them into which *shifting forks* fit loosely. The forks do not interfere with these parts turning around, but they can be used to slide them endwise.

Then we connect the forks to the gearshift lever in the driver's compartment in such a way that he can select either one and move it in either direction. Thus with the one lever he can

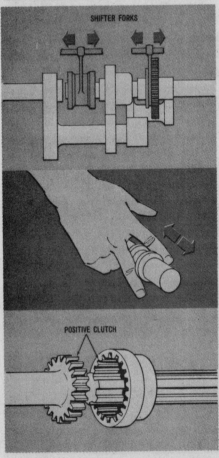

SHIFTER FORKS

POSITIVE CLUTCH

take his choice of any one of the four positions of the gears—five, counting neutral.

We have to disengage the main friction clutch when we shift gears. Otherwise there would be jerks and much loud clashing of gears. Some gears are running and some are standing still, or they are running at different speeds. Also there is considerable pressure on the gear teeth when they are driving, so the gears do not slide apart easily. And of course it gives the clutch a chance to cushion the shock or jerk of suddenly changing the ratio between the engine and the rear wheels.

There has been a lot of work done to make it easier to shift gears. The most successful result has been the development of gear synchronizers, or *synchronous transmissions*. This is a refinement of the constant mesh type we have described. Synchronizers are used for all forward speeds in the majority of today's manual shift transmissions, although some transmissions use synchronizers only for second and third speeds. There are several types, but they all have the same object.

Most of the trouble in shifting gears comes from the gears or clutches running at different speeds. If we could synchronize them, get them running at approximately the same speed before we tried to mesh the teeth, there would be little clash or clatter. This is just what we do. When the second and high speed clutch slides on the shaft—in either direction—it does not mesh with the teeth on the other half of the clutch right away. Instead a small friction clutch takes hold first. (The illustrations show only the general principle of it; the parts do not look anything like those shown.) This is a cone-shaped clutch, with metal faces, but it acts like the friction clutches we have described. It can slip enough to prevent a shock, but almost immediately it is solidly engaged. In doing this it has brought the speed of the gear up to the speed of the shaft.

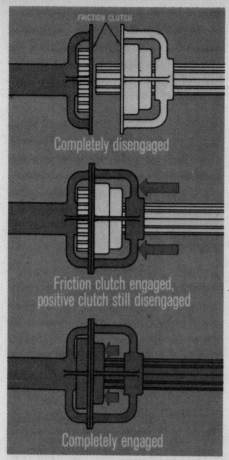

Completely disengaged

Friction clutch engaged,
positive clutch still disengaged

Completely engaged

As soon as they are turning at the same speed, it is easy to push in the toothed part of the clutch which gives a positive connection. The first part of the motion engages the friction clutch, and the second part engages the positive toothed

clutch. This arrangement enables even a new driver to shift gears without trouble.

All manual shift transmissions do not look like those we have shown. Some have a greater number of forward speeds, particularly trucks, and the gears may be arranged in a different order on the shafts. Most manual transmissions, however, operate on the principles discussed. There are a number of gears which can be connected together in different ways to give us the different ratios we want. Except when it is in direct drive, a certain amount of torque comes in at the front end from the clutch shaft, and a different amount goes out the back end to the propeller shaft.

We have described to some extent the main parts of the power path in a car with a manual shift transmission. These are the clutch and transmission gearing. We covered the propeller shaft, universal joints, axles, differential, and wheels and tires earlier. We will soon discuss automatic transmissions and how they make the power path different from those in cars with manual shift transmissions. Before we do that, however, it would be best to spend a little time talking about planetary gears since they play such an important role in the operation of an automatic transmission.

POWER FLOW THROUGH A
THREE SPEED TRANSMISSION

This shows how a three speed, constant mesh transmission operates in its various positions. The color indicates the path of the power through the transmission, from the engine on the left to the rear axle on the right. It shows which gears are actually working in each speed.

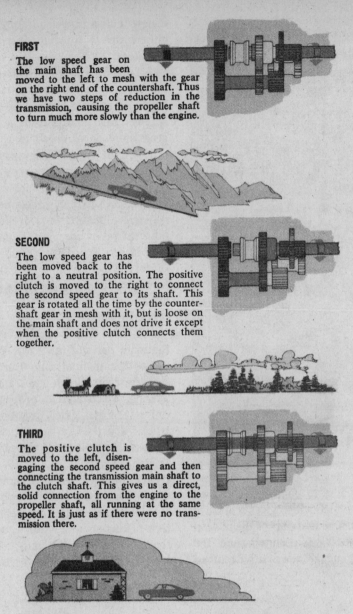

FIRST

The low speed gear on the main shaft has been moved to the left to mesh with the gear on the right end of the countershaft. Thus we have two steps of reduction in the transmission, causing the propeller shaft to turn much more slowly than the engine.

SECOND

The low speed gear has been moved back to the right to a neutral position. The positive clutch is moved to the right to connect the second speed gear to its shaft. This gear is rotated all the time by the countershaft gear in mesh with it, but is loose on the main shaft and does not drive it except when the positive clutch connects them together.

THIRD

The positive clutch is moved to the left, disengaging the second speed gear and then connecting the transmission main shaft to the clutch shaft. This gives us a direct, solid connection from the engine to the propeller shaft, all running at the same speed. It is just as if there were no transmission there.

REVERSE

With the transmission in neutral, we move the low speed gear on the main shaft to the right. It meshes with one gear of the reverse idler, which is rotated all the time by the countershaft but does not do anything until it is connected to the main shaft in this way. It can be seen that the shaft to the rear wheels is now turning in the opposite direction.

PLANETARY GEARS

Planetary gears are used in a variety of arrangements in the automobile. Probably the main reason for this is that we can make them do a number of different things, depending on how we connect them into the power system. This is what makes a planetary gear set so interesting. But, first, let us look at one and see what it is.

In its simplest form, a planetary gear

set is comprised of three gears. There is a *sun gear,* or pinion, in the center. Then there is a small *planet gear* meshing with it. (We show two of them here but usually there are three or four.) On the outside is the *ring gear,* an internal gear meshing with the planets. The planet gears are fastened together by the *planet carrier.* This holds them in place but lets them rotate. Just how these gears and carriers are fastened to the shafts depends on what we want the mechanism to do. We will explain one of the forms here, and others are shown on page 156.

Suppose we connect the sun gear to the input, or driving shaft, and the planet carrier to the output, or driven shaft. We put a brake band around the outside of the ring gear and hold it tight so it cannot move.

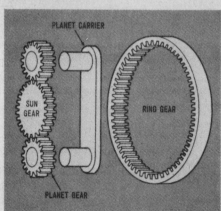

If the engine drives the sun gear, the planet gears must turn around. But they cannot stand still and rotate on their shafts because that would mean the ring gear must move, and we are holding

that with the brake. So they have to move around the ring gear and the planet carrier moves with them. It is something like the differential we described. There are two motions in the planet gears. Each one is rotating about its own shaft, and at the same time they are all moving around in a circle on the teeth of the ring gear. This is where this type of gearing gets its name.

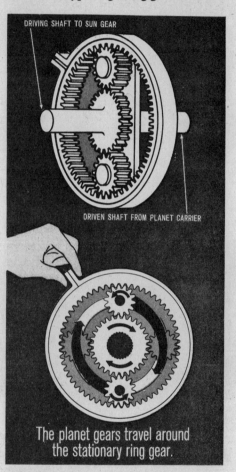

The planet gears travel around the stationary ring gear.

The motion is much the same as the Earth and other planets about the sun. Each one rotates on its own axis, but they also continually circle around the sun.

The planet carrier, and thus the driven shaft, is turning much more slowly than the sun gear and drive shaft and in the same direction. Just what the ratio is depends on the size of the gears, and we will not go into the details of how it is figured. As an example, how-

PLANETARY GEAR COMBINATIONS

There are three units in a planetary gear—sun gear, planet gears and carrier, and ring gear. To get various results we can hold any one of these units stationary, and either of the other two can be the driving or driven member. So there are six possible combinations. We show them here, with colors indicating the driving, driven, and locked members, and the labels telling what kind of gear results from each arrangement.

They are all planetary gears, but a number of different results are obtained by hooking them up differently.

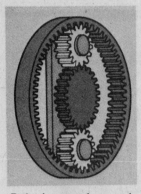

Reduction gear—less speed, more torque.

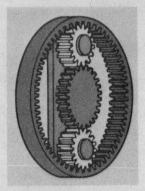

Reversing reduction gear — less speed, more torque, turns backward.

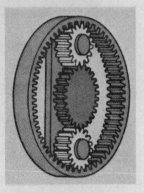

Reduction gear—less speed, more torque.

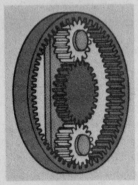

Reversing overdrive — more speed, less torque, turns backward.

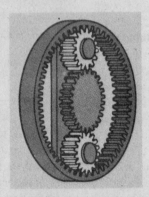

Overdrive—more speed, less torque.

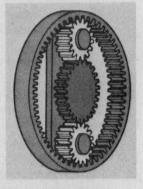

Overdrive—more speed, less torque.

■ DRIVING   ■ DRIVEN   ■ LOCKED

ever, with the smallest practical planets the ratio cannot be less than 2½ to 1. When the planets and the sun gear are the same size, the ratio is 4 to 1. This of course means that the speed is reduced to ¼, and the torque increased 4 times.

To shift into direct drive, we release the brake on the ring gear and engage a clutch connecting the drive shaft directly to the driven shaft. If we wish, this can be done by clutching the planet carrier to either the sun gear or ring gear. In either case none of the gears can turn on each other, so the whole mechanism is locked and rotates all together without affecting the drive.

We mentioned that we can get various results with a planetary transmission by connecting it up in different

ways. If we drive the ring gear and hold the sun gear still, we will still increase torque as we did in the case just described, but it will not be increased so much. By other arrangements we can increase the speed and reduce the torque, and by still other means we can get reverse. We have three units, any one of which we can hold stationary, and either of the other two can be the driving or driven member. So there are six possible combinations, shown on page 156. Practically all of them are used in transmissions in one way or another.

There are various modifications of this simple planetary gear. There are some with double planets of different sizes, and there are compound planetary gears, which consist of two planetary gear-sets with certain gears of one connected to certain gears of the other. These act in fundamentally the same way as the simple planetary, but following the power flow through them is rather complicated and figuring the gear ratio is not worth the trouble unless we are in the business of designing transmissions.

Planetary gears are used in automobiles mostly in automatic or semi-automatic transmissions. In the next section we will show how they work in the hydraulic torque converter type of automatic transmissions used in many cars built today.

AUTOMATIC TRANSMISSION

The name *automatic transmission* has been used to cover a lot of different things. Ordinarily it means any arrangement which will change the ratio between the engine and the wheels *by itself*—without the driver having to do anything.

In discussing the manual shift transmission, the first part after the engine in the power path was the clutch. In automatic power transmission systems, the clutch—or its replacement—also must be automatic. We must have a device that does the work of the friction clutch without requiring the driver to operate it.

Various ways have been tried to make the clutch work automatically, that is, to engage and disengage without effort on the part of the driver. Some early designs used vacuum power to operate the linkage of a standard clutch. In others, the clutch itself was changed to operate centrifugally. We won't go into the details of it. The principle remains the same, but centrifugal weights were arranged to engage the clutch when the engine reached a certain speed, then disengaged it when it dropped below a certain speed.

Hydraulic Coupling

Another device to replace the friction clutch is the *hydraulic coupling,* sometimes called the *fluid flywheel.* Some early automatic power transmission systems used the hydraulic coupling to replace the clutch entirely. In other arrangements, the coupling was placed just behind the engine, followed by a friction clutch, and finally the transmission. The hydraulic coupling does not do everything the friction clutch can do, but does some things the clutch cannot. The coupling can be called a centrifugal clutch because of the way it operates. If we run the engine slowly, it will not start the drive wheels turning. When we speed up the engine, it gradually takes hold until finally the engine is driving the wheels with practically no slip.

How does it work? Suppose we start

with a simple example. If we shoot steel balls at the blades of a paddle wheel, each ball will give the wheel a little push, will try to turn it around. If we can shoot them fast enough and hard enough, the wheel will keep spinning.

Now if we think of water or oil as being made up of a lot of small liquid balls, we can shoot these at the wheel and get the same results. You probably have seen water wheels which worked much like this, driven by the water falling over a dam or by the flow of a swift stream. This is about what we do in a fluid flywheel. But in an automobile we have to make an artificial stream. What it amounts to is a pump forcing oil against a turbine, or hydraulic motor. Many years ago it was found that the most efficient way to do this was to get the pump and motor close together, to more or less combine them. The result was a hydraulic coupling essentially the same as the fluid flywheel.

The working parts of a hydraulic coupling look very much like a doughnut. But the doughnut is sliced down the middle, so there is no connection between the two halves. One half is fastened to the engine crankshaft; the other to the clutch, or transmission, or some part eventually leading to the rear wheels. The doughnut is hollow, but each half has a number of straight radial blades leading from the hub to the outside edge. Very often a section of each blade is cut away, and in that space is put a metal plate or guide ring shaped like half of another, smaller doughnut. The two halves of the hydraulic coupling are just alike. When

we put them together we have what looks like a skinny doughnut inside a fat one, with thin blades connecting the two.

To make this complete we put a cover around it all, the cover often being fastened solidly to one of the rotating members. Then we fill it almost full of oil. Now if the engine is running, the first half of the hydraulic coupling, the *driving member,* is turning with it. If it is turning fairly fast, the oil is being thrown toward the outside of the doughnut by centrifugal force, just like marbles on a phonograph turntable. When it gets to the outside it wants to keep on going, and the only place it can go is across into the other half of the

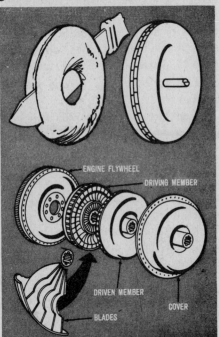

ENGINE FLYWHEEL
DRIVING MEMBER
DRIVEN MEMBER
COVER
BLADES

doughnut, the *driven member*.

All this time that the oil is being forced outward, it is also being whirled around in the other direction by the blades of the driving member. Consequently, when it crosses over into the driven member, it hits against those blades just as in the water wheel we mentioned and pushes them around. This tends to slow up the drops of oil, and they travel toward the hub, or center, of the driven member, then across the driving member and repeat the whole process. Thus we have the oil continually circulating, outward in the driving member, inward in the driven member. And at the same time it is traveling in a direction at right angles to this, being pushed by the blades of the driving member and pushing on the blades of the driven member.

The driven member can never go quite as fast as the driving member.

Driving member turning faster, driven member turning slowly.

Both members turning at approximately same speed.

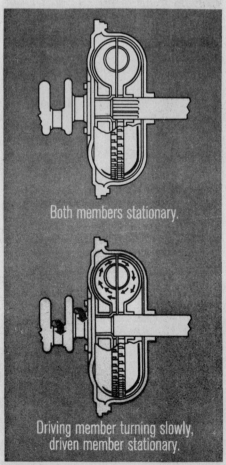

Both members stationary.

Driving member turning slowly, driven member stationary.

There is always a certain amount of slip no matter how fast they are turning. But at ordinary driving speeds this may amount to less than one per cent so it is not serious. When we get below a certain speed however, this slip begins to get greater. Finally it gets down to the point where the driven member does not turn at all. There is still some torque being applied to it, but it is not enough to make the rear wheels turn and move the car. This means that we can stand at a traffic signal with the transmission in gear and the car will stand still just as if a friction clutch were disengaged. Then as we speed up the engine, the driven member begins to turn, gradually picks up speed, and finally is running at approximately the same speed as the engine.

We mentioned that the driving member and driven member were just alike. There may be slight differences in them, but they are enough alike that a hydraulic coupling can drive in one direction as well as the other. The oil just circulates in the opposite direction, from what was the driven member to the driving member. Thus if the car is coasting or being pushed, the wheels drive the engine just about the same as if there were a solid connection there.

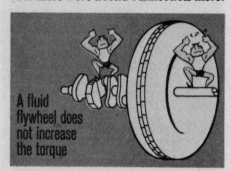

A fluid flywheel does not increase the torque

The use of a hydraulic coupling gives smoother pickup and makes it impossible to stall the engine when starting or climbing a hill. It also smooths out jerks, especially at low speeds, and in some ways acts as a centrifugal clutch. As we will see later, those characteristics let us use certain types of transmissions and shift gears in certain ways

which would not be satisfactory without a fluid flywheel. But we must remember that this is just a clutch. It is not a transmission. It cannot replace the transmission because it does not increase the torque—it only transmits the torque which the engine delivers to it. We will see later on in this book a mechanism that looks very much like it and which does multiply torque. But it is different. We will point out just how it is different when we get there.

Coupling-Planetary Combination

When automatic transmissions first came into wide use, the majority used a hydraulic coupling in combination with planetary gear sets. Although this design is no longer used today, it is worthwhile to discuss briefly how it operated since it was used so widely.

The hydraulic coupling-planetary gear combination was a four-speed automatic transmission, the top gear being direct drive, and a low rear axle ratio was used. A low axle ratio usually means slower pickup or acceleration in high gear, so third speed was arranged so that it could be brought into use at almost any speed when more acceleration was desired.

The transmission consisted of two planetary gear sets, one behind the other. Each planetary had two speeds, a reduction ratio and direct drive, but the reduction ratios were not the same. We could get the four speeds we wanted by choosing the proper ratios. In low gear, both planetaries were in action, giving us a double reduction. In second

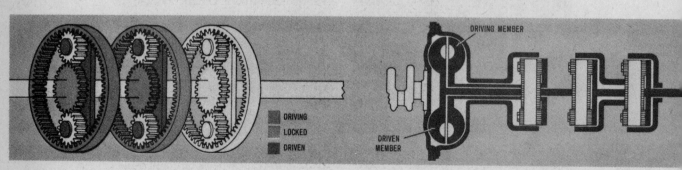

DRIVING
LOCKED
DRIVEN

DRIVING MEMBER

DRIVEN MEMBER

speed the front unit was in direct drive, and the rear unit alone gave a reduction of about 2½ to 1. In third speed we did just the opposite; the rear unit was in direct drive and the front unit was working. This had a ratio of approximately 1½ to 1. In fourth speed, both units were in direct drive, so engine torque flowed straight through to the rear axle. There also was a reverse gear which was a third planetary unit behind the other two. It acted in combination with the other two units to furnish a low ratio in the reverse direction.

The hydraulic coupling was a very important part of this combination. It was located between the engine and the transmission, but the flow of power from the engine actually went first to the front planetary unit, then to the fluid coupling, and then to the second planetary unit. The effect was just the same, however, except that the coupling was at a reduced speed at certain times, which had advantages. There was no friction clutch. The transmission shifted from one speed to another under load, without being disconnected from the engine. This was possible because the fluid flywheel cushioned the shock, and

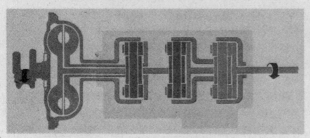

First speed
3¾ to 1

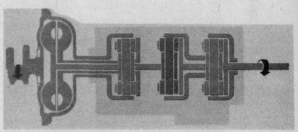

Second speed
2½ to 1

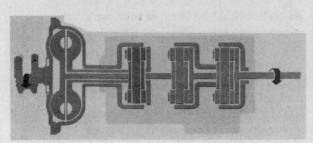

Third speed
1½ to 1

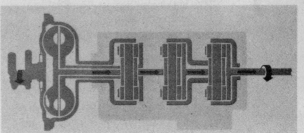

Fourth speed
1 to 1

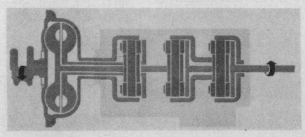

Reverse
4¼ to 1

■ REDUCTION GEAR

was one of the big differences between this and most other transmissions, even some which used a fluid flywheel.

The planetary gears were controlled by brake bands and friction clutches. A brake band held the proper member stationary in each unit when it was in low ratio, and a clutch locked each unit together when direct drive was needed in that unit. Oil pressure made these brakes and clutches work at the right time, depending on how fast the car was going and how far the accelerator pedal was pushed down. All the driver had to do was control the speed of the engine, and the gear shifting took care of itself.

Hydraulic Torque Converter

In our discussion of the hydraulic coupling, we pointed out that it is simply a hydraulic clutch which cannot deliver any more torque than is put into it. It is a very useful addition to a transmission, but it cannot replace the transmission because it is not a torque multiplier.

But we can make a torque multiplier out of it, and most automatic transmissions built today are of the multiplying type, commonly designated as *three-element hydraulic torque converters.*

In principle, all we have to do to a hydraulic coupling to make a torque converter is add another set of blades— *stationary* blades. There is the old rule that for every force there must be an equal and opposite reacting force. In transmissions this means that we cannot multiply torque unless we have some solid point to push on. We usually say we must have a reaction member, some stationary part connected to the frame of the vehicle. In a manual shift transmission the whole casing is fastened solidly and this holds the shafts in place. In the planetary gear set we have to grab hold of one of the three members before we can multiply torque—we have to hold it stationary in relation to the

frame. And we have the same situation here. In a hydraulic coupling the whole thing turns around together. But if we put in a new part, a set of blades tied solidly to the frame, we have something to take the reaction, to furnish the reacting force. Then it can multiply torque.

We show here the simplest arrangement. We have the pump, or driving element, and the turbine, or driven element, just as in the hydraulic coupling. But between them we add a *stator,* the reaction element. The casing is filled with oil which circulates in the usual manner, outward from the pump, inward through the turbine, and then

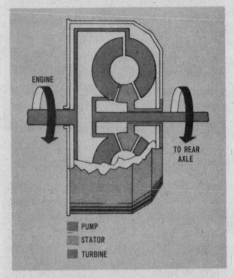

ENGINE

TO REAR AXLE

- ■ PUMP
- ■ STATOR
- ■ TURBINE

through the stator back to the pump.

The blades are not straight and flat however. If we could spread the three members out flat and look down on them, we would get an idea of their shape and how the liquid flows through them. The pump pushes the oil in the direction it is turning, and this oil hits the turbine and forces it to turn in the same direction. In doing this the oil bounces off the turbine blades in the opposite direction, and is flowing somewhat backward when it reaches the stator. If this reaction member were free to turn it would turn backward, but it is held tight. So it straightens out the oil and gets it moving in a forward direction again before it returns to the pump. In this way the motion of the oil assists the pump, and that is why such an arrangement can multiply torque.

A hydraulic torque converter is completely automatic in itself. It furnishes the greatest multiplication of torque when the car is starting from standstill, and this becomes less as the car picks up speed. The torque converter does not shift. It just smoothly changes from one

would be wasting fuel. The stationary blades are necessary for multiplying torque, but when we are cruising along they just get in the way and churn up the oil. The curvature of the blades in all three elements is important, and if we design them for one condition they may not be so good for others. It is difficult to get as much torque multiplication as we desire to give good performance in starting up, and if the designer concentrates on this problem, he must sacrifice something else.

The approach used to improve the efficiency is to mount the stator on a one-way, or roller, clutch. This prevents the stator from turning backward, and

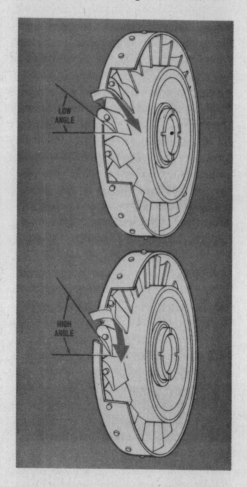

ratio to another and to another in a continuous fashion, without definite steps. It is what we know as a continuously variable transmission.

This seems like the perfect way to drive a car, but there are some problems. If we tried to use the simple design we have shown, the results would be disappointing. Such an arrangement gives maximum efficiency at only one speed, and a large part of the time we

thus it can act as the reaction element for multiplying torque. When the car speed reaches the point at which no further torque multiplication is needed, however, there is no backward force on the blades and the stator turns forward, or free-wheels, with the oil flow. What this actually means is that the torque converter now operates as a hydraulic coupling which wastes very little power under these conditions.

In some converter designs, the blades of the stator are mounted on pivots. This arrangement, known as variable pitch control, allows the angle at which the oil impinges on the stator blades to be changed to a low angle position for maximum efficiency of the converter and economical cruising or to a high angle position when more torque multiplication is needed for increased acceleration or pull. The blade angles can be changed automatically by means of a hydraulically controlled mechanism that is activated by the engine's throttle linkage.

If we wanted a simple form of automatic transmission, we could use the three-element torque converter by itself and connect the turbine shaft directly to the propeller shaft. Such an arrangement might satisfy a car's normal speed and torque requirements. But, unfortunately, the needs of an automatic transmission are more demanding than this. We need some way to provide additional torque multiplication, a reverse gear to back the car, and a neutral gear. We can do all these things with planetary gears.

Today's three-element torque converter transmissions use compound planetary gear sets, which means that gears of both sets are interconnected. The planetary gears, along with the necessary clutches and bands, give the added torque multiplication needed as the car accelerates through the forward speed gear ratios. They also provide a low gear for slowing down the car or for hard pulling, such as when going either down or up a steep hill, and the necessary reverse gear and neutral.

The forward speed gear ratios provided by the planetary gears are changed automatically, and at exactly the right time. This is done by means of a hydraulic system that is an integral part of the torque converter-planetary gear transmission assembly. The hydraulic system applies the clutches and bands that grab or release the gears of the planetary set, as we explained earlier, to provide the proper gear ratio and control the automatic shifting. The hydraulic pressure that activates the specific bands and clutches used in the transmission varies with car speed and torque input to the transmission. An explanation of exactly how this is done is too complex for the scope of this booklet. We would have to get into a discussion on governor valves, servos, accumulator pistons, modulator valves and other components that make up the hydraulic system. For our purposes, it is sufficient to say that the system is designed to make sure that the gears are shifted (clutches and bands are held or released) at the proper time for all conditions of car speed and torque requirements.

The accompanying cut-away diagram shows how the components are arranged in a typical three-element torque converter transmission that provides three forward gear ratios and one reverse. Because of the difficulty in showing exactly how each part looks, simple shapes have been used for illustration. The diagram, however, indicates where the various components are located. Also, only the upper half of the overall transmission is shown, since the bottom half, of course, would look the same.

The flow of power from the engine to the rear wheels is through the torque converter assembly (pump, turbine, stator), the turbine shaft, mainshaft, the various clutches indicated, the com-

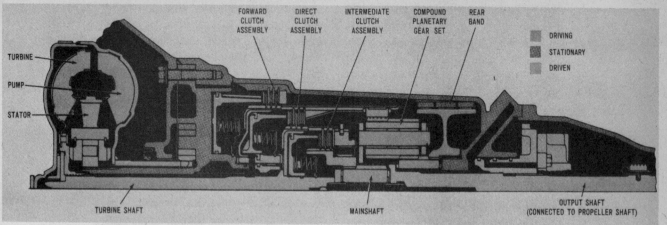

FORWARD CLUTCH ASSEMBLY | DIRECT CLUTCH ASSEMBLY | INTERMEDIATE CLUTCH ASSEMBLY | COMPOUND PLANETARY GEAR SET | REAR BAND

DRIVING
STATIONARY
DRIVEN

TURBINE
PUMP
STATOR

TURBINE SHAFT

MAINSHAFT

OUTPUT SHAFT
(CONNECTED TO PROPELLER SHAFT)

pound planetary gear set, and finally the output shaft connected to the propeller shaft. Let's see what happens when the engine is running and the driver places the transmission selector lever in the Drive position.

As soon as the lever is placed in the Drive position, the forward clutch assembly is applied and the transmission is in first gear. This clutch is connected to both the turbine shaft and the mainshaft. The mainshaft, in turn, is connected to the planetary gear sets. As the accelerator pedal is depressed and car speed increases, power flows through the turbine shaft and into the mainshaft which causes the gears in the planetary set to rotate and provide the proper gear reduction (about 2.5 to 1) and the proper torque to the output shaft. As car speed increases, less torque multiplication is needed and the hydraulic system receives a signal to apply the intermediate clutch. The transmission is now in second gear. This action results in the planetary gearing providing a lower gear ratio of about 1.5 to 1.

As the car continues to accelerate, we eventually get to a speed where no more torque multiplication is needed. When this point is reached, the hydraulic system applies the direct clutch and the car is in direct drive or third gear. The planetary gear set rotates as a unit and there is a ratio of 1 to 1, since the output shaft now rotates at the same

speed as the turbine shaft.

The forward clutch not only provides the means for obtaining the proper gear reduction ratio for the first gear, but also lets the transmission be placed in Neutral. When the transmission selector lever is placed in Neutral, the forward clutch is released. This interrupts the flow of power from the turbine shaft to the mainshaft and, in turn, the output shaft.

The rear band assembly is used for reverse gear. When the transmission selector is placed in Reverse, the front and intermediate clutches are released and the direct clutch and rear band are applied. The direct clutch lets torque from the turbine be transmitted through the turbine shaft and into the planetary gear set (the mainshaft is by-passed). The rear band makes the planetary gears rotate opposite to the way they rotated for the forward speed gear ratios. This causes a similar change in output shaft and propeller shaft rotation.

Most torque converter transmissions also provide an intermediate and low gear range which can aid to brake the car when coming down steep hills or for hard pulling. When the transmission selector is placed in the intermediate range (this might be indicated as D_1, S, or L_2 on the quadrant), the transmission immediately shifts to second gear. The front band is applied to the direct clutch assembly to keep the transmission in second gear. When the driver's foot is taken off the accelerator pedal, the car will decelerate by using engine compression as the braking force.

The low gear provides even greater engine braking. Actually, low gear is the same as first gear—that is, moving the transmission to Lo, or L, on the quadrant places the transmission in first gear. (Shifting the transmission into the Lo range can only be done below a certain speed). When the transmission shifts into the low gear, the rear band and forward clutch assemblies are applied and the direct and intermediate clutch assemblies are released. The transmission will stay in the low gear range regardless of car speed until the driver shifts the transmission.

The automatic transmission also provides a Park position. This locks the output shaft and prevents the car from moving. Because the output shaft is mechanically locked to prevent its rotation, the Park position is never selected until the car is completely stopped.

We have now discussed all of the common ways of transmitting power in automotive vehicles. We have seen that there are many different ways of doing it. There are various types of mechanical drives and hydraulic devices. But if we look at them more closely, we find that they are simply entirely different ways of doing exactly the same thing. In all of them we are just transmitting power from one place to another, and providing something which will change the speed and torque when necessary.

We get a certain twist from the engine crankshaft and we carry that back to where it can apply a certain different twist to the wheels. To go a step further, we carry it back until it can apply a certain backward force to the ground, which makes the vehicle move forward. Just as there are different ways to transmit the engine's power to the rear wheels, so are there different ways in which the various components used to transmit this power are arranged in an automobile. We'll examine these arrangements in the next section.

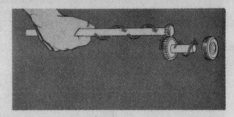

POWER TRAIN CONFIGURATIONS

Most of the automobiles we see on the road today—whether they have manual shift or automatic transmissions—have the engine located in the front with the power transferred to the rear drive wheels. This is the kind of power train configuration we have been talking about in this section.

Other automobiles are manufactured with different power train configurations. This means that while the engine and power transmission system are doing the same job, the arrangement of the system's components in the car, as well as the shape or form of each component, may be different.

In this section we'll discuss three other common power train configurations—front wheel drive, rear engine cars, and four and six-wheel drive.

Front Wheel Drive

Pulling a car by providing power at the front wheels instead of pushing it with the rear wheels is not a new idea. During the early days of automobiles, several models were produced with front wheel drive. But as cars became larger and more powerful, this power transmission system configuration became impractical.

It was not until recently that the knowledge of design, materials, and manufacturing had advanced enough to make front wheel drive practical on a modern, large-sized car with automatic transmission. In this section we will discuss only the power transmission system used on one of the present

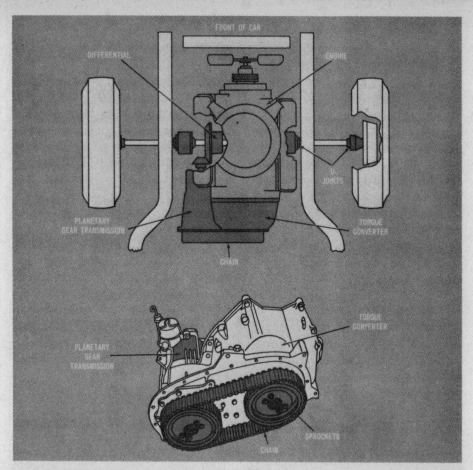

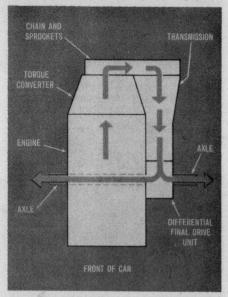

day front wheel drive cars and show how power from the engine can be transferred to the front wheels.

In this car, we are taking power from one place and putting it to work in another, just as we did before. Most of the components of the power train are the same as those in rear wheel drive cars. But now we are driving the front wheels. So, instead of being stretched out in a line from the engine back to the rear wheels, the power train is arranged to bend from the back of the engine forward to the front wheels.

The engine is located in the usual position, but there are major changes in the transmission. As we saw earlier, the usual automatic transmission has the torque converter attached to the engine with the rest of the transmission extending behind it. In the front wheel drive car, the transmission is split be-

tween the converter and the other section, which contains the planetary gear-

ing. The converter is attached to the back of the engine, but the other section is swung around alongside the engine—like the hinged lid of a cigarette lighter that has been opened all the way.

Now what used to be the back of the transmission is facing the front of the car. But something else is needed. We must connect the converter and the rest of the transmission where we split them. One way to do this is with a chain and sprockets, which work something like those on a bicycle would if its sprockets were the same size. By attaching one sprocket to the torque converter and the other to the rest of the transmission where we split it, we have two sprockets of equal size side by side. When we put a chain around these sprockets, we can keep the power flowing through both parts of the split transmission.

Now the power comes from the engine through the torque converter, and is transferred into the transmission gearing. From there it flows directly into the final drive. Thus, we see another advantage of front wheel drive—the long propeller shaft has been replaced by a direct connection between the transmission and the differential.

The differential is located directly in front of the transmission gearing. A separate axle runs from the differential to each front wheel. Since the front wheels must pivot to steer the car as well as provide the drive, they undergo a wide range of movement while under power. To handle this, two universal joints are placed on each axle—one at each end.

This power transmission system is typical of those used in the large, front wheel drive cars being made today. Some smaller cars also are made with front wheel drive, and use a manual shift transmission in the power train. But we won't go into the details. The arrangement of their components is similar to what we have described.

Rear Engine Cars

Another power train configuration found in many cars—especially small cars—is one with the engine and power transmission system in the rear of the vehicle. This arrangement gives a compact power train that can be thought of as a single unit, much like the front wheel drive arrangement already described.

Although there are several ways to arrange the power transmission components in a rear engine car, we'll discuss only one. It gives us a good idea of how power can be transferred from an engine in the rear of the car to the rear drive wheels.

As with front wheel drive, putting the entire power train in the rear of the car makes finding room a problem. The car we're going to look at solves this problem by placing the engine and transmission on opposite sides of the rear axle.

The engine is the rearmost power train component. In this car, its output shaft faces the front of the vehicle. Attached to the engine is the clutch. Then directly in front of the clutch is the final drive, and beyond it the transmission.

Now we know that in the power path the transmission must come between the clutch and the final drive. Although in this car the physical units themselves are not arranged in this order, a mechanical arrangement makes sure that the actual flow of power is.

This is done by using concentric shafts—a smaller shaft that is free to turn inside a larger, hollow shaft, which also is free to turn. In this way, each shaft can be used to transmit power without having any effect on or being affected by the other. Different ratios of power can be transferred in opposite directions at the same time.

In this car, the hollow shaft is the pinion shaft that carries power from the transmission to the differential. Running inside this shaft and passing completely through the differential is

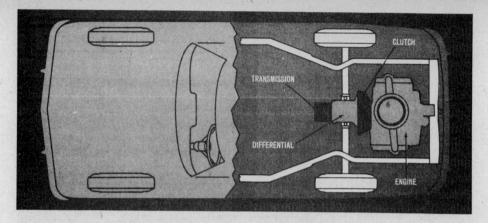

the shaft connecting the clutch with the transmission.

Thus, power flows from the engine through the clutch and into the transmission by way of the "inside" shaft. Then, after the power ratio is changed in the transmission, it flows by way of the "outside" shaft back into the differential. Finally, it goes through the axles to the rear wheels.

On rear engine cars with automatic transmissions, the torque converter takes the place of the clutch, while the transmission planetary gearing and controls occupy the position of the standard transmission.

Again, the car we have described is only one of several rear engine cars. And its power train configuration is only one of several. But it shows us how power in a rear engine can be transferred to the rear wheels successfully.

Four-Wheel and Six-Wheel Drive

Trucks and other utility vehicles often are driven in places where the going is rough. Sometimes better traction than usual is needed. For example, two wheels might get stuck in a mud hole and not be able to pull out of it. So instead of having the engine drive just two wheels, it drives four wheels or six wheels. A four-wheel vehicle driving on all four wheels is known as a 4 × 4, and one with six wheels, all driving, is a 6 × 6. A 4 × 6 is a six-wheel truck with four driving wheels.

To get such a drive we use a *transfer case*. In back of the regular transmission is another set of gears. Essentially this consists of three gears meshing together in series, extending out to one side of the transmission. The first and third gears are the same size. From each side of the third gear a propeller

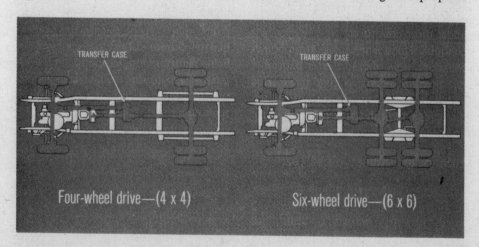

Four-wheel drive—(4 x 4) Six-wheel drive—(6 x 6)

shaft extends, one forward to the front axle, one back to the rear axle. Each axle is driven just as we have shown in the two-wheel drive, except that in the front axle we must have some universal joints in order to steer.

For a six-wheel drive a third propeller shaft extends straight back from the first gear in the transfer case; that is, in line with the regular transmission.

Thus, we have one input shaft into the transfer case and three output shafts.

With the first and third gears the same size we have no change of speed or torque in the transfer case. Usually, however, there is another pair of gears in it which can be shifted to give us a different ratio. A two-speed transfer case doubles the number of gear ratios available in the regular transmission.

(Courtesy: General Motors Corporation.)

ELECTRICAL THEORY
AND WORK

Definition of Electricity. Electricity is an invisible force which we only know about through the effects it produces. While the exact nature of electricity is not known, the laws governing electrical phenomena are clearly understood and defined, just as the laws of gravitation are known, although we cannot define the nature of gravity.

The Movement of Electricity. In many ways electricity in motion is like flowing water, and electrical phenomena can be more easily understood if this analogy is borne in mind. In dealing with the flow of electricity and the flow of water, we consider three factors: (a) Current (Flow of electricity, usually along a conductor); (b) Pressure (that which causes the current to flow); (c) Resistance (that which regulates the flow of current).

Electrical Current or Flow. If we want to know about the flow of water in a pipe, we would determine how many gallons of water flow through the pipe in a second. In exactly the same way, the electrician determines the number of *coulombs* of electricity that flow through a wire in a second. Just as the gallon is a measure of the quantity of water, the coulomb is a measure of the quantity of electricity. There is an abbreviated method of describing the flow of electrical current. The electrician speaks of the *ampere,* which means one coulomb per second, and is thus saved the trouble of saying "per second" every time he wants to describe the current flow.

Electrical Pressure. Water pressure is measured in pounds per square inch. There is also a measure of electrical pressure. This electrical pressure has a definite effect upon the number of amperes flowing along a wire. The electrical unit of pressure is the volt. A volt means the same thing in speaking of a current of electricity that a pound-per-square-inch pressure does in speaking of a current of water. Just as a higher pressure is required to force the same current of water through a small pipe than through a large pipe, so a higher electrical pressure is required to force the same current of electricity through a small wire than through a large wire. The voltage (pressure) between two points in an electric circuit is sometimes spoken of as the difference in potential, or the drop in potential, or merely the "drop" between those two points.

The distinction between amperes and volts should now be plain. The amperes represent the amount of the current flowing through a circuit; the volts represent the pressure causing it to flow.

Electrical Resistance. The electrical unit of resistance is the ohm. We say a wire has one ohm resistance when a pressure of one volt forces a current of one ampere through it.

Ohm's Law. In any circuit through which a current is flowing, the three following factors are present: (1) The pressure or potential difference, expressed in volts, causing the current to flow; (2) the opposition or resistance of the circuit, expressed in ohms, which must be overcome; (3) the current strength, expressed in amperes, which is maintained in the circuit as a result of the pressure overcoming the resistance. A definite and exact relation exists between three factors; pressure, current strength, and resistance in any circuit, whereby the value of any one factor may always be calculated when the values of the other two factors are known. This relation, known as Ohm's Law, is very important, since it forms the basis for all calculations in electrical engineering. It may be summarized as follows:

The current in any electric circuit is equal to the electromotive force applied to the circuit, divided by the resistance of the circuit.

Let E = E. M. F. or available pressure, expressed in volts, applied to any circuit.
   R = resistance of the circuit, expressed in ohms,
   I = current strength, expressed in amperes, to be maintained through circuit.

Then, by the above statement of Ohm's Law,

$$\text{Current} = \frac{\text{(Pressure)}}{\text{Resistance}} \text{ or}$$

$$\text{Amperes} = \frac{\text{volts}}{\text{ohms}} \text{ or } I = \frac{E}{R}$$

The Circuit. Electricity is not as simple as water in that it can not be piped from one point to another. In order to flow, electricity must be sent along a closed circuit. Except through a generator or a battery cell, electricity always flows from a higher to a lower level. The higher level, or positive, is marked +, and the lower level, or negative, is marked −, in order to indicate the direction in which the current is flowing. A given point is + to all points below its level, and − to all points above its level.

If any of the wires leading from the + to the − terminal is broken, the current cannot flow, for the circuit has been interrupted and is incomplete.

Measuring Electrical Current. In order to find out how much current is flowing through an electric circuit, we insert a current meter into the circuit so that all the current which we wish to measure flows through the meter. Since an instrument which measures an electric current must read in amperes, such a current meter is called an ammeter. The ammeter must be of very low resistance in order not to hinder the current. Such an instrument is very delicate and must be handled carefully.

Measurement of Electrical Pressure. When it is necessary to measure the pressure which is causing an electric current to flow through a circuit, the terminals of a *voltmeter* are tapped on to that circuit in such a way that the voltmeter is made to register not current but pressure. The method of attaching a voltmeter is different from that used in attaching an ammeter. The ammeter becomes a part of the circuit. The voltmeter does not become a part of the circuit.

Measurement of Electrical Resistance. In order to find the resistance of an electrical piece, the voltmeter reading is divided by the ammeter reading.

Regulating and Controlling Electrical Current. The usual method of regulating and controlling the current required for various electrical purposes is by inserting or removing resistance from a circuit. An adjustable resistance, or any apparatus for changing the resistance without opening the circuit, is called a rheostat. The function of a rheostat is to absorb electrical energy; and this energy, which appears as heat, is wasted instead of performing any useful work. A rheostat may be constructed of coils of iron wire, iron plates or strips; of carbon, either pulverized in tubes or in the form of solid rods or disks; German silver, platinoid, or wires of other alloys wound on spools; columns of liquids, as water and mercury, etc. The cross-sectional area of the material must be sufficient to carry the current without excessive heating. In rheostats used for regulating the current in commercial electrical circuits no great degree of accuracy of the resistance coils is required, as is the case with laboratory rheostats.

The Effects of a Current. A current of electricity is believed to be a transfer of electrons through a circuit, and since these carriers are so minute, a direct measurement of them is impractical. Consequently, an electric current is measured by the effects it produces, all of which are commercially utilized. The effects manifested by a current of electricity are: Heating Effect, Magnetic Effect, Chemical Effect, and Physiological Effect.

Heating Effect. Every wire which conducts a current of electricity becomes heated to some extent as a result of the current, because the best conductors offer some opposition (resistance) to the flow of the current, and it is in overcoming this resistance that the heat is developed. If the wire is large in cross-sectional area and the current small, the heat developed will be so small in amount as not to be recognized by the touch; nevertheless, the wire releases some heat energy. On the other hand, with a small wire and a large current, it becomes quite hot.

Magnetic Effect. A wire carrying a current of electricity deflects a magnetic needle. When the wire is insulated and coiled around an iron core, the current magnetizes the core.

Chemical Effect. Electrical current is capable of decomposing certain chemical compounds when it is passed through them, breaking up the compounds into their constituent parts. In the production of electrical energy by a simple primary cell, electrolytic decomposition takes place inside the cell when the current is flowing. Electroplating, or the art of depositing a coating of metal upon any object, is based upon the principles of electrolytic decomposition.

Physiological Effect. A current of electricity passed through the body produces muscular contractions which are due to the physiological effects of an electrical current. Electrotherapeutics deals with the study of this effect.

Direct and Alternating Current. A direct or continuous current flows always in the same direction. In many cases it has a constant strength for definite periods of time. A pulsating current has a uniform direction, but the current strength varies. Most direct current generators furnish pulsating current; but since the pulsations are very small, the current is practically constant.

An alternating current of electricity is one that changes its direction of flow at regular intervals of time. These intervals are usually much shorter than one second. During an interval, the current strength is capable of varying in any way. In practice, the strength rises and then falls smoothly. Most electricity today comes in the form of alternating current. This is so because high voltage can more easily be obtained with alternating current than with direct current. High voltages, of course, are much more cheaply transmitted over power lines than are low voltages.

The Dynamo and Electromagnetic Induction. The electrical generator and the electric motor are intimately related. The term dynamo is applied to machines which convert either mechanical energy into electrical energy or electrical energy into mechanical energy by utilizing the principles of electromagnetic induction. A dynamo is called a generator when mechanical energy supplied in the form of rotation is converted into electrical energy. When the energy conversion takes place in the reverse order the dynamo is called a motor. Thus a dynamo is a reversible machine capable of operation as a generator or motor as desired.

The generator consists fundamentally of a number of loops of insulated wires revolving in a strong magnetic field in such a way that these wires cut across the lines of magnetic force. This cutting of the lines of force sets up an electromotive force along the wires.

We have shown that wherever there is an electric current present, there is also present a magnetic field. It is not true that wherever a magnetic field exists, there also exists an electric current, in the ordinary sense; but we can say that wherever a conductor moves in a magnetic field in such a way as to cut lines of force, an electromotive force is set up. It is on this principle that the electric generator works.

SECOND MODEL EXAM

ANSWER SHEET—SECOND MODEL EXAM

PART 1—GENERAL SCIENCE

1 Ⓐ Ⓑ Ⓒ Ⓓ	6 Ⓐ Ⓑ Ⓒ Ⓓ	11 Ⓐ Ⓑ Ⓒ Ⓓ	16 Ⓐ Ⓑ Ⓒ Ⓓ	21 Ⓐ Ⓑ Ⓒ Ⓓ
2 Ⓐ Ⓑ Ⓒ Ⓓ	7 Ⓐ Ⓑ Ⓒ Ⓓ	12 Ⓐ Ⓑ Ⓒ Ⓓ	17 Ⓐ Ⓑ Ⓒ Ⓓ	22 Ⓐ Ⓑ Ⓒ Ⓓ
3 Ⓐ Ⓑ Ⓒ Ⓓ	8 Ⓐ Ⓑ Ⓒ Ⓓ	13 Ⓐ Ⓑ Ⓒ Ⓓ	18 Ⓐ Ⓑ Ⓒ Ⓓ	23 Ⓐ Ⓑ Ⓒ Ⓓ
4 Ⓐ Ⓑ Ⓒ Ⓓ	9 Ⓐ Ⓑ Ⓒ Ⓓ	14 Ⓐ Ⓑ Ⓒ Ⓓ	19 Ⓐ Ⓑ Ⓒ Ⓓ	24 Ⓐ Ⓑ Ⓒ Ⓓ
5 Ⓐ Ⓑ Ⓒ Ⓓ	10 Ⓐ Ⓑ Ⓒ Ⓓ	15 Ⓐ Ⓑ Ⓒ Ⓓ	20 Ⓐ Ⓑ Ⓒ Ⓓ	25 Ⓐ Ⓑ Ⓒ Ⓓ

PART 2—ARITHMETIC REASONING

1 Ⓐ Ⓑ Ⓒ Ⓓ	7 Ⓐ Ⓑ Ⓒ Ⓓ	13 Ⓐ Ⓑ Ⓒ Ⓓ	19 Ⓐ Ⓑ Ⓒ Ⓓ	25 Ⓐ Ⓑ Ⓒ Ⓓ
2 Ⓐ Ⓑ Ⓒ Ⓓ	8 Ⓐ Ⓑ Ⓒ Ⓓ	14 Ⓐ Ⓑ Ⓒ Ⓓ	20 Ⓐ Ⓑ Ⓒ Ⓓ	26 Ⓐ Ⓑ Ⓒ Ⓓ
3 Ⓐ Ⓑ Ⓒ Ⓓ	9 Ⓐ Ⓑ Ⓒ Ⓓ	15 Ⓐ Ⓑ Ⓒ Ⓓ	21 Ⓐ Ⓑ Ⓒ Ⓓ	27 Ⓐ Ⓑ Ⓒ Ⓓ
4 Ⓐ Ⓑ Ⓒ Ⓓ	10 Ⓐ Ⓑ Ⓒ Ⓓ	16 Ⓐ Ⓑ Ⓒ Ⓓ	22 Ⓐ Ⓑ Ⓒ Ⓓ	28 Ⓐ Ⓑ Ⓒ Ⓓ
5 Ⓐ Ⓑ Ⓒ Ⓓ	11 Ⓐ Ⓑ Ⓒ Ⓓ	17 Ⓐ Ⓑ Ⓒ Ⓓ	23 Ⓐ Ⓑ Ⓒ Ⓓ	29 Ⓐ Ⓑ Ⓒ Ⓓ
6 Ⓐ Ⓑ Ⓒ Ⓓ	12 Ⓐ Ⓑ Ⓒ Ⓓ	18 Ⓐ Ⓑ Ⓒ Ⓓ	24 Ⓐ Ⓑ Ⓒ Ⓓ	30 Ⓐ Ⓑ Ⓒ Ⓓ

PART 3—WORD KNOWLEDGE

1 Ⓐ Ⓑ Ⓒ Ⓓ	8 Ⓐ Ⓑ Ⓒ Ⓓ	15 Ⓐ Ⓑ Ⓒ Ⓓ	22 Ⓐ Ⓑ Ⓒ Ⓓ	29 Ⓐ Ⓑ Ⓒ Ⓓ
2 Ⓐ Ⓑ Ⓒ Ⓓ	9 Ⓐ Ⓑ Ⓒ Ⓓ	16 Ⓐ Ⓑ Ⓒ Ⓓ	23 Ⓐ Ⓑ Ⓒ Ⓓ	30 Ⓐ Ⓑ Ⓒ Ⓓ
3 Ⓐ Ⓑ Ⓒ Ⓓ	10 Ⓐ Ⓑ Ⓒ Ⓓ	17 Ⓐ Ⓑ Ⓒ Ⓓ	24 Ⓐ Ⓑ Ⓒ Ⓓ	31 Ⓐ Ⓑ Ⓒ Ⓓ
4 Ⓐ Ⓑ Ⓒ Ⓓ	11 Ⓐ Ⓑ Ⓒ Ⓓ	18 Ⓐ Ⓑ Ⓒ Ⓓ	25 Ⓐ Ⓑ Ⓒ Ⓓ	32 Ⓐ Ⓑ Ⓒ Ⓓ
5 Ⓐ Ⓑ Ⓒ Ⓓ	12 Ⓐ Ⓑ Ⓒ Ⓓ	19 Ⓐ Ⓑ Ⓒ Ⓓ	26 Ⓐ Ⓑ Ⓒ Ⓓ	33 Ⓐ Ⓑ Ⓒ Ⓓ
6 Ⓐ Ⓑ Ⓒ Ⓓ	13 Ⓐ Ⓑ Ⓒ Ⓓ	20 Ⓐ Ⓑ Ⓒ Ⓓ	27 Ⓐ Ⓑ Ⓒ Ⓓ	34 Ⓐ Ⓑ Ⓒ Ⓓ
7 Ⓐ Ⓑ Ⓒ Ⓓ	14 Ⓐ Ⓑ Ⓒ Ⓓ	21 Ⓐ Ⓑ Ⓒ Ⓓ	28 Ⓐ Ⓑ Ⓒ Ⓓ	35 Ⓐ Ⓑ Ⓒ Ⓓ

PART 4—PARAGRAPH COMPREHENSION

1 Ⓐ Ⓑ Ⓒ Ⓓ	5 Ⓐ Ⓑ Ⓒ Ⓓ	9 Ⓐ Ⓑ Ⓒ Ⓓ	13 Ⓐ Ⓑ Ⓒ Ⓓ
2 Ⓐ Ⓑ Ⓒ Ⓓ	6 Ⓐ Ⓑ Ⓒ Ⓓ	10 Ⓐ Ⓑ Ⓒ Ⓓ	14 Ⓐ Ⓑ Ⓒ Ⓓ
3 Ⓐ Ⓑ Ⓒ Ⓓ	7 Ⓐ Ⓑ Ⓒ Ⓓ	11 Ⓐ Ⓑ Ⓒ Ⓓ	15 Ⓐ Ⓑ Ⓒ Ⓓ
4 Ⓐ Ⓑ Ⓒ Ⓓ	8 Ⓐ Ⓑ Ⓒ Ⓓ	12 Ⓐ Ⓑ Ⓒ Ⓓ	

PART 5—NUMERICAL OPERATIONS

1 Ⓐ Ⓑ Ⓒ Ⓓ	11 Ⓐ Ⓑ Ⓒ Ⓓ	21 Ⓐ Ⓑ Ⓒ Ⓓ	31 Ⓐ Ⓑ Ⓒ Ⓓ	41 Ⓐ Ⓑ Ⓒ Ⓓ
2 Ⓐ Ⓑ Ⓒ Ⓓ	12 Ⓐ Ⓑ Ⓒ Ⓓ	22 Ⓐ Ⓑ Ⓒ Ⓓ	32 Ⓐ Ⓑ Ⓒ Ⓓ	42 Ⓐ Ⓑ Ⓒ Ⓓ
3 Ⓐ Ⓑ Ⓒ Ⓓ	13 Ⓐ Ⓑ Ⓒ Ⓓ	23 Ⓐ Ⓑ Ⓒ Ⓓ	33 Ⓐ Ⓑ Ⓒ Ⓓ	43 Ⓐ Ⓑ Ⓒ Ⓓ
4 Ⓐ Ⓑ Ⓒ Ⓓ	14 Ⓐ Ⓑ Ⓒ Ⓓ	24 Ⓐ Ⓑ Ⓒ Ⓓ	34 Ⓐ Ⓑ Ⓒ Ⓓ	44 Ⓐ Ⓑ Ⓒ Ⓓ
5 Ⓐ Ⓑ Ⓒ Ⓓ	15 Ⓐ Ⓑ Ⓒ Ⓓ	25 Ⓐ Ⓑ Ⓒ Ⓓ	35 Ⓐ Ⓑ Ⓒ Ⓓ	45 Ⓐ Ⓑ Ⓒ Ⓓ
6 Ⓐ Ⓑ Ⓒ Ⓓ	16 Ⓐ Ⓑ Ⓒ Ⓓ	26 Ⓐ Ⓑ Ⓒ Ⓓ	36 Ⓐ Ⓑ Ⓒ Ⓓ	46 Ⓐ Ⓑ Ⓒ Ⓓ
7 Ⓐ Ⓑ Ⓒ Ⓓ	17 Ⓐ Ⓑ Ⓒ Ⓓ	27 Ⓐ Ⓑ Ⓒ Ⓓ	37 Ⓐ Ⓑ Ⓒ Ⓓ	47 Ⓐ Ⓑ Ⓒ Ⓓ
8 Ⓐ Ⓑ Ⓒ Ⓓ	18 Ⓐ Ⓑ Ⓒ Ⓓ	28 Ⓐ Ⓑ Ⓒ Ⓓ	38 Ⓐ Ⓑ Ⓒ Ⓓ	48 Ⓐ Ⓑ Ⓒ Ⓓ
9 Ⓐ Ⓑ Ⓒ Ⓓ	19 Ⓐ Ⓑ Ⓒ Ⓓ	29 Ⓐ Ⓑ Ⓒ Ⓓ	39 Ⓐ Ⓑ Ⓒ Ⓓ	49 Ⓐ Ⓑ Ⓒ Ⓓ
10 Ⓐ Ⓑ Ⓒ Ⓓ	20 Ⓐ Ⓑ Ⓒ Ⓓ	30 Ⓐ Ⓑ Ⓒ Ⓓ	40 Ⓐ Ⓑ Ⓒ Ⓓ	50 Ⓐ Ⓑ Ⓒ Ⓓ

PART 6—CODING SPEED

1 Ⓐ Ⓑ Ⓒ Ⓓ Ⓔ	15 Ⓐ Ⓑ Ⓒ Ⓓ Ⓔ	29 Ⓐ Ⓑ Ⓒ Ⓓ Ⓔ	43 Ⓐ Ⓑ Ⓒ Ⓓ Ⓔ	57 Ⓐ Ⓑ Ⓒ Ⓓ Ⓔ	71 Ⓐ Ⓑ Ⓒ Ⓓ Ⓔ
2 Ⓐ Ⓑ Ⓒ Ⓓ Ⓔ	16 Ⓐ Ⓑ Ⓒ Ⓓ Ⓔ	30 Ⓐ Ⓑ Ⓒ Ⓓ Ⓔ	44 Ⓐ Ⓑ Ⓒ Ⓓ Ⓔ	58 Ⓐ Ⓑ Ⓒ Ⓓ Ⓔ	72 Ⓐ Ⓑ Ⓒ Ⓓ Ⓔ
3 Ⓐ Ⓑ Ⓒ Ⓓ Ⓔ	17 Ⓐ Ⓑ Ⓒ Ⓓ Ⓔ	31 Ⓐ Ⓑ Ⓒ Ⓓ Ⓔ	45 Ⓐ Ⓑ Ⓒ Ⓓ Ⓔ	59 Ⓐ Ⓑ Ⓒ Ⓓ Ⓔ	73 Ⓐ Ⓑ Ⓒ Ⓓ Ⓔ
4 Ⓐ Ⓑ Ⓒ Ⓓ Ⓔ	18 Ⓐ Ⓑ Ⓒ Ⓓ Ⓔ	32 Ⓐ Ⓑ Ⓒ Ⓓ Ⓔ	46 Ⓐ Ⓑ Ⓒ Ⓓ Ⓔ	60 Ⓐ Ⓑ Ⓒ Ⓓ Ⓔ	74 Ⓐ Ⓑ Ⓒ Ⓓ Ⓔ
5 Ⓐ Ⓑ Ⓒ Ⓓ Ⓔ	19 Ⓐ Ⓑ Ⓒ Ⓓ Ⓔ	33 Ⓐ Ⓑ Ⓒ Ⓓ Ⓔ	47 Ⓐ Ⓑ Ⓒ Ⓓ Ⓔ	61 Ⓐ Ⓑ Ⓒ Ⓓ Ⓔ	75 Ⓐ Ⓑ Ⓒ Ⓓ Ⓔ
6 Ⓐ Ⓑ Ⓒ Ⓓ Ⓔ	20 Ⓐ Ⓑ Ⓒ Ⓓ Ⓔ	34 Ⓐ Ⓑ Ⓒ Ⓓ Ⓔ	48 Ⓐ Ⓑ Ⓒ Ⓓ Ⓔ	62 Ⓐ Ⓑ Ⓒ Ⓓ Ⓔ	76 Ⓐ Ⓑ Ⓒ Ⓓ Ⓔ
7 Ⓐ Ⓑ Ⓒ Ⓓ Ⓔ	21 Ⓐ Ⓑ Ⓒ Ⓓ Ⓔ	35 Ⓐ Ⓑ Ⓒ Ⓓ Ⓔ	49 Ⓐ Ⓑ Ⓒ Ⓓ Ⓔ	63 Ⓐ Ⓑ Ⓒ Ⓓ Ⓔ	77 Ⓐ Ⓑ Ⓒ Ⓓ Ⓔ
8 Ⓐ Ⓑ Ⓒ Ⓓ Ⓔ	22 Ⓐ Ⓑ Ⓒ Ⓓ Ⓔ	36 Ⓐ Ⓑ Ⓒ Ⓓ Ⓔ	50 Ⓐ Ⓑ Ⓒ Ⓓ Ⓔ	64 Ⓐ Ⓑ Ⓒ Ⓓ Ⓔ	78 Ⓐ Ⓑ Ⓒ Ⓓ Ⓔ
9 Ⓐ Ⓑ Ⓒ Ⓓ Ⓔ	23 Ⓐ Ⓑ Ⓒ Ⓓ Ⓔ	37 Ⓐ Ⓑ Ⓒ Ⓓ Ⓔ	51 Ⓐ Ⓑ Ⓒ Ⓓ Ⓔ	65 Ⓐ Ⓑ Ⓒ Ⓓ Ⓔ	79 Ⓐ Ⓑ Ⓒ Ⓓ Ⓔ
10 Ⓐ Ⓑ Ⓒ Ⓓ Ⓔ	24 Ⓐ Ⓑ Ⓒ Ⓓ Ⓔ	38 Ⓐ Ⓑ Ⓒ Ⓓ Ⓔ	52 Ⓐ Ⓑ Ⓒ Ⓓ Ⓔ	66 Ⓐ Ⓑ Ⓒ Ⓓ Ⓔ	80 Ⓐ Ⓑ Ⓒ Ⓓ Ⓔ
11 Ⓐ Ⓑ Ⓒ Ⓓ Ⓔ	25 Ⓐ Ⓑ Ⓒ Ⓓ Ⓔ	39 Ⓐ Ⓑ Ⓒ Ⓓ Ⓔ	53 Ⓐ Ⓑ Ⓒ Ⓓ Ⓔ	67 Ⓐ Ⓑ Ⓒ Ⓓ Ⓔ	81 Ⓐ Ⓑ Ⓒ Ⓓ Ⓔ
12 Ⓐ Ⓑ Ⓒ Ⓓ Ⓔ	26 Ⓐ Ⓑ Ⓒ Ⓓ Ⓔ	40 Ⓐ Ⓑ Ⓒ Ⓓ Ⓔ	54 Ⓐ Ⓑ Ⓒ Ⓓ Ⓔ	68 Ⓐ Ⓑ Ⓒ Ⓓ Ⓔ	82 Ⓐ Ⓑ Ⓒ Ⓓ Ⓔ
13 Ⓐ Ⓑ Ⓒ Ⓓ Ⓔ	27 Ⓐ Ⓑ Ⓒ Ⓓ Ⓔ	41 Ⓐ Ⓑ Ⓒ Ⓓ Ⓔ	55 Ⓐ Ⓑ Ⓒ Ⓓ Ⓔ	69 Ⓐ Ⓑ Ⓒ Ⓓ Ⓔ	83 Ⓐ Ⓑ Ⓒ Ⓓ Ⓔ
14 Ⓐ Ⓑ Ⓒ Ⓓ Ⓔ	28 Ⓐ Ⓑ Ⓒ Ⓓ Ⓔ	42 Ⓐ Ⓑ Ⓒ Ⓓ Ⓔ	56 Ⓐ Ⓑ Ⓒ Ⓓ Ⓔ	70 Ⓐ Ⓑ Ⓒ Ⓓ Ⓔ	84 Ⓐ Ⓑ Ⓒ Ⓓ Ⓔ

PART 7—AUTO & SHOP INFORMATION

1 Ⓐ Ⓑ Ⓒ Ⓓ	6 Ⓐ Ⓑ Ⓒ Ⓓ	11 Ⓐ Ⓑ Ⓒ Ⓓ	16 Ⓐ Ⓑ Ⓒ Ⓓ	21 Ⓐ Ⓑ Ⓒ Ⓓ
2 Ⓐ Ⓑ Ⓒ Ⓓ	7 Ⓐ Ⓑ Ⓒ Ⓓ	12 Ⓐ Ⓑ Ⓒ Ⓓ	17 Ⓐ Ⓑ Ⓒ Ⓓ	22 Ⓐ Ⓑ Ⓒ Ⓓ
3 Ⓐ Ⓑ Ⓒ Ⓓ	8 Ⓐ Ⓑ Ⓒ Ⓓ	13 Ⓐ Ⓑ Ⓒ Ⓓ	18 Ⓐ Ⓑ Ⓒ Ⓓ	23 Ⓐ Ⓑ Ⓒ Ⓓ
4 Ⓐ Ⓑ Ⓒ Ⓓ	9 Ⓐ Ⓑ Ⓒ Ⓓ	14 Ⓐ Ⓑ Ⓒ Ⓓ	19 Ⓐ Ⓑ Ⓒ Ⓓ	24 Ⓐ Ⓑ Ⓒ Ⓓ
5 Ⓐ Ⓑ Ⓒ Ⓓ	10 Ⓐ Ⓑ Ⓒ Ⓓ	15 Ⓐ Ⓑ Ⓒ Ⓓ	20 Ⓐ Ⓑ Ⓒ Ⓓ	25 Ⓐ Ⓑ Ⓒ Ⓓ

PART 8—MATHEMATICS KNOWLEDGE

1 Ⓐ Ⓑ Ⓒ Ⓓ	6 Ⓐ Ⓑ Ⓒ Ⓓ	11 Ⓐ Ⓑ Ⓒ Ⓓ	16 Ⓐ Ⓑ Ⓒ Ⓓ	21 Ⓐ Ⓑ Ⓒ Ⓓ
2 Ⓐ Ⓑ Ⓒ Ⓓ	7 Ⓐ Ⓑ Ⓒ Ⓓ	12 Ⓐ Ⓑ Ⓒ Ⓓ	17 Ⓐ Ⓑ Ⓒ Ⓓ	22 Ⓐ Ⓑ Ⓒ Ⓓ
3 Ⓐ Ⓑ Ⓒ Ⓓ	8 Ⓐ Ⓑ Ⓒ Ⓓ	13 Ⓐ Ⓑ Ⓒ Ⓓ	18 Ⓐ Ⓑ Ⓒ Ⓓ	23 Ⓐ Ⓑ Ⓒ Ⓓ
4 Ⓐ Ⓑ Ⓒ Ⓓ	9 Ⓐ Ⓑ Ⓒ Ⓓ	14 Ⓐ Ⓑ Ⓒ Ⓓ	19 Ⓐ Ⓑ Ⓒ Ⓓ	24 Ⓐ Ⓑ Ⓒ Ⓓ
5 Ⓐ Ⓑ Ⓒ Ⓓ	10 Ⓐ Ⓑ Ⓒ Ⓓ	15 Ⓐ Ⓑ Ⓒ Ⓓ	20 Ⓐ Ⓑ Ⓒ Ⓓ	25 Ⓐ Ⓑ Ⓒ Ⓓ

PART 9—MECHANICAL COMPREHENSION

1 Ⓐ Ⓑ Ⓒ Ⓓ	6 Ⓐ Ⓑ Ⓒ Ⓓ	11 Ⓐ Ⓑ Ⓒ Ⓓ	16 Ⓐ Ⓑ Ⓒ Ⓓ	21 Ⓐ Ⓑ Ⓒ Ⓓ
2 Ⓐ Ⓑ Ⓒ Ⓓ	7 Ⓐ Ⓑ Ⓒ Ⓓ	12 Ⓐ Ⓑ Ⓒ Ⓓ	17 Ⓐ Ⓑ Ⓒ Ⓓ	22 Ⓐ Ⓑ Ⓒ Ⓓ
3 Ⓐ Ⓑ Ⓒ Ⓓ	8 Ⓐ Ⓑ Ⓒ Ⓓ	13 Ⓐ Ⓑ Ⓒ Ⓓ	18 Ⓐ Ⓑ Ⓒ Ⓓ	23 Ⓐ Ⓑ Ⓒ Ⓓ
4 Ⓐ Ⓑ Ⓒ Ⓓ	9 Ⓐ Ⓑ Ⓒ Ⓓ	14 Ⓐ Ⓑ Ⓒ Ⓓ	19 Ⓐ Ⓑ Ⓒ Ⓓ	24 Ⓐ Ⓑ Ⓒ Ⓓ
5 Ⓐ Ⓑ Ⓒ Ⓓ	10 Ⓐ Ⓑ Ⓒ Ⓓ	15 Ⓐ Ⓑ Ⓒ Ⓓ	20 Ⓐ Ⓑ Ⓒ Ⓓ	25 Ⓐ Ⓑ Ⓒ Ⓓ

PART 10—ELECTRONICS INFORMATION

1 Ⓐ Ⓑ Ⓒ Ⓓ	6 Ⓐ Ⓑ Ⓒ Ⓓ	11 Ⓐ Ⓑ Ⓒ Ⓓ	16 Ⓐ Ⓑ Ⓒ Ⓓ
2 Ⓐ Ⓑ Ⓒ Ⓓ	7 Ⓐ Ⓑ Ⓒ Ⓓ	12 Ⓐ Ⓑ Ⓒ Ⓓ	17 Ⓐ Ⓑ Ⓒ Ⓓ
3 Ⓐ Ⓑ Ⓒ Ⓓ	8 Ⓐ Ⓑ Ⓒ Ⓓ	13 Ⓐ Ⓑ Ⓒ Ⓓ	18 Ⓐ Ⓑ Ⓒ Ⓓ
4 Ⓐ Ⓑ Ⓒ Ⓓ	9 Ⓐ Ⓑ Ⓒ Ⓓ	14 Ⓐ Ⓑ Ⓒ Ⓓ	19 Ⓐ Ⓑ Ⓒ Ⓓ
5 Ⓐ Ⓑ Ⓒ Ⓓ	10 Ⓐ Ⓑ Ⓒ Ⓓ	15 Ⓐ Ⓑ Ⓒ Ⓓ	20 Ⓐ Ⓑ Ⓒ Ⓓ

PART 1

GENERAL SCIENCE

The general science part of your examination asks questions based upon the science you learned in high school. For each question there are four possible answers. Only one answer is correct. Choose the answer which you think is correct and mark the corresponding space on your answer sheet. Try these questions.

1. Of the following methods, the one which is correct to use in converting a steel knitting needle into a permanent magnet is

1-A heating
1-B jarring
1-C stroking with a magnet
1-D passing electricity through it

1. Ⓐ Ⓑ Ⓒ Ⓓ

1-C STROKING WITH A MAGNET is the correct answer. A permanent magnet may be created by stroking a steel needle with a magnet, always in one direction. This action organizes the electrons in the needle so that they concentrate themselves at one end. That end is the negative pole of the needle. The other end is positive. Heating (A) and jarring (B) both lead to disorganization of the electrons and might destroy the magnet. Passing electricity through a wire which is wound around a steel needle creates an electromagnet (D). An electromagnet is not a permanent magnet. When the electricity is cut off, the magnetism disappears.

2. Proteins are used by the body *chiefly* to:

2-A build cells
2-B develop antibodies
2-C maintain body heat
2-D produce nutrients

2. Ⓐ Ⓑ Ⓒ Ⓓ

2-A BUILD CELLS is the correct answer. Proteins are called the building blocks of the body. They are essential parts of all living cells. Proteins do play a role in the development of antibodies (B), the body's defenses against specific diseases, and they may be burned to maintain body heat (C) when other sources of calories are not available, but these are not their *chief* uses. Proteins are nutrients (D), they do not produce nutrients.

3. The "wind chill factor" as reported by weather forecasters affects

3-A the speed of the wind
3-B the freezing point of water
3-C the amount of snow likely
3-D how cold you feel

3. Ⓐ Ⓑ Ⓒ Ⓓ

3-D HOW COLD YOU FEEL is the correct answer. The wind chill factor is based on a mathematical formula which describes the effect upon the senses of the combined temperature and wind speed. The wind chill factor is affected by the speed of the wind (A), not vice-versa. Water freezes at 32° F or 0° C (B). The amount of snowfall (C) is not dependent on the wind chill factor.

DO NOT TURN THE PAGE UNTIL YOU ARE TOLD TO DO SO

GENERAL SCIENCE

TIME: 11 Minutes—25 Questions

1. The only pouched mammal native to the United States is the

   1-A kangaroo
   1-B armadillo
   1-C opossum
   1-D raccoon

2. What temperature is shown on a Fahrenheit thermometer when a centigrade thermometer reads 0°?

   2-A $-40°$
   2-B $-32°$
   2-C $0°$
   2-D $+32°$

3. The major chemical constituent of a cell (by weight) is

   3-A protein
   3-B ash
   3-C water
   3-D carbohydrates

4. The Wassermann test may indicate the presence of

   4-A syphilis
   4-B tuberculosis
   4-C measles
   4-D polio

5. Alcoholic beverages contain

   5-A wood alcohol
   5-B isopropyl alcohol
   5-C glyceryl alcohol
   5-D grain alcohol

6. The air around us is composed mostly of

   6-A carbon
   6-B nitrogen
   6-C hydrogen
   6-D oxygen

7. The process which is responsible for the continuous removal of carbon dioxide from the atmosphere is

   7-A respiration
   7-B oxidation
   7-C metabolism
   7-D photosynthesis

8. Ringworm is caused by a(n)

   8-A alga
   8-B fungus
   8-C bacterium
   8-D protozoan

9. Among the following, the invertebrate is the

   9-A dinosaur
   9-B python
   9-C pigeon
   9-D starfish

10. Saliva contains an enzyme which acts on

    10-A carbohydrates
    10-B proteins
    10-C minerals
    10-D vitamins

11. The vitamin which helps coagulation of the blood is

    11-A C
    11-B E
    11-C D
    11-D K

12. Of the following, the part of a ship which gives it stability by lowering the center of gravity is the

    12-A bulkhead
    12-B keel
    12-C anchor
    12-D prow

13. To reduce soil acidity a farmer should use

    13-A lime
    13-B phosphate

13-C manure
13-D peat moss

14. Which of the following minerals is restored to the soil by plants of the pea and bean family?

14-A sulfates
14-B carbonates
14-C nitrates
14-D phosphates

15. In the production of sounds, the greater the number of vibrations per second

15-A the greater the volume
15-B the higher the tone
15-C the lower the volume
15-D the lower the tone

16. Of the following, the food which contains the largest amount of Vitamin C is

16-A carrots
16-B sweet potatoes
16-C lima beans
16-D tomatoes

17. The cyclotron is used to

17-A measure radioactivity
17-B measure the speed of the earth's rotation
17-C split atoms
17-D store radioactive energy

18. In four hours the earth rotates

18-A 20 degrees
18-B 60 degrees
18-C 40 degrees
18-D 120 degrees

19. A person is more buoyant when swimming in salt water than in fresh water because

19-A he keeps his head out of salt water
19-B salt coats his body with a floating membrane

19-C salt water has greater tensile strength
19-D salt water weighs more than an equal volume of fresh water

20. A volcanic eruption is caused by

20-A sunspots
20-B pressure inside the earth
20-C nuclear fallout
20-D boiling lava

21. The vitamin manufactured by the skin with the help of the sun is

21-A A
21-B B_6
21-C B_{12}
21-D D

22. A tumor is

22-A cancer
22-B a growth
22-C a sore spot
22-D a kind of mushroom

23. All types of steel contain

23-A iron
23-B chromium
23-C nickel
23-D tungsten

24. The *most important* provision for a hike in hot, dry countryside is

24-A dried meat
24-B raisins
24-C fresh fruit
24-D water

25. Of the following animals, the one which is most closely related to the extinct dinosaur is the

25-A sloth
25-B lizard
25-C elephant
25-D whale

STOP

IF YOU FINISH THIS PART BEFORE THE TIME IS UP, CHECK OVER YOUR WORK ON THIS PART ONLY. DO NOT TURN THE PAGE UNTIL YOU ARE TOLD TO DO SO.

ARITHMETIC REASONING

The arithmetic reasoning questions require careful thinking as well as arithmetic calculation. Some problems require more than one step for their solutions. You must decide exactly what the question asks; then you must determine the best method for finding the answer; finally you must work out the problem on your scratch paper. Be sure to mark the letter of the correct answer on your answer sheet. Try these questions.

1. If a plane travels 1,000 miles in 5 hours 30 minutes, what is its average speed in miles per hour?

1-A $181\frac{9}{11}$
1-B 200
1-C 215
1-D $191\frac{1}{2}$

1. Ⓐ Ⓑ Ⓒ Ⓓ

1-A 5 hours 30 minutes = $5\frac{1}{2}$ hours

1000 mph ÷ $5\frac{1}{2}$ hours

$\qquad = 1000 \div \frac{11}{2} = 1000 \times \frac{2}{11} = 181\frac{9}{11}$ mph

2. A jacket that normally sells for $35 can be purchased on sale for 2,975 pennies. What is the rate of discount represented by the sale price?

2-A 5%
2-B 10%
2-C 15%
2-D 20%

2. Ⓐ Ⓑ Ⓒ Ⓓ

2-C 2,975 pennies = $29.75

$35.00 − $29.75 = $5.25 saved

$$\text{Rate of discount} = \frac{5.25}{35} \times 100 = .15 \times 100$$

$$= 15\%$$

3. Perform the indicated operations and express your answer in inches: 12 feet, minus 7 inches, plus 2 feet 1 inch, minus 7 feet, minus 1 yard, plus 2 yards 1 foot 3 inches.

3-A 130 inches
3-B 128 inches
3-C 129 inches
3-D 131 inches

3. Ⓐ Ⓑ Ⓒ Ⓓ

3-C First convert all the yards and feet into inches so that all addition and subtraction can be done using the same units.

12 feet =	144 inches
−7 inches = −	7 inches
+2 feet, 1 inch = +	25 inches
−7 feet = −	84 inches
−1 yard = −	36 inches
+2 yards, 1 foot, 3 inches = +	87 inches
	129 inches

DO NOT TURN THE PAGE UNTIL YOU ARE TOLD TO DO SO

ARITHMETIC REASONING

TIME: 36 Minutes—30 Questions

1. A man owned 75 shares of stock worth $50 each. The corporation declared a dividend of 8%, payable in stock. How many shares did he then own?

   1-A 81 shares
   1-B 90 shares
   1-C 80 shares
   1-D 85 shares

2. If a scow is towed at the rate of three miles an hour, it will need how many hours to go 28 miles?

   2-A 10 hrs. 30 min.
   2-B 9 hrs. 20 min.
   2-C 12 hrs.
   2-D 9 hrs. 15 min.

3. If a fire truck is 60 feet away from a hydrant, it is how many feet nearer to the hydrant than a truck that is 100 feet away?

   3-A 60 ft.
   3-B 50 ft.
   3-C 40 ft.
   3-D 20 ft.

4. A clerk divided his 35 hour work week as follows: $\frac{1}{5}$ of his time in sorting mail; $\frac{1}{2}$ of his time in filing letters; and $\frac{1}{7}$ of his time in reception work. The rest of his time was devoted to messenger work. The percentage of time spent on messenger work by the clerk during the week was most nearly

   4-A 6%
   4-B 14%
   4-C 10%
   4-D 16%

5. A dealer bought some bicycles for $4000. He sold them for $6200, making $50 on each bicycle. How many bicycles were there?

   5-A 40
   5-B 43
   5-C 38
   5-D 44

6. Twelve clerks are assigned to enter certain data on index cards. This number of clerks could perform the task in 18 days. After these clerks have worked on this assignment for 6 days, 4 more clerks are added to the staff to do this work. Assuming that all the clerks work at the same rate of speed, the entire task, instead of taking 18 days, will be performed in

   6-A 14 days
   6-B 17 days
   6-C 12 days
   6-D 16 days

7. Six gross of special drawing pencils were purchased for use in a City department. If the pencils were used at the rate of 24 a week, the maximum number of weeks that the six gross of pencils would last is

   7-A 6 weeks
   7-B 24 weeks
   7-C 12 weeks
   7-D 36 weeks

8. A stock clerk had 600 pads on hand. He then issued $\frac{3}{8}$ of his supply of pads to Division X, $\frac{1}{4}$ to Division Y, and $\frac{1}{6}$ to Division Z. The number of pads remaining in stock is

   8-A 48
   8-B 240
   8-C 125
   8-D 475

9. The local music shop had a record sale. The records normally cost $6.98 each. The sale price was $12.50 for 2 records. Pete bought

4 records at the sale price. How much money did Pete save by buying the records at the sale price?

9-A $2.98
9-B $2.92
9-C $2.50
9-D $1.46

10. A teenager had to walk 2 miles to school. If he walked at an average of 3 miles per hour, how many minutes did it take him to walk to school?

10-A 40
10-B 20
10-C 50
10-D 45

11. Two sailors traveled by bus from one point to another. The trip took 15 hours, and they left their point of origin at 8 a.m. What time did they arrive at their destination?

11-A 11 a.m.
11-B 10 p.m.
11-C 11 p.m.
11-D 12 a.m.

12. Gary went to the store and bought a toy harmonica for $1.95 and an instruction booklet for $.35. He gave the clerk $2.50. How much change did Gary get?

12-A $.20
12-B $.25
12-C $.30
12-D $.15

13. A man deposited a check for $1000 to open an account. Shortly after that, he withdrew $941.20. How much did he have left in his account?

13-A $56.72
13-B $58.80
13-C $59.09
13-D $60.60

14. A shopper bought 4 pillow cases that cost $4.98 apiece, 2 fitted bottom sheets that cost $8.29 apiece, and 2 fitted top sheets that cost $8.09 apiece. What was her total bill?

14-A $52.58
14-B $51.68
14-C $52.68
14-D $21.36

15. After an employer figures out an employee's weekly salary of $190.57, he deducts $13.05 for social security and $5.68 for pension. What is the amount of the check after these deductions?

15-A $171.84
15-B $171.92
15-C $172.84
15-D $172.99

16. The temperature yesterday at noon was 68.5 degrees. Today at noon it was 59.9 degrees. What was the difference in temperature?

16-A 8.4 degrees
16-B 8.5 degrees
16-C 8.6 degrees
16-D 8.7 degrees

17. The Youth Fellowship decided to have a hayride. Five girls and five boys went on the trip. The parents of two of the children went along as chaperons. How many children went on the trip?

17-A 12
17-B 10
17-C 8
17-D 14

18. A student was planning a trip to Europe. She had a total of $700 available for expenses. If the plane ticket cost $372 how much money did she have left?

18-A $338.00
18-B $248.00
18-C $438.00
18-D $328.00

19. A woman bought a house dress for $17.95, a purse for $10.95, and a warm hat for $7.95.

What is the total amount she had to pay for these items?

19-A $35.75
19-B $36.85
19-C $26.85
19-D $34.85

20. A skier started a fire in the fireplace. Each log she put on burned for a half-hour. If she started with 10 logs, for how many hours could the fire burn?

20-A 5 hrs.
20-B $8\frac{1}{2}$ hrs.
20-C 10 hrs.
20-D 7 hrs.

21. To go from Poughkeepsie, New York, to West Palm Beach, Florida, you must travel 1,400 miles. If you can average a driving speed of 50 miles an hour, how many hours must you drive to make this trip?

21-A 25
21-B 28
21-C 30
21-D $27\frac{1}{2}$

22. A woman bowled 3 games. Her scores were 136, 133, and 139. She had an average of 133 before bowling these 3 games. What is her average now?

22-A 136
22-B 138
22-C 135
22-D 134

23. If a boy had $15 and spent $13.72, how do you find how much money he had left?

23-A add
23-B divide
23-C multiply
23-D subtract

24. Fred had a coupon worth $2.00 on the purchase of one record. Each record cost $5.98, and Fred bought two records. How much did Fred have to pay?

24-A $3.98
24-B $7.96
24-C $9.96
24-D $10.98

25. An officer traveled 1200 miles in 20 hours. How many miles per hour did she average?

25-A 45
25-B 60
25-C 50
25-D 65

26. A boy sold $88.50 worth of stationery. If he received a $33\frac{1}{3}\%$ commission, what was the amount of his commission?

26-A $29.50
26-B $40.00
26-C $50.00
26-D $62.50

27. What is the shortest board a man must buy in order to cut three sections from it each 4 feet, 8 inches long?

27-A 12 ft.
27-B 14 ft.
27-C 16 ft.
27-D 18 ft.

28. A girl had to buy a sweater, a blouse, and a scarf. The sweater cost $21.00, the blouse $14.98, and the scarf $4.97. What was the total cost of her purchases?

28-A $35.50
28-B $40.85
28-C $30.85
28-D $40.95

29. Don and Frank started from the same point and drove in opposite directions. Don's rate of speed was 50 miles per hour. Frank's rate of speed was 40 miles per hour. How many miles apart were they at the end of 2 hours?

29-A 90
29-B 160

29-C 140
29-D 180

30. A decorator went to a department store and ordered curtains for 5 windows. One pair of curtains cost $14.28, 2 pairs cost $33.26 apiece, and the remaining 2 pairs cost $65.38 apiece. What was the retail cost of the five pairs of curtains?

30-A $211.46
30-B $211.56
30-C $112.92
30-D $110.82

END OF PART 2

IF YOU FINISH BEFORE THE TIME IS UP, CHECK TO BE CERTAIN THAT YOU HAVE MARKED ALL OF YOUR ANSWERS ON THE ANSWER SHEET. THEN CHECK OVER YOUR WORK ON THIS PART ONLY. DO NOT RETURN TO PART ONE. DO NOT TURN THE PAGE UNTIL YOU ARE TOLD TO DO SO.

PART 3

WORD KNOWLEDGE

The questions in this part test how well you understand the meanings of words. Each question has an underlined word. Read all four possible answers and decide which one has a meaning closest to the meaning of the underlined word. On your answer sheet mark the letter of the answer you choose. Try these questions.

1. Exterminate most nearly means

   1-A destroy
   1-B classify
   1-C experiment with
   1-D drive away

1. Ⓐ Ⓑ Ⓒ Ⓓ

1-A DESTROY is the correct answer. *To exterminate* means *to get rid of by killing off. Driving away* (D) might be a way to get rid of, but it would not be extermination. (B) and (C) are wrong.

2. The military vehicles travelled in a convoy.

   2-A hearse
   2-B thunderstorm
   2-C jeep
   2-D group

2. Ⓐ Ⓑ Ⓒ Ⓓ

2-D GROUP is the correct answer. A *jeep* (C) may be part of a *convoy*. A *convoy* is a group travelling together for protection or convenience. You have probably seen *convoys* of military vehicles travelling single-file up the highway toward summer reserve camp. (A) and (B) are wrong.

3. The rent bill is payable on the first of the month.

   3-A late
   3-B profitable
   3-C due
   3-D paid

3. Ⓐ Ⓑ Ⓒ Ⓓ

3-C DUE is the only correct answer. A bill which is *payable* is *due;* it is not yet *late* (A) nor has it been *paid* (D). *Profitable* (B) is not the meaning of *payable.*

4. Lyrics most nearly means

   4-A music
   4-B words
   4-C rhyme
   4-D song

4. Ⓐ Ⓑ Ⓒ Ⓓ

4-B WORDS is the correct answer. The *lyrics* are the *words* of a *song* (D), not the song itself nor the *music* (A). The *lyrics* may *rhyme* (C).

5. Adopt most nearly means

   5-A baby
   5-B change
   5-C legal
   5-D accept

5. Ⓐ Ⓑ Ⓒ Ⓓ

5-D ACCEPT is the correct answer. The actual *adoption* is the *acceptance* as one's own. The object of *adoption* is very often a *baby* (A) and the formal process for *adoption* is a *legal* (C) one. If you answered (B) *change,* you were confusing *adopt* with *adapt,* which does mean *change.*

DO NOT TURN THE PAGE UNTIL YOU ARE TOLD TO DO SO

WORD KNOWLEDGE

TIME: 11 Minutes—35 Questions

1. <u>Revenue</u> most nearly means

    1-A taxes
    1-B income
    1-C expenses
    1-D produce

2. <u>Convene</u> most nearly means

    2-A meet
    2-B debate
    2-C agree
    2-D drink

3. The machine has <u>manual</u> controls.

    3-A self-acting
    3-B simple
    3-C hand-operated
    3-D handmade

4. <u>Deportment</u> most nearly means

    4-A attendance
    4-B intelligence
    4-C neatness
    4-D behavior

5. I could not go to the party because I had a <u>prior</u> engagement.

    5-A personal
    5-B more urgent
    5-C more attractive
    5-D earlier

6. <u>Grimy</u> most nearly means

    6-A ill-fitting
    6-B poorly made
    6-C dirty
    6-D ragged

7. <u>Approximate</u> most nearly means

    7-A mathematically correct
    7-B nearly exact
    7-C remarkable
    7-D worthless

8. The man <u>survived</u> his three sisters.

    8-A outlived
    8-B envied
    8-C excelled
    8-D destroyed

9. <u>Competent</u> most nearly means

    9-A busy
    9-B capable
    9-C friendly
    9-D good-natured

10. All air traffic was <u>suspended</u> during the emergency.

    10-A turned back
    10-B checked carefully
    10-C regulated strictly
    10-D stopped temporarily

11. The <u>territory</u> is too large for one platoon to defend.

    11-A region
    11-B swamp
    11-C ranch
    11-D beach

12. <u>Huge</u> most nearly means

    12-A ugly
    12-B tall
    12-C wide
    12-D immense

13. <u>Prevented</u> most nearly means

    13-A allowed
    13-B suggested
    13-C hindered
    13-D urged

14. All mail is to be <u>forwarded</u> to our new address.

14-A sent
14-B returned
14-C canceled
14-D received

15. <u>Vacant</u> most nearly means

15-A quiet
15-B dark
15-C available
15-D empty

16. <u>Irritating</u> most nearly means

16-A nervous
16-B unsuitable
16-C annoying
16-D noisy

17. The cyclist pedaled at a <u>uniform</u> rate.

17-A increasing
17-B unchanging
17-C unusual
17-D very slow

18. <u>Power</u> most nearly means

18-A size
18-B ambition
18-C force
18-D success

19. The sailors reached the <u>shore</u> in a landing barge.

19-A gulf
19-B coast
19-C inlet
19-D alien

20. <u>Flexible</u> most nearly means

20-A pliable
20-B rigid
20-C weak
20-D athletic

21. <u>Comprehend</u> most nearly means

21-A hear
21-B listen
21-C agree
21-D understand

22. <u>Instructor</u> most nearly means

22-A expert
22-B assistant
22-C teacher
22-D foreman

23. The boy scouts were <u>commended</u> for their actions at the scene of the accident.

23-A reprimanded
23-B praised
23-C promoted
23-D blamed

24. <u>Revolving</u> most nearly means

24-A rocking
24-B working
24-C vibrating
24-D turning

25. <u>Alert</u> most nearly means

25-A watchful
25-B busy
25-C helpful
25-D honest

26. The computer did not <u>function</u> yesterday.

26-A finish
26-B stop
26-C operate
26-D overheat

27. <u>Hazard</u> most nearly means

27-A damage
27-B choice
27-C opportunity
27-D danger

28. The <u>blemish</u> on the tomato appears to be caused by disease.

28-A color
28-B insect
28-C flaw
28-D design

29. The package will be <u>conveyed</u> by Greyhound bus.

    29-A carried
    29-B guarded
    29-C refused
    29-D damaged

30. <u>Pedestrian</u> most nearly means

    30-A passenger
    30-B street-crosser
    30-C walker
    30-D traffic light

31. <u>Attorney</u> most nearly means

    31-A banker
    31-B lawyer
    31-C foot doctor
    31-D accountant

32. <u>Obsolete</u> most nearly means

    32-A out-of-date
    32-B broken down

    32-C as good as new
    32-D improved

33. The old-fashioned classroom has <u>stationary</u> desks.

    33-A heavy
    33-B carved
    33-C written-upon
    33-D not movable

34. The only sound was the <u>steady</u> ticking of the clock.

    34-A noisy
    34-B eerie
    34-C tiresome
    34-D regular

35. The letter <u>emphasized</u> two important ideas.

    35-A introduced
    35-B overlooked
    35-C contrasted
    35-D stressed

END OF PART 3

IF YOU FINISH BEFORE TIME IS UP, CHECK YOUR WORK ON THIS PART ONLY. DO NOT GO BACK TO EITHER PREVIOUS PART. DO NOT GO ON TO THE NEXT PART UNTIL YOU ARE TOLD TO DO SO.

PART 4

PARAGRAPH COMPREHENSION

The paragraph comprehension part of your test battery requires concentration and attention to detail. First you must read and understand the paragraph. Then you must read and understand each of the answer choices, noticing the differences of meaning or emphasis that are imparted by little words. There is one question based upon each paragraph. You must answer that question on the basis of what is stated or implied in the passage, even if you know a better answer and even if the information in the paragraph is contrary to fact. In some cases more than one answer might be correct, but you must choose the BEST answer and mark its letter on your answer sheet. Try these questions.

1. Some fire-resistant buildings, although wholly constructed of materials that will not burn, may be completely gutted by the spread of fire through their contents by way of hallways and other openings. They may even suffer serious structural damage by the collapse of metal beams and columns.

The paragraph best supports the statement that some fire-resistant buildings

1-A can be damaged seriously by fire
1-B have specially constructed halls and doors
1-C afford less protection to their contents than would ordinary buildings
1-D will burn readily

1. Ⓐ Ⓑ Ⓒ Ⓓ

1-A The paragraph presents the problems of fire in fire-resistant buildings. It suggests that the contents of the buildings may burn even though the structural materials themselves do not, and the ensuing fire may even cause the collapse of the buildings. The paragraph does not compare the problem of fire in fire-resistant buildings with that of fire in ordinary buildings.

2. It is probably safe to assume that for most people mental growth cases somewhere between fourteen and a half and sixteen. After that, any increase in ability to meet novel situations is gained from experience. Intellectual growth is likewise ascribed to wider experience and more information, rather than to an increase in mental capacity.

Most individuals somewhere between fourteen and a half and sixteen

2-A make demands on mere experience rather than on native ability
2-B show an increase rather than a decrease in general mental capacity
2-C have achieved their total mental growth
2-D cease to show increased capacity to meet novel situations

2. Ⓐ Ⓑ Ⓒ Ⓓ

2-C The first sentence states that for most people mental growth ceases between the ages of fourteen and a half and sixteen. The remainder of the paragraph explains that what may later appear to be increased capacity must be ascribed to greater experience and information.

DO NOT TURN THE PAGE UNTIL YOU ARE TOLD TO DO SO

PARAGRAPH COMPREHENSION

TIME: 13 Minutes—15 Questions

1. The indiscriminate or continual use of any drug without medical supervision is dangerous. Even drugs considered harmless may result in chronic poisoning if used for a period of years. Prescriptions should not be refilled without consulting your doctor. He prescribed a given amount because he wished to limit your use of the drug to a certain time. Never use a drug prescribed for someone else just because your symptoms appear similar. There may be differences, apparent to an expert but hidden from you, which indicate an entirely different ailment requiring different medication.

The paragraph best supports the statement that

1-A the use of drugs is very dangerous
1-B if a physician prescribes a drug it is safe to refill the prescription
1-C people with similar symptoms are usually suffering from the same ailment
1-D a drug considered harmless may be dangerous if taken over a long period of time without supervision

2. Although rural crime reporting is spottier and less efficient than city and town reporting, sufficient data is collected to support the statement that rural crime rates are lower than those of urban communities.

The paragraph best supports the statement that

2-A better reporting of crime occurs in rural areas than in cities
2-B there appears to be a lower proportion of crime in rural areas than in cities
2-C cities have more crime than towns
2-D no conclusions can be drawn regarding crime in rural areas because of inadequate reporting

3. Telegrams should be clear, concise, and brief. Omit all unnecessary words. The parts of speech most often used in telegrams are nouns, verbs, adjectives, and adverbs. If possible, do without pronouns, prepositions, articles, and copulative verbs. Use simple sentences, rather than complex and compound.

In writing telegrams one should always use

3-A common and simple words
3-B only nouns, verbs, adjectives, and adverbs
3-C incomplete sentences
3-D only words essential to the meaning

4. The Suggestion System is conducted to give thorough and understanding study to ideas presented by postal employees for promoting the welfare of postal personnel and for improving mail handling and other postal business; and to encourage and reward postal employees who think out, develop, and present acceptable ideas and plans. Through this system the talent and ability of postal employees are to be used for improving postal service and reducing expenses.

One purpose of the Suggestion System is to

4-A maintain a unit of experienced employees to plan and develop improvements
4-B obtain ideas that will help postal employees improve their work
4-C offer promotions to postal employees who suggest useful changes in service
4-D provide pay raises for employees who increase their output

5. Economy once in a while is just not enough. I expect to find it at every level of responsibility, from cabinet member to the newest and youngest recruit. Controlling waste is something like bailing a boat; you have to keep at it. I have no intention of easing up on my insistence on getting a dollar of value for each dollar we spend.

The paragraph best supports the statement that

5-A we need not be concerned about items which cost less than a dollar
5-B it is advisable to buy the cheaper of two items
5-C the responsibility of economy is greater at high levels than at low levels
5-D economy is a continuing responsibility

6. Many industrial processes are dangerous to the health of workers and give rise to occupational disease. The state, as the guardian of public health and welfare, has a legitimate interest in conserving the vitality of industrial workers and may, to this end, make appropriate laws, and give to boards or departments authority to make regulations to carry out the law. Such laws and rules may prohibit dangerous conditions, regulate the plant or the person, or compensate for injuries received.

The paragraph best supports the statement that

6-A workmen's compensation laws are in force in practically all states
6-B government regulation of industry is highly desirable
6-C the state is interested in lessening the occurrence of occupational disease
6-D the state compensates the worker for injuries received while carrying out the duties of his occupation

7. The Federal investigator must direct his whole effort toward success in his work. If he wishes to succeed in each investigation, his work will be by no means easy, smooth, or peaceful; on the contrary, he will have to devote himself completely and continuously to a task that requires all his ability.

An investigator's success depends most upon

7-A ambition to advance rapidly in the service
7-B persistence in the face of difficulty
7-C training and experience
7-D willingness to obey orders without delay

8. Salt has always been important in our diet as a flavoring for food, but recently doctors have come to recognize it as an absolute necessity. Most living things contain salt and it is almost impossible to eat a normal diet without getting some. However, that "some" may not be enough. Now doctors recommend that those who normally use little salt step up their salt consumption in hot weather, when more than the usual salt intake is required.

The paragraph best supports the statement that

8-A salt is necessary if flavor is to be maintained
8-B people living on a normal diet have an intake of salt which is sufficient to maintain good blood pressure
8-C the body needs more salt in summer than in winter
8-D all organic life contains salt in one form or another

9. The dangers of the ancient triple menace of the operating room—shock, hemorrhage, and infection—have been virtually eliminated. Transfusion of blood is employed to combat shock and hemorrhage. It is also used to build up a patient so weakened by disease that an operation would otherwise be impossible.

The paragraph best supports the statement that

9-A asepsis has removed the danger from infection

9-B operations are no longer as dangerous as they once were

9-C a blood transfusion usually precedes a serious operation

9-D operating technique has greatly improved due to the rise in standards of medical schools

10. Iron is used in making our bridges and skyscrapers, subways and steamships, railroads and automobiles, and nearly all kinds of machinery—besides millions of small articles varying from the farmer's scythe to the woman's needle.

The paragraph best supports the statement that iron

10-A is the most abundant of the metals

10-B has many different uses

10-C is the strongest of all metals

10-D is the only material used in building skyscrapers and bridges

11. The labor required to produce a bushel of wheat in 1830 was three hours. Today it takes less than ten minutes. Further, it has been estimated that fifty men, employing modern farm machinery and agricultural methods, can do the work of five hundred peasants toiling under the conditions of the eighteenth century.

On the basis of the facts presented above, one could best conclude that

11-A the increase of efficiency in agriculture is almost as great as that in manufacturing

11-B modern farm machinery has resulted in serious unemployment among farmers

11-C more than 18 times as much wheat is produced today than in 1830

11-D modern farm machinery is labor-saving

12. In the business districts of cities, collections from street letter boxes are made at stated hours, and collectors are required to observe these hours exactly. Any businessman using these boxes can rely with certainty upon the time of the next collection.

The paragraph best supports the statement that

12-A mail collections in business districts are more frequent during the day than at night

12-B mail collectors are required to observe safety regulations exactly

12-C mail collections are made often in business districts

12-D mail is collected in business districts on a regular schedule

13. Statutes to prevent and penalize adulteration of foods, and to provide for sanitary food preparation, are in force in every state. Such legislation has been upheld as proper under the police power of the state, since this legislation is obviously designed to promote the health and general welfare of the people.

The paragraph best supports the statement that

13-A the state provides for drastic measures to deal with violations of the pure food laws

13-B to make laws for the purpose of promoting the general health and general welfare of the people is a proper function of the state

13-C adulterated food is an outstanding menace to public health

13-D the right of the state to penalize adulteration of foods has never been questioned

14. Certain chemical changes, such as fermentation, are due to the action of innumerable living micro-organisms known as bacteria. Bacteria also cause the decomposition of sewage.

Certain chemical changes are due to

14-A bacteria

14-B oxidation

14-C   fermentation
14-D   decomposition

15. The rates of vibration perceived by the ears as musical tones lie between fairly well-defined limits. In the ear, as in the eye, there are individual variations. However, variations are more marked in the ear, since its range of perception is greater.

The ear

15-A   is limited by the nature of its variations
15-B   is the most sensitive of the auditory organs
15-C   differs from the eye in its broader range of perception
15-D   is sensitive to a great range of musical volume

END OF PART 4

IF YOU COMPLETE YOUR WORK BEFORE TIME IS UP, CHECK OVER YOUR ANSWERS ON THIS PART ONLY. DO NOT GO BACK TO ANY PREVIOUS PART. DO NOT TURN TO THE NEXT PART UNTIL YOU ARE TOLD TO DO SO.

PART 5

NUMERICAL OPERATIONS

The numerical operations part of your test battery consists of fifty very simple arithmetic questions that must be answered in only three minutes. Obviously, speed is a very important factor. You should not attempt to compute these answers using pencil and scratch paper. Instead, solve each problem in your head, then choose the correct answer from among the four choices and mark the letter of the correct answer on your answer sheet. If you are not sure of an answer, guess and go on to the next question. Do not skip any questions. You will most certainly not have time to go back to fill in. Since a wrong answer will not count against you, it cannot hurt to guess. Many people cannot complete all fifty questions in the three minutes allowed. Do not be upset if you cannot finish. Just answer as many questions as you can. Try these questions.

1. 6 + 8 =

    1-A 11
    1-B 12
    1-C 13
    1-D 14

    1. Ⓐ Ⓑ Ⓒ Ⓓ

1-D 6 + 8 = 14

2. 5 − 3 =

    2-A 8
    2-B 15
    2-C 2
    2-D 4

    2. Ⓐ Ⓑ Ⓒ Ⓓ

2-C 5 − 3 = 2

3. 6 + 6 =

    3-A 0
    3-B 1
    3-C 8
    3-D 12

    3. Ⓐ Ⓑ Ⓒ Ⓓ

3-D 6 + 6 = 12

4. 9 − 1 =

    4-A 10
    4-B 9
    4-C 8
    4-D 0

    4. Ⓐ Ⓑ Ⓒ Ⓓ

4-C 9 − 1 = 8

5. 16 ÷ 4 =

    5-A 12
    5-B 10
    5-C 4
    5-D 2

    5. Ⓐ Ⓑ Ⓒ Ⓓ

5-C 16 ÷ 4 = 4

6. 3 × 2 =

    6-A 6
    6-B 4
    6-C 1
    6-D 5

    6. Ⓐ Ⓑ Ⓒ Ⓓ

6-A 3 × 2 = 6

DO NOT TURN THE PAGE UNTIL YOU ARE TOLD TO DO SO

NUMERICAL OPERATIONS

TIME: 3 Minutes—50 Questions

1. $60 \div 10 =$

  1-A 5
  1-B 6
  1-C 10
  1-D 16

2. $5 + 2 =$

  2-A 3
  2-B 6
  2-C 7
  2-D 9

3. $3 \times 4 =$

  3-A 7
  3-B 12
  3-C 15
  3-D 21

4. $8 - 6 =$

  4-A 12
  4-B 5
  4-C 4
  4-D 2

5. $4 + 8 =$

  5-A 6
  5-B 10
  5-C 12
  5-D 14

6. $6 \times 8 =$

  6-A 24
  6-B 48
  6-C 42
  6-D 36

7. $3 + 9 =$

  7-A 12
  7-B 11
  7-C 13
  7-D 14

8. $7 + 8 =$

  8-A 12
  8-B 15
  8-C 17
  8-D 19

9. $3 \times 8 =$

  9-A 5
  9-B 13
  9-C 24
  9-D 32

10. $16 \div 2 =$

  10-A 8
  10-B 12
  10-C 9
  10-D 6

11. $9 \times 3 =$

  11-A 21
  11-B 25
  11-C 27
  11-D 29

12. $3 + 4 =$

  12-A 1
  12-B 7
  12-C 9
  12-D 11

13. $10 - 6 =$

13-A 4
13-B 8
13-C 14
13-D 16

14. $1 + 5 =$

14-A 0
14-B 4
14-C 5
14-D 6

15. $4 \times 2 =$

15-A 6
15-B 16
15-C 12
15-D 8

16. $49 \div 7 =$

16-A 6
16-B 7
16-C 8
16-D 9

17. $3 \times 10 =$

17-A 7
17-B 13
17-C 15
17-D 30

18. $8 + 0 =$

18-A 8
18-B 0
18-C 1
18-D 80

19. $5 + 8 =$

19-A 11
19-B 12
19-C 13
19-D 15

20. $7 - 6 =$

20-A 5
20-B 1
20-C 11
20-D 13

21. $8 + 3 =$

21-A 5
21-B 11
21-C 12
21-D 13

22. $2 \times 2 =$

22-A 2
22-B 4
22-C 6
22-D 8

23. $6 + 1 =$

23-A 16
23-B 15
23-C 7
23-D 5

24. $6 \div 2 =$

24-A 12
24-B 8
24-C 4
24-D 3

25. $4 + 5 =$

25-A 25
25-B 20
25-C 11
25-D 9

26. $7 \times 8 =$

26-A 56
26-B 48
26-C 42
26-D 72

27. $9 + 6 =$

27-A 13
27-B 14
27-C 15
27-D 16

28. 2 + 3 =

    28-A 5
    28-B 7
    28-C 1
    28-D 6

29. 7 − 1 =

    29-A 8
    29-B 0
    29-C 7
    29-D 6

30. 8 ÷ 8 =

    30-A 8
    30-B 0
    30-C 16
    30-D 1

31. 2 × 9 =

    31-A 17
    31-B 19
    31-C 18
    31-D 16

32. 7 + 3 =

    32-A 4
    32-B 10
    32-C 13
    32-D 11

33. 30 ÷ 3 =

    33-A 33
    33-B 11
    33-C 12
    33-D 10

34. 6 + 8 =

    34-A 14
    34-B 15
    34-C 17
    34-D 19

35. 9 + 2 =

    35-A 10
    35-B 7
    35-C 11
    35-D 12

36. 1 × 5 =

    36-A 5
    36-B 1
    36-C 6
    36-D 10

37. 3 + 6 =

    37-A 3
    37-B 8
    37-C 9
    37-D 18

38. 4 × 8 =

    38-A 24
    38-B 28
    38-C 32
    38-D 42

39. 5 + 5 =

    39-A 25
    39-B 10
    39-C 5
    39-D 1

40. 7 − 4 =

    40-A 11
    40-B 9
    40-C 6
    40-D 3

41. 4 − 0 =

    41-A 0
    41-B 4
    41-C 1
    41-D 5

42. 1 + 2 =

    42-A 1
    42-B 2
    42-C 3
    42-D 4

43. 16 ÷ 4 =

    43-A 4
    43-B 8
    43-C 12
    43-D 20

44. 9 × 9 =

    44-A 99
    44-B 0
    44-C 72
    44-D 81

45. 5 + 7 =

    45-A 11
    45-B 2
    45-C 12
    45-D 13

46. 10 − 4 =

    46-A 4
    46-B 6
    46-C 8
    46-D 14

47. 4 + 7 =

    47-A 3
    47-B 21
    47-C 12
    47-D 11

48. 9 × 5 =

    48-A 45
    48-B 47
    48-C 55
    48-D 36

49. 20 ÷ 2 =

    49-A 40
    49-B 22
    49-C 18
    49-D 10

50. 8 − 7 =

    50-A 56
    50-B 15
    50-C 5
    50-D 1

END OF PART 5

IF YOU FINISH THIS PART BEFORE THE TIME IS UP, CHECK OVER YOUR WORK ON THIS PART ONLY. DO NOT GO ON UNTIL YOU ARE TOLD TO DO SO.

PART 6

CODING SPEED

The coding part of your exam is different from all other parts of the exam. Nothing that you have learned enters into your answering of these questions. Coding is a test of your memory, your eye-hand coordination and your working speed.

Before each set of questions you will find a "key." The key consists of ten words listed in alphabetical order. Each word has a four-digit code number assigned to it.

In the set of questions you will find the same ten words, scrambled and sometimes repeated. Following each word in the test are *five* answer choices in columns labelled A to E. Each answer choice is a four-digit number. The answer choices are in ascending order; that is, the lowest number is always in column A, the next higher number is in column B and so on to the highest number in column E. You must look at the word, find the correct code number among the choices and mark on your answer sheet the letter of the column in which you found the correct code number.

On the actual examination you must work very quickly. You have only seven minutes in which to try to answer eighty-four questions. Use the sample questions that follow to develop a system that works for you—memorization, some sort of word-number association, a mathematical formula or any private method that helps you work up speed and accuracy. Many people cannot finish the coding test in the time allowed. Do not be upset if you cannot finish. Just do your best. Try these questions.

Key

clay 5813	fudge 1875	kiss 7871
dungeon 6214	gentle 9432	loft 4630
elf 3185	hand 5500	sock 8902
	jump 2864	

Answers

		A	B	C	D	E	
1.	gentle	2864	4630	5813	7871	9432	1. Ⓐ Ⓑ Ⓒ Ⓓ Ⓔ
2.	loft	1875	3185	4630	6214	8902	2. Ⓐ Ⓑ Ⓒ Ⓓ Ⓔ
3.	elf	1875	2864	3185	5813	8902	3. Ⓐ Ⓑ Ⓒ Ⓓ Ⓔ
4.	kiss	2864	4630	5500	7871	9432	4. Ⓐ Ⓑ Ⓒ Ⓓ Ⓔ
5.	fudge	1875	3185	5500	5813	6214	5. Ⓐ Ⓑ Ⓒ Ⓓ Ⓔ
6.	jump	2864	5813	6214	7871	8902	6. Ⓐ Ⓑ Ⓒ Ⓓ Ⓔ
7.	hand	4630	5500	5813	6214	7871	7. Ⓐ Ⓑ Ⓒ Ⓓ Ⓔ
8.	dungeon	1875	3185	4630	6214	8902	8. Ⓐ Ⓑ Ⓒ Ⓓ Ⓔ
9.	sock	2864	4630	5500	8902	9432	9. Ⓐ Ⓑ Ⓒ Ⓓ Ⓔ
10.	clay	5500	5813	6214	7871	9432	10. Ⓐ Ⓑ Ⓒ Ⓓ Ⓔ
11.	hand	1875	3185	4630	5500	5813	11. Ⓐ Ⓑ Ⓒ Ⓓ Ⓔ
12.	kiss	2864	4630	7871	8902	9432	12. Ⓐ Ⓑ Ⓒ Ⓓ Ⓔ

The correct answers are:

1-E	4-D	7-B	10-B
2-C	5-A	8-D	11-D
3-C	6-A	9-D	12-C

Key

bubble 3393	eat 6912	oval 8003
crown 1465	hose 7577	steer 5665
dentist 3290	juice 2012	yellow 6872
	lap 4755	

Answers

		A	B	C	D	E	
13.	dentist	2012	3290	3393	6872	8003	13. Ⓐ Ⓑ Ⓒ Ⓓ Ⓔ
14.	yellow	3393	4755	5665	6872	7577	14. Ⓐ Ⓑ Ⓒ Ⓓ Ⓔ
15.	oval	3290	5665	6912	7577	8003	15. Ⓐ Ⓑ Ⓒ Ⓓ Ⓔ
16.	crown	1465	2012	3290	5665	6872	16. Ⓐ Ⓑ Ⓒ Ⓓ Ⓔ
17.	hose	3290	3393	4755	6912	7577	17. Ⓐ Ⓑ Ⓒ Ⓓ Ⓔ
18.	lap	1465	2012	3290	3393	4755	18. Ⓐ Ⓑ Ⓒ Ⓓ Ⓔ
19.	steer	1465	4755	5665	6872	6912	19. Ⓐ Ⓑ Ⓒ Ⓓ Ⓔ
20.	juice	2012	3290	4755	6872	6912	20. Ⓐ Ⓑ Ⓒ Ⓓ Ⓔ
21.	eat	4755	5665	6872	6912	7577	21. Ⓐ Ⓑ Ⓒ Ⓓ Ⓔ
22.	bubble	3290	3393	4755	5665	6912	22. Ⓐ Ⓑ Ⓒ Ⓓ Ⓔ
23.	dentist	1465	2012	3290	3393	6912	23. Ⓐ Ⓑ Ⓒ Ⓓ Ⓔ
24.	hose	2012	4755	5665	7577	8003	24. Ⓐ Ⓑ Ⓒ Ⓓ Ⓔ

The correct answers are:

13-B	16-A	19-C	22-B
14-D	17-E	20-A	23-C
15-E	18-E	21-D	24-D

DO NOT TURN THE PAGE UNTIL YOU ARE TOLD TO DO SO

CODING SPEED

TIME: 7 Minutes—84 Questions

Key

button 5266	flu 3838	mail 6234
chop 1817	gold 8351	pot 7007
dawn 9745	iris 4658	puppy 6606
	love 2456	

Answers

		A	B	C	D	E
1.	button	2456	4658	5266	6234	8351
2.	puppy	1817	2456	5266	6234	6606
3.	gold	1817	3838	6234	8351	9745
4.	mail	2456	4658	5266	6234	8351
5.	flu	3838	5266	6234	6606	9745
6.	iris	2456	4658	5266	6234	8351
7.	pot	3838	5266	6606	7007	9745
8.	chop	1817	3838	6234	6606	8351
9.	love	2456	4658	5266	6234	9745
10.	iris	1817	3838	4658	6234	7007
11.	dawn	2456	3838	6234	6606	9745
12.	mail	2456	4658	6234	8351	9745

Key

axle 5614	guitar 4379	noose 7867
baby 9846	lamp 6686	trip 8968
club 1090	mop 2545	waste 4886
	muffin 3939	

Answers

		A	B	C	D	E
13.	guitar	3939	4379	4886	6686	7867
14.	waste	1090	2545	3939	4379	4886
15.	axle	4379	4886	5614	6686	8968
16.	mop	1090	2545	4379	7867	9846
17.	trip	3939	4886	6686	8968	9846
18.	lamp	2545	3939	4886	5614	6686
19.	club	1090	4379	4886	5614	7867
20.	muffin	2545	3939	4379	7867	8968
21.	noose	4379	5614	7867	8968	9846
22.	lamp	1090	3939	4886	6686	8968
23.	baby	4379	4886	6686	7867	9846
24.	noose	1090	6686	7867	8968	9846

Key

aunt	7959	dove	1918	ladle	3344
couch	4790	hail	1929	mark	6776
deer	8812	iron	2458	pistol	9434
		judge	5761		

Answers

		A	B	C	D	E
25.	pistol	1918	1929	4790	7959	9434
26.	iron	1929	2458	3344	6776	7959
27.	mark	3344	4790	5761	6776	7959
28.	judge	1918	1929	2458	4790	5761
29.	ladle	2458	3344	6776	7959	9434
30.	couch	4790	5761	6776	8812	9434
31.	deer	1918	2458	5761	7959	8812
32.	aunt	3344	5761	7959	8812	9434
33.	pistol	1929	3344	4790	7959	9434
34.	dove	1918	1929	2458	3344	4790
35.	mark	4790	6776	7959	8812	9434
36.	hail	1929	2458	5761	6776	7959

Key

coach	4589	gun	1118	root	6943
coal	9260	lunch	2024	stable	3377
eagle	5583	marble	6874	top	7337
		oven	1418		

Answers

		A	B	C	D	E
37.	marble	2024	4589	5583	6874	6943
38.	stable	1418	3377	5583	7337	9260
39.	eagle	1118	2024	3377	5583	6874
40.	lunch	1118	1418	2024	6943	9260
41.	oven	1418	3377	4589	6943	7337
42.	coal	2024	4589	6874	6943	9260
43.	root	5583	6874	6943	7337	9260
44.	coach	1118	2024	3377	4589	6874
45.	top	1418	3377	5583	6943	7337
46.	gun	1118	1418	4589	7337	9260
47.	eagle	2024	3377	5583	6943	7337
48.	root	1418	2024	6943	7337	9260

Key

bed 4814	elbow 5511	index 6904
coat 3765	fence 2026	kick 7546
doll 9086	gift 1683	lump 2826
	girl 8797	

Answers

		A	B	C	D	E
49.	index	2026	2826	3765	6904	9086
50.	coat	1683	3765	4814	5511	7546
51.	lump	2826	3765	6904	7546	8797
52.	fence	1683	2026	4814	5511	6904
53.	kick	1683	3765	6904	7546	8797
54.	doll	2026	2826	6904	8797	9086
55.	bed	4814	5511	7546	8797	9086
56.	elbow	1683	4814	5511	6904	7546
57.	gift	1683	2026	3765	4814	6904
58.	girl	2826	3765	6904	7546	8797
59.	coat	1683	2026	2826	3765	4814
60.	kick	2026	2826	3765	4814	7546

Key

air 1230	day 1010	island 9064
brush 8800	edge 6010	knee 3369
cabin 5254	fate 7946	lever 2125
	goose 4656	

Answers

		A	B	C	D	E
61.	island	1010	3369	7946	8800	9064
62.	goose	1230	2125	4656	5254	6010
63.	knee	2125	3369	5254	7946	8800
64.	fate	1010	1230	3369	4656	7946
65.	brush	2125	4656	5254	8800	9064
66.	lever	1010	1230	2125	6010	8800
67.	cabin	3369	4656	5254	7946	9064
68.	edge	1230	2125	4656	6010	8800
69.	air	1230	3369	5254	7946	9064
70.	knee	1010	1230	2125	3369	4656
71.	cabin	1230	2125	3369	4656	5254
72.	day	1010	1230	6010	8800	9064

Key

bell 5458	echo 1978	jewel 6877
cable 1058	fuss 4363	mug 7613
dash 4844	height 2984	tub 3439
	iron 9100	

Answers

		A	B	C	D	E
73.	height	1058	1978	2984	7613	9100
74.	jewel	1978	4844	5458	6877	7613
75.	bell	2984	3439	4363	4844	5458
76.	dash	2984	3439	4363	4844	6877
77.	cable	1058	1978	6877	7613	9100
78.	fuss	3439	4363	4844	5458	7613
79.	mug	2984	4363	5458	6877	7613
80.	echo	1978	2984	5458	7613	9100
81.	tub	3439	4363	4844	6877	7613
82.	iron	1058	1978	4363	7613	9100
83.	bell	1978	2984	5458	6877	7613
84.	dash	4363	4844	5458	7613	9100

END OF PART 6

IF YOU FINISH BEFORE TIME IS UP, CHECK TO BE SURE THAT ALL YOUR ANSWERS ARE CLEARLY MARKED. DO NOT RETURN TO ANY PREVIOUS PART. DO NOT GO ON TO THE NEXT PART UNTIL YOU ARE TOLD TO DO SO.

PART 7

AUTO & SHOP INFORMATION

The auto and shop information questions test your knowledge and understanding of automobiles and of tools and shop practices. The answers to many questions come straight from your life experience. However, if this is not your area of interest, there will be questions to which you do not know the answer. Make the most sensible guess. Answer all questions. Mark the letter of your choice on your answer sheet. Try these questions.

1. Wheels should be balanced

   1-A only when they are new
   1-B whenever air pressure is low
   1-C every 10,000 miles
   1-D whenever tires are put onto rims

1. Ⓐ Ⓑ Ⓒ Ⓓ

1-D EACH TIME A TIRE IS PUT ONTO A RIM the wheel must be balanced. If you take your regular tires off the rims and mount snow tires on those same rims, the wheels must be balanced, even though the tires may not be new (A). If you answered (C), you were probably thinking of tire rotation, which is done according to schedule.

2. The main advantage of four-wheel drive is

   2-A higher speed
   2-B better traction
   2-C better gas mileage
   2-D greater durability of the vehicle

2. Ⓐ Ⓑ Ⓒ Ⓓ

2-B Since power from the engine is transmitted to both the front wheels and the back wheels, a four-wheel drive vehicle has much BETTER TRACTION. Four-wheel drive is especially useful in mud, sand and very uneven terrain. While four-wheel drive tends to be a feature of durable vehicles (D), like jeeps, it is not the four-wheel drive that makes them durable.

3.

The tool above is a

   3-A screw
   3-B screwdriver
   3-C drill bit
   3-D corkscrew

3. Ⓐ Ⓑ Ⓒ Ⓓ

3-C The tool is a DRILL BIT. The smooth end is inserted into the drill chuck and is tightened so that it is very secure. When the drill motor goes, the bit turns very fast and drills holes wherever it is applied.

4. The proper place for rope storage is

   4-A a dry, cool closet
   4-B a hot, dry attic
   4-C in the open air
   4-D a covered container of water

4. Ⓐ Ⓑ Ⓒ Ⓓ

4-A A DRY, COOL CLOSET is the best place to store rope. There it should not dry out and become brittle, as it might in a hot attic, yet it would be protected from weather and weakening moisture.

DO NOT TURN THE PAGE UNTIL YOU ARE TOLD TO DO SO

AUTO & SHOP INFORMATION

TIME: 11 Minutes—25 Questions

1. An engine, such as is most often used in automobiles, is called a(n)

   1-A diesel engine
   1-B external-combustion engine
   1-C internal-combustion engine
   1-D three cycle engine

2. In the four stroke cycle gasoline engine, the sequence of the steps in each cylinder to complete a cycle is which one of the following?

   2-A Intake stroke, power stroke, compression stroke, exhaust stroke
   2-B Intake stroke, compression stroke, exhaust stroke, power stroke
   2-C Intake stroke, exhaust stroke, compression stroke, power stroke
   2-D Intake stroke, compression stroke, power stroke, exhaust stroke

3. Vapor-lock in a gasoline engine is most likely due to

   3-A an over-rich gas-air mixture
   3-B fuel forming bubbles in the gas line
   3-C a tear in the fuel pump diaphragm
   3-D the carburetor being clogged with dirt

4. When the level of the liquid in a battery gets too low, it is necessary to put in some more

   4-A battery acid
   4-B hydroxide
   4-C water
   4-D antifreeze

5. After brakes have been severely overheated, what should be checked for?

   5-A water condensation in brake fluid
   5-B glazed brake shoes
   5-C wheels out of alignment
   5-D crystallized wheel bearings

6. A number 10 wood screw is

   6-A thicker than a number 6
   6-B longer than a number 6
   6-C shorter than a number 6
   6-D thinner than a number 6

7. Paint is "thinned" with

   7-A linseed oil
   7-B varnish
   7-C turpentine
   7-D gasoline

8.

   The tool shown above is

   8-A an offset wrench
   8-B a box wrench
   8-C a spanner wrench
   8-D an open end wrench

9. A brad is similar in shape to a

   9-A box nail
   9-B finishing nail
   9-C common nail
   9-D tack

10. The type of screwdriver that will develop the greatest turning force is a

    10-A screwdriver-bit and brace
    10-B straight handle with ratchet
    10-C standard straight handle
    10-D spiral push-type

11.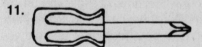

    The tool shown above is used to

11-A ream holes in wood
11-B countersink holes in soft metals
11-C turn Philips-head screws
11-D drill holes in concrete

12. A jointer plane is

12-A used for making close fits
12-B used for heavy rough work
12-C usually less than 12 inches long
12-D used for treaching

13. A good lubricant for locks is

13-A graphite
13-B grease
13-C mineral oil
13-D motor oil

14. If the "charge and discharge" indicator, whether a meter or a light, suddenly indicates "discharge" while a car is in normal operation, it is best that the car be

14-A stopped immediately and then be towed in for repairs
14-B stopped immediately and have a new battery installed on the spot
14-C driven as usual and the incident ignored
14-D driven to the nearest garage for inspection and repair

15. Manifolds are used to conduct

15-A gases out of an engine only
15-B gases into an engine only
15-C gases into or out of an engine
15-D heat into the piston

16. What forces fuel from the carburetor into the cylinder?

16-A the fuel pump
16-B atmospheric pressure
16-C temperature difference
16-D the distributor

17. The most probable cause of a complete loss of oil pressure while driving is

17-A a crankcase oil level which is too low
17-B a crankcase oil level which is too high

17-C the use of too thick an oil
17-D dirty oil

18. To test for leaks around the intake manifold of an idling engine, the mechanic would most likely use

18-A soap bubbles
18-B talc powder
18-C oil
18-D heavy grease

19. What is used to fasten ceramic tiles to walls?

19-A putty
19-B caulking
19-C plaster of paris
19-D mastic

20. With which of these screw heads do you use an "Allen" wrench?

20-A

20-B

20-C

20-D

21. When sanding wood by hand, best results are usually obtained in finishing the surface when the sanding block is worked

21-A across the grain
21-B in a diagonal to the grain
21-C in a circular motion
21-D with the grain

22. A 6-point saw is one which

22-A weighs 6 ounces per foot
22-B is made of no. 6 gauge steel
22-C has 6 teeth per inch
22-D has 6 styles of teeth for universal work

23. If the intake manifold of a gasoline engine is warped to the extent that it leaks, the engine will most likely tend to

    23-A check out with a vacuum gauge as running on a rich mixture

    23-B miss on one cylinder

    23-C perform better on acceleration

    23-D have a fast idle

24. The carpenter's "hand screw" is

24-A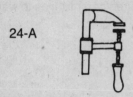

24-B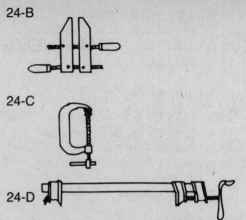

24-C

24-D

25. Of the following tools, the one which is least like the others is

    25-A brace and bit

    25-B plane

    25-C draw-knife

    25-D spoke-shave

END OF PART 7

IF YOU FINISH BEFORE TIME IS UP, CHECK OVER YOUR WORK ON THIS PART ONLY. DO NOT RETURN TO ANY PREVIOUS PART. DO NOT GO ON UNTIL YOU ARE TOLD TO DO SO.

PART 8

MATHEMATICS KNOWLEDGE

To solve the problems in this part, you must draw upon your knowledge of high school mathematics. The problems require you to use simple algebra and geometry along with arithmetic skills and reasoning power. Some questions can be answered in your head. Others will require the use of scratch paper. If you use scratch paper for your calculations, be sure to mark the letter of the correct answer on your answer sheet. Try these questions.

1. What is the value of x when $5x = 5 \times 4 \times 2 \times 0$?

  1-A 6
  1-B 8
  1-C 0
  1-D 1

  1. Ⓐ Ⓑ Ⓒ Ⓓ

1-C Any number multiplied by 0 equals 0. Since one multiplier on one side of the = sign is 0, the product on that side of the sign must be 0. The value on the other side of the = sign must also be 0.

$5x = 5 \times 4 \times 2 \times 0$
$5x = 40 \times 0$
$5x = 0$
$x = 0$

2. A square has an area of 49 sq. in. The number of inches in its perimeter is

  2-A 7
  2-B 28
  2-C 14
  2-D 98

  2. Ⓐ Ⓑ Ⓒ Ⓓ

2-B Area of a square $= s^2$

$49 = 7^2$
one side $= 7$ inches
$P = 4s$
$P = 4'' \times 7'' = 28$ inches

3. $(3 + 4)^3 =$

  3-A 21
  3-B 91
  3-C 343
  3-D 490

  3. Ⓐ Ⓑ Ⓒ Ⓓ

3-C First perform the operation within the parentheses. To cube a number, multiply it by itself two times.

$(3 + 4)^3 = (7)^3 = 7 \times 7 \times 7 = 343$

4. Change $\frac{5}{8}$ to a percent

  4-A 60%
  4-B $62\frac{1}{2}$%
  4-C 75%
  4-D 65%

  4. Ⓐ Ⓑ Ⓒ Ⓓ

4-B To change a fraction to a percent, multiply the fraction by 100; reduce, if possible; then add a percent sign. Thus,

$\frac{5}{8} \times 100 = 500/8 = 62\frac{1}{2}$%

5. If Mary is "x" years old now and her sister is 3 years younger, then 5 years from now her sister will be what age?

  5-A x + 5 years
  5-B x + 3 years
  5-C x + 2 years
  5-D   8 years

  5. Ⓐ Ⓑ Ⓒ Ⓓ

5-C Mary's age now $= x$
Her sister's age now $= x - 3$
In five years her sister's age will be
$x - 3 + 5 = x + 2$

DO NOT TURN THE PAGE UNTIL YOU ARE TOLD TO DO SO

MATHEMATICS KNOWLEDGE

TIME: 24 Minutes—25 Questions

1. A box contains 3 black, 4 red, and 5 white marbles. If one marble is to be picked at random, what is the probability that it will be red?

   1-A 1/5
   1-B 1/2
   1-C 1/3
   1-D 1/4

2.

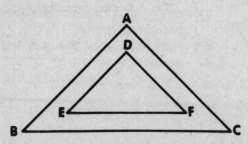

   In the figure above, the sides of △ABC are respectively parallel to the sides of triangle DEF. If the complement of A is 40°, then the complement of D is

   2-A 20°
   2-B 50°
   2-C 40°
   2-D 60°

3. In a class of 24 students there are 14 boys. What fractional part of the class is girls?

   3-A $\frac{4}{12}$
   3-B $\frac{6}{12}$
   3-C $\frac{7}{12}$
   3-D 2.5/6

4. If $A^2 + B^2 = A^2 + X^2$, then B equals

   4-A X
   4-B $X^2 - 2A^2$
   4-C A
   4-D $A^2 + X^2$

5. If $6 + x + y = 20$, and $x + y = k$, then $20 - k =$

   5-A 6
   5-B 0
   5-C 14
   5-D 20

6. What is the maximum number of books each $\frac{1}{4}$ inch thick that can be placed standing on a shelf 4 feet long?

   6-A 16
   6-B 192
   6-C 48
   6-D 96

7. $\sqrt{960}$ is a number between

   7-A 20 and 30
   7-B 60 and 70
   7-C 80 and 90
   7-D 30 and 40

8. $(6 + 8) - (21 - 4) =$

   8-A 14×17
   8-B $14 - 3$
   8-C $14 + 17$
   8-D $14 - 17$

9. 60 is what percent of $\frac{1}{2}$?

   9-A 25
   9-B 12,000
   9-C 1,000
   9-D 24,000

10. How many pints are equal to 2 gallons?

    10-A 8
    10-B 16

10-C 4
10-D 24

11. If x = y, find the value of 8 + 5(x − y).

  11-A 8 + 5x − 5y
  11-B 8 + 5xy
  11-C 13x − 13y
  11-D 8

12.

Triangle R is 3 times triangle S.
Triangle S is 3 times triangle T.
If triangle S = 1, what is the sum of the three triangles?

  12-A $2\frac{1}{3}$
  12-B $3\frac{1}{3}$
  12-C $4\frac{1}{3}$
  12-D 6

13. A boy has 5 pairs of slacks, and 3 sport jackets. How many different combinations can he wear?

  13-A 3
  13-B 5
  13-C 8
  13-D 15

14. Divide 1.672 by .08

  14-A 200.9
  14-B 20.9
  14-C 2.9
  14-D .29

15. If D = R × T, then R =

  15-A D × T
  15-B T ÷ R
  15-C T − D
  15-D D ÷ T

16. To find the radius of a circle whose circumference is 60 inches

  16-A multiply 60 by π
  16-B divide 60 by 2π
  16-C divide 30 by 2π
  16-D divide 60 by π and extract the square root of the result

17. A prime number is a number that can be divided only by itself and one. Which is *not* a prime number?

  17-A 23
  17-B 37
  17-C 87
  17-D 53

18. A is older than B. With the passage of time

  18-A the ratio of the ages of A and B remains unchanged
  18-B the ratio of the ages of A and B increases
  18-C the ratio of the ages of A and B decreases
  18-D the difference in their ages varies

19. The pages of a typewritten report are numbered from 1 to 100 by hand. How many times will it be necessary to write the number 5?

  19-A 10
  19-B 11
  19-C 12
  19-D 20

20. A desk was listed at $90.00 and was bought for $75.00. What was the rate of discount?

  20-A 15%
  20-B $16\frac{2}{3}$%
  20-C 18%
  20-D 20%

21. The sum of −24 and −3 is

  21-A 8
  21-B 21
  21-C −8
  21-D −27

22. The area of the figure shown can be determined by the formula

22-A $ac \div b$

22-B $\frac{1}{2}bh$

22-C $bc \div a$

22-D bh^2

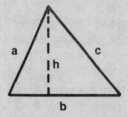

23. If psychological studies of college students show K percent to be emotionally unstable, the number of college students not emotionally unstable per one hundred college students is

23-A 100 minus K

23-B 1 minus K

23-C K minus 1

23-D 100 $\div$ K

24. A cog wheel having 8 cogs plays into another cog wheel having 24 cogs. When the small wheel has made 42 revolutions, how many has the larger wheel made?

24-A 14

24-B 16

24-C 20

24-D 10

25. Angle ABD is

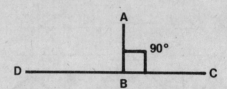

25-A a straight angle and contains 180°

25-B an acute angle and contains 35°

25-C a right angle and contains 90°

25-D a right angle and contains 45°

END OF PART 8

IF YOU FINISH BEFORE THE TIME IS UP, MAKE CERTAIN THAT YOU HAVE MARKED ALL YOUR ANSWERS ON THE ANSWER SHEET. THEN CHECK OVER YOUR WORK ON THIS PART ONLY. DO NOT GO BACK TO ANY PREVIOUS PART. DO NOT GO ON UNTIL YOU ARE TOLD TO DO SO.

MECHANICAL COMPREHENSION

Part 9 consists of questions about your understanding of general mechanical and physical principles. Your understanding of these principles will come from your own observations, from experience in working with mechanical devices and from your reading and school courses. Answer all the questions as best you can, marking the letter of your choice on your answer sheet. Try these questions.

1.

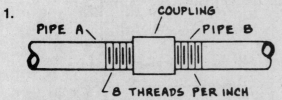

If both pipes A and B are free to move back and forth but are held so they cannot turn, and the coupling is turned 4 revolutions with a wrench, the overall length of the pipes and coupling will:

1-A   decrease $\frac{1}{2}''$
1-B   remain the same
1-C   increase or decrease 1″ depending upon the direction of turning
1-D   increase $\frac{1}{2}''$

1. Ⓐ Ⓑ Ⓒ Ⓓ

1-B If the coupling is turned, but the pipes are held firm so that they cannot turn, then the coupling will move along the length of one or the other pipes, but the overall length of the three pieces will remain the same.

2.

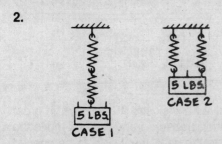

In the figure above, all 4 springs are identical. In Case 1 with the springs end to end, the stretch of each spring caused by the five lb. weight is

2-A $\frac{1}{2}$ as much as in Case 2
2-B   the same as in Case 2

2-C   twice as much as in Case 2
2-D   four times as much as in Case 2

2. Ⓐ Ⓑ Ⓒ Ⓓ

2-C In Case 2, each spring bears one-half of the weight of the five pound weight. Each spring in Case 2 is therefore stretched by two and one-half pounds. In Case 1, each spring bears a full five pound load. Each spring in Case 1 must be stretched twice as much as each spring in Case 2.

3.

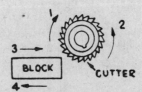

The figure above shows a cutter and a steel block. For proper cutting, they should move respectively in directions

3-A   1 and 4
3-B   2 and 3
3-C   1 and 3
3-D   2 and 4

3. Ⓐ Ⓑ Ⓒ Ⓓ

3-C Common sense should give you the answer to this question. In order for the cutter to cut the block, the two must be in contact. Obviously, the block must move in direction 3 in order to make contact with the cutter. For a cutter to cut, it must move in a direction so that the sharp edge of its teeth bites into the object being cut. In direction 1 the teeth will bite into the block. In direction 2 the back edge of the teeth would just slide off the block.

DO NOT TURN THE PAGE UNTIL YOU ARE TOLD TO DO SO

MECHANICAL COMPREHENSION

TIME: 19 Minutes—25 Questions

1.

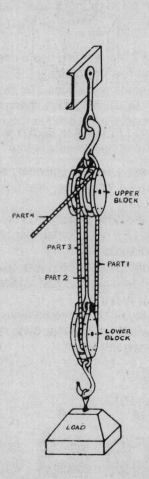

When a load is hoisted by means of the tackle shown above, the part that remains stationary is

1-A   the load
1-B   the lower block
1-C   the lower hook
1-D   the upper block

2.

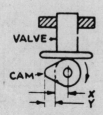

The figure above shows a cam and a valve. For each cam revolution, the vertical valve rise equals distance

2-A   Y
2-B   X
2-C   X plus Y
2-D   twice X

3.

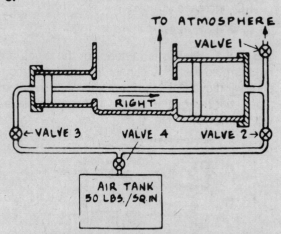

If all valves are closed at the start, in order to have air pressure from the tank move the pistons to the right, the valves to be opened are

3-A   2 and 4
3-B   2, 3, and 4
3-C   1 and 2
3-D   1, 3 and 4

4. Automatic operation of a sump pump is controlled by the

    4-A   pneumatic switch
    4-B   float
    4-C   foot valve
    4-D   centrifugal driving unit

5.

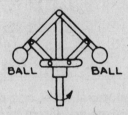

The figure above shows a governor on a rotating shaft. As the shaft speeds up, the governor balls will

    5-A   move down
    5-B   move upward and inward
    5-C   move upward
    5-D   move inward

6.

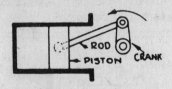

The figure above shows a crank and piston. The piston moves from mid-position to the extreme right if the crank

    6-A   makes $\frac{1}{2}$ turn
    6-B   makes a $\frac{3}{4}$ turn
    6-C   makes one turn
    6-D   makes $1\frac{1}{2}$ turns

7.

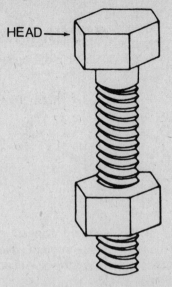

Referring to the figure above, which one of the following statements is true?

    7-A   If the nut is held stationary and the head turned clockwise, the bolt will move down.
    7-B   If the head of the bolt is held stationary and the nut is turned clockwise, the nut will move down.
    7-C   If the head of the bolt is held stationary and the nut is turned clockwise, the nut will move up.
    7-D   If the nut is held stationary and the head turned counter-clockwise, the bolt will move up.

8.

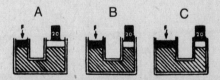

Which hydraulic press requires the least force to lift the weight?

    8-A   A
    8-B   B
    8-C   C
    8-D   All three require the same force.

9. The try-cocks of steam boilers are used to

9-A   act as safety valves
9-B   empty the boiler of water
9-C   test steam pressure in the boiler
9-D   find the height of water in the boiler

10.

In the case of the standard flanged pipe shown, the maximum angle through which it would be necessary to rotate the pipe in order to line up the holes is

10-A   22.5 degrees
10-B   45 degrees
10-C   30 degrees
10-D   60 degrees

11.

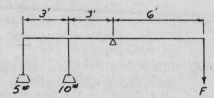

The force F needed to balance the lever is, in lbs., most nearly

11-A   7.5
11-B   12.5
11-C   10
11-D   15

12.

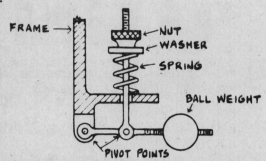

If the ball and spring mechanism are balanced in the position shown, the ball will move upward if

12-A   the nut is loosened
12-B   ball is moved away from the frame
12-C   the nut is loosened and the ball moved away from the frame
12-D   the nut is tightened

13.

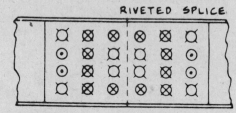

In the structural steel splice the different types of rivets are shown by different symbols. The number of different types of rivets is

13-A   6
13-B   4
13-C   5
13-D   3

14. The main purpose of baffle plates in a furnace is to

14-A   change the direction of flow of heated gases
14-B   retard the burning of gases
14-C   increase combustion rate of the fuel
14-D   prevent escape of flue gases through furnace openings

15.

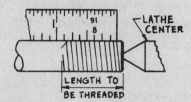

A very light cut (trace) is being measured as a check before cutting the thread on the lathe. The number of threads per inch shown is:

15-A   12
15-B   14
15-C   13
15-D   15

16. A characteristic of a rotary pump is

16-A a rapidly rotating impeller moves the liquid through the discharge piping

16-B two gears, meshed together and revolving in opposite directions, move the liquid to the discharge pipe

16-C valves are required on the discharge side of the pump

16-D it is usually operated at high speeds up to 3600 rpm

17.

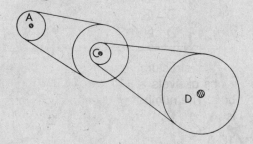

In the diagram above, pulley "A" drives a system of pulleys. Pulleys "B" and "C" are keyed to the same shaft. Use the following diameters in your computations: A = 1 inch; B = 2 inches; C = $\frac{1}{2}$ inch; and D = 4 inches. When pulley "A" runs at an RPM of 2000, pulley "D" will make

17-A 125 RPM

17-B 500 RPM

17-C 250 RPM

17-D 8000 RPM

18. Analysis of the flue gases shows that as the percentage of excess air

18-A increases, the percentage of CO_2 increases

18-B increases, the percentage of oxygen decreases

18-C increases, the percentage of CO_2 decreases

18-D decreases, the percentage of oxygen decreases

19. The symbol ℄ 1.5 on a drawing means:

19-A load center

19-B combination angle

19-C clearance limit

19-D center line

20.

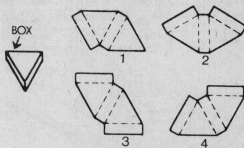

The flat sheet metal pattern which can be bent along the dotted lines to form the completely closed triangular box is

20-A 1

20-B 3

20-C 2

20-D 4

21. If the float of a flush tank leaks and fills with water, the most probable result will be

21-A no water in the tank

21-B ball cock will remain open

21-C water will flow over tank rim onto floor

21-D flush ball will not seat properly

22.

If the block on which the lever is resting is moved closer to the brick

22-A the brick will be easier to lift and will be lifted higher

22-B the brick will be harder to lift and will be lifted higher

22-C the brick will be easier to lift but will not be lifted as high

22-D the brick will be harder to lift and will not be lifted as high

23.

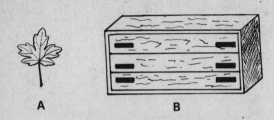

A   B

C   D

If all of these are the same temperature, which will feel coldest?

23-A   A
23-B   B
23-C   C
23-D   D

24.

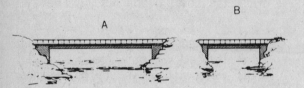

A   B

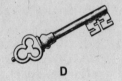

C

Which bridge is the strongest?

24-A   A
24-B   B
24-C   C
24-D   All are equally strong

25.

If both cyclists pedal at the same rate on the same surface, the cyclist in front will

25-A   travel at the same speed as the cyclist behind
25-B   move faster than the cyclist behind
25-C   move more slowly than the other cyclist
25-D   have greater difficulty steering

END OF PART 9

IF YOU FINISH BEFORE TIME IS UP, CHECK OVER YOUR WORK ON THIS PART ONLY. DO NOT RETURN TO ANY PREVIOUS PART. DO NOT GO ON UNTIL YOU ARE TOLD TO DO SO.

ELECTRONICS INFORMATION

The questions in this part test your knowledge and understanding of electricity, radio and electronics. To answer some of the questions all you need is common sense. Other questions can be answered on the basis of experience, courses and reading. Answer all the questions. Mark the letter of your answer on the answer sheet. Try these questions.

1. An electric light bulb operated at *more* than its rated voltage will result in a

  1-A longer life and dimmer light
  1-B longer life and brighter light
  1-C shorter life and brighter light
  1-D shorter life and dimmer light

  1. Ⓐ Ⓑ Ⓒ Ⓓ

1-C If an electric lightbulb is operated at more than its rated voltage, the extra surge of electricity will cause the bulb to burn more brightly. However, the same excess electrical force will weaken the filament and cause the bulb to burn out more quickly.

2. Light fixtures suspended from chains should be wired so that the

  2-A wires do not support the fixture
  2-B wires help support the fixture
  2-C chains have an insulated link
  2-D chain is not grounded to prevent short circuits

  2. Ⓐ Ⓑ Ⓒ Ⓓ

2-A The answer to this question is pure common sense. Electrical wires should serve only one purpose—to supply electricity. If electrical wires are required to support weight there is danger of breakage in the wires and of damage to the fixture itself caused by tension at the connections.

3. A piece of electrical equipment that serves the same purpose as a fuse is a

  3-A transformer
  3-B generator
  3-C switch
  3-D circuit breaker

  3. Ⓐ Ⓑ Ⓒ Ⓓ

3-D In new construction or in the upgrading of old electrical installations, a breaker box is substituted for a fuse box. The circuit breakers serve exactly the same function as a fuse. If a circuit becomes overloaded for any reason, the breaker will "trip" and break the circuit. If a circuit breaker "trips" the circuit must be checked. There is no possibility of a "tired" fuse. Use of a circuit breaker avoids the possibility of running out of fuses. It also makes it impossible to substitute a higher rated fuse or a copper penny and to thus lose the protection of the fuse.

4. A thermostat is caused to operate by changes in

  4-A air pressure
  4-B moisture
  4-C temperature
  4-D speed of rotation

  4. Ⓐ Ⓑ Ⓒ Ⓓ

4-C The action of a thermostat in opening and closing a circuit is directed by changes in temperature. *Thermo* comes from a Greek word meaning *heat*. It is the same root found in *thermometer*.

DO NOT TURN THE PAGE UNTIL YOU ARE TOLD TO DO SO

ELECTRONICS INFORMATION

TIME: 9 Minutes—20 Questions

1. In lights controlled by three-way switches, the switches should be treated and put in as

   1-A   flush switches
   1-B   single pole switches
   1-C   three double pole switches
   1-D   three pole switches

2. When working on live 600-volt equipment where rubber gloves might be damaged, an electrician should

   2-A   work without gloves
   2-B   carry a spare pair of rubber gloves
   2-C   reinforce the fingers of the rubber gloves with rubber tape
   2-D   wear leather gloves over the rubber gloves

3. A "mil" measures

   3-A   an eighth of an inch
   3-B   a millionth of an inch
   3-C   a thousandth of an inch
   3-D   a ten-thousandth of an inch

4.

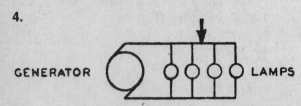

EACH LAMP TAKES 1 AMPERE

   The current in the wire at the point indicated by the arrow is

   4-A   1 ampere
   4-B   2 amperes
   4-C   3 amperes
   4-D   4 amperes

5. If a fuse of higher than the required current rating is used in an electrical circuit

   5-A   better protection will be afforded
   5-B   the fuse will blow more often since it carries more current
   5-C   serious damage may result to the circuit from overload
   5-D   maintenance of the large fuse will be higher

6. The electrical contacts in the tuner of a television set are usually plated with silver. Silver is used to

   6-A   avoid tarnish
   6-B   improve conductivity
   6-C   improve appearance
   6-D   avoid arcing

7. The following equipment is required for a "2-line return-call" electric bell circuit:

   7-A   2 bells, 2 metallic lines, 2 ordinary push buttons, and one set of batteries
   7-B   2 bells, 2 metallic lines, 2 return-call push buttons and 2 sets of batteries
   7-C   2 bells, 2 metallic lines, 2 return-call push buttons and one set of batteries
   7-D   2 bells, 2 metallic lines, one ordinary push button, one return-call push button and one set of batteries

8.

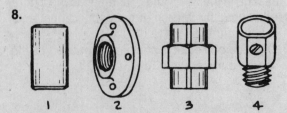

   1   2   3   4

The standard coupling for rigid electrical conduit is

8-A 1
8-B 2
8-C 3
8-D 4

9. Metal cabinets used for lighting circuits are grounded to

9-A eliminate electrolysis
9-B assure that the fuse in a defective circuit will blow
9-C reduce shock hazard
9-D simplify wiring

10. Low Potential is a trade term which refers to

10-A 700 volts
10-B 600 volts or less
10-C 1200 volts
10-D 900 volts

11. The purpose of having a rheostat in the field circuit of a d.c. shunt motor is to

11-A control the speed of the motor
11-B minimize the starting current
11-C limit the field current to a safe value
11-D reduce sparking at the brushes

12. A polarized plug generally has

12-A two parallel prongs of the same size
12-B prongs at an angle with one another
12-C magnetized prongs
12-D prongs marked plus and minus

13.

The reading of the kilowatt-hour meter is

13-A 7972
13-B 1786
13-C 2786
13-D 6872

14. Commutators are found on

14-A mercury rectifiers
14-B D.C. motors
14-C circuit breakers
14-D alternators

15. Neutral wire can be quickly recognized by the

15-A greenish color
15-B bluish color
15-C natural or whitish color
15-D black color

16. The term which is NOT applicable in describing the *construction* of a microphone is

16-A dynamic
16-B carbon
16-C crystal
16-D feedback

17.

The fitting shown is used in electrical construction to

17-A clamp two adjacent junction boxes together
17-B act as a ground clamp for the conduit system
17-C attach flexible metallic conduit to a junction box
17-D protect exposed wires where they pass through a wall

18. A good magnetic material is

18-A copper
18-B iron
18-C tin
18-D brass

19. Rosin is a material generally used

19-A in batteries
19-B for high voltage insulation
19-C as a dielectric
19-D as a soldering flux

20. The letters RIWP when applied to electrical
wire indicate the wire

    20-A has a solid conductor
    20-B has rubber insulation
    20-C is insulated with paper
    20-D has lead sheath

END OF EXAMINATION

**IF YOU FINISH BEFORE TIME IS UP, CHECK OVER YOUR WORK ON
THIS PART ONLY. DO NOT GO BACK TO ANY PREVIOUS PART.**

CORRECT ANSWERS—SECOND MODEL EXAM

PART 1—GENERAL SCIENCE

1. C	5. D	8. B	11. D	14. C	17. C	20. B	23. A
2. D	6. B	9. D	12. B	15. B	18. B	21. D	24. D
3. C	7. D	10. B	13. A	16. D	19. D	22. B	25. B
4. A							

PART 2—ARITHMETIC REASONING

1. A	5. D	9. B	13. B	17. B	21. B	25. B	28. D
2. B	6. A	10. A	14. C	18. D	22. A	26. A	29. D
3. C	7. D	11. C	15. A	19. B	23. D	27. B	30. B
4. D	8. C	12. A	16. C	20. A	24. C		

PART 3—WORD KNOWLEDGE

1. B	6. C	11. A	16. C	20. A	24. D	28. C	32. A
2. A	7. B	12. D	17. B	21. D	25. A	29. A	33. D
3. C	8. A	13. C	18. C	22. C	26. C	30. C	34. D
4. D	9. B	14. A	19. B	23. B	27. D	31. B	35. D
5. D	10. D	15. D					

PART 4—PARAGRAPH COMPREHENSION

1. D	3. D	5. D	7. B	9. B	11. D	13. B	15. C
2. B	4. B	6. C	8. C	10. B	12. D	14. A	

PART 5—NUMERICAL OPERATIONS

1. B	8. B	15. D	21. B	27. C	33. D	39. B	45. C
2. C	9. C	16. B	22. B	28. A	34. A	40. D	46. B
3. B	10. A	17. D	23. C	29. D	35. C	41. B	47. D
4. D	11. C	18. A	24. D	30. D	36. A	42. C	48. A
5. C	12. B	19. C	25. D	31. C	37. C	43. A	49. D
6. B	13. A	20. B	26. A	32. B	38. C	44. D	50. D
7. A	14. D						

PART 6—CODING SPEED

1. C	12. C	23. E	34. A	45. E	55. A	65. D	75. E
2. E	13. B	24. C	35. B	46. A	56. C	66. C	76. D
3. D	14. E	25. E	36. A	47. C	57. A	67. C	77. A
4. D	15. C	26. B	37. D	48. C	58. E	68. D	78. B
5. A	16. B	27. D	38. B	49. D	59. D	69. A	79. E
6. B	17. D	28. E	39. D	50. B	60. E	70. D	80. A
7. D	18. E	29. B	40. C	51. A	61. E	71. E	81. A
8. A	19. A	30. A	41. A	52. B	62. C	72. A	82. E
9. A	20. B	31. E	42. E	53. D	63. B	73. C	83. C
10. C	21. C	32. C	43. C	54. E	64. E	74. D	84. B
11. E	22. D	33. E	44. D				

PART 7—AUTO & SHOP INFORMATION

1. C	5. B	8. D	11. C	14. D	17. A	20. C	23. D
2. D	6. A	9. B	12. A	15. C	18. C	21. D	24. B
3. B	7. C	10. A	13. A	16. B	19. D	22. C	25. A
4. C							

PART 8—MATHEMATICS KNOWLEDGE

1. C	5. A	8. D	11. D	14. B	17. C	20. B	23. A
2. C	6. B	9. B	12. C	15. D	18. C	21. D	24. A
3. D	7. D	10. B	13. D	16. B	19. D	22. B	25. C
4. A							

PART 9—MECHANICAL COMPREHENSION

1. D	5. C	8. A	11. C	14. A	17. A	20. B	23. D
2. A	6. B	9. D	12. D	15. C	18. C	21. B	24. C
3. D	7. C	10. A	13. B	16. B	19. D	22. C	25. B
4. B							

PART 10—ELECTRONICS INFORMATION

1. B	4. B	7. B	10. B	13. D	15. C	17. C	19. D
2. D	5. C	8. A	11. A	14. B	16. D	18. B	20. B
3. C	6. B	9. C	12. B				

SCORE SHEET—SECOND MODEL EXAM

PART	NUMBER CORRECT		NUMBER OF QUESTIONS	
GENERAL SCIENCE	_____ ÷ 25 =	_____	× 100 =	_____%
ARITHMETIC REASONING	_____ ÷ 30 =	_____	× 100 =	_____%
WORD KNOWLEDGE	_____ ÷ 35 =	_____	× 100 =	_____%
PARAGRAPH COMPREHENSION	_____ ÷ 15 =	_____	× 100 =	_____%
NUMERICAL OPERATIONS	_____ ÷ 50 =	_____	× 100 =	_____%
CODING SPEED	_____ ÷ 84 =	_____	× 100 =	_____%
AUTO & SHOP INFORMATION	_____ ÷ 25 =	_____	× 100 =	_____%
MATHEMATICS KNOWLEDGE	_____ ÷ 25 =	_____	× 100 =	_____%
MECHANICAL COMPREHENSION	_____ ÷ 25 =	_____	× 100 =	_____%
ELECTRONICS INFORMATION	_____ ÷ 20 =	_____	× 100 =	_____%
TOTAL	_____ ÷ 334 =	_____	× 100 =	_____%

PROGRESS CHART

	Exam I	Exam II
GENERAL SCIENCE	%	%
ARITHMETIC REASONING	%	%
WORD KNOWLEDGE	%	%
PARAGRAPH COMPREHENSION	%	%
NUMERICAL OPERATIONS	%	%
CODING SPEED	%	%
AUTO & SHOP INFORMATION	%	%
MATHEMATICS KNOWLEDGE	%	%
MECHANICAL COMPREHENSION	%	%
ELECTRONICS INFORMATION	%	%
TOTAL	%	%

THIRD MODEL EXAM

ANSWER SHEET—THIRD MODEL EXAM

PART 1—GENERAL SCIENCE

1 Ⓐ Ⓑ Ⓒ Ⓓ   6 Ⓐ Ⓑ Ⓒ Ⓓ   11 Ⓐ Ⓑ Ⓒ Ⓓ   16 Ⓐ Ⓑ Ⓒ Ⓓ   21 Ⓐ Ⓑ Ⓒ Ⓓ
2 Ⓐ Ⓑ Ⓒ Ⓓ   7 Ⓐ Ⓑ Ⓒ Ⓓ   12 Ⓐ Ⓑ Ⓒ Ⓓ   17 Ⓐ Ⓑ Ⓒ Ⓓ   22 Ⓐ Ⓑ Ⓒ Ⓓ
3 Ⓐ Ⓑ Ⓒ Ⓓ   8 Ⓐ Ⓑ Ⓒ Ⓓ   13 Ⓐ Ⓑ Ⓒ Ⓓ   18 Ⓐ Ⓑ Ⓒ Ⓓ   23 Ⓐ Ⓑ Ⓒ Ⓓ
4 Ⓐ Ⓑ Ⓒ Ⓓ   9 Ⓐ Ⓑ Ⓒ Ⓓ   14 Ⓐ Ⓑ Ⓒ Ⓓ   19 Ⓐ Ⓑ Ⓒ Ⓓ   24 Ⓐ Ⓑ Ⓒ Ⓓ
5 Ⓐ Ⓑ Ⓒ Ⓓ   10 Ⓐ Ⓑ Ⓒ Ⓓ   15 Ⓐ Ⓑ Ⓒ Ⓓ   20 Ⓐ Ⓑ Ⓒ Ⓓ   25 Ⓐ Ⓑ Ⓒ Ⓓ

PART 2—ARITHMETIC REASONING

1 Ⓐ Ⓑ Ⓒ Ⓓ   7 Ⓐ Ⓑ Ⓒ Ⓓ   13 Ⓐ Ⓑ Ⓒ Ⓓ   19 Ⓐ Ⓑ Ⓒ Ⓓ   25 Ⓐ Ⓑ Ⓒ Ⓓ
2 Ⓐ Ⓑ Ⓒ Ⓓ   8 Ⓐ Ⓑ Ⓒ Ⓓ   14 Ⓐ Ⓑ Ⓒ Ⓓ   20 Ⓐ Ⓑ Ⓒ Ⓓ   26 Ⓐ Ⓑ Ⓒ Ⓓ
3 Ⓐ Ⓑ Ⓒ Ⓓ   9 Ⓐ Ⓑ Ⓒ Ⓓ   15 Ⓐ Ⓑ Ⓒ Ⓓ   21 Ⓐ Ⓑ Ⓒ Ⓓ   27 Ⓐ Ⓑ Ⓒ Ⓓ
4 Ⓐ Ⓑ Ⓒ Ⓓ   10 Ⓐ Ⓑ Ⓒ Ⓓ   16 Ⓐ Ⓑ Ⓒ Ⓓ   22 Ⓐ Ⓑ Ⓒ Ⓓ   28 Ⓐ Ⓑ Ⓒ Ⓓ
5 Ⓐ Ⓑ Ⓒ Ⓓ   11 Ⓐ Ⓑ Ⓒ Ⓓ   17 Ⓐ Ⓑ Ⓒ Ⓓ   23 Ⓐ Ⓑ Ⓒ Ⓓ   29 Ⓐ Ⓑ Ⓒ Ⓓ
6 Ⓐ Ⓑ Ⓒ Ⓓ   12 Ⓐ Ⓑ Ⓒ Ⓓ   18 Ⓐ Ⓑ Ⓒ Ⓓ   24 Ⓐ Ⓑ Ⓒ Ⓓ   30 Ⓐ Ⓑ Ⓒ Ⓓ

PART 3—WORD KNOWLEDGE

1 Ⓐ Ⓑ Ⓒ Ⓓ   8 Ⓐ Ⓑ Ⓒ Ⓓ   15 Ⓐ Ⓑ Ⓒ Ⓓ   22 Ⓐ Ⓑ Ⓒ Ⓓ   29 Ⓐ Ⓑ Ⓒ Ⓓ
2 Ⓐ Ⓑ Ⓒ Ⓓ   9 Ⓐ Ⓑ Ⓒ Ⓓ   16 Ⓐ Ⓑ Ⓒ Ⓓ   23 Ⓐ Ⓑ Ⓒ Ⓓ   30 Ⓐ Ⓑ Ⓒ Ⓓ
3 Ⓐ Ⓑ Ⓒ Ⓓ   10 Ⓐ Ⓑ Ⓒ Ⓓ   17 Ⓐ Ⓑ Ⓒ Ⓓ   24 Ⓐ Ⓑ Ⓒ Ⓓ   31 Ⓐ Ⓑ Ⓒ Ⓓ
4 Ⓐ Ⓑ Ⓒ Ⓓ   11 Ⓐ Ⓑ Ⓒ Ⓓ   18 Ⓐ Ⓑ Ⓒ Ⓓ   25 Ⓐ Ⓑ Ⓒ Ⓓ   32 Ⓐ Ⓑ Ⓒ Ⓓ
5 Ⓐ Ⓑ Ⓒ Ⓓ   12 Ⓐ Ⓑ Ⓒ Ⓓ   19 Ⓐ Ⓑ Ⓒ Ⓓ   26 Ⓐ Ⓑ Ⓒ Ⓓ   33 Ⓐ Ⓑ Ⓒ Ⓓ
6 Ⓐ Ⓑ Ⓒ Ⓓ   13 Ⓐ Ⓑ Ⓒ Ⓓ   20 Ⓐ Ⓑ Ⓒ Ⓓ   27 Ⓐ Ⓑ Ⓒ Ⓓ   34 Ⓐ Ⓑ Ⓒ Ⓓ
7 Ⓐ Ⓑ Ⓒ Ⓓ   14 Ⓐ Ⓑ Ⓒ Ⓓ   21 Ⓐ Ⓑ Ⓒ Ⓓ   28 Ⓐ Ⓑ Ⓒ Ⓓ   35 Ⓐ Ⓑ Ⓒ Ⓓ

PART 4—PARAGRAPH COMPREHENSION

1 Ⓐ Ⓑ Ⓒ Ⓓ   5 Ⓐ Ⓑ Ⓒ Ⓓ   9 Ⓐ Ⓑ Ⓒ Ⓓ   13 Ⓐ Ⓑ Ⓒ Ⓓ
2 Ⓐ Ⓑ Ⓒ Ⓓ   6 Ⓐ Ⓑ Ⓒ Ⓓ   10 Ⓐ Ⓑ Ⓒ Ⓓ   14 Ⓐ Ⓑ Ⓒ Ⓓ
3 Ⓐ Ⓑ Ⓒ Ⓓ   7 Ⓐ Ⓑ Ⓒ Ⓓ   11 Ⓐ Ⓑ Ⓒ Ⓓ   15 Ⓐ Ⓑ Ⓒ Ⓓ
4 Ⓐ Ⓑ Ⓒ Ⓓ   8 Ⓐ Ⓑ Ⓒ Ⓓ   12 Ⓐ Ⓑ Ⓒ Ⓓ

PART 5–NUMERICAL OPERATIONS

1 Ⓐ Ⓑ Ⓒ Ⓓ	11 Ⓐ Ⓑ Ⓒ Ⓓ	21 Ⓐ Ⓑ Ⓒ Ⓓ	31 Ⓐ Ⓑ Ⓒ Ⓓ	41 Ⓐ Ⓑ Ⓒ Ⓓ
2 Ⓐ Ⓑ Ⓒ Ⓓ	12 Ⓐ Ⓑ Ⓒ Ⓓ	22 Ⓐ Ⓑ Ⓒ Ⓓ	32 Ⓐ Ⓑ Ⓒ Ⓓ	42 Ⓐ Ⓑ Ⓒ Ⓓ
3 Ⓐ Ⓑ Ⓒ Ⓓ	13 Ⓐ Ⓑ Ⓒ Ⓓ	23 Ⓐ Ⓑ Ⓒ Ⓓ	33 Ⓐ Ⓑ Ⓒ Ⓓ	43 Ⓐ Ⓑ Ⓒ Ⓓ
4 Ⓐ Ⓑ Ⓒ Ⓓ	14 Ⓐ Ⓑ Ⓒ Ⓓ	24 Ⓐ Ⓑ Ⓒ Ⓓ	34 Ⓐ Ⓑ Ⓒ Ⓓ	44 Ⓐ Ⓑ Ⓒ Ⓓ
5 Ⓐ Ⓑ Ⓒ Ⓓ	15 Ⓐ Ⓑ Ⓒ Ⓓ	25 Ⓐ Ⓑ Ⓒ Ⓓ	35 Ⓐ Ⓑ Ⓒ Ⓓ	45 Ⓐ Ⓑ Ⓒ Ⓓ
6 Ⓐ Ⓑ Ⓒ Ⓓ	16 Ⓐ Ⓑ Ⓒ Ⓓ	26 Ⓐ Ⓑ Ⓒ Ⓓ	36 Ⓐ Ⓑ Ⓒ Ⓓ	46 Ⓐ Ⓑ Ⓒ Ⓓ
7 Ⓐ Ⓑ Ⓒ Ⓓ	17 Ⓐ Ⓑ Ⓒ Ⓓ	27 Ⓐ Ⓑ Ⓒ Ⓓ	37 Ⓐ Ⓑ Ⓒ Ⓓ	47 Ⓐ Ⓑ Ⓒ Ⓓ
8 Ⓐ Ⓑ Ⓒ Ⓓ	18 Ⓐ Ⓑ Ⓒ Ⓓ	28 Ⓐ Ⓑ Ⓒ Ⓓ	38 Ⓐ Ⓑ Ⓒ Ⓓ	48 Ⓐ Ⓑ Ⓒ Ⓓ
9 Ⓐ Ⓑ Ⓒ Ⓓ	19 Ⓐ Ⓑ Ⓒ Ⓓ	29 Ⓐ Ⓑ Ⓒ Ⓓ	39 Ⓐ Ⓑ Ⓒ Ⓓ	49 Ⓐ Ⓑ Ⓒ Ⓓ
10 Ⓐ Ⓑ Ⓒ Ⓓ	20 Ⓐ Ⓑ Ⓒ Ⓓ	30 Ⓐ Ⓑ Ⓒ Ⓓ	40 Ⓐ Ⓑ Ⓒ Ⓓ	50 Ⓐ Ⓑ Ⓒ Ⓓ

PART 6—CODING SPEED

1 Ⓐ Ⓑ Ⓒ Ⓓ Ⓔ	15 Ⓐ Ⓑ Ⓒ Ⓓ Ⓔ	29 Ⓐ Ⓑ Ⓒ Ⓓ Ⓔ	43 Ⓐ Ⓑ Ⓒ Ⓓ Ⓔ	57 Ⓐ Ⓑ Ⓒ Ⓓ Ⓔ	71 Ⓐ Ⓑ Ⓒ Ⓓ Ⓔ
2 Ⓐ Ⓑ Ⓒ Ⓓ Ⓔ	16 Ⓐ Ⓑ Ⓒ Ⓓ Ⓔ	30 Ⓐ Ⓑ Ⓒ Ⓓ Ⓔ	44 Ⓐ Ⓑ Ⓒ Ⓓ Ⓔ	58 Ⓐ Ⓑ Ⓒ Ⓓ Ⓔ	72 Ⓐ Ⓑ Ⓒ Ⓓ Ⓔ
3 Ⓐ Ⓑ Ⓒ Ⓓ Ⓔ	17 Ⓐ Ⓑ Ⓒ Ⓓ Ⓔ	31 Ⓐ Ⓑ Ⓒ Ⓓ Ⓔ	45 Ⓐ Ⓑ Ⓒ Ⓓ Ⓔ	59 Ⓐ Ⓑ Ⓒ Ⓓ Ⓔ	73 Ⓐ Ⓑ Ⓒ Ⓓ Ⓔ
4 Ⓐ Ⓑ Ⓒ Ⓓ Ⓔ	18 Ⓐ Ⓑ Ⓒ Ⓓ Ⓔ	32 Ⓐ Ⓑ Ⓒ Ⓓ Ⓔ	46 Ⓐ Ⓑ Ⓒ Ⓓ Ⓔ	60 Ⓐ Ⓑ Ⓒ Ⓓ Ⓔ	74 Ⓐ Ⓑ Ⓒ Ⓓ Ⓔ
5 Ⓐ Ⓑ Ⓒ Ⓓ Ⓔ	19 Ⓐ Ⓑ Ⓒ Ⓓ Ⓔ	33 Ⓐ Ⓑ Ⓒ Ⓓ Ⓔ	47 Ⓐ Ⓑ Ⓒ Ⓓ Ⓔ	61 Ⓐ Ⓑ Ⓒ Ⓓ Ⓔ	75 Ⓐ Ⓑ Ⓒ Ⓓ Ⓔ
6 Ⓐ Ⓑ Ⓒ Ⓓ Ⓔ	20 Ⓐ Ⓑ Ⓒ Ⓓ Ⓔ	34 Ⓐ Ⓑ Ⓒ Ⓓ Ⓔ	48 Ⓐ Ⓑ Ⓒ Ⓓ Ⓔ	62 Ⓐ Ⓑ Ⓒ Ⓓ Ⓔ	76 Ⓐ Ⓑ Ⓒ Ⓓ Ⓔ
7 Ⓐ Ⓑ Ⓒ Ⓓ Ⓔ	21 Ⓐ Ⓑ Ⓒ Ⓓ Ⓔ	35 Ⓐ Ⓑ Ⓒ Ⓓ Ⓔ	49 Ⓐ Ⓑ Ⓒ Ⓓ Ⓔ	63 Ⓐ Ⓑ Ⓒ Ⓓ Ⓔ	77 Ⓐ Ⓑ Ⓒ Ⓓ Ⓔ
8 Ⓐ Ⓑ Ⓒ Ⓓ Ⓔ	22 Ⓐ Ⓑ Ⓒ Ⓓ Ⓔ	36 Ⓐ Ⓑ Ⓒ Ⓓ Ⓔ	50 Ⓐ Ⓑ Ⓒ Ⓓ Ⓔ	64 Ⓐ Ⓑ Ⓒ Ⓓ Ⓔ	78 Ⓐ Ⓑ Ⓒ Ⓓ Ⓔ
9 Ⓐ Ⓑ Ⓒ Ⓓ Ⓔ	23 Ⓐ Ⓑ Ⓒ Ⓓ Ⓔ	37 Ⓐ Ⓑ Ⓒ Ⓓ Ⓔ	51 Ⓐ Ⓑ Ⓒ Ⓓ Ⓔ	65 Ⓐ Ⓑ Ⓒ Ⓓ Ⓔ	79 Ⓐ Ⓑ Ⓒ Ⓓ Ⓔ
10 Ⓐ Ⓑ Ⓒ Ⓓ Ⓔ	24 Ⓐ Ⓑ Ⓒ Ⓓ Ⓔ	38 Ⓐ Ⓑ Ⓒ Ⓓ Ⓔ	52 Ⓐ Ⓑ Ⓒ Ⓓ Ⓔ	66 Ⓐ Ⓑ Ⓒ Ⓓ Ⓔ	80 Ⓐ Ⓑ Ⓒ Ⓓ Ⓔ
11 Ⓐ Ⓑ Ⓒ Ⓓ Ⓔ	25 Ⓐ Ⓑ Ⓒ Ⓓ Ⓔ	39 Ⓐ Ⓑ Ⓒ Ⓓ Ⓔ	53 Ⓐ Ⓑ Ⓒ Ⓓ Ⓔ	67 Ⓐ Ⓑ Ⓒ Ⓓ Ⓔ	81 Ⓐ Ⓑ Ⓒ Ⓓ Ⓔ
12 Ⓐ Ⓑ Ⓒ Ⓓ Ⓔ	26 Ⓐ Ⓑ Ⓒ Ⓓ Ⓔ	40 Ⓐ Ⓑ Ⓒ Ⓓ Ⓔ	54 Ⓐ Ⓑ Ⓒ Ⓓ Ⓔ	68 Ⓐ Ⓑ Ⓒ Ⓓ Ⓔ	82 Ⓐ Ⓑ Ⓒ Ⓓ Ⓔ
13 Ⓐ Ⓑ Ⓒ Ⓓ Ⓔ	27 Ⓐ Ⓑ Ⓒ Ⓓ Ⓔ	41 Ⓐ Ⓑ Ⓒ Ⓓ Ⓔ	55 Ⓐ Ⓑ Ⓒ Ⓓ Ⓔ	69 Ⓐ Ⓑ Ⓒ Ⓓ Ⓔ	83 Ⓐ Ⓑ Ⓒ Ⓓ Ⓔ
14 Ⓐ Ⓑ Ⓒ Ⓓ Ⓔ	28 Ⓐ Ⓑ Ⓒ Ⓓ Ⓔ	42 Ⓐ Ⓑ Ⓒ Ⓓ Ⓔ	56 Ⓐ Ⓑ Ⓒ Ⓓ Ⓔ	70 Ⓐ Ⓑ Ⓒ Ⓓ Ⓔ	84 Ⓐ Ⓑ Ⓒ Ⓓ Ⓔ

PART 7—AUTO & SHOP INFORMATION

1 Ⓐ Ⓑ Ⓒ Ⓓ	6 Ⓐ Ⓑ Ⓒ Ⓓ	11 Ⓐ Ⓑ Ⓒ Ⓓ	16 Ⓐ Ⓑ Ⓒ Ⓓ	21 Ⓐ Ⓑ Ⓒ Ⓓ
2 Ⓐ Ⓑ Ⓒ Ⓓ	7 Ⓐ Ⓑ Ⓒ Ⓓ	12 Ⓐ Ⓑ Ⓒ Ⓓ	17 Ⓐ Ⓑ Ⓒ Ⓓ	22 Ⓐ Ⓑ Ⓒ Ⓓ
3 Ⓐ Ⓑ Ⓒ Ⓓ	8 Ⓐ Ⓑ Ⓒ Ⓓ	13 Ⓐ Ⓑ Ⓒ Ⓓ	18 Ⓐ Ⓑ Ⓒ Ⓓ	23 Ⓐ Ⓑ Ⓒ Ⓓ
4 Ⓐ Ⓑ Ⓒ Ⓓ	9 Ⓐ Ⓑ Ⓒ Ⓓ	14 Ⓐ Ⓑ Ⓒ Ⓓ	19 Ⓐ Ⓑ Ⓒ Ⓓ	24 Ⓐ Ⓑ Ⓒ Ⓓ
5 Ⓐ Ⓑ Ⓒ Ⓓ	10 Ⓐ Ⓑ Ⓒ Ⓓ	15 Ⓐ Ⓑ Ⓒ Ⓓ	20 Ⓐ Ⓑ Ⓒ Ⓓ	25 Ⓐ Ⓑ Ⓒ Ⓓ

PART 8—MATHEMATICS KNOWLEDGE

1 Ⓐ Ⓑ Ⓒ Ⓓ	6 Ⓐ Ⓑ Ⓒ Ⓓ	11 Ⓐ Ⓑ Ⓒ Ⓓ	16 Ⓐ Ⓑ Ⓒ Ⓓ	21 Ⓐ Ⓑ Ⓒ Ⓓ
2 Ⓐ Ⓑ Ⓒ Ⓓ	7 Ⓐ Ⓑ Ⓒ Ⓓ	12 Ⓐ Ⓑ Ⓒ Ⓓ	17 Ⓐ Ⓑ Ⓒ Ⓓ	22 Ⓐ Ⓑ Ⓒ Ⓓ
3 Ⓐ Ⓑ Ⓒ Ⓓ	8 Ⓐ Ⓑ Ⓒ Ⓓ	13 Ⓐ Ⓑ Ⓒ Ⓓ	18 Ⓐ Ⓑ Ⓒ Ⓓ	23 Ⓐ Ⓑ Ⓒ Ⓓ
4 Ⓐ Ⓑ Ⓒ Ⓓ	9 Ⓐ Ⓑ Ⓒ Ⓓ	14 Ⓐ Ⓑ Ⓒ Ⓓ	19 Ⓐ Ⓑ Ⓒ Ⓓ	24 Ⓐ Ⓑ Ⓒ Ⓓ
5 Ⓐ Ⓑ Ⓒ Ⓓ	10 Ⓐ Ⓑ Ⓒ Ⓓ	15 Ⓐ Ⓑ Ⓒ Ⓓ	20 Ⓐ Ⓑ Ⓒ Ⓓ	25 Ⓐ Ⓑ Ⓒ Ⓓ

PART 9—MECHANICAL COMPREHENSION

1 Ⓐ Ⓑ Ⓒ Ⓓ	6 Ⓐ Ⓑ Ⓒ Ⓓ	11 Ⓐ Ⓑ Ⓒ Ⓓ	16 Ⓐ Ⓑ Ⓒ Ⓓ	21 Ⓐ Ⓑ Ⓒ Ⓓ
2 Ⓐ Ⓑ Ⓒ Ⓓ	7 Ⓐ Ⓑ Ⓒ Ⓓ	12 Ⓐ Ⓑ Ⓒ Ⓓ	17 Ⓐ Ⓑ Ⓒ Ⓓ	22 Ⓐ Ⓑ Ⓒ Ⓓ
3 Ⓐ Ⓑ Ⓒ Ⓓ	8 Ⓐ Ⓑ Ⓒ Ⓓ	13 Ⓐ Ⓑ Ⓒ Ⓓ	18 Ⓐ Ⓑ Ⓒ Ⓓ	23 Ⓐ Ⓑ Ⓒ Ⓓ
4 Ⓐ Ⓑ Ⓒ Ⓓ	9 Ⓐ Ⓑ Ⓒ Ⓓ	14 Ⓐ Ⓑ Ⓒ Ⓓ	19 Ⓐ Ⓑ Ⓒ Ⓓ	24 Ⓐ Ⓑ Ⓒ Ⓓ
5 Ⓐ Ⓑ Ⓒ Ⓓ	10 Ⓐ Ⓑ Ⓒ Ⓓ	15 Ⓐ Ⓑ Ⓒ Ⓓ	20 Ⓐ Ⓑ Ⓒ Ⓓ	25 Ⓐ Ⓑ Ⓒ Ⓓ

PART 10—ELECTRONICS INFORMATION

1 Ⓐ Ⓑ Ⓒ Ⓓ	6 Ⓐ Ⓑ Ⓒ Ⓓ	11 Ⓐ Ⓑ Ⓒ Ⓓ	16 Ⓐ Ⓑ Ⓒ Ⓓ
2 Ⓐ Ⓑ Ⓒ Ⓓ	7 Ⓐ Ⓑ Ⓒ Ⓓ	12 Ⓐ Ⓑ Ⓒ Ⓓ	17 Ⓐ Ⓑ Ⓒ Ⓓ
3 Ⓐ Ⓑ Ⓒ Ⓓ	8 Ⓐ Ⓑ Ⓒ Ⓓ	13 Ⓐ Ⓑ Ⓒ Ⓓ	18 Ⓐ Ⓑ Ⓒ Ⓓ
4 Ⓐ Ⓑ Ⓒ Ⓓ	9 Ⓐ Ⓑ Ⓒ Ⓓ	14 Ⓐ Ⓑ Ⓒ Ⓓ	19 Ⓐ Ⓑ Ⓒ Ⓓ
5 Ⓐ Ⓑ Ⓒ Ⓓ	10 Ⓐ Ⓑ Ⓒ Ⓓ	15 Ⓐ Ⓑ Ⓒ Ⓓ	20 Ⓐ Ⓑ Ⓒ Ⓓ

PART 1

GENERAL SCIENCE

The general science part of your examination asks questions based upon the science you learned in high school. For each question there are four possible answers. Only one answer is correct. Choose the answer that you think is correct and mark the corresponding space on your answer sheet. Try these questions.

1. Of the following, the *most important* function performed for man by the bee is to

1-A produce beeswax
1-B pollinate plants
1-C produce honey
1-D destroy harmful insects

1. Ⓐ Ⓑ Ⓒ Ⓓ

1-B POLLINATE PLANTS is the correct answer. The words "most important" are key words in choosing the answer to this question. Bees do produce beeswax (A) and honey (C), both of which are useful to man, but their most important function is pollinating plants. Bees destroy other insects (D) only if those insects are threatening the nest.

2. Cholesterol is

2-A a basic part of bone structure
2-B a carbohydrate
2-C a substance found in blood
2-D the cause of colitis .

2. Ⓐ Ⓑ Ⓒ Ⓓ

2-C A SUBSTANCE FOUND IN BLOOD is the correct answer. Cholesterol is an alcohol formed in the body. While cholesterol is important to the proper function of nerves, excess amounts in the blood may cause the clogging of arteries and lead to heart attacks. In some individuals dietary fat contributes to the buildup of cholesterol in the blood. The substance basic to bones (A) is calcium. Cholesterol is not a carbohydrate (B), nor is it known to be a cause of colitis (D), inflamation of the large intestine.

3. A blood transfusion may be very dangerous if the person receiving the transfusion

3-A is unconscious
3-B has hemophilia
3-C has had hepatitis
3-D has a blood type different from that of the donor

3. Ⓐ Ⓑ Ⓒ Ⓓ

3-D BLOOD TRANSFUSED FROM ONE PERSON TO ANOTHER MUST BE OF THE SAME GROUP AND TYPE. If the blood is not accurately matched, the recipient may have a very drastic reaction which may even lead to death. There is no harm in giving a transfusion to an unconscious (A) person. A person who has hemophilia, bleeder's disease, (B) is likely to need blood badly. The hepatitis virus (C) remains in the blood even when the person has recovered, so it is dangerous to *give* the blood of a person who has had hepatitis, but a person who has had hepatitis may safely *receive* a transfusion.

DO NOT TURN THE PAGE UNTIL YOU ARE TOLD TO DO SO

GENERAL SCIENCE

TIME: 11 Minutes—25 Questions

1. Which one of the following is *not* a fruit?

   1-A potato
   1-B tomato
   1-C cucumber
   1-D green pepper

2. The hammer, anvil, and stirrup bones lie in the

   2-A knee
   2-B hip
   2-C ear
   2-D elbow

3. Of the following, a condition *not* associated with heavy cigarette smoking is

   3-A shorter life span
   3-B slowing of the heartbeat
   3-C cancer of the lung
   3-D heart disease

4. You are most likely to develop hypothermia when

   4-A it is very hot and you have nothing to drink
   4-B you are bitten by a rabid dog
   4-C you fall asleep with a thermometer in your mouth
   4-D it is very cold and your clothes are wet

5. If you are caught away from home during a thunderstorm, the safest place to be is

   5-A in a car
   5-B under a tree
   5-C in an open field
   5-D at the top of a small hill

6. During what season is hail most likely to occur during thunderstorms?

   6-A fall
   6-B spring
   6-C winter
   6-D summer

7. Of the following, a human blood disease which has been definitely shown to be due to a hereditary factor or factors is

   7-A pernicious anemia
   7-B polyscythemia
   7-C sickle cell anemia
   7-D leukemia

8. The number of degrees on the Fahrenheit thermometer between the freezing point and the boiling point of water is

   8-A 100 degrees
   8-B 212 degrees
   8-C 180 degrees
   8-D 273 degrees

9. The time that it takes for the earth to complete a 60 degree rotation is

   9-A 1 hour
   9-B 6 hours
   9-C 4 hours
   9-D 24 hours

10. Of the following, the gas which is needed for burning is

    10-A carbon dioxide
    10-B nitrogen
    10-C oxygen
    10-D argon

11. Of the following, the only safe blood transfusion would be

   11-A Group A blood into a Group O person
   11-B Group B blood into a Group A person
   11-C Group O blood into a Group AB person
   11-D Group AB blood into a Group B person

12. Of the following, the statement that best describes a "high" on a weather map is

   12-A the air extends farther up than normal
   12-B the air pressure is greater than normal
   12-C the air temperature is higher than normal
   12-D the air moves faster than normal

13. If all pork were thoroughly cooked before being eaten, there would be very few cases of

   13-A cancer
   13-B hookworm
   13-C trichinosis
   13-D ringworm

14. Narcotics may be dangerous if used without supervision, but they are useful in medicine because they

   14-A increase production of red blood cells
   14-B kill bacteria
   14-C relieve pain
   14-D stimulate the heart

15. The primary reason why fungi are often found growing in abundance deep in the forest is that there

   15-A it is cooler
   15-B it is warmer
   15-C they have little exposure to sunlight for photosynthesis
   15-D they have a plentiful supply of organic matter

16. The presence of coal deposits in Alaska shows that at one time Alaska

   16-A had a tropical climate
   16-B was covered with ice
   16-C was connected to Asia
   16-D was formed by volcanic action

17. If a person has been injured in an accident and damage to the back and neck is suspected, it is best to

   17-A roll the person over so that he does not lie on his back
   17-B rush the person to the nearest hospital
   17-C force the person to drink water to replace body fluids
   17-D wait for professional help

18. A 1000-ton ship must displace a weight of water equal to

   18-A 500 tons
   18-B 1500 tons
   18-C 1000 tons
   18-D 2000 tons

19. Which of the following birds would most probably *not* be found in a wooded area?

   19-A thrush
   19-B green heron
   19-C barred owl
   19-D towhee

20. Of the following phases of the moon, the invisible one is called

   20-A crescent
   20-B new moon
   20-C full moon
   20-D waxing and waning

21. The normal height of a mercury barometer at sea level is

   21-A 15 inches
   21-B 32 feet
   21-C 30 inches
   21-D 34 feet

22. Nitrogen-fixing bacteria are found in nodules on the roots of the

   22-A beet
   22-B potato
   22-C carrot
   22-D clover

23. The vascular system of the body is concerned with:

23-A   respiration
23-B   sense of touch
23-C   circulation of blood
23-D   enzymes

24. Of the following substances, the one which is non-magnetic is

24-A   iron
24-B   aluminum
24-C   nickel
24-D   cobalt

25. A well-balanced meal would include meat, bread, milk and

25-A   fish
25-B   spaghetti
25-C   jello
25-D   string beans

STOP

IF YOU FINISH THIS PART BEFORE THE TIME IS UP, CHECK OVER YOUR WORK ON THIS PART ONLY. DO NOT GO ON UNTIL YOU ARE TOLD TO DO SO.

ARITHMETIC REASONING

The arithmetic reasoning questions require careful thinking as well as arithmetic calculation. Some problems require more than one step for their solutions. You must decide exactly what the question asks; then you must determine the best method for finding the answer; finally you must work out the problem on your scratch paper. Be sure to mark the letter of the correct answer on your answer sheet. Try these questions.

1. Two cars start from the same point at the same time. One drives north at 20 miles an hour and the other drives south on the same straight road at 36 miles an hour. How many miles apart are they after 30 minutes?

1-A less than 10
1-B between 10 and 20
1-C between 20 and 30
1-D between 30 and 40

1. Ⓐ Ⓑ Ⓒ Ⓓ

1-C One car went 20 mph for $\frac{1}{2}$ hour = 10 miles. The other car went 36 mph for $\frac{1}{2}$ hour = 18 miles. Since they went in opposite directions, add the two distances to find the total number of miles apart. 10 + 18 = 28

2. A sportswriter claims that his football predictions are accurate 60% of the time. During football season, a fan kept records and found that the writer was inaccurate for a total of 16 games, although he did maintain his 60% accuracy. For how many games was the sportswriter accurate?

2-A 15
2-B 24
2-C 40
2-D 5

2. Ⓐ Ⓑ Ⓒ Ⓓ

2-B If 60% of the games were predicted accurately, then 40% of the games were predicted inaccurately.

Let x = games played
.40x = 16
   x = 40 games played
40 − 16 = 24 games won

Therefore, the sportswriter was accurate for 24 games.

3. In making a bracelet a girl uses three 10-inch strips of cord. How many bracelets can she make from a 5-yard roll of cord?

3-A 2
3-B 5
3-C 6
3-D 15

3. Ⓐ Ⓑ Ⓒ Ⓓ

N

↑ 10 miles

X

↓ 18 miles

S

3-C 10 inches × 3 strips = 30 inches per bracelet; 36 inches per yard × 5 yards of cord = 180 inches in the roll; 180 ÷ 30 = 6 bracelets can be made from the roll.

4. The net profits of a department store decreased from $650,000 to $400,000 in five years. What was the average decrease in net profit?

4-A $5000
4-B $25,000
4-C $50,000
4-D $200,000

4. Ⓐ Ⓑ Ⓒ Ⓓ

4-C $650,000 − $400,000 = $250,000 decrease in profit over 5 years. $250,000 ÷ 5 = $50,000 per year.

DO NOT TURN THE PAGE UNTIL YOU ARE TOLD TO DO SO

ARITHMETIC REASONING

TIME: 36 Minutes—30 Questions

1. If pencils are bought at 35 cents per dozen and sold at 3 for 10 cents the total profit on $5\frac{1}{2}$ dozen is

   1-A 25 cents
   1-B $27\frac{1}{2}$ cents
   1-C $28\frac{1}{2}$ cents
   1-D $31\frac{1}{2}$ cents

2. A certain type of siding for a house costs $10.50 per square yard. What does it cost for the siding for a wall 4 yards wide and 60 feet long?

   2-A $800
   2-B $840
   2-C $2520
   2-D $3240

3. If a woman bought some pillow cases for a total cost of $8.46, and the average per unit cost was $2.82, how many pillow cases did she buy?

   3-A 4
   3-B 2
   3-C 3
   3-D 5

4. A typist uses lengthwise a sheet of paper 9 inches by 12 inches. She leaves a 1-inch margin on each side and a $1\frac{1}{2}$-inch margin on top and bottom. What fractional part of the page is used for typing?

   4-A $\frac{21}{22}$
   4-B $\frac{7}{12}$
   4-C $\frac{5}{9}$
   4-D $\frac{3}{4}$

5. A carpenter needs four boards, each 2 feet, 9 inches long. If wood is sold only by the foot, how many feet must he buy?

   5-A 9
   5-B 10
   5-C 11
   5-D 12

6. One-sixth of an audience consisted of boys and $\frac{1}{3}$ of it consisted of girls. What percent of the audience consisted of children?

   6-A $66\frac{2}{3}$
   6-B 50
   6-C $37\frac{1}{2}$
   6-D 40

7. On a house plan on which 2 inches represents 5 feet, the length of a room measures $7\frac{1}{2}$ inches. The actual length of the room is

   7-A $12\frac{1}{2}$ feet
   7-B $17\frac{1}{2}$ feet
   7-C $15\frac{3}{4}$ feet
   7-D $18\frac{3}{4}$ feet

8. A girl earns twice as much in December as in each of the other months. What part of her entire year's earnings does she earn in December?

   8-A $\frac{2}{11}$
   8-B $\frac{2}{13}$
   8-C $\frac{3}{14}$
   8-D $\frac{1}{6}$

9. It costs 31 cents a square foot to lay linoleum. To lay 20 square yards of linoleum it will cost

   9-A $16.20
   9-B $18.60
   9-C $55.80
   9-D $62.00

10. A piece of wood 35 feet, 6 inches long was used to make 4 shelves of equal length. The

length of each shelf was

10-A 9 feet, $1\frac{1}{2}$ inches
10-B 8 feet, $10\frac{1}{2}$ inches
10-C 7 feet, $10\frac{1}{2}$ inches
10-D 7 feet, $1\frac{1}{2}$ inches

11. A team won 2 games and lost 10. The fraction of its games won is correctly expressed as

11-A 1/6
11-B 1/5
11-C 4/5
11-D 5/6

12. What is the simple interest on $600 at 4% for 2 years?

12-A $36
12-B $52
12-C $48
12-D $56

13. A change purse contained 3 half dollars, 8 quarters, 7 dimes, 6 nickels and 9 pennies. Express in dollars and cents the total amount of money in the purse.

13-A $3.78
13-B $4.32
13-C $3.95
13-D $4.59

14. How much does a salesperson earn for selling $68 worth of writing paper if she is paid a commission of 40% on her sales?

14-A $20.40
14-B $25.60
14-C $22.80
14-D $27.20

15. A team played 24 games of which it won 18. What percent of the games played did it win?

15-A 50%
15-B 80%
15-C 75%
15-D 85%

16. Patty went to the store and bought a bottle of cologne, 2 tubes of lipstick, and 1 box of powder. The cologne cost $4.98 a bottle, lipstick $2.29 each, and the powder $1.89 a box. What was the amount Patty had to pay

for these cosmetics?

16-A $9.16
16-B $9.45
16-C $11.45
16-D $11.89

17. A man had $25.00. He saw some ties that cost $4.95 apiece. How many of these ties could he buy?

17-A Six
17-B Seven
17-C Five
17-D Three

18. A man earns $20.56 on Monday; $32.90 on Tuesday; $20.78 on Wednesday. He spends half of all that he earns during the three days. How much has he left?

18-A $29.19
18-B $31.23
18-C $34.27
18-D $37.12

19. How many packages of candy containing $\frac{3}{4}$ of a pound each can be filled from 15 pounds of candy?

19-A 10
19-B 20
19-C 15
19-D 25

20. A champion runner ran the 100-yard dash in three track meets. The first time he ran it in 10.2 seconds; the second in 10.4 seconds; and the third in 10 seconds. What was his average time?

20-A 10.2 seconds
20-B 10.3 seconds
20-C 10.35 seconds
20-D 10.4 seconds

21. A boy saved up $4.56 the first month, $3.82 the second month, and $5.06 the third month. How much did he save altogether?

21-A $12.56
21-B $13.28
21-C $13.44
21-D $14.02

22. A woman bought a lamp for $37.50. She gave the clerk $40.00. How much change did she get?

22-A $3.50
22-B $2.50
22-C $2.75
22-D $3.25

23. A girl purchased a blouse for $10.98. She returned the blouse the next day and selected a better one costing $12.50. She gave the clerk a five-dollar bill to pay for the difference in price. How much change should she receive?

23-A $3.58
23-B $3.48
23-C $2.52
23-D $1.52

24. The daily almanac report for one day during the summer stated that the sun rose at 6:14 a.m. and set at 6:06 p.m. Find the number of hours and minutes in the time between the rising and setting of the sun on that day.

24-A 11 hr. 52 min.
24-B 11 hr. 2 min.
24-C 12 hr. 8 min.
24-D 12 hr. 48 min.

25. In a 45 minute gym class, 30 boys want to play basketball. Only 10 can play at once. If each player is to play the same length of time, how many minutes should each play?

25-A 8
25-B 12
25-C 15
25-D 20

26. The library charges 5¢ for the first day and 2¢ for each additional day that a book is overdue. If a borrower paid 65¢ in late charges, for how many days was the book overdue?

26-A 15
26-B 20
26-C 30
26-D 31

27. How many slices of bread, each weighing 2 ounces, are needed to balance 2 pounds of apples?

27-A 8
27-B 12
27-C 16
27-D 24

28. If $\frac{1}{2}$ cup of spinach contains 80 calories and the same amount of peas contains 300 calories, how many cups of spinach have the same caloric content as $\frac{2}{3}$ cup of peas?

28-A $\frac{2}{5}$
28-B $1\frac{1}{3}$
28-C 2
28-D $2\frac{1}{2}$

29. If it takes 30 minutes to type 6 pages, how many hours will it take to type 126 pages at the same rate?

29-A 6.3
29-B 10.5
29-C 15
29-D 25

30. A night watchman must check a certain storage area every 45 minutes. If he first checks the area as he begins a 9-hour tour of duty, how many times will he have checked this storage area?

30-A 10
30-B 11
30-C 12
30-D 13

END OF PART 2

IF YOU FINISH BEFORE THE TIME IS UP, CHECK TO BE CERTAIN THAT YOU HAVE MARKED ALL OF YOUR ANSWERS ON THE ANSWER SHEET. THEN CHECK OVER YOUR WORK ON THIS PART ONLY. DO NOT RETURN TO PART ONE. DO NOT GO ON UNTIL YOU ARE TOLD TO DO SO.

PART 3

WORD KNOWLEDGE

The questions in this part test how well you understand the meanings of words. Each question has an underlined word. Read all four possible answers and decide which one has a meaning closest to the meaning of the underlined word. On your answer sheet mark the letter of the answer you choose. Try these questions.

1. Explode most nearly means

1-A crash
1-B cave in
1-C crumble
1-D burst

1. Ⓐ Ⓑ Ⓒ Ⓓ

1-D BURST is the correct answer. *Crash* (A), *cave in* (B), and *crumble* (C) are common results of an *explosion*. When an object *explodes,* it *bursts.*

2. Because of a death in the family, the private's leave was extended.

2-A denied
2-B lengthened
2-C dreary
2-D publicized

2. Ⓐ Ⓑ Ⓒ Ⓓ

2-B LENGTHENED is the correct answer. *To extend* means *to stretch out* or *to lengthen.* Under the circumstances the private's leave may well have been *dreary,* but that is not the meaning of *extended.* (A) and (D) are wrong.

3. Reservoir most nearly means

3-A lake
3-B water
3-C storage place
3-D dam

3. Ⓐ Ⓑ Ⓒ Ⓓ

3-C STORAGE PLACE is the correct answer. A *reservoir* need not be a place for *storing water* (B), though that is its most familiar use. A *reservoir* for *water* is often created by a *dam* (D) and takes the form of an artificial *lake* (A).

4. Tenant most nearly means

4-A occupant
4-B landlord
4-C owner
4-D farmer

4. Ⓐ Ⓑ Ⓒ Ⓓ

4-A OCCUPANT is the correct answer. The most common sense of the word *tenant* is *renter.* As such, the *tenant* is never the *landlord* (B). The *owner* (C) may well be an *occupant* (A), but unless he *occupies* on a very temporary basis he is not considered a *tenant.* A *tenant farmer* (D) lives on and cultivates the land of another.

5. The novice skier broke his ankle when he fell.

5-A competitive
5-B clumsy
5-C aged
5-D beginning

5. Ⓐ Ⓑ Ⓒ Ⓓ

5-D BEGINNING is the correct answer. A *novice* is a *beginner.* A *novice* may, of course, be *competitive* (A), *clumsy* (B) or *aged* (D), but it is his being a *beginner* that makes him a *novice.*

DO NOT TURN THE PAGE UNTIL YOU ARE TOLD TO DO SO

WORD KNOWLEDGE

TIME: 11 Minutes—35 Questions

1. Superiority most nearly means

   1-A abundance
   1-B popularity
   1-C permanence
   1-D excellence

2. Absurd most nearly means

   2-A disgusting
   2-B foolish
   2-C reasonable
   2-D very old

3. Be careful, that liquid is inflammable!

   3-A poisonous
   3-B valuable
   3-C explosive
   3-D likely to give off fumes

4. Conscious most nearly means

   4-A surprised
   4-B afraid
   4-C disappointed
   4-D aware

5. Exhibit most nearly means

   5-A display
   5-B trade
   5-C sell
   5-D label

6. We assumed that our candidate had been elected.

   6-A knew
   6-B wished
   6-C decided
   6-D supposed

7. Counterfeit most nearly means

   7-A mysterious
   7-B false
   7-C unreadable
   7-D priceless

8. Expertly most nearly means

   8-A awkwardly
   8-B quickly
   8-C skillfully
   8-D unexpectedly

9. Marshy most nearly means

   9-A swampy
   9-B sandy
   9-C wooded
   9-D rocky

10. Each morning the children pledge allegiance to the flag.

   10-A freedom
   10-B homeland
   10-C protection
   10-D loyalty

11. The cashier yearned for a vacation.

   11-A begged
   11-B longed
   11-C saved
   11-D applied

12. Summit most nearly means

12-A face
12-B top
12-C base
12-D side

13. The driver heeded the traffic signals.

13-A worried about
13-B ignored
13-C disagreed with
13-D took notice of

14. Vigorously most nearly means

14-A sleepily
14-B thoughtfully
14-C energetically
14-D sadly

15. Imitate most nearly means

15-A copy
15-B attract
15-C study
15-D appreciate

16. The severity of their criticism upset us.

16-A harshness
16-B suddenness
16-C method
16-D unfairness

17. Incredible most nearly means

17-A thrilling
17-B convincing
17-C uninteresting
17-D unbelievable

18. With a full month for vacation, we made a very leisurely trip to California.

18-A roundabout
18-B unhurried
18-C unforgetable
18-D tiresome

19. Gratitude most nearly means

19-A thankfulness
19-B excitement
19-C disappointment
19-D sympathy

20. Familiar most nearly means

20-A welcome
20-B dreaded
20-C rare
20-D well-known

21. He had an acute pain in his back.

21-A dull
21-B slight
21-C alarming
21-D sharp

22. Bewildered most nearly means

22-A worried
22-B offended
22-C puzzled
22-D delighted

23. Conclusion most nearly means

23-A theme
23-B suspense
23-C end
23-D beginning

24. Don't you like the aroma of fresh-brewed coffee?

24-A flavor
24-B warmth
24-C fragrance
24-D steam

25. Nonessential most nearly means

25-A damaged
25-B unnecessary
25-C expensive
25-D foreign-made

26. Amplified most nearly means

26-A expanded
26-B summarized
26-C analyzed
26-D shouted

27. One of the cars in the accident remained in-tact.

    27-A unattended
    27-B undamaged
    27-C a total loss
    27-D unmoved

28. Penicillin is a potent drug when used cor-rectly.

    28-A harmless
    28-B possible
    28-C effective
    28-D drinkable

29. Terminate most nearly means

    29-A continue
    29-B go by train
    29-C begin
    29-D end

30. The face on the poster was that of a notorious bank robber,

    30-A convicted
    30-B dangerous
    30-C well-known
    30-D escaped

31. Fatal most nearly means

    31-A accidental
    31-B deadly
    31-C dangerous
    31-D beautiful

32. Indigent people are entitled to food stamps.

    32-A poor
    32-B lazy
    32-C angry
    32-D homeless

33. Technique most nearly means

    33-A computed
    33-B engineered
    33-C calculation
    33-D method

34. Vocation most nearly means

    34-A school
    34-B examination
    34-C occupation
    34-D carpentry

35. One should eat only mature fruits.

    35-A edible
    35-B washed
    35-C ripe
    35-D sprayed

END OF PART 3

IF YOU FINISH BEFORE THE TIME IS UP, CHECK OVER YOUR WORK ON THIS PART ONLY. DO NOT RETURN TO EITHER PREVIOUS PART. DO NOT GO ON TO THE NEXT PAGE UNTIL YOU ARE TOLD TO DO SO.

PART 4

PARAGRAPH COMPREHENSION

The paragraph comprehension part of your test battery requires concentration and attention to detail. First you must read and understand the paragraph. Then you must read and understand each of the answer choices, noticing the differences of meaning or emphasis which are imparted by little words. There is one question based upon each paragraph. You must answer that question on the basis of what is stated or implied in the passage, even if you know a better answer and even if you know the information in the paragraph to be wrong. In some cases more than one answer might be correct, but you must choose the BEST answer and mark its letter on your answer sheet. Try these questions.

1. Since duplicating machines are being changed constantly, the person who is in the market for such a machine should not purchase offhand the kind with which he is most familiar or the one recommended by the first salesman who calls on him. Instead he should analyze his particular equipment situation and then investigate all the possibilities.

When duplicating equipment is being purchased,

1-A the purchaser should choose equipment that he can use with the least extra training

1-B the needs of the purchaser's office should determine the selection

1-C the buyer should have his needs analyzed by an office-equipment salesman

1-D the recommendations of salesmen should usually be ignored

1. Ⓐ Ⓑ Ⓒ Ⓓ

1-B The last sentence answers the question. It recommends that specific office needs be analyzed and that all types of equipment be investigated. Since the office-equipment salesman is necessarily biased toward whatever he sells, he is not the one to do the analysis.

2. Neither the revolution in manufacturing nor that in agriculture could have proceeded without those brilliant inventions in transportation and communication which have bound country to city, nation to nation, and continent to continent.

The paragraph best supports the statement that

2-A nations have been brought together more closely by transportation than by manufacturing and agriculture

2-B progress in communication and transportation has been essential to progress in manufacturing and agriculture

2-C changes in manufacturing and agriculture are characterized by a revolutionary process

2-D industrial changes must be preceded by brilliant inventions in agriculture

2. Ⓐ Ⓑ Ⓒ Ⓓ

2-B Within the context of this paragraph, the meaning of the word "revolution" is "radical progress." Hence, the passage is stating that neither manufacturing nor agriculture could have progressed without inventions in transportation and communication. The effects of improved transportation and communication, other than their effects upon manufacturing and agriculture, are irrelevant to the meaning of the paragraph.

DO NOT TURN THE PAGE UNTIL YOU ARE TOLD TO DO SO

PARAGRAPH COMPREHENSION

TIME: 13 Minutes—15 Questions

1. Prior to the Civil War, the steamboat was the center of life in the thriving Mississippi towns. With the war came the railroads. River traffic dwindled and the white-painted vessels rotted at the wharves. During World War I, the government decided to relieve rail congestion by reviving the long-forgotten waterways. Today, steamers, diesels, and barges ply the Mississippi.

The paragraph best supports the statement that

1-A the volume of river transportation was greater than the volume of rail transportation during World War I

1-B growth of river transportation greatly increased the congestion on the railroads

1-C business found river transportation more profitable than railroad transportation during World War I

1-D since the Civil War, the volume of transportation on the Mississippi has varied

2. Specialization could not exist without the process of exchange. A farmer might specialize in raising corn. In the course of a year he would produce many more bushels of corn than he and his family could possibly consume. However, being a specialist, he can neither grow the other foods he needs, nor produce such necessities of life as clothing, shelter, newspapers, and machinery. What he does in effect is exchange his corn for those products.

As a result of specialization

2-A the process of exchange has been greatly accelerated

2-B the farm has become a business

2-C the farmer's produce must be sent to the open market for distribution

2-D food products become the specialized field of the farmer

3. In large organizations some standardized, simple, inexpensive method of giving employees information about company policies and rules, as well as specific instructions regarding their duties, is practically essential. This is the purpose of all office manuals of whatever type.

The paragraph best supports the statement that office manuals

3-A are all about the same

3-B should be simple enough for the average employee to understand

3-C are necessary to large organizations

3-D act as constant reminders to the employee of his duties

4. What gave this country the isolation it enjoyed in the 19th century was the statesmanship of Jefferson, Adams, Madison, and Monroe on this side of the Atlantic and of men like Canning on the other side. American independence of the European system did not exist in the two centuries before the Monroe Doctrine of 1823, and it has not existed in the century which began in 1914.

The paragraph best supports the statement that

4-A America enjoyed greater isolation from European affairs from 1823 to 1914 than before or after

4-B the isolation of this country from European affairs was, prior to 1914, the result of our geographic position

4-C Canning was a statesman living in the 20th century

4-D America is less isolated today than it has ever been

5. Just as municipal corporations acting in a governmental capacity are free from accident liability, so also are private corporations or

associations exempt from liability when carrying on welfare or charitable enterprises not for profit.

The paragraph best supports the statement that

5-A municipal and charitable corporations are exempt from taxes
5-B a private hospital or clinic that treats indigent patients without making a charge would not be liable for injuries caused
5-C municipal corporations do not operate for profit
5-D an individual hurt in an automobile accident by a city chauffeur cannot sue the city if the chauffeur is incorporated

6. The X-ray has gone into business. Developed primarily to aid in diagnosing human ills, the machine now works in packing plants, in foundries, in service stations, and in a dozen ways contributes to precision and accuracy in industry.

The X-ray

6-A was first developed to aid business
6-B is being used to improve the functioning of industry
6-C is more accurate for packing plants than for foundries
6-D increases the output of such industries as service stations

7. In almost every community, fortunately, there are certain men and women known to be public-spirited. Others, however, may be selfish and act only as their private interests seem to require.

The paragraph suggests that those citizens who disregard others are

7-A needed
7-B found only in small communities
7-C not known
7-D not public-spirited

8. Whenever two groups of people whose interests at the moment conflict meet to discuss a solution of that conflict, there is laid a basis for an interchange of facts and ideas which increases the total range of knowledge of both parties and tends to break down the barrier that their restricted field of information has helped to create.

Conflicts between two parties may be brought closer to a settlement through

8-A the exchange of accusations
8-B gaining a wider knowledge of facts
8-C submitting the dispute to an impartial judge
8-D limiting discussion to plans acceptable to both groups

9. Unfortunately, specialization in industry creates workers who lack versatility. When a laborer is trained to perform only one task, he is almost entirely dependent for employment upon the demand for that particular skill. If anything happens to interrupt that demand he is unemployed.

The paragraph best supports the statement that

9-A the demand for labor of a particular type is constantly changing
9-B the average laborer is not capable of learning more than one task at a time
9-C some cases of unemployment are due to laborers' lack of versatility
9-D too much specialization is as dangerous as too little

10. Scientific judgments as opposed to legal judgments are more impartial, objective, and precise. They are more subject to verification by any competent observer.

Scientific judgments

10-A can be verified by competent observers
10-B can be tested by advanced laboratory methods
10-C accept no opinion until validated
10-D are usually propounded by experts in their fields

11. Even when sheep are raised as a principal business rather than a farm by-product, it is extremely difficult to produce wool of uniform quality. On a single sheep there are at least four grades. In one season, no two sheep in a flock yield exactly the same grade of wool.

In addition, since quality is affected by the food the sheep eat, by the soil over which they graze, and by the weather, no two flocks in one year produce the same grade of wool.

The paragraph best supports the statement that

11-A soil is a factor in the quality of wool
11-B sheep raising is always a by-product of the meat-producing industries
11-C in one season all sheep yield exactly the same grade of wool
11-D there is a consistent change in the seasonal quality of wool

12. Since the government can spend only what it obtains from the people and this amount is ultimately limited by their capacity and willingness to pay taxes, it is very important that the people be given full information about the work of the government.

The paragraph best supports the statement that

12-A governmental employees should be trained not only in their own work, but also in how to perform the duties of other employees in their agency
12-B taxation by the government rests upon the consent of the people
12-C the release of full information on the work of the government will increase the efficiency of governmental operations
12-D the work of the government, in recent years, has been restricted because of reduced tax collections

13. The increasing size of business organizations has resulted in less personal contact between superior and subordinate. Consequently, business executives today depend more upon records and reports to secure information and exercise control over the operations of various departments.

The increasing size of business organizations

13-A has caused a complete cleavage between employer and employee
13-B has resulted in less personal contact between superior and subordinate
13-C has tended toward class distinctions in large organizations
13-D has resulted in a better means of controlling the operations of various departments

14. In humid climates a thick growth of vegetation with a mattress of interlacing roots usually protects the moist soil from wind. But in dry regions vegetation is either wholly lacking, or scant growths are found huddled in detached clumps, leaving patches of unprotected ground. Since there is little or no moisture present to hold the soil particles together, they are readily lifted and scattered by the wind.

The main point of the paragraph is that

14-A vegetation is always present in humid climates
14-B lack of moisture increases cohesion
14-C moisture is an important element in soil and rock erosion
14-D wind is the chief agent in the dispersal of topsoil

15. Influenza, the flu, travels exactly as fast as man. In oxcart days its progress was slow. In 1918 man could girdle the globe in eight weeks, and that is exactly the time it took influenza to complete its encirclement of the earth. Today, by jets and air transport, man moves at higher speed. This modern speed makes influenza's advent unpredictable from day to day.

The purpose of this paragraph is to describe

15-A influenza around the world
15-B the world epidemic of influenza in 1918
15-C the unpredictability of influenza
15-D the effect of speed upon the spread of influenza

END OF PART 4

IF YOU FINISH BEFORE TIME IS UP, DO NOT GO ON.

PART 5

NUMERICAL OPERATIONS

The numerical operations part of your test battery consists of fifty very simple arithmetic questions that must be answered in only three minutes. Obviously, speed is a very important factor. You should not attempt to compute these answers using pencil and scratch paper. Instead, solve each problem in your head, then choose the correct answer from among the four choices and mark the letter of the correct answer on your answer sheet. If you are not sure of an answer, guess and go on to the next question. Do not skip any questions. You will most certainly not have time to go back to fill in. Since a wrong answer will not count against you, it cannot hurt to guess. Many people cannot complete all fifty questions in the three minutes allowed. Do not be upset if you cannot finish. Just answer as many questions as you can. Try these questions.

1. 7 + 6 =

   1-A 11
   1-B 13
   1-C 15
   1-D 19

   1. Ⓐ Ⓑ Ⓒ Ⓓ

1-B 7 + 6 = 13

2. 8 − 3 =

   2-A 6
   2-B 11
   2-C 4
   2-D 5

   2. Ⓐ Ⓑ Ⓒ Ⓓ

2-D 8 − 3 = 5

3. 4 × 2 =

   3-A 6
   3-B 8
   3-C 16
   3-D 2

   3. Ⓐ Ⓑ Ⓒ Ⓓ

3-B 4 × 2 = 8

4. 12 ÷ 4 =

   4-A 3
   4-B 8
   4-C 16
   4-D 2

   4. Ⓐ Ⓑ Ⓒ Ⓓ

4-A 12 ÷ 4 = 3

5. 9 × 1 =

   5-A 0
   5-B 10
   5-C 1
   5-D 9

   5. Ⓐ Ⓑ Ⓒ Ⓓ

5-D 9 × 1 = 9

6. 6 + 2 =

   6-A 12
   6-B 4
   6-C 8
   6-D 16

   6. Ⓐ Ⓑ Ⓒ Ⓓ

6-C 6 + 2 = 8

DO NOT TURN THE PAGE UNTIL YOU ARE TOLD TO DO SO

NUMERICAL OPERATIONS

TIME: 3 Minutes—50 Questions

1. $2 + 5 =$

   1-A 3
   1-B 7
   1-C 9
   1-D 10

2. $18 \div 2 =$

   2-A 3
   2-B 6
   2-C 9
   2-D 11

3. $10 - 8 =$

   3-A 2
   3-B 9
   3-C 16
   3-D 18

4. $3 \times 3 =$

   4-A 6
   4-B 9
   4-C 30
   4-D 33

5. $1 + 8 =$

   5-A 18
   5-B 80
   5-C 7
   5-D 9

6. $9 \times 8 =$

   6-A 56
   6-B 64
   6-C 72
   6-D 76

7. $4 \times 5 =$

   7-A 20
   7-B 24
   7-C 28
   7-D 30

8. $3 + 7 =$

   8-A 37
   8-B 21
   8-C 10
   8-D 4

9. $9 - 5 =$

   9-A 7
   9-B 14
   9-C 12
   9-D 4

10. $3 + 9 =$

   10-A 3
   10-B 6
   10-C 12
   10-D 15

11. $50 \div 5 =$

   11-A 5
   11-B 10
   11-C 55
   11-D 11

12. $8 - 6 =$

   12-A 14
   12-B 4
   12-C 3
   12-D 2

13. $6 \div 3 =$

13-A 3
13-B 2
13-C 18
13-D 24

14. $2 \times 9 =$

14-A 7
14-B 17
14-C 18
14-D 19

15. $4 + 8 =$

15-A 4
15-B 10
15-C 12
15-D 16

16. $7 \times 9 =$

16-A 45
16-B 63
16-C 72
16-D 75

17. $5 + 6 =$

17-A 11
17-B 13
17-C 15
17-D 7

18. $0 + 8 =$

18-A 0
18-B 1
18-C 8
18-D 18

19. $4 + 5 =$

19-A 6
19-B 1
19-C 9
19-D 11

20. $64 \div 8 =$

20-A 6
20-B 7
20-C 8
20-D 9

21. $7 - 1 =$

21-A 6
21-B 7
21-C 8
21-D 0

22. $2 \times 3 =$

22-A 5
22-B 1
22-C 9
22-D 6

23. $9 - 7 =$

23-A 6
23-B 5
23-C 2
23-D 4

24. $6 + 8 =$

24-A 16
24-B 12
24-C 15
24-D 14

25. $10 \div 2 =$

25-A 2
25-B 5
25-C 20
25-D 12

26. $6 \times 3 =$

26-A 3
26-B 9
26-C 12
26-D 18

27. $5 + 9 =$

27-A 14
27-B 16
27-C 17
27-D 18

28. $7 + 7 =$

28-A 49
28-B 77

28-C 0
28-D 14

29. 6 − 6 =

29-A 0
29-B 1
29-C 6
29-D 12

30. 9 × 6 =

30-A 15
30-B 54
30-C 45
30-D 72

31. 7 + 9 =

31-A 12
31-B 15
31-C 16
31-D 17

32. 5 − 4 =

32-A 9
32-B 20
32-C 3
32-D 1

33. 4 + 4 =

33-A 1
33-B 4
33-C 8
33-D 16

34. 10 − 5 =

34-A 50
34-B 15
34-C 9
34-D 5

35. 7 × 4 =

35-A 21
35-B 28
35-C 36
35-D 42

36. 36 ÷ 6 =

36-A 11
36-B 9
36-C 10
36-D 6

37. 8 × 3 =

37-A 24
37-B 21
37-C 29
37-D 32

38. 2 + 4 =

38-A 6
38-B 2
38-C 16
38-D 8

39. 8 − 1 =

39-A 9
39-B 8
39-C 7
39-D 6

40. 1 + 5 =

40-A 6
40-B 5
40-C 4
40-D 1

41. 90 ÷ 9 =

41-A 9
41-B 10
41-C 11
41-D 12

42. 2 − 2 =

42-A 1
42-B 4
42-C 2
42-D 0

43. 7 + 8 =

    43-A 9
    43-B 19
    43-C 17
    43-D 15

44. 4 − 0 =

    44-A 1
    44-B 4
    44-C 5
    44-D 8

45. 8 + 3 =

    45-A 5
    45-B 15
    45-C 13
    45-D 11

46. 3 − 2 =

    46-A 1
    46-B 2
    46-C 5
    46-D 6

47. 5 + 8 =

    47-A 12
    47-B 11
    47-C 13
    47-D 17

48. 3 ÷ 3 =

    48-A 0
    48-B 1
    48-C 3
    48-D 6

49. 9 + 1 =

    49-A 19
    49-B 9
    49-C 10
    49-D 11

50. 4 × 6 =

    50-A 28
    50-B 24
    50-C 23
    50-D 18

END OF PART 5

IF YOU FINISH THIS PART BEFORE THE TIME IS UP, CHECK OVER YOUR WORK ON THIS PART ONLY. DO NOT GO ON UNTIL YOU ARE TOLD TO DO SO.

PART 6

CODING SPEED

The coding part of your exam is different from all other parts of the exam. Nothing that you have learned enters into your answering of these questions. Coding is a test of your memory, your eye-hand coordination and your working speed.

Before each set of questions you will find a "key." The key consists of ten words listed in alphabetical order. Each word has a four-digit code number assigned to it.

In the set of questions you will find the same ten words, scrambled and sometimes repeated. Following each word in the test are *five* answer choices in columns labelled A to E. Each answer choice is a four-digit number. The answer choices are in ascending order, that is, the lowest number is always in column A, the next higher number is in column B and so on to the highest number in column E. You must look at the word, find the correct code number among the choices and mark on your answer sheet the letter of the column in which you found the correct code number.

On the actual examination you must work very quickly. You have only seven minutes in which to try to answer eighty-four questions. Use the sample questions which follow to develop a system which works for you—memorization, some sort of word-number association, a mathematical formula or any private method which helps you work up speed and accuracy. Many people cannot finish the coding test in the time allowed. Do not be upset if you cannot finish. Just do your best. Try these questions.

Key

bay 7100	dark 1872	mole 4386
brain 3600	half 1492	nest 6663
calf 9012	igloo 1776	shoe 8080
	lemon 5486	

Answers

		A	B	C	D	E	
1.	brain	1776	3600	4386	6663	8080	1. Ⓐ Ⓑ Ⓒ Ⓓ Ⓔ
2.	igloo	1492	1776	1872	7100	9012	2. Ⓐ Ⓑ Ⓒ Ⓓ Ⓔ
3.	shoe	3600	4386	5486	6663	8080	3. Ⓐ Ⓑ Ⓒ Ⓓ Ⓔ
4.	mole	1872	3600	4386	5486	7100	4. Ⓐ Ⓑ Ⓒ Ⓓ Ⓔ
5.	calf	1776	4386	6663	8080	9012	5. Ⓐ Ⓑ Ⓒ Ⓓ Ⓔ
6.	lemon	3600	5486	7100	8080	9012	6. Ⓐ Ⓑ Ⓒ Ⓓ Ⓔ
7.	nest	1776	3600	6663	7100	8080	7. Ⓐ Ⓑ Ⓒ Ⓓ Ⓔ
8.	dark	1872	3600	5486	6663	7100	8. Ⓐ Ⓑ Ⓒ Ⓓ Ⓔ
9.	bay	1776	1872	4386	5486	7100	9. Ⓐ Ⓑ Ⓒ Ⓓ Ⓔ
10.	half	1492	1872	3600	4386	6663	10. Ⓐ Ⓑ Ⓒ Ⓓ Ⓔ
11.	lemon	3600	4386	5486	6663	9012	11. Ⓐ Ⓑ Ⓒ Ⓓ Ⓔ
12.	mole	1872	4386	5486	8080	9012	12. Ⓐ Ⓑ Ⓒ Ⓓ Ⓔ

The correct answers are:

1-B	4-C	7-C	10-A
2-B	5-E	8-A	11-C
3-E	6-B	9-E	12-B

Key

arrow 7813	deed 4957	noon 8695
bride 1012	gray 5858	nun 9486
cave 6590	infant 1212	pig 2342
	junk 3666	

Answers

	A	B	C	D	E	
13. gray	2342	3666	5858	6590	9486	13. Ⓐ Ⓑ Ⓒ Ⓓ Ⓔ
14. infant	1012	1212	3666	5858	8695	14. Ⓐ Ⓑ Ⓒ Ⓓ Ⓔ
15. nun	2342	4957	6590	8695	9486	15. Ⓐ Ⓑ Ⓒ Ⓓ Ⓔ
16. junk	1212	2342	3666	4957	8695	16. Ⓐ Ⓑ Ⓒ Ⓓ Ⓔ
17. arrow	1012	3666	5858	7813	9486	17. Ⓐ Ⓑ Ⓒ Ⓓ Ⓔ
18. cave	1212	2342	6590	7813	8695	18. Ⓐ Ⓑ Ⓒ Ⓓ Ⓔ
19. pig	2342	3666	4957	6590	7813	19. Ⓐ Ⓑ Ⓒ Ⓓ Ⓔ
20. deed	4957	5858	6590	7813	8695	20. Ⓐ Ⓑ Ⓒ Ⓓ Ⓔ
21. cave	1012	1212	3666	4957	6590	21. Ⓐ Ⓑ Ⓒ Ⓓ Ⓔ
22. noon	1212	2342	4957	7813	8695	22. Ⓐ Ⓑ Ⓒ Ⓓ Ⓔ
23. bride	1012	1212	2342	4957	5858	23. Ⓐ Ⓑ Ⓒ Ⓓ Ⓔ
24. junk	1212	3666	4957	5858	6590	24. Ⓐ Ⓑ Ⓒ Ⓓ Ⓔ

The correct answers are:

13-C	16-C	19-A	22-E
14-B	17-D	20-A	23-A
15-E	18-C	21-E	24-B

DO NOT TURN THE PAGE UNTIL YOU ARE TOLD TO DO SO

CODING SPEED

TIME: 7 Minutes—84 Questions

Key

apron 4341	date 2024	jet 7699
bridge 3636	earth 9229	knot 6157
canoe 1936	face 5678	lizard 5163
	germm 8606	

(germ .... 8606)

Answers

		A	B	C	D	E
1.	lizard	2024	3636	4341	5163	7699
2.	jet	1936	5163	5678	6157	7699
3.	bridge	1936	3636	4341	7699	8606
4.	face	5678	6157	7699	8606	9229
5.	knot	1936	2024	4341	5163	6157
6.	apron	2024	4341	5163	6157	9229
7.	canoe	1936	3636	4341	5163	5678
8.	date	2024	5163	6157	7699	8606
9.	germ	2024	3636	6157	7699	8606
10.	earth	1936	4341	5163	6157	9229
11.	face	2024	3636	4341	5163	5678
12.	knot	1936	4341	6157	8606	9229

Key

bank 3029	eel 2270	luck 1654
candle 5605	farm 9564	mule 9984
dinner 8002	hill 6883	tuba 7240
	husk 4488	

Answers

		A	B	C	D	E
13.	candle	2270	3029	4488	5605	7240
14.	hill	1654	5605	6883	8002	9984
15.	farm	3029	4488	6883	7240	9564
16.	bank	2270	3029	5605	6883	8002
17.	dinner	4488	7240	8002	9564	9984
18.	luck	1654	3029	4488	6883	7240
19.	husk	4488	6883	7240	8002	9564
20.	mule	3029	4488	8002	9564	9984
21.	eel	2270	3029	4488	6883	8002
22.	dinner	3029	4488	6883	8002	9984
23.	tuba	5605	7240	8002	9564	9984
24.	husk	1654	2270	3029	4488	6883

Key

army	9234	land	1620	paint	7677
coast	4532	line	1854	rug	5600
disc	6957	man	3002	test	8406
		pain	2610		

Answers

		A	B	C	D	E
25.	disc	1620	3002	5600	6957	8406
26.	paint	1854	2610	4532	6957	7677
27.	line	1620	1854	2610	3002	5600
28.	test	1854	4532	6957	8406	9234
29.	pain	2610	3002	5600	7677	8406
30.	army	1620	2610	3002	6957	9234
31.	rug	4532	5600	6957	8406	9234
32.	man	3002	4532	6957	7677	8406
33.	paint	1620	2610	7677	8406	9234
34.	coast	2610	3002	4532	5600	6957
35.	land	1620	1854	2610	3002	5600
36.	rug	2610	4532	5600	6957	9234

Key

author	6509	card	7074	pin	8768
blood	3348	fire	1886	shore	5135
cake	2988	frog	9492	time	6852
		hunter	4141		

Answers

		A	B	C	D	E
37.	hunter	1886	2988	4141	5135	8768
38.	shore	2988	3348	5135	6509	7074
39.	frog	3348	4141	6852	8768	9492
40.	author	2988	5135	6509	6852	8768
41.	blood	1886	3348	4141	6852	7074
42.	cake	2988	3348	5135	6509	6852
43.	card	1886	4141	7074	8768	9492
44.	pin	2988	3348	5135	6852	8768
45.	fire	1886	2988	4141	6509	7074
46.	time	3348	4141	5135	6509	6852
47.	author	1886	3348	4141	6509	6852
48.	shore	5135	6509	6852	7074	9492

Key

book 3498	guard 5249	pie 6765
boy 1518	hotel 9804	sea 7602
exam 2412	motel 8940	thing 5521
	navy 4404	

Answers

		A	B	C	D	E
49.	guard	1518	4404	5249	5521	6765
50.	exam	1518	2412	5521	7602	9804
51.	thing	2412	5521	5249	6765	8940
52.	motel	3498	4404	6765	8940	9804
53.	sea	5249	6765	7602	8940	9804
54.	boy	1518	2412	4404	5521	7602
55.	navy	2412	3498	4404	5249	6765
56.	book	3498	5249	5521	7602	8940
57.	hotel	1518	2412	6765	8940	9804
58.	pie	5521	6765	7602	8940	9804
59.	navy	4404	5249	5521	6765	7602
60.	book	1518	2412	3498	4404	9804

Key

art 2679	flag 4855	nation 5897
basket 4562	gas 1499	nature 7004
crust 9911	link 3964	razor 8282
	music 6242	

Answers

		A	B	C	D	E
61.	basket	1499	4562	4855	5897	6242
62.	nation	1499	2679	3964	4855	5897
63.	music	4562	6242	7004	8282	9911
64.	nature	2679	3964	4855	6242	7004
65.	gas	1499	3964	4562	4855	9911
66.	link	1499	2679	3964	5897	6242
67.	flag	4562	4855	5897	6242	8282
68.	razor	2679	4562	6242	8282	9911
69.	art	2679	3964	4855	5897	6242
70.	crust	1499	4562	4855	7004	9911
71.	nature	2679	5897	7004	8282	9911
72.	flag	1499	2679	3964	4562	4855

Key

acorn 4745	desk 7621	star 5704
bear 1086	ego 2190	steak 6667
camel 8808	fly 9266	wax 7512
	halo 3835	

Answers

		A	B	C	D	E
73.	steak	3835	4745	5704	6667	7621
74.	ego	2190	5704	7512	7621	8808
75.	halo	1086	2190	3835	4745	6667
76.	fly	4745	5704	7512	8808	9266
77.	wax	3835	4745	5704	7512	7621
78.	camel	1086	2190	5704	6667	8808
79.	bear	1086	2190	6667	8808	9266
80.	desk	4745	5704	6667	7512	7621
81.	acorn	3835	4745	5704	7621	9266
82.	star	1086	2190	3835	4745	5704
83.	camel	2190	3835	6667	8808	9266
84.	steak	4745	5704	6667	7512	7621

END OF PART 6

IF YOU FINISH BEFORE TIME IS UP, CHECK TO BE SURE THAT YOUR ANSWERS ARE CLEARLY MARKED. DO NOT GO BACK TO ANY PREVIOUS PART. DO NOT TURN THE PAGE UNTIL YOU ARE TOLD TO DO SO.

PART 7

AUTO & SHOP INFORMATION

The auto and shop information questions test your knowledge and understanding of automobiles and of tools and shop practices. The answers to many questions come straight from your life experience. However, if this is not your area of interest, there will be questions to which you do not know the answer. Make the most sensible guess. Answer all questions. Mark the letter of your choice on your answer sheet. Try these questions.

1. The function of the generator or alternator is to

1-A start the engine
1-B carry electricity from the battery to the engine
1-C keep the battery charged
1-D control production of hydrocarbons

1. Ⓐ Ⓑ Ⓒ Ⓓ

1-C The GENERATOR or ALTERNATOR is operated by the car's engine. It produces electricity which flows to the battery and keeps the battery charged.

2. Black smoke coming from the muffler means that

2-A there is too much lubricating oil
2-B the car needs an oil change
2-C the carburetor is delivering too rich a mixture
2-D the carburetor is delivering too weak a mixture

2. Ⓐ Ⓑ Ⓒ Ⓓ

2-C If the carburetor is sending to the engine a mixture that contains TOO MUCH GASOLINE with TOO LITTLE AIR, the mixture is said to be *too rich* and black smoke will come from the muffler. If there is too much lubricating oil (A), bluish-gray smoke will come from the tailpipe.

3.

You might use the instrument above if you wanted to

3-A pitch a tent
3-B poke holes in a fabric
3-C locate studs in a wall
3-D drill holes at equal short distances along a board

3. Ⓐ Ⓑ Ⓒ Ⓓ

3-D The *compass* above would be very useful in marking out equal short distances on a board. The compass would not, of course, be of use in the actual drilling.

4. The solvent that should be used to clean a brush immediately after it was used to apply rubber base paint is

4-A turpentine
4-B mineral oil
4-C alcohol
4-D warm water

4. Ⓐ Ⓑ Ⓒ Ⓓ

4-D Clean-up for latex or rubber based paint is plain water. Turpentine (A) is a solvent for oil paints. Alcohol (C) is used for shellac base paint.

DO NOT TURN THE PAGE UNTIL YOU ARE TOLD TO DO SO

AUTO & SHOP INFORMATION

TIME: 11 Minutes—25 Questions

1. Burned engine bearings are due to

    1-A lack of oil in the engine
    1-B lack of water in the engine
    1-C too much oil in the engine
    1-D too much water in the engine

2. If the temperature gauge indicates the engine is getting overheated

    2-A allow it to cool down
    2-B pour cold water in immediately
    2-C pour hot water in immediately
    2-D pour in a cooling anti-freeze at once

3. Cam ground pistons are used primarily because

    3-A they can be used in badly worn engines without reboring the cylinders
    3-B their use increases the compression ratio
    3-C their use aids in the lubrication of the cylinder walls
    3-D they eliminate piston slap in engine warm-up and permit expansion

4. What happens if cylinder head torquing is not done in proper sequence?

    4-A It warps the piston rings.
    4-B It cracks the intake manifold.
    4-C It distorts the head.
    4-D It reduces valve clearance.

5. Water sludge in engine crankcase oil is most usually caused by

    5-A using a low viscosity oil
    5-B condensation in the crankcase
    5-C mixing different brands of motor oil
    5-D using a high viscosity oil

6. When painting, nail holes and cracks should be

    6-A filled with putty before starting
    6-B filled with putty after the priming coat is applied
    6-C filled with paint by careful working
    6-D ignored

7.

The tool shown above is a

    7-A punch
    7-B drill holder
    7-C Philips-type screwdriver
    7-D socket wrench

8. The length of a flat head screw is defined as the length

    8-A of the threaded portion
    8-B of the shank plus the threaded portion
    8-C of the complete screw
    8-D between the bottom of the head and the point

9. If the head of a hammer has become loose on the handle, it should properly be tightened by

    9-A driving the handle further into the head
    9-B driving a nail alongside the present wedge
    9-C using a slightly larger wedge
    9-D soaking the handle in water

10. End grain of wood should be sanded

    10-A crosswise
    10-B with the grain
    10-C obliquely
    10-D with a circular motion

11.

The tool shown above is

11-A   an Allen-head wrench
11-B   a double scraper
11-C   an offset screwdriver
11-D   a nail puller

12. To install an expansion shield in a concrete wall, of the following, the proper tool to use is a

12-A   bull nose chisel
12-B   star drill
12-C   chrome vanadium alloy cold chisel
12-D   rock wedge

13. A method that can be used to prevent the forming of "skin" on a partially used can of oil paint is to

13-A   turn the can upside down every few months
13-B   pour a thin layer of solvent over the top of the paint
13-C   store the paint in a well ventilated room
13-D   avoid shaking the can after it has been sealed

14. A car slows down, lacks power, and a popping sound can be heard. The trouble is likely to be

14-A   a faulty fuel supply
14-B   a shorted sparkplug
14-C   pitted breaker points
14-D   faulty distributor timing

15. Setting the spark plug gap opening closer than normally required would probably result in

15-A   smoother idling and increase in top engine speed
15-B   rougher idling and decrease in top engine speed
15-C   smoother idling and decrease in top engine speed
15-D   rougher idling and increase in top engine speed

16. If a gasoline engine is continued in operation with the contact points of a reverse current relay or "cut-out" being fused together, the result would most likely be to

16-A   "run down" the battery
16-B   reverse the current through the voltage coils
16-C   demagnetize the relay iron core
16-D   overcharge the battery

17. Upon dismantling a gasoline engine, it was found that the piston rings were stuck in the grooves, not being free to rotate. This was most likely caused by

17-A   operating the engine with spark setting in advanced position
17-B   the thermostat maintaining too low an engine temperature
17-C   dirty or contaminated lubricating oil
17-D   using the wrong type of spark plugs in the engine

18. Upon the complete loss of oil pressure while a car is in operation it is best that the car be

18-A   pulled over to the side of the road and the engine stopped immediately for inspection
18-B   pulled over to the side of the road, and a repair truck called to install a new oil pump
18-C   driven a few miles to your favorite garage
18-D   driven as usual for the entire day and be dropped off at the garage in the evening

19. Which of the saws is used to make curved cuts?

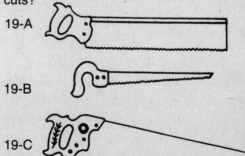

19-A

19-B

19-C

19-D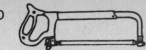

20. A screw is broken off in a tapped hole. The proper tools to use in removing the broken screw from the hole are

20-A hammer and cold chisel
20-B drill and EZY-out
20-C acetylene and oxygen torch
20-D screw driver and pliers

21. "Blistering" is generally caused by applying paint

21-A over a primer that has not completely dried
21-B containing an improper binder for the pigment
21-C that has been thinned too much
21-D over a surface that has excessive moisture

22. The plane to use in shaping a curved edge on wood is known as

22-A jack
22-B spoke shave
22-C smooth
22-D rabbet

23. The wrench that is used principally for pipe work is

23-A

23-B

23-C

23-D

24. If an expander is used under an oil ring it must be

24-A of the diagonal joint type
24-B a rigid type
24-C of the step joint type
24-D of the vented type

25. A squeegee is a tool that is used in

25-A drying windows after washing
25-B cleaning inside boiler surfaces
25-C the central vacuum cleaning system
25-D clearing stoppages in waste lines

END OF PART 7

IF YOU FINISH BEFORE TIME IS UP, CHECK OVER YOUR WORK ON THIS PART ONLY. DO NOT RETURN TO ANY PREVIOUS PART. DO NOT GO ON UNTIL YOU ARE TOLD TO DO SO.

MATHEMATICS KNOWLEDGE

To solve the problems in this part, you must draw upon your knowledge of high school mathematics. The problems require you to use simple algebra and geometry along with arithmetic skills and reasoning power. Some questions can be answered in your head. Others will require the use of scratch paper. If you use scratch paper for your calculations, be sure to mark the letter of the correct answer on your answer sheet. Try these questions.

1. A section of pavement which is 10 feet long and 8 feet wide contains how many square feet?

1-A 80 sq. ft.
1-B 92 sq. ft.
1-C 800 sq. ft.
1-D 18 sq. ft.

1. Ⓐ Ⓑ Ⓒ Ⓓ

1-A Area equals Length times Width
  $A = L \times W$
  $A = 10 \text{ ft.} \times 8 \text{ ft.}$
  $A = 80 \text{ sq. ft.}$

2. $r = 35 - (3 + 6)(-n)$
  $n = 2$
  $r =$

2-A 53
2-B 17
2-C −53
2-D −17

2. Ⓐ Ⓑ Ⓒ Ⓓ

2-A $r = 35 - (9)(-n)$
  $r = 35 - (9)(-2)$
  $r = 35 - (-18)$
  $r = 35 + 18 = 53$

To subtract signed numbers, change the sign of the subtrahend and proceed as in algebraic addition.

3. If an engine pumps G gallons of water per minute, then the number of gallons pumped in half an hour may be found by

3-A taking one-half of G
3-B dividing 60 by G
3-C multiplying G by 30
3-D dividing 30 by G

3. Ⓐ Ⓑ Ⓒ Ⓓ

3-C One half hour = 30 minutes
Amount = rate (G) × time (30 minutes)

4. When one-fifth is added to one-third the sum is

4-A $\frac{1}{4}$
4-B $\frac{1}{8}$
4-C eight-fifteenths
4-D one-fifteenth

4. Ⓐ Ⓑ Ⓒ Ⓓ

4-C First find the lowest common denominator, in this case 15. Then change each fraction to a fraction with 15 as its denominator by multiplying the numerator and the denominator by the same number. Then add.

  $1/5 = 3/15$
  $+\ 1/3 = 5/15$
  $\overline{\qquad\quad 8/15}$

DO NOT TURN THE PAGE UNTIL YOU ARE TOLD TO DO SO

MATHEMATICS KNOWLEDGE

TIME: 24 Minutes—25 Questions

1. If two numbers are multiplied together, the result is 3752. If one of the two numbers is 56, the other number is

   1-A 41
   1-B 15
   1-C 67
   1-D 76

2. When $2x - 1$ is multiplied by 10 the result is 70. What is the value of x?

   2-A 2
   2-B 12
   2-C 3
   2-D 4

3. If the circumference of a circle has the same numbered value as its area, then the radius of the circle must be

   3-A 1
   3-B 5
   3-C 2
   3-D 0

4. R is what percent of 1000?

   4-A .001R
   4-B 1R
   4-C .01R
   4-D .1R

5. A car owner finds he needs 12 gallons of gas for each 120 miles he drives. If he has his carburetor adjusted, he will need only 80% as much gas. How many miles will 12 gallons of gas then last him?

   5-A 90
   5-B 150
   5-C 96
   5-D 160

6. What fraction of 63 is $\frac{2}{7}$ of 21?

   6-A $\frac{1}{42}$
   6-B $\frac{7}{6}$
   6-C $\frac{2}{21}$
   6-D $\frac{1}{3}$

7. When $2x + 3$ is multiplied by 10, the result is 55. What is the value of x?

   7-A $1\frac{1}{4}$
   7-B 4
   7-C 2
   7-D 3

8.

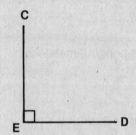

   In the diagram above, CE $\perp$ ED. If CE = 7 and ED = 6, what is the shortest distance from C to D?

   8-A 6
   8-B $4\sqrt{12}$
   8-C 7
   8-D $\sqrt{85}$

9. 5% of 5% of 100 is

   9-A 25
   9-B .25
   9-C 2.5
   9-D 10

10. If $\frac{3}{8}$ of a number is 96, the number is

   10-A 132

10-B 36
10-C 256
10-D 156

11. A line of print in a magazine article contains an average of 6 words. There are 5 lines to the inch. If 8 inches are available for an article which contains 270 words, how must the article be changed?

11-A Add 30 words
11-B Delete 30 words
11-C Delete 40 words
11-D Add 60 words

12. $9\overline{)111111111}$ =

12-A 12345678
12-B 11111119
12-C 11191119
12-D 12345679

13. If $\frac{2}{3}$ of a jar is filled with water in one minute, how many minutes longer will it take to fill the jar?

13-A $\frac{1}{4}$
13-B $\frac{1}{3}$
13-C $\frac{1}{2}$
13-D $\frac{2}{3}$

14. If $2 - x = x - 2$, then x =

14-A -2
14-B 2
14-C 0
14-D $\frac{1}{2}$

15. What is the correct time if the hour hand is exactly $\frac{2}{3}$ of the way between 5 and 6?

15-A 5:25
15-B 5:40
15-C 5:30
15-D 5:45

16. A square is changed into a rectangle by increasing its length 10% and decreasing its width 10%. Its area

16-A remains the same
16-B decreases by 10%
16-C increases by 1%
16-D decreases by 1%

17. If all P are S and no S are Q, it necessarily follows that

17-A all Q are S
17-B all Q are P
17-C no P are Q
17-D no S are P

18. How many of the numbers between 100 and 300 begin or end with 2?

18-A 40
18-B 180
18-C 100
18-D 110

19. If $\frac{5}{4}x = \frac{5}{4}$, then $1 - x$ =

19-A $-\frac{5}{4}$
19-B 1
19-C 0
19-D -1

20. If a piece of wood measuring 4 feet 2 inches is divided into three equal parts, each part is

20-A 1 foot $4\frac{2}{3}$ inches
20-B 1 foot $2\frac{1}{3}$ inches
20-C 1 foot 4 inches
20-D 1 foot $\frac{7}{18}$ inch

21. When 5.1 is divided by 0.017 the quotient is

21-A 30
21-B 300
21-C 3,000
21-D 30,000

22. The area of circle O is 64π. The perimeter of square ABCD is

22-A 32
22-B 32π
22-C 64
22-D 16

23. The number of digits in the square root of 64,048,009 is

23-A 4
23-B 5
23-C 6
23-D 7

24. If 9 is 9% of x, then x =

24-A .01

24-B 100
24-C 1
24-D 9

25. 75% of 4 is the same as what percent of 9?

25-A 36
25-B 25
25-C 40
25-D $33\frac{1}{3}$

END OF PART 8

IF YOU FINISH BEFORE TIME IS UP, MAKE CERTAIN THAT YOU HAVE MARKED ALL YOUR ANSWERS ON THE ANSWER SHEET. THEN CHECK OVER YOUR WORK ON THIS PART ONLY. DO NOT RETURN TO ANY PREVIOUS PART. DO NOT GO ON TO THE NEXT PART UNTIL YOU ARE TOLD TO DO SO.

PART 9

MECHANICAL COMPREHENSION

Part 9 consists of questions about your understanding of general mechanical and physical principles. Your understanding of these principles will come from your own observations, from experience in working with mechanical devices and from your reading and school courses. Answer all the questions as best you can, marking the letter of your choice on your answer sheet. Try these questions.

1.

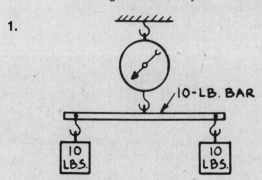

The reading on the weighing scale will be approximately

1-A   zero
1-B   20 lbs.
1-C   10 lbs.
1-D   30 lbs.

1. Ⓐ Ⓑ Ⓒ Ⓓ

1-D The scale is supporting the weight of two 10-pound weights and a 10-pound bar. Since 30 pounds is suspended from the scale, it should read 30 pounds. In actuality, the scale should read just slightly more than 30 pounds, because it will also register the weight of the hardware used for suspension.

2.

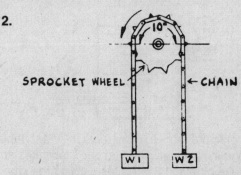

One complete revolution of the sprocket wheel will bring weight W2 higher than weight W1 by

2-A   20″
2-B   40″
2-C   30″
2-D   50″

2. Ⓐ Ⓑ Ⓒ Ⓓ

2-B One-half the circumference of the sprocket wheel is ten inches, therefore the entire circumference is twenty inches. In one complete revolution of the wheel, the chain will move twenty inches. As weight 2 moves up twenty inches, weight 1 will move down twenty inches. The difference between the heights of the two weights will be forty inches.

DO NOT TURN THE PAGE UNTIL YOU ARE TOLD TO DO SO

MECHANICAL COMPREHENSION

TIME: 19 Minutes—25 Questions

1.

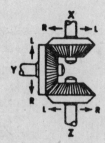

Which of the following is correct if gear Z is turned to the right (R)?

1-A Gear Y turns L, and gear X turns R.
1-B Gear Y turns R, and gear X turns R.
1-C Gear Y turns L, and gear X turns L.
1-D Gear Y turns R, and gear X turns L.

2.

The figure above represents a water tank containing water. The number 1 indicates an intake pipe and 2 indicates a discharge pipe. Of the following, the statement which is *least* accurate is that the

2-A tank will eventually overflow if water flows through the intake pipe at a faster rate than it flows out through the discharge pipe
2-B tank will empty completely if the intake pipe is closed and the discharge pipe is allowed to remain open
2-C water in the tank will remain at a constant level if the rate of intake is equal to the rate of discharge
2-D water in the tank will rise if the intake pipe is operating when the discharge pipe is closed

3.

In the figure above, the threaded block can slide in the slot but cannot revolve. If the hand wheel is turned 20 revolutions clockwise, the threaded block will move

3-A one inch to the left
3-B $\frac{1}{2}$ inch to the left
3-C one inch to the right
3-D $\frac{1}{2}$ inch to the right

4.

What is the function of A and B in the crankshaft shown in the drawing?

4-A They strengthen the crankshaft by increasing its weight.
4-B They make it easier to remove the crankshaft for repairs.
4-C They are necessary to maintain the proper balance of the crankshaft.
4-D They hold grease for continuous lubrication of the crankshaft.

5. Sweating usually occurs on pipes that

5-A contain cold water
5-B contain hot water
5-C are chrome plated
5-D require insulation

6.

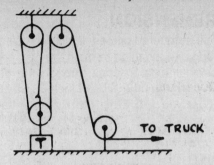

TO TRUCK

The tank "T" is to be raised as shown by attaching the pull rope to a truck. If the tank is to be raised ten feet, the truck will have to move

6-A   20 feet
6-B   40 feet
6-C   30 feet
6-D   50 feet

7.

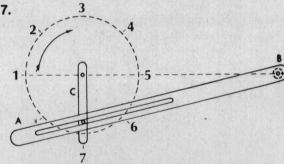

In the diagram above, crank arm "C" revolves at a constant speed of 400 RPM and drives the lever "AB". When lever "AB" is moving the fastest, arm "C" will be in position

7-A   1
7-B   6
7-C   5
7-D   7

8. Assume that the color of the flame from a gas stove is bright yellow. To correct this, you should

8-A   close the air flap
8-B   increase the size of the gas opening
8-C   increase the gas pressure
8-D   open the air flap

9.

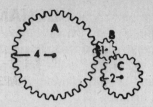

If gear A makes one clockwise revolution per minute, which of the following is true?

9-A   Gear B makes one counterclockwise revolution every 4 minutes.
9-B   Gear C makes two clockwise revolutions every minute.
9-C   Gear B makes four clockwise revolutions every minute.
9-D   Gear C makes one counterclockwise revolution every 8 minutes.

10.

PRESSURE GAGE

The reading shown on the gage is

10-A   10.35
10-B   13.5
10-C   10.7
10-D   17.0

11.

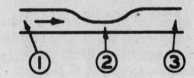

The figure above represents a pipe through which water is flowing in the direction of the arrow. There is a constriction in the pipe at the point indicated by the number 2. Water is being pumped into the pipe at a constant rate of 350 gallons per minute. Of the following, the most accurate statement is that

11-A   the velocity of the water at point 2 is the same as the velocity of the water at point 3
11-B   a greater volume of water is flowing past point 1 in a minute than is flowing past point 2

11-C the velocity of the water at point 1 is greater than the velocity at point 2

11-D the volume of water flowing past point 2 in a minute is the same as the volume of water flowing past point 1 in a minute

12.

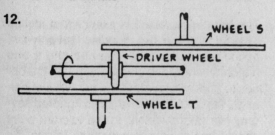

With the wheels in the position shown

12-A wheels S and T will rotate in opposite directions

12-B wheels S and T will rotate at the same speed

12-C wheels S and T will rotate in the same direction

12-D wheel S will rotate at exactly the same speed as the driver wheel

13. The main purpose of a float in a flush tank is to regulate the

13-A water pressure
13-B water velocity
13-C rate of discharge
13-D water supply

14.

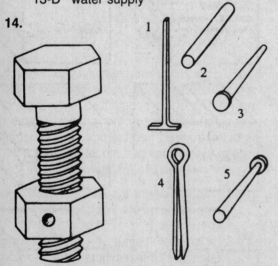

The figure at 14 shows a bolt and nut and five numbered pieces. If all of the pieces are long enough to go through the bolt, and if the circular hole extends through the bolt and through the other side of the nut, which piece must you use to fix the nut in a stationary position?

14-A 1
14-B 3
14-C 2
14-D 4

15. Assume that a gear and pinion have a ratio of 3 to 1. If the gear is rotating at 300 revolutions per minute, the speed of the pinion in revolutions per minute is most nearly

15-A 100
15-B 900
15-C 300
15-D 1800

16.

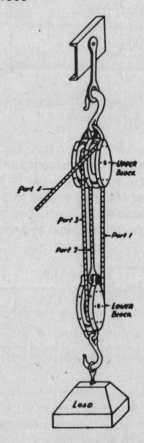

Determine which part of the rope is fastened directly to the block.

16-A Part 1
16-B Part 3
16-C Part 2
16-D Part 4

17.

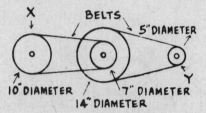

A double belt drive is shown in the figure above. If the pulley marked "X" is revolving at 100 R.P.M., the speed of pulley "Y" is

17-A 800 R.P.M.
17-B 200 R.P.M.
17-C 400 R.P.M.
17-D 25 R.P.M.

18. The best reason for having gaskets on manholes of a boiler is to

18-A prevent leakage from the boiler
18-B provide an emergency exit for excessive steam pressure
18-C provide easy access to the boiler for cleaning
18-D prevent corrosion at the manholes

19.

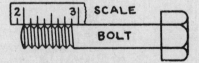

The number of threads per inch on the bolt is:

19-A 16
19-B 8
19-C 10
19-D 7

20.

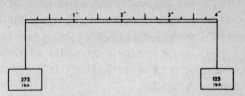

The bar above, which is exactly four inches in length, has a two hundred seventy-five pound weight hung on one end and a one hundred twenty-five pound weight on the opposite end. In order that the bar will just balance, the distance from the two hundred seventy-five pound weight to the fulcrum point should be (In your computation ignore the weight of the bar.)

20-A $\frac{1}{2}$ inch
20-B 1 inch
20-C $\frac{3}{4}$ inch
20-D $1\frac{1}{4}$ inches

21. In order to stop a faucet from dripping, your first act should be to replace the

21-A cap nut
21-B seat
21-C washer
21-D spindle

22.

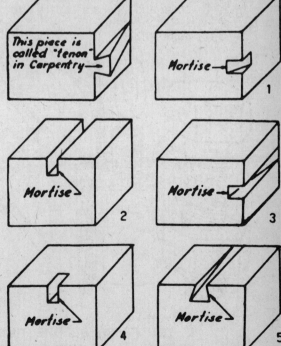

Examine the tenon and the numbered mortises previously shown. The tenon best fits into the mortise numbered

22-A 1
22-B 3
22-C 2
22-D 5

23.

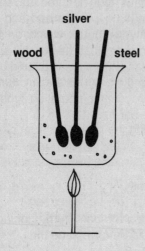

Which spoon is hottest?

23-A wood
23-B silver
23-C steel
23-D silver and steel are equally hot

24.

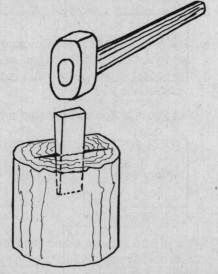

The simple machine pictured at 24 is a form of

24-A inclined plane
24-B pulley
24-C spur gear
24-D torque

25.

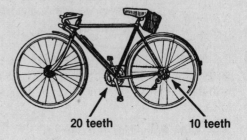

There are twenty teeth on the front sprocket and ten teeth on the rear sprocket on the bicycle above. Each time the pedals go around, the rear wheel will

25-A go half way around
25-B go around once
25-C go around twice
25-D go around four times

END OF PART 9

IF YOU FINISH BEFORE TIME IS UP, CHECK YOUR WORK ON THIS PART ONLY. DO NOT RETURN TO ANY PREVIOUS PART. DO NOT GO ON UNTIL YOU ARE TOLD TO DO SO.

ELECTRONICS INFORMATION

The questions in this part test your knowledge and understanding of electricity, radio and electronics. To answer some of the questions all you need is common sense. Other questions can be answered on the basis of experience, courses and reading. Answer all the questions. Mark the letter of your answer on the answer sheet. Try these questions.

1. If a co-worker is not breathing after receiving an electric shock but is no longer in contact with the electricity, it is most important for you to

1-A wrap the victim in a blanket
1-B force him to take hot liquids
1-C start artificial respiration promptly
1-D avoid moving him

1. Ⓐ Ⓑ Ⓒ Ⓓ

1-C Once a victim of electric shock is no longer in contact with the electricity, whether from a turn-off of the current or from falling or being thrown from the source of the shock, it is no longer dangerous to come into contact with that person. Breathing is absolutely essential to life. The oxygen starved person will die within minutes. Therefore, if a person is not breathing, you must start artificial respiration IMMEDIATELY, no matter what the weather or the extent of his other injuries.

2. A battery consisting of four two-volt cells in series will have a voltage of

2-A ½ volt
2-B 4 volts
2-C 2 volts
2-D 8 volts

2. Ⓐ Ⓑ Ⓒ Ⓓ

2-D In a series connection, each member draws from or contributes equally to the voltage. Thus five light bulbs connected in series to a 300 volt source would each draw 60 volts. In this case,

the four two-volt cells connected in series will produce 8 volts.

3. When removing the insulation from a wire before making a splice, care should be taken to avoid nicking the wire mainly because the

3-A current carrying capacity will be reduced
3-B resistance will be increased
3-C wire tinning will be injured
3-D wire is more likely to break

3. Ⓐ Ⓑ Ⓒ Ⓓ

3-D A nick in wire can be dangerous because it weakens the wire at that point and can lead to breakage. If the wire is nicked during stripping, you should cut off the weakened portion and begin again. Later breakage from an unnoticed weakness can lead to a short circuit.

4. Safety regulations prohibit testing even a 20-volt light socket with the fingers to see whether the socket is alive. The main reason for this prohibition is that

4-A such action can become a bad working habit
4-B sockets usually have sharp edges
4-C a 20-volt shock is often fatal
4-D the skin will become less sensitive to higher voltages

4. Ⓐ Ⓑ Ⓒ Ⓓ

4-A It is hard to break a bad habit, far more sensible to not develop the bad habit in the first place. Sticking a finger into a socket, any socket, to find out if it is live is foolish.

DO NOT TURN THE PAGE UNTIL YOU ARE TOLD TO DO SO

ELECTRONICS INFORMATION

TIME: 9 Minutes—20 Questions

1. Boxes and fittings intended for outdoor use should be of

   1-A weatherproof type
   1-B stamped steel of not less than No. 16
   1-C standard gauge
   1-D stamped steel plated with cadmium

2. A direct-current supply may be obtained from an alternating-current source by means of

   2-A a frequency changer set
   2-B an inductance-capacitance filter
   2-C a tungar bulb rectifier
   2-D none of the devices mentioned above

3.

1   2   3   4

The shape of nut most commonly used on electrical terminals is

   3-A 1
   3-B 2
   3-C 3
   3-D 4

4. When working near lead acid storage batteries extreme care should be taken to guard against sparks, essentially to avoid

   4-A overheating the electrolyte
   4-B an electric shock
   4-C a short circuit
   4-D an explosion

5. A load is missing from a D.C. shunt wound motor. If you happen to open the field circuit

   5-A the speed of the motor will slow down greatly

   5-B the speed of the motor will be much greater
   5-C the speed will be the same
   5-D the motor will cease to operate

6.

The outlet that will accept the plug is

   6-A 1
   6-B 2
   6-C 3
   6-D 4

7. Receptacles in a house-lighting system are regularly connected in

   7-A parallel
   7-B series
   7-C diagonal
   7-D perpendicular

8. If a live conductor is contacted accidentally, the severity of the electrical shock is determined primarily by

   8-A the size of the conductor
   8-B the current in the conductor
   8-C whether the current is a.c. or d.c.
   8-D the contact resistance

9. Locknuts are frequently used in making electrical connections on terminal boards. The purpose of the locknuts is to

   9-A eliminate the use of flat washers

9-B prevent unauthorized personnel from tampering with the connections

9-C keep the connections from loosening through vibration

9-D increase the contact area at the connection point

10. If a condenser is connected across the make-and-break contact of an ordinary electric bell, the effect will be to

10-A speed up the action of the clapper

10-B reduce the amount of arcing at the contact

10-C slow down the action of the clapper

10-D reduce the load on the bell transformer or battery

11. A material *not* used in the make-up of lighting wires or cables is

11-A rubber

11-B paper

11-C lead

11-D cotton

12.

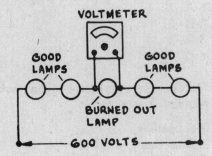

The reading of the voltmeter should be

12-A 600

12-B 300

12-C 120

12-D zero

13. Silver is a better conductor of electricity than copper; however copper is generally used for electrical conductors. The main reason for using copper instead of silver is its

13-A cost

13-B weight

13-C strength

13-D melting point

14. Direct current arcs are "hotter" and harder to extinguish than alternating current arcs, so that electrical appliances which include a thermostat are frequently marked for use on "a.c. only." One appliance which might be so marked *because it includes a thermostat* is a

14-A soldering iron

14-B floor waxer

14-C vacuum cleaner

14-D household iron

15. An alternator is

15-A an a.c. generator

15-B a frequency meter

15-C a ground detector device

15-D a choke coil

16. Operating an incandescent electric light bulb at less than its rated voltage will result in

16-A shorter life and brighter light

16-B brighter light and longer life

16-C longer life and dimmer light

16-D dimmer light and shorter life

17.

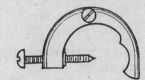

The device shown above is a

17-A C-clamp

17-B test clip

17-C battery connector

17-D ground clamp

18. When the electric refrigerator in a certain household kitchen starts up, the kitchen light at first dims down considerably and then it increases somewhat in brightness while the refrigerator motor is running; the light finally returns to full brightness when the refrigerator shuts off. This behavior of the light shows that most likely the

18-A circuit wires are too small

18-B refrigerator motor is defective

18-C circuit fuse is too small
18-D kitchen lamp is too large

19. A circular mil is a measure of electrical conductor

19-A length
19-B area
19-C volume
19-D weight

20. The instrument by which electric power may be measured is a

20-A rectifier
20-B scanner drum
20-C ammeter
20-D wattmeter

END OF EXAMINATION

IF YOU FINISH BEFORE THE TIME IS UP, CHECK OVER YOUR WORK ON THIS PART ONLY. DO NOT GO BACK TO ANY PREVIOUS PART.

CORRECT ANSWERS—THIRD MODEL EXAM

PART 1—GENERAL SCIENCE

1. A	5. A	8. C	11. C	14. C	17. D	20. B	23. C
2. C	6. D	9. C	12. B	15. D	18. C	21. C	24. B
3. B	7. C	10. C	13. C	16. A	19. B	22. D	25. D
4. D							

PART 2—ARITHMETIC REASONING

1. B	5. C	9. C	13. D	17. C	21. C	25. C	28. D
2. B	6. B	10. B	14. D	18. D	22. B	26. D	29. B
3. C	7. D	11. A	15. C	19. B	23. B	27. C	30. D
4. B	8. B	12. C	16. C	20. A	24. A		

PART 3—WORD KNOWLEDGE

1. D	6. D	11. B	16. A	20. D	24. C	28. C	32. A
2. B	7. B	12. B	17. D	21. D	25. B	29. D	33. D
3. C	8. C	13. D	18. B	22. C	26. A	30. C	34. C
4. D	9. A	14. C	19. A	23. C	27. B	31. B	35. C
5. A	10. D	15. A					

PART 4—PARAGRAPH COMPREHENSION

1. D	3. C	5. B	7. D	9. C	11. A	13. B	15. D
2. A	4. A	6. B	8. B	10. A	12. B	14. D

PART 5—NUMERICAL OPERATIONS

1. B	8. C	15. C	21. A	27. A	33. C	39. C	45. D
2. C	9. D	16. B	22. D	28. D	34. D	40. A	46. A
3. A	10. C	17. A	23. C	29. A	35. B	41. B	47. C
4. B	11. B	18. C	24. D	30. B	36. D	42. D	48. B
5. D	12. D	19. C	25. B	31. C	37. A	43. D	49. C
6. C	13. B	20. C	26. D	32. D	38. A	44. B	50. B
7. A	14. C						

PART 6—CODING SPEED

1. D	12. C	23. B	34. C	45. A	55. C	65. A	75. C
2. E	13. D	24. D	35. A	46. E	56. A	66. C	76. E
3. B	14. C	25. D	36. C	47. D	57. E	67. B	77. D
4. A	15. E	26. E	37. C	48. A	58. B	68. D	78. E
5. E	16. B	27. B	38. C	49. C	59. A	69. A	79. A
6. B	17. C	28. D	39. E	50. B	60. C	70. E	80. E
7. A	18. A	29. A	40. C	51. B	61. B	71. C	81. B
8. A	19. A	30. E	41. B	52. D	62. E	72. E	82. E
9. E	20. E	31. B	42. A	53. C	63. B	73. D	83. D
10. E	21. A	32. A	43. C	54. A	64. E	74. A	84. C
11. E	22. D	33. C	44. E				

PART 7—AUTO & SHOP INFORMATION

1. A	5. B	8. C	11. C	14. A	17. C	20. B	23. C
2. A	6. B	9. C	12. B	15. D	18. A	21. D	24. D
3. D	7. D	10. A	13. B	16. D	19. B	22. B	25. A
4. C							

PART 8—MATHEMATICS KNOWLEDGE

1. C	5. B	8. D	11. B	14. B	17. C	20. A	23. A
2. D	6. C	9. B	12. D	15. B	18. D	21. B	24. B
3. A	7. A	10. C	13. C	16. D	19. C	22. C	25. D
4. D							

PART 9—MECHANICAL COMPREHENSION

1. A	5. A	8. D	11. D	14. D	17. C	20. D	23. B
2. B	6. C	9. B	12. C	15. B	18. A	21. C	24. A
3. C	7. C	10. D	13. D	16. C	19. B	22. D	25. C
4. C							

PART 10—ELECTRONICS INFORMATION

1. A	4. D	7. A	10. B	13. A	15. A	17. D	19. B
2. C	5. B	8. D	11. B	14. D	16. C	18. A	20. D
3. B	6. C	9. C	12. A				

SCORE SHEET—THIRD MODEL EXAM

PART	NUMBER CORRECT		NUMBER OF QUESTIONS		
GENERAL SCIENCE	_____	÷ 25 =	_____	× 100 =	_____%
ARITHMETIC REASONING	_____	÷ 30 =	_____	× 100 =	_____%
WORD KNOWLEDGE	_____	÷ 35 =	_____	× 100 =	_____%
PARAGRAPH COMPREHENSION	_____	÷ 15 =	_____	× 100 =	_____%
NUMERICAL OPERATIONS	_____	÷ 50 =	_____	× 100 =	_____%
CODING SPEED	_____	÷ 84 =	_____	× 100 =	_____%
AUTO & SHOP INFORMATION	_____	÷ 25 =	_____	× 100 =	_____%
MATHEMATICS KNOWLEDGE	_____	÷ 25 =	_____	× 100 =	_____%
MECHANICAL COMPREHENSION	_____	÷ 25 =	_____	× 100 =	_____%
ELECTRONICS INFORMATION	_____	÷ 20 =	_____	× 100 =	_____%
TOTAL	_____	÷ 334 =	_____	× 100 =	_____%

PROGRESS CHART

	Exam I	Exam II	Exam III
GENERAL SCIENCE	%	%	%
ARITHMETIC REASONING	%	%	%
WORD KNOWLEDGE	%	%	%
PARAGRAPH COMPREHENSION	%	%	%
NUMERICAL OPERATIONS	%	%	%
CODING SPEED	%	%	%
AUTO & SHOP INFORMATION	%	%	%
MATHEMATICS KNOWLEDGE	%	%	%
MECHANICAL COMPREHENSION	%	%	%
ELECTRONICS INFORMATION	%	%	%
TOTAL	%	%	%

WHAT ABOUT ASVAB-5?

ASVAB-5 is the high school version of the ASVAB exam. At one time, ASVAB-5 was the only exam administered both to military recruits and to high school students. With the development of the newer exam, described in this book up to this point, ASVAB-5 has been limited to use in the high school testing program. The testing program is widely used in high schools as an aid to vocational counseling. The high school counselor may request this service, and, free of charge, military personnel will administer the exam and assist with its interpretation. The Military Enlistment Processing Command has prepared charts and tables which help the counselor to compare the student's scores on each part with those of other high school students and with those of military men successful in the various training areas. The pattern of subscores—individual part scores and combined scores of certain parts—helps to define a student's areas of interest, aptitude and ability. This information is useful whether the student is considering a military or a civilian career. With the information provided by the student's ASVAB-5 scores and pattern of scores, the school counselor can be of greater assistance in helping the student to establish realistic goals and to choose the best path for attaining them.

A student who has taken ASVAB-5 in high school does not have to take another exam should he choose to enter the service right after graduation. Although versions of the exam differ slightly, the information they give is comparable and each service is able to interpret ASVAB-5 scores for its own purposes.

If you are still in high school and are planning a military career, try the full-length specimen ASVAB-5 which follows. Carefully follow all directions and time limits. Score yourself and compare your scores on this exam with your scores on the three model exams you did earlier in the book. If you find that you are happier with General Information, Attention to Detail, and Space Perception than you are with Paragraph Comprehension and Coding Speed, then you might discuss with your counselor the possibility of taking ASVAB-5 in school. On the other hand, you are *not required* to offer ASVAB-5 scores even though you are still in high school. If you prefer the newer exam, you may take it as well, and offer its scores for training school placement. Follow your recruiter's instructions. He/she will direct you to the enlistment testing center for your area and will tell you when to report for testing.

If you are no longer in high school, you cannot take ASVAB-5. We suggest that you just skip over General Information, Attention to Detail, and Space Perception, none of which will appear on your exam. However, we do recommend that you answer all the remaining questions in the Specimen ASVAB-5. These questions are similar to questions on the exam you will take, and answering them will give you valuable extra practice.

SPECIMEN ASVAB-5

ANSWER SHEET—SPECIMEN ASVAB-5

PART 1—GENERAL INFORMATION

1 Ⓐ Ⓑ Ⓒ Ⓓ   6 Ⓐ Ⓑ Ⓒ Ⓓ   11 Ⓐ Ⓑ Ⓒ Ⓓ   16 Ⓐ Ⓑ Ⓒ Ⓓ

2 Ⓐ Ⓑ Ⓒ Ⓓ   7 Ⓐ Ⓑ Ⓒ Ⓓ   12 Ⓐ Ⓑ Ⓒ Ⓓ   17 Ⓐ Ⓑ Ⓒ Ⓓ

3 Ⓐ Ⓑ Ⓒ Ⓓ   8 Ⓐ Ⓑ Ⓒ Ⓓ   13 Ⓐ Ⓑ Ⓒ Ⓓ   18 Ⓐ Ⓑ Ⓒ Ⓓ

4 Ⓐ Ⓑ Ⓒ Ⓓ   9 Ⓐ Ⓑ Ⓒ Ⓓ   14 Ⓐ Ⓑ Ⓒ Ⓓ   19 Ⓐ Ⓑ Ⓒ Ⓓ

5 Ⓐ Ⓑ Ⓒ Ⓓ   10 Ⓐ Ⓑ Ⓒ Ⓓ   15 Ⓐ Ⓑ Ⓒ Ⓓ   20 Ⓐ Ⓑ Ⓒ Ⓓ

PART 2—NUMERICAL OPERATIONS

21 Ⓐ Ⓑ Ⓒ Ⓓ   31 Ⓐ Ⓑ Ⓒ Ⓓ   41 Ⓐ Ⓑ Ⓒ Ⓓ   51 Ⓐ Ⓑ Ⓒ Ⓓ   61 Ⓐ Ⓑ Ⓒ Ⓓ

22 Ⓐ Ⓑ Ⓒ Ⓓ   32 Ⓐ Ⓑ Ⓒ Ⓓ   42 Ⓐ Ⓑ Ⓒ Ⓓ   52 Ⓐ Ⓑ Ⓒ Ⓓ   62 Ⓐ Ⓑ Ⓒ Ⓓ

23 Ⓐ Ⓑ Ⓒ Ⓓ   33 Ⓐ Ⓑ Ⓒ Ⓓ   43 Ⓐ Ⓑ Ⓒ Ⓓ   53 Ⓐ Ⓑ Ⓒ Ⓓ   63 Ⓐ Ⓑ Ⓒ Ⓓ

24 Ⓐ Ⓑ Ⓒ Ⓓ   34 Ⓐ Ⓑ Ⓒ Ⓓ   44 Ⓐ Ⓑ Ⓒ Ⓓ   54 Ⓐ Ⓑ Ⓒ Ⓓ   64 Ⓐ Ⓑ Ⓒ Ⓓ

25 Ⓐ Ⓑ Ⓒ Ⓓ   35 Ⓐ Ⓑ Ⓒ Ⓓ   45 Ⓐ Ⓑ Ⓒ Ⓓ   55 Ⓐ Ⓑ Ⓒ Ⓓ   65 Ⓐ Ⓑ Ⓒ Ⓓ

26 Ⓐ Ⓑ Ⓒ Ⓓ   36 Ⓐ Ⓑ Ⓒ Ⓓ   46 Ⓐ Ⓑ Ⓒ Ⓓ   56 Ⓐ Ⓑ Ⓒ Ⓓ   66 Ⓐ Ⓑ Ⓒ Ⓓ

27 Ⓐ Ⓑ Ⓒ Ⓓ   37 Ⓐ Ⓑ Ⓒ Ⓓ   47 Ⓐ Ⓑ Ⓒ Ⓓ   57 Ⓐ Ⓑ Ⓒ Ⓓ   67 Ⓐ Ⓑ Ⓒ Ⓓ

28 Ⓐ Ⓑ Ⓒ Ⓓ   38 Ⓐ Ⓑ Ⓒ Ⓓ   48 Ⓐ Ⓑ Ⓒ Ⓓ   58 Ⓐ Ⓑ Ⓒ Ⓓ   68 Ⓐ Ⓑ Ⓒ Ⓓ

29 Ⓐ Ⓑ Ⓒ Ⓓ   39 Ⓐ Ⓑ Ⓒ Ⓓ   49 Ⓐ Ⓑ Ⓒ Ⓓ   59 Ⓐ Ⓑ Ⓒ Ⓓ   69 Ⓐ Ⓑ Ⓒ Ⓓ

30 Ⓐ Ⓑ Ⓒ Ⓓ   40 Ⓐ Ⓑ Ⓒ Ⓓ   50 Ⓐ Ⓑ Ⓒ Ⓓ   60 Ⓐ Ⓑ Ⓒ Ⓓ   70 Ⓐ Ⓑ Ⓒ Ⓓ

PART 3—ATTENTION TO DETAIL

71 ⑪ ⑫ ⑬ ⑭ ⑮   77 ⑪ ⑫ ⑬ ⑭ ⑮   83 ⑪ ⑫ ⑬ ⑭ ⑮   89 ⑪ ⑫ ⑬ ⑭ ⑮   95 ⑪ ⑫ ⑬ ⑭ ⑮

72 ⑪ ⑫ ⑬ ⑭ ⑮   78 ⑪ ⑫ ⑬ ⑭ ⑮   84 ⑪ ⑫ ⑬ ⑭ ⑮   90 ⑪ ⑫ ⑬ ⑭ ⑮   96 ⑪ ⑫ ⑬ ⑭ ⑮

73 ⑪ ⑫ ⑬ ⑭ ⑮   79 ⑪ ⑫ ⑬ ⑭ ⑮   85 ⑪ ⑫ ⑬ ⑭ ⑮   91 ⑪ ⑫ ⑬ ⑭ ⑮   97 ⑪ ⑫ ⑬ ⑭ ⑮

74 ⑪ ⑫ ⑬ ⑭ ⑮   80 ⑪ ⑫ ⑬ ⑭ ⑮   86 ⑪ ⑫ ⑬ ⑭ ⑮   92 ⑪ ⑫ ⑬ ⑭ ⑮   98 ⑪ ⑫ ⑬ ⑭ ⑮

75 ⑪ ⑫ ⑬ ⑭ ⑮   81 ⑪ ⑫ ⑬ ⑭ ⑮   87 ⑪ ⑫ ⑬ ⑭ ⑮   93 ⑪ ⑫ ⑬ ⑭ ⑮   99 ⑪ ⑫ ⑬ ⑭ ⑮

76 ⑪ ⑫ ⑬ ⑭ ⑮   82 ⑪ ⑫ ⑬ ⑭ ⑮   88 ⑪ ⑫ ⑬ ⑭ ⑮   94 ⑪ ⑫ ⑬ ⑭ ⑮   100 ⑪ ⑫ ⑬ ⑭ ⑮

PART 4—WORD KNOWLEDGE

1 Ⓐ Ⓑ Ⓒ Ⓓ	7 Ⓐ Ⓑ Ⓒ Ⓓ	13 Ⓐ Ⓑ Ⓒ Ⓓ	19 Ⓐ Ⓑ Ⓒ Ⓓ	25 Ⓐ Ⓑ Ⓒ Ⓓ
2 Ⓐ Ⓑ Ⓒ Ⓓ	8 Ⓐ Ⓑ Ⓒ Ⓓ	14 Ⓐ Ⓑ Ⓒ Ⓓ	20 Ⓐ Ⓑ Ⓒ Ⓓ	26 Ⓐ Ⓑ Ⓒ Ⓓ
3 Ⓐ Ⓑ Ⓒ Ⓓ	9 Ⓐ Ⓑ Ⓒ Ⓓ	15 Ⓐ Ⓑ Ⓒ Ⓓ	21 Ⓐ Ⓑ Ⓒ Ⓓ	27 Ⓐ Ⓑ Ⓒ Ⓓ
4 Ⓐ Ⓑ Ⓒ Ⓓ	10 Ⓐ Ⓑ Ⓒ Ⓓ	16 Ⓐ Ⓑ Ⓒ Ⓓ	22 Ⓐ Ⓑ Ⓒ Ⓓ	28 Ⓐ Ⓑ Ⓒ Ⓓ
5 Ⓐ Ⓑ Ⓒ Ⓓ	11 Ⓐ Ⓑ Ⓒ Ⓓ	17 Ⓐ Ⓑ Ⓒ Ⓓ	23 Ⓐ Ⓑ Ⓒ Ⓓ	29 Ⓐ Ⓑ Ⓒ Ⓓ
6 Ⓐ Ⓑ Ⓒ Ⓓ	12 Ⓐ Ⓑ Ⓒ Ⓓ	18 Ⓐ Ⓑ Ⓒ Ⓓ	24 Ⓐ Ⓑ Ⓒ Ⓓ	30 Ⓐ Ⓑ Ⓒ Ⓓ

PART 5—ARITHMETIC REASONING

31 Ⓐ Ⓑ Ⓒ Ⓓ	35 Ⓐ Ⓑ Ⓒ Ⓓ	39 Ⓐ Ⓑ Ⓒ Ⓓ	43 Ⓐ Ⓑ Ⓒ Ⓓ	47 Ⓐ Ⓑ Ⓒ Ⓓ
32 Ⓐ Ⓑ Ⓒ Ⓓ	36 Ⓐ Ⓑ Ⓒ Ⓓ	40 Ⓐ Ⓑ Ⓒ Ⓓ	44 Ⓐ Ⓑ Ⓒ Ⓓ	48 Ⓐ Ⓑ Ⓒ Ⓓ
33 Ⓐ Ⓑ Ⓒ Ⓓ	37 Ⓐ Ⓑ Ⓒ Ⓓ	41 Ⓐ Ⓑ Ⓒ Ⓓ	45 Ⓐ Ⓑ Ⓒ Ⓓ	49 Ⓐ Ⓑ Ⓒ Ⓓ
34 Ⓐ Ⓑ Ⓒ Ⓓ	38 Ⓐ Ⓑ Ⓒ Ⓓ	42 Ⓐ Ⓑ Ⓒ Ⓓ	46 Ⓐ Ⓑ Ⓒ Ⓓ	50 Ⓐ Ⓑ Ⓒ Ⓓ

PART 6—SPACE PERCEPTION

51 Ⓐ Ⓑ Ⓒ Ⓓ	55 Ⓐ Ⓑ Ⓒ Ⓓ	59 Ⓐ Ⓑ Ⓒ Ⓓ	63 Ⓐ Ⓑ Ⓒ Ⓓ	67 Ⓐ Ⓑ Ⓒ Ⓓ
52 Ⓐ Ⓑ Ⓒ Ⓓ	56 Ⓐ Ⓑ Ⓒ Ⓓ	60 Ⓐ Ⓑ Ⓒ Ⓓ	64 Ⓐ Ⓑ Ⓒ Ⓓ	68 Ⓐ Ⓑ Ⓒ Ⓓ
53 Ⓐ Ⓑ Ⓒ Ⓓ	57 Ⓐ Ⓑ Ⓒ Ⓓ	61 Ⓐ Ⓑ Ⓒ Ⓓ	65 Ⓐ Ⓑ Ⓒ Ⓓ	69 Ⓐ Ⓑ Ⓒ Ⓓ
54 Ⓐ Ⓑ Ⓒ Ⓓ	58 Ⓐ Ⓑ Ⓒ Ⓓ	62 Ⓐ Ⓑ Ⓒ Ⓓ	66 Ⓐ Ⓑ Ⓒ Ⓓ	70 Ⓐ Ⓑ Ⓒ Ⓓ

PART 7—MATHEMATICS KNOWLEDGE

71 Ⓐ Ⓑ Ⓒ Ⓓ	75 Ⓐ Ⓑ Ⓒ Ⓓ	79 Ⓐ Ⓑ Ⓒ Ⓓ	83 Ⓐ Ⓑ Ⓒ Ⓓ	87 Ⓐ Ⓑ Ⓒ Ⓓ
72 Ⓐ Ⓑ Ⓒ Ⓓ	76 Ⓐ Ⓑ Ⓒ Ⓓ	80 Ⓐ Ⓑ Ⓒ Ⓓ	84 Ⓐ Ⓑ Ⓒ Ⓓ	88 Ⓐ Ⓑ Ⓒ Ⓓ
73 Ⓐ Ⓑ Ⓒ Ⓓ	77 Ⓐ Ⓑ Ⓒ Ⓓ	81 Ⓐ Ⓑ Ⓒ Ⓓ	85 Ⓐ Ⓑ Ⓒ Ⓓ	89 Ⓐ Ⓑ Ⓒ Ⓓ
74 Ⓐ Ⓑ Ⓒ Ⓓ	78 Ⓐ Ⓑ Ⓒ Ⓓ	82 Ⓐ Ⓑ Ⓒ Ⓓ	86 Ⓐ Ⓑ Ⓒ Ⓓ	90 Ⓐ Ⓑ Ⓒ Ⓓ

PART 8—ELECTRONICS INFORMATION

91 Ⓐ Ⓑ Ⓒ Ⓓ	97 Ⓐ Ⓑ Ⓒ Ⓓ	103 Ⓐ Ⓑ Ⓒ Ⓓ	109 Ⓐ Ⓑ Ⓒ Ⓓ	115 Ⓐ Ⓑ Ⓒ Ⓓ
92 Ⓐ Ⓑ Ⓒ Ⓓ	98 Ⓐ Ⓑ Ⓒ Ⓓ	104 Ⓐ Ⓑ Ⓒ Ⓓ	110 Ⓐ Ⓑ Ⓒ Ⓓ	116 Ⓐ Ⓑ Ⓒ Ⓓ
93 Ⓐ Ⓑ Ⓒ Ⓓ	99 Ⓐ Ⓑ Ⓒ Ⓓ	105 Ⓐ Ⓑ Ⓒ Ⓓ	111 Ⓐ Ⓑ Ⓒ Ⓓ	117 Ⓐ Ⓑ Ⓒ Ⓓ
94 Ⓐ Ⓑ Ⓒ Ⓓ	100 Ⓐ Ⓑ Ⓒ Ⓓ	106 Ⓐ Ⓑ Ⓒ Ⓓ	112 Ⓐ Ⓑ Ⓒ Ⓓ	118 Ⓐ Ⓑ Ⓒ Ⓓ
95 Ⓐ Ⓑ Ⓒ Ⓓ	101 Ⓐ Ⓑ Ⓒ Ⓓ	107 Ⓐ Ⓑ Ⓒ Ⓓ	113 Ⓐ Ⓑ Ⓒ Ⓓ	119 Ⓐ Ⓑ Ⓒ Ⓓ
96 Ⓐ Ⓑ Ⓒ Ⓓ	102 Ⓐ Ⓑ Ⓒ Ⓓ	108 Ⓐ Ⓑ Ⓒ Ⓓ	114 Ⓐ Ⓑ Ⓒ Ⓓ	120 Ⓐ Ⓑ Ⓒ Ⓓ

PART 9—MECHANICAL COMPREHENSION

121 Ⓐ Ⓑ Ⓒ Ⓓ	125 Ⓐ Ⓑ Ⓒ Ⓓ	129 Ⓐ Ⓑ Ⓒ Ⓓ	133 Ⓐ Ⓑ Ⓒ Ⓓ	137 Ⓐ Ⓑ Ⓒ Ⓓ
122 Ⓐ Ⓑ Ⓒ Ⓓ	126 Ⓐ Ⓑ Ⓒ Ⓓ	130 Ⓐ Ⓑ Ⓒ Ⓓ	134 Ⓐ Ⓑ Ⓒ Ⓓ	138 Ⓐ Ⓑ Ⓒ Ⓓ
123 Ⓐ Ⓑ Ⓒ Ⓓ	127 Ⓐ Ⓑ Ⓒ Ⓓ	131 Ⓐ Ⓑ Ⓒ Ⓓ	135 Ⓐ Ⓑ Ⓒ Ⓓ	139 Ⓐ Ⓑ Ⓒ Ⓓ
124 Ⓐ Ⓑ Ⓒ Ⓓ	128 Ⓐ Ⓑ Ⓒ Ⓓ	132 Ⓐ Ⓑ Ⓒ Ⓓ	136 Ⓐ Ⓑ Ⓒ Ⓓ	140 Ⓐ Ⓑ Ⓒ Ⓓ

PART 10—GENERAL SCIENCE

141 Ⓐ Ⓑ Ⓒ Ⓓ	145 Ⓐ Ⓑ Ⓒ Ⓓ	149 Ⓐ Ⓑ Ⓒ Ⓓ	153 Ⓐ Ⓑ Ⓒ Ⓓ	157 Ⓐ Ⓑ Ⓒ Ⓓ
142 Ⓐ Ⓑ Ⓒ Ⓓ	146 Ⓐ Ⓑ Ⓒ Ⓓ	150 Ⓐ Ⓑ Ⓒ Ⓓ	154 Ⓐ Ⓑ Ⓒ Ⓓ	158 Ⓐ Ⓑ Ⓒ Ⓓ
143 Ⓐ Ⓑ Ⓒ Ⓓ	147 Ⓐ Ⓑ Ⓒ Ⓓ	151 Ⓐ Ⓑ Ⓒ Ⓓ	155 Ⓐ Ⓑ Ⓒ Ⓓ	159 Ⓐ Ⓑ Ⓒ Ⓓ
144 Ⓐ Ⓑ Ⓒ Ⓓ	148 Ⓐ Ⓑ Ⓒ Ⓓ	152 Ⓐ Ⓑ Ⓒ Ⓓ	156 Ⓐ Ⓑ Ⓒ Ⓓ	160 Ⓐ Ⓑ Ⓒ Ⓓ

PART 11—SHOP INFORMATION

161 Ⓐ Ⓑ Ⓒ Ⓓ	165 Ⓐ Ⓑ Ⓒ Ⓓ	169 Ⓐ Ⓑ Ⓒ Ⓓ	173 Ⓐ Ⓑ Ⓒ Ⓓ	177 Ⓐ Ⓑ Ⓒ Ⓓ
162 Ⓐ Ⓑ Ⓒ Ⓓ	166 Ⓐ Ⓑ Ⓒ Ⓓ	170 Ⓐ Ⓑ Ⓒ Ⓓ	174 Ⓐ Ⓑ Ⓒ Ⓓ	178 Ⓐ Ⓑ Ⓒ Ⓓ
163 Ⓐ Ⓑ Ⓒ Ⓓ	167 Ⓐ Ⓑ Ⓒ Ⓓ	171 Ⓐ Ⓑ Ⓒ Ⓓ	175 Ⓐ Ⓑ Ⓒ Ⓓ	179 Ⓐ Ⓑ Ⓒ Ⓓ
164 Ⓐ Ⓑ Ⓒ Ⓓ	168 Ⓐ Ⓑ Ⓒ Ⓓ	172 Ⓐ Ⓑ Ⓒ Ⓓ	176 Ⓐ Ⓑ Ⓒ Ⓓ	180 Ⓐ Ⓑ Ⓒ Ⓓ

PART 12—AUTOMOTIVE INFORMATION

181 Ⓐ Ⓑ Ⓒ Ⓓ	185 Ⓐ Ⓑ Ⓒ Ⓓ	189 Ⓐ Ⓑ Ⓒ Ⓓ	193 Ⓐ Ⓑ Ⓒ Ⓓ	197 Ⓐ Ⓑ Ⓒ Ⓓ
182 Ⓐ Ⓑ Ⓒ Ⓓ	186 Ⓐ Ⓑ Ⓒ Ⓓ	190 Ⓐ Ⓑ Ⓒ Ⓓ	194 Ⓐ Ⓑ Ⓒ Ⓓ	198 Ⓐ Ⓑ Ⓒ Ⓓ
183 Ⓐ Ⓑ Ⓒ Ⓓ	187 Ⓐ Ⓑ Ⓒ Ⓓ	191 Ⓐ Ⓑ Ⓒ Ⓓ	195 Ⓐ Ⓑ Ⓒ Ⓓ	199 Ⓐ Ⓑ Ⓒ Ⓓ
184 Ⓐ Ⓑ Ⓒ Ⓓ	188 Ⓐ Ⓑ Ⓒ Ⓓ	192 Ⓐ Ⓑ Ⓒ Ⓓ	196 Ⓐ Ⓑ Ⓒ Ⓓ	200 Ⓐ Ⓑ Ⓒ Ⓓ

PART 1

GENERAL INFORMATION

TIME: 7 Minutes. 20 Questions.

This is a test to find out how much you know about different kinds of things. Pick the best answer for each question, then blacken the space on your separate answer form which has the same number and letter as your choice.

1. A rose is a kind of

   1-A   animal.
   1-B   bird.
   1-C   flower.
   1-D   fish.

2. An ally of the United States during WWII was

   2-A   Japan.
   2-B   Germany.
   2-C   Italy.
   2-D   Great Britain.

3. How many degrees apart are the foul lines on a baseball field?

   3-A   60⁰
   3-B   90⁰
   3-C   120⁰
   3-D   180⁰

4. For which of the following taxes was it necessary to amend the US Constitution?

   4-A   Income.
   4-B   Sales.
   4-C   Liquor.
   4-D   Tobacco.

5. Picasso was a famous

   5-A   poet.
   5-B   painter.
   5-C   philosopher.
   5-D   soldier.

6. Which one of the following states does **not** border Canada?

   6-A   Washington.
   6-B   Idaho.
   6-C   Wyoming.
   6-D   New York.

7. The Rosetta stone provided the key for translating

   7-A   The Mosaic Tablets.
   7-B   Babylonian Cuneiform.
   7-C   New Testament Papyri.
   7-D   Egyptian Hieroglyphs.

8. A women writer famous for her books about China is

   8-A   Pearl Buck.
   8-B   Ellen Glasgow.
   8-C   Willa Cather.
   8-D   Edith Wharton.

9. During the period from 1963 to 1974 which collegiate basketball team won the most NCAA titles?

   9-A   North Carolina State University.
   9-B   Marquette University.
   9-C   University of California at Los Angeles.
   9-D   University of Houston.

10. Which flower below is grown from a bulb?

    10-A Petunia.
    10-B Cosmos.
    10-C Gladiola.
    10-D Poppy.

11. A fabric woven from smooth surface yarn spun from long, stapled wool is

    11-A Gingham.
    11-B Convert Cloth.
    11-C Worsted.
    11-D Shetland Tweed.

12. Which city below has a Spanish name?

    12-A New Orleans.
    12-B Sault Ste. Marie.
    12-C Seattle.
    12-D Monterey.

13. A coarse acid bread made of unbolted rye is called

    13-A Black bread.
    13-B Pumpernickel.
    13-C French bread.
    13-D Vienna bread.

14. Citrus fruits include

    14-A Apples.
    14-B Bananas.
    14-C Oranges.
    14-D Peaches.

15. Margaret Chase Smith is a noted

    15-A Interior decorator.
    15-B Political figure.
    15-C Business executive.
    15-D Television commentator.

16. Cork is obtained from

    16-A An animal skeleton.
    16-B A tree.
    16-C A mineral.
    16-D A deep-sea plant.

17. The author of the Pulitzer prize winning play "Death of a Salesman" is

    17-A Arthur Miller.
    17-B Henry Miller.
    17-C Sidney Miller.
    17-D Mitchell Miller.

18. The state which has the smallest area is

    18-A Nevada.
    18-B Rhode Island.
    18-C Connecticut.
    18-D Delaware.

19. A man of the Renaissance who worked in many fields of art and science was

    19-A Niccolo Machiavelli.
    19-B Sir Thomas More.
    19-C Erasmus.
    19-D Francis Bacon.

20. In the United Nations, one difference between the General Assembly and the Security Council is that the General Assembly

    20-A Permits use of the veto.
    20-B Includes Communist China.
    20-C Does not deal with military matters.
    20-D Gives more power to the smaller nations.

STOP!

IF YOU FINISH THIS PART BEFORE THE TIME IS UP, CHECK OVER YOUR WORK ON THIS PART ONLY. DO NOT GO ON UNTIL YOU ARE TOLD TO DO SO.

PART 2

NUMERICAL OPERATIONS

TIME: 3 Minutes. 50 Questions.

This is a test to see how rapidly and accurately you can do arithmetic problems. Each problem is followed by four answers, only one of which is correct. Decide which answer is correct, then blacken the space on your answer form which has the same number and letter as your choice.

This is a speed test, so work as fast as you can without making mistakes. Do each problem as it comes. If you finish before time is up, go back and check your work.

21. 2 + 3 =

21-A 1
21-B 4
21-C 5
21-D 6

22. 8 − 5 =

22-A 3
22-B 1
22-C 4
22-D 2

23. 9 ÷ 3 =

23-A 2
23-B 3
23-C 6
23-D 4

24. 4 × 2 =

24-A 2
24-B 4
24-C 6
24-D 8

25. 7 − 3 =

25-A 5
25-B 3
25-C 2
25-D 4

26. 9 + 1 =

26-A 10
26-B 8
26-C 2
26-D 7

27. 8 − 4 =

27-A 4
27-B 12
27-C 10
27-D 2

28. 2 × 8 =

28-A 10
28-B 6
28-C 16
28-D 4

29. 9 − 6 =

29-A 1
29-B 2
29-C 3
29-D 4

30. 3 − 2 =

30-A 1
30-B 2
30-C 3
30-D 4

31. 1 − 1 =

31-A 2
31-B 3
31-C 0
31-D 1

32. 2 × 9 =

32-A 16
32-B 17
32-C 18
32-D 20

33. 9 + 3 =

33-A 3
33-B 7
33-C 11
33-D 12

34. 8 + 6 =

34-A 2
34-B 10
34-C 12
34-D 14

35. 9 − 4 =

35-A 3
35-B 5
35-C 6
35-D 7

36. 10 ÷ 2 =

36-A 8
36-B 7
36-C 6
36-D 5

37. 7 − 2 =

37-A 5
37-B 7
37-C 9
37-D 10

38. 3 − 3 =

38-A 0
38-B 5
38-C 6
38-D 9

39. 4 − 3 =

39-A 0
39-B 1
39-C 2
39-D 4

40. 8 − 3 =

40-A 3
40-B 4
40-C 5
40-D 6

41. 7 × 4 =

41-A 28
41-B 30
41-C 32
41-D 34

42. 5 + 8 =

42-A 3
42-B 7
42-C 12
42-D 13

43. 20 ÷ 2 =

43-A 6
43-B 8
43-C 10
43-D 12

44. 15 − 7 =

44-A 5
44-B 8
44-C 10
44-D 12

45. 6 ÷ 2 =

   45-A 3
   45-B 4
   45-C 5
   45-D 8

46. 9 − 1 =

   46-A 2
   46-B 5
   46-C 6
   46-D 8

47. 10 − 2 =

   47-A 8
   47-B 7
   47-C 5
   47-D 4

48. 1 + 6 =

   48-A 5
   48-B 7
   48-C 8
   48-D 9

49. 4 × 5 =

   49-A 8
   49-B 10
   49-C 16
   49-D 20

50. 7 − 7 =

   50-A 14
   50-B 10
   50-C 1
   50-D 0

51. 5 + 5 =

   51-A 0
   51-B 10
   51-C 15
   51-D 20

52. 5 × 3 =

   52-A 8
   52-B 10
   52-C 13
   52-D 15

53. 16 ÷ 4 =

   53-A 2
   53-B 4
   53-C 6
   53-D 7

54. 7 + 9 =

   54-A 2
   54-B 13
   54-C 16
   54-D 18

55. 5 × 5 =

   55-A 10
   55-B 15
   55-C 20
   55-D 25

56. 4 − 3 =

   56-A 1
   56-B 5
   56-C 7
   56-D 9

57. 7 + 3 =

   57-A 4
   57-B 5
   57-C 9
   57-D 10

58. 9 + 3 =

   58-A 3
   58-B 6
   58-C 12
   58-D 13

59. 6 + 4 =

   59-A 10
   59-B 12
   59-C 14
   59-D 16

60. 10 + 2 =

   60-A 4
   60-B 5
   60-C 8
   60-D 12

61. 2 + 8 =

   61-A 6
   61-B 8
   61-C 10
   61-D 12

62. 8 − 2 =

   62-A 4
   62-B 6
   62-C 8
   62-D 10

63. 2 + 2 =

   63-A 4
   63-B 5
   63-C 6
   63-D 8

64. 3 × 5 =

   64-A 8
   64-B 10
   64-C 12
   64-D 15

65. 25 ÷ 5 =

   65-A 4
   65-B 5
   65-C 6
   65-D 7

66. 30 ÷ 5 =

   66-A 5
   66-B 6
   66-C 7
   66-D 8

67. 7 + 5 =

   67-A 12
   67-B 13
   67-C 14
   67-D 15

68. 3 × 6 =

   68-A 3
   68-B 9
   68-C 15
   68-D 18

69. 9 − 6 =

   69-A 3
   69-B 7
   69-C 14
   69-D 15

70. 4 × 6 =

   70-A 10
   70-B 20
   70-C 24
   70-D 26

STOP!

IF YOU FINISH THIS PART BEFORE THE TIME IS UP, CHECK OVER YOUR WORK ON THIS PART ONLY. DO NOT GO ON UNTIL YOU ARE TOLD TO DO SO.

PART 3

ATTENTION TO DETAIL

TIME: 5 Minutes

This is a test of your ability to find an important detail. For each problem in the test, there are five possible answers. There is only one correct answer for each problem. Look at each problem carefully, and decide which one of the five answers is correct.

Now look at Sample Problem S1

O O C O C O O O O C O O O O O O O O C O O O O C O C C O O O C O O O O O O O O O
O O O O O C O O O O O O C O O O C O O C O O C O O C O O O O O O O C O O O O O O O O

There are two lines of O's with some C's mixed in. You are to count the total number of C's in both lines of the problem. There are 14 C's in both lines of Sample Problem S1, so 14 is the correct answer. After the number S1, below, are five numbers: 11, 12, 13, 14, and 15. The space under the number 14 is blackened out to show that 14 is the correct answer.

S1   11   12   13   14   15
     O   O   O   ●   O

Now look at Sample Problem S2.

O C O O O O O C O O O O C O O O O O O O O C O O O O O C O O O O O O O O O C O O O
O O O O O O O O C O C O O C O O O O O O O O O O O O C O O O C O O O O C O O O O O

Count the number of C's in both lines of the problem. You may find 11, 12, 13, 14, or 15 C's. Do this now.

There are 12 C's, so 12 is the correct answer.

This is a speed test, so work as fast as you can without making mistakes.

71. O O O O O O O C O O O O C O O O O O O O C O O O O O O C O O O O O O O O O O O C O O O
    O O O O O C O O O C O O O O O C O O O O O O O O C O O O C O O C O O C O O C O O O O O C O

72. O C O O O C O O O O O C O O O C O O O O O O C O C O O O O C O O O O O O O O C O O O O
    O O O O O C O C O C O O O O O O O O O C O O O O O O C O O O O O O O O O O O O O O O O O

73. O O O O O O O O O C O C O O C O C O O O O O O O O O O O O C O O O C O O O O O C O O O O O
    O O C O O O O O O O O O O C O O O O O C O O O O O C O O O C O O O O O O O O O C O O O O O

74. O O O O O O O C O C O O O O O C O O O O O O O O O O O O O O O O O C O O O O O O O O O O O
    O O O O O O O C O O O C O O O O O C O O O O O C O O O O O O O O O O O O O O C O O C O O C O

75. C O O O O O O O O C O O O O O C O O O O O O O C O O O C O O O O O O O C O O O O O O O
    O C O O O O O O C O C O O O O O O O C O O O O O O O O C O O O O O O O O C O O O C O O

76. O O C O O O O O C O O C O O O C O O O O O C O O O O O C O O O O O C O O O O O O O O O
    C O O O O O O O C O O O C O O O C O O O O O C O O O O C O O O O O O C O O O O O C O O O O O

77. O O O O O C O O C O O O O O O O O C O O O O O O O O O O O C O O C O O C O O C O C O O O
    O C O O O C O O O O O O C O C O O O O O C O O O O O O O O C C O O O O O O C O O O O

78. C O O C O O O O O C O O O O O C O O O O O C O C O O O O O O O C O O O O O O O O O O C O O
    O O O C C O O C O O O O C O O O O O C O O O O O O O O O O O O O C O O O O O O O O O

79. O C O O O O O C O O O O O O O C C O O O O O C O O O O O O O O C O O O C O O O C O O O O O
    O O O O O O O O C O O O O C O O C O O C O O O O C O O O O O C O O O O O O O O O O O O

80. O O C C C O O O O C O O C O O O O O O O O C O O O C O O O O O C O C O O O O O O
    C O O O O C O O O O O O O O O C O O O O C O O O O O O O O O O O C O O O O O O

81. C O O C O O O C O O O O O O O O O O C O O O O O O O O O C O O C O O O O O C O O
    O O C O O O C O O O O O O O O O O O O O C O O C C C O O O C O C O O O O O O O

82. O O O O C O O O C O C O O O O C O O C O O O O O C O O O O O O O O C O O O C O O
    O O O O C O O O C O O C O O O O O O O O C O O C O O O O O O O C C O O O O O

83. O C O O O O O O O C O O O O O C O O O O O O O O C O O O C O O O O O O O O O O
    O O C O O O O O O O C O C C O O O O O O O C O O O O C O O O O O C O O O C O O

84. C O C O O C O O O O O O O C O O C O O O O O O O O C O O O O C O O O O O C O O O
    C O O O O O O O C O O C O O O O O O O O C O O O C O O O O O C O O O O O C O O

85. O O C O O O O C O O O O O O C O O O O O C O O C O O O O O O O C O O C O O O C O O
    O O O C O O C O O O O O O O O C O O O C O C O O O O O O O O O O C O O O O

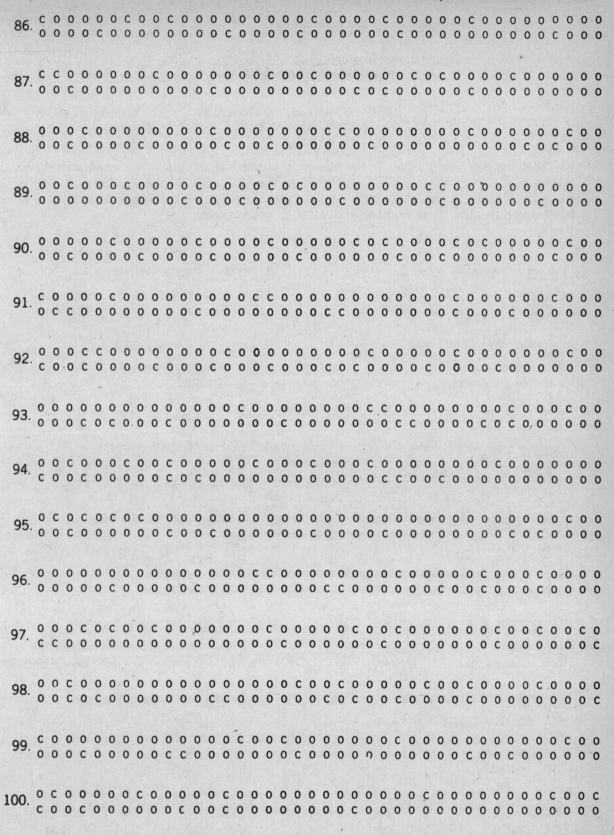

PART 4

WORD KNOWLEDGE

TIME: 10 Minutes. 30 Questions.

This test has questions about the meanings of words. Each question has an underlined boldface word. You are to decide which one of the four words in the choices most nearly means the same as the underlined boldface word, then mark the space on your answer form which has the same number and letter as your choice.

1. **Inform** most nearly means

   1-A Ask.   1-B Heed.
   1-C Tell.   1-D Ignore.

2. **Crimson** most nearly means

   2-A Crisp.
   2-B Neatly Pressed.
   2-C Reddish.
   2-D Colorful.

3. **Caution** most nearly means

   3-A Signals.   3-B Care.
   3-C Traffic.   3-D Haste.

4. **Intermittently** most nearly means

   4-A Constantly.
   4-B Annually.
   4-C Using intermediaries (to stay).
   4-D At irregular intervals.

5. **Occurrence** most nearly means

   5-A Event.   5-B Place.
   5-C Occupation.   5-D Opinion.

6. **Deception** most nearly means

   6-A Secrets.
   6-B Fraud.
   6-C Mistrust.
   6-D Hatred.

7. **Cease** most nearly means

   7-A Start.   7-B Change.
   7-C Continue.   7-D Stop.

8. **Acclaim** most nearly means

   8-A Amazement.   8-B Laughter.
   8-C Booing.   8-D Applause.

9. **Erect** most nearly means

   9-A Paint.
   9-B Design.
   9-C Destroy.
   9-D Construct.

10. **Relish** most nearly means

    10-A Care.   10-B Speed.
    10-C Amusement.   10-D Enjoy.

11. **Sufficient** most nearly means

    11-A Durable.
    11-B Substitution.
    11-C Expendable.
    11-D Appropriate.

12. **Fortnight** most nearly means

    12-A Two weeks.   12-B One week.
    12-C Two months. 12-D One month.

13. **Blemish** most nearly means

    13-A Defect
    13-B Mixture.
    13-C Accusation.
    13-D Decoration.

14. **Impose** most nearly means

    14-A Disguise.   14-B Escape.
    14-C Require.   14-D Purchase.

15. **Jeer** most nearly means

    15-A Peek.
    15-B Scoff.
    15-C Turn.
    15-D Judge.

16. **Alias** most nearly means

    16-A Enemy.
    16-B Sidekick.
    16-C Hero.
    16-D Other name.

17. **Impair** most nearly means.

    17-A Direct.
    17-B Improve.
    17-C Weaken.
    17-D Stimulate.

18. **Itinerant** most nearly means.

    18-A Traveling.
    18-B Shrewd.
    18-C Insurance.
    18-D Aggressive.

19. **Abandon** most nearly means.

    19-A Relinguish.
    19-B Encompass.
    19-C Infiltrate.
    19-D Quarantine.

20. **Resolve** most nearly means.

    20-A End.
    20-B Understand.
    20-C Recall.
    20-D Forget.

21. **Ample** means

    21-A Plentiful.
    21-B Enthusiastic.
    21-C Well shaped.
    21-D Fat.

22. **Stench** most nearly means.

    22-A Puddle of slimy water.
    22-B Pile of debris.
    22-C Foul odor.
    22-D Dead animal.

23. **Sullen** most nearly means.

    23-A Grayish yellow.
    23-B Soaking wet.
    23-C Very dirty.
    23-D Angrily silent.

24. **Rudiments** most nearly means.

    24-A Basic methods and procedures.
    24-B Politics.
    24-C Promotion opportunities.
    24-D Minute details.

25. **Clash** most nearly means:

    25-A Applaud.
    25-B Fasten.
    25-C Conflict.
    25-D Punish.

26. **Camaraderie** most nearly means.

    26-A Interest in photography.
    26-B Close friendship.
    26-C Petty jealousies.
    26-D Arts and crafts projects.

27. **Superficial** most nearly means.

    27-A Excellent.
    27-B Official.
    27-C Profound.
    27-D Cursory.

28. **Tapestry** most nearly means.

    28-A Fabric of woven designs.
    28-B Tent
    28-C Piece of elaborate jewelry.
    28-D Exquisite painting.

29. **Terse** most nearly means.

    29-A Pointed.
    29-B Trivial.
    29-C Oral.
    29-D Lengthy.

30. **Concoction** most nearly means.

    30-A Combination of ingredients.
    30-B Appetizer.
    30-C Drink made of wine and spices.
    30-D Relish tray.

PART 5

ARITHMETIC REASONING

TIME: 20 Minutes. 20 Questions.

This test has questions about arithmetic. Each question is followed by four possible answers. Decide which answer is correct, then blacken the space on your answer form which has the same number and letter as your choice. Use your scratch paper for any figuring you wish to do.

Your score on this test will be based on the number of questions you answer correctly. You should try to answer every question. Do not spend too much time on any one question.

31. A fruit picker gets $2.00 an hour plus 48¢ for every bushel over 40 that he picks in a day. If he works 8 hours and picks 50 bushels, how much will he get?

31-A $16.00
31-B $19.84
31-C $20.80
31-D $24.00

32. How many 36 passenger buses will it take to carry 144 people?

32-A 4
32-B 3
32-C 5
32-D 6

33. A gallon contains 4 quarts. A cartoning machine can fill 120 one-quart cartons a minute. How long will it take to put 600 gallons of orange juice into cartons?

33-A 1 minute and 15 seconds
33-B 5 minutes
33-C 10 minutes
33-D 20 minutes

34. A man who runs a filling station greased 168 cars in 28 days. What was his daily average of cars greased?

34-A 5
34-B 6
34-C 7
34-D 8

35. What is the fifth term in the series: 4½; 8¾; 13; 17¼; _____?

35-A 20¾
35-B 21
35-C 21½
35-D 21¾

36. Three girls assemble 360 switches per hour, but 5% of the switches are defective. How many good (nondefective) switches will these 3 girls assemble in an 8-hour shift?

36-A 2736
36-B 2880
36-C 2944
36-D 3000

37. The butcher made 22½ pounds of beef into hamburger and wrapped it in 1¼-pound packages. How many packages did he make?

37-A 15
37-B 16
37-C 17
37-D 18

38. A car-renting agency charges a fixed rate of $8 per day plus 8 cents per mile. If a family paid the agency $260 for the use of a car on a 2,450-mile trip, how many days was the car used?

38-A 8 days   38-B 24½ days
38-C 26 days   38-D 32 days

39. It cost a boy $13.50 to take a girl out for the evening. Sixty per cent of this was for theater tickets. What was the cost for each ticket?

   39-A $3.95
   39-B $4.05
   39-C $5.40
   39-D $8.10

40. Soap, ordinarily priced at 2 bars for $0.66, may be purchased in lots of one dozen for $3.48. What is the saving per bar when it is purchased in this way?

   40-A 4 cents
   40-B 8 cents
   40-C 16 cents
   40-D 19 cents

41. Twenty men contribute $25 each for a Christmas party. Forty percent of the money is spent for food and drinks. How much is left for other expenses?

   41-A $125
   41-B $200
   41-C $300
   41-D $375

42. A pole 24 feet high has a shadow 8 feet long. A nearby pole is 72 feet high. How long is its shadow?

   42-A 16 feet
   42-B 24 feet
   42-C 32 feet
   42-D 56 feet

43. The price of a $250 item after successive discounts of 20% and 30% is

   43-A $125
   43-B $130
   43-C $140
   43-D $180

44. If the following series will continue in the same pattern, what is the next number in the series 1, 10, 7, 16, _____?

   44-A 10
   44-B 13
   44-C 14
   44-D 25

45. A home has a tax rate of 2%. If the tax is $550.00, what is the assessed value of the home?

   45-A $1,100.00
   45-B $2,750.00
   45-C $11,000.00
   45-D $27,500.00

46. The parcel post rate in the local zone is 18 cents for the first pound and 1½ cents for each additional pound. How many pounds can be sent in the local zone for $1.50?

   46-A 88
   46-B 89
   46-C 100
   46-D 225

47. The minute hand fell off a watch but the watch continued to work accurately. What time was it when the hour hand was at the 17-minute mark?

   47-A 3:02
   47-B 3:17
   47-C 3:24
   47-D 4:17

48. A dressmaker has 3,375 yards of material on hand. If the average dress takes 3⅜ yards of material, how many dresses can he make?

   48-A 844
   48-B 1000
   48-C 1125
   48-D 1250

49. It cost $0.50 per square yard to waterproof canvas. What will it cost to waterproof a canvas truck cover that is 15′ x 24′?

   49-A $6.67
   49-B $18.00
   49-C $20.00
   49-D $180.00

50. Mary put in a total of 16½ hours baby-sitting during 5 days of the past week. What was her average work day?

   50-A 3 hours
   50-B 3 hours, 15 minutes
   50-C 3 hours, 18 minutes
   50-D 3 hours, 25 minutes

PART 6

SPACE PERCEPTION

TIME: 12 Minutes. 20 Questions.

This test has questions about folding cardboard patterns into boxes. The first row of pictures below shows what this means. The dotted lines show where folds are to be made. The last picture shows the box that has been made by folding.

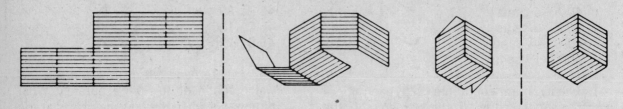

In the test, the first picture in each row shows a cardboard pattern that is to be folded. There are also four boxes in each row, labeled A, B, C, D. Your job is to find which box could be made by folding the pattern.

Look at the sample question. Which box could this pattern make?

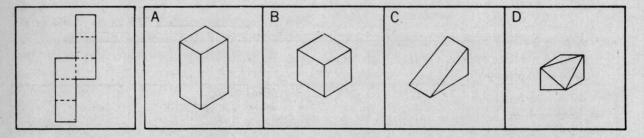

The B answer is correct.

Here is another type of question. Which of the four patterns would result when the box is unfolded?

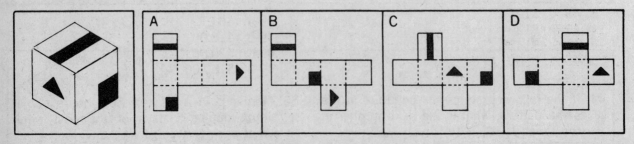

The D answer is correct.

Your score on this test will be based on the number of questions you answer correctly. You should try to answer every question. Do not spend too much time on any one question.

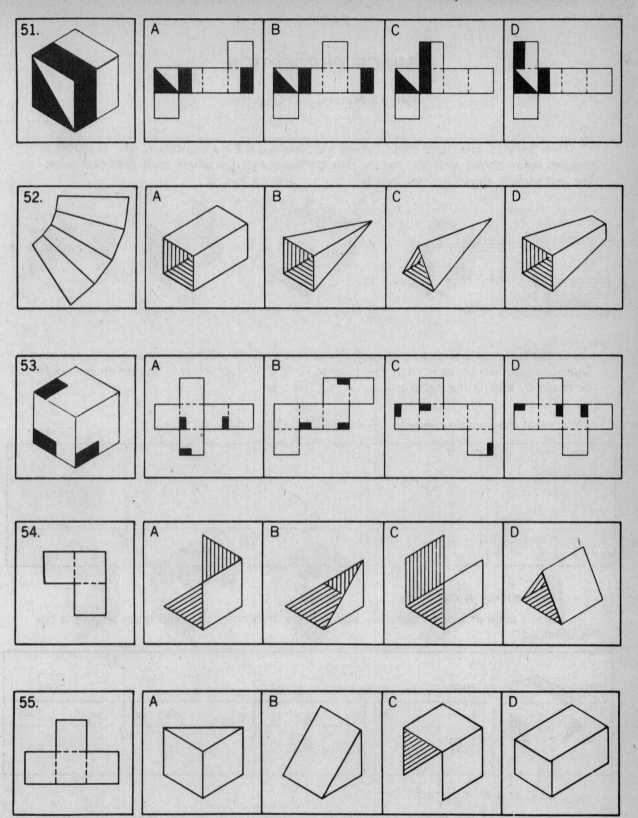

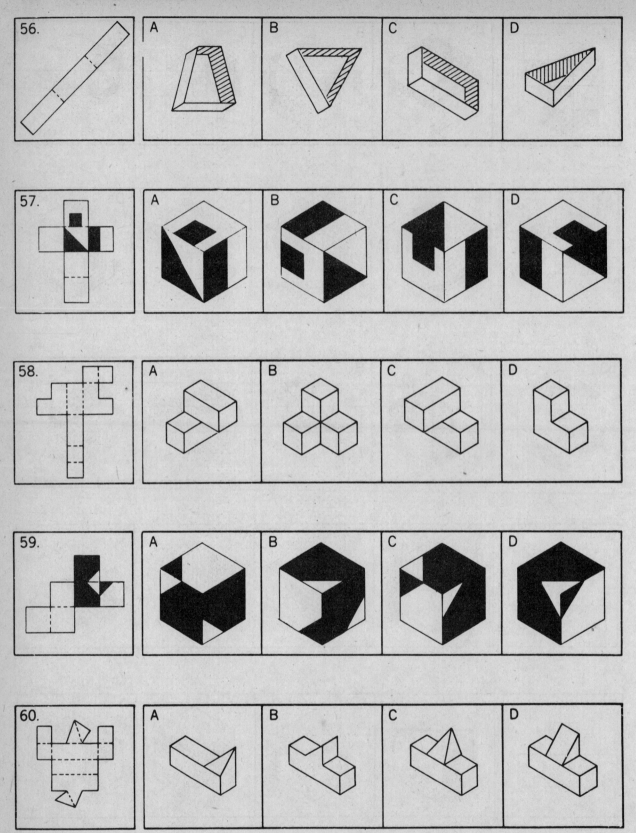

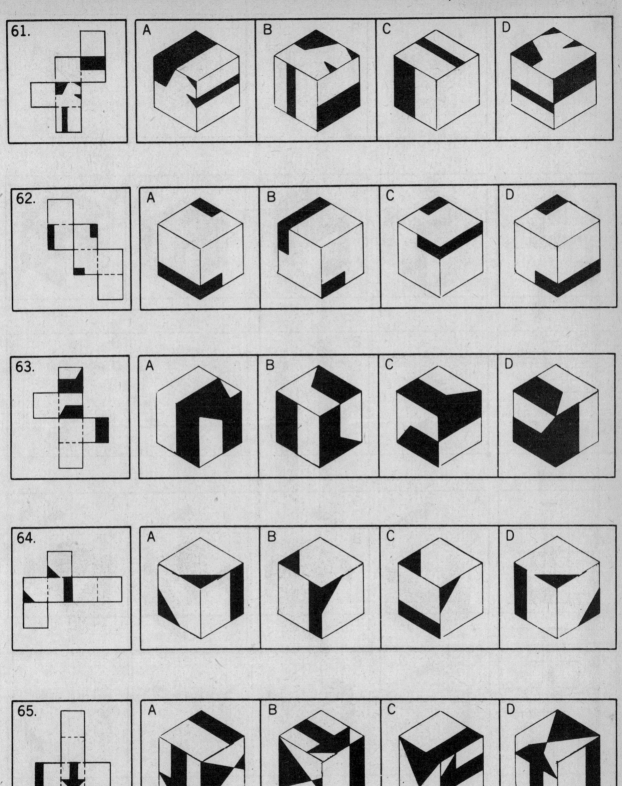

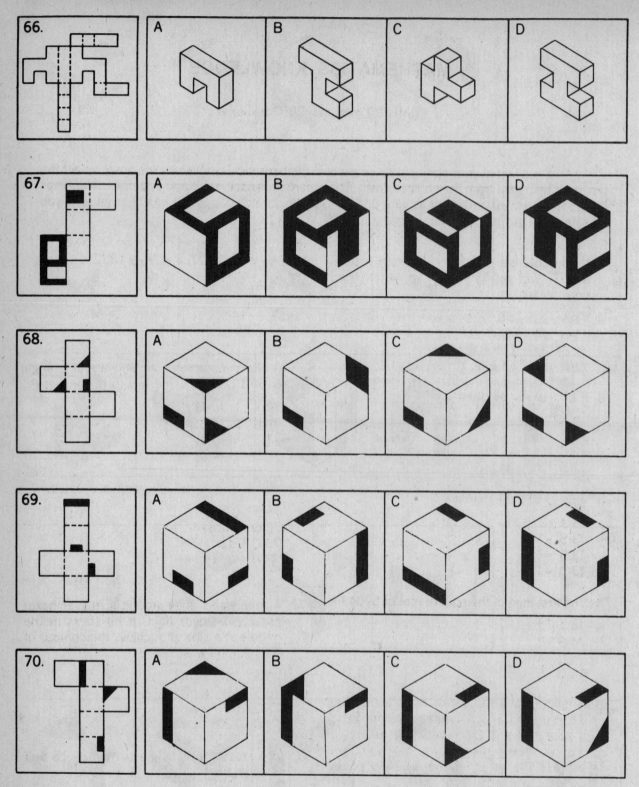

PART 7

MATHEMATICS KNOWLEDGE

TIME: 20 Minutes. 20 Questions.

This is a test of your ability to solve general mathematical problems. You are to select the correct response from the choices given. Then mark the space on your answer form which has the same number and letter as your choice. Use the scratch paper that has been given to you to do any figuring that you wish.

71. If you subtract 6a – 4b + 3c from a polynomial, you get 4a + 9b – 5c. What is the polynomial?

  71-A 10a – 5b + 2c
  71-B 10a + 5b – 2c
  71-C 2a + 13b – 8c
  71-D 2a + 5b + 8c

72. If 50% of x = 66, then x =

  72-A 33
  72-B 99
  72-C 122
  72-D None of these

73. If 3x = –5, then x equals

  73-A 3/5
  73-B – 5/3
  73-C – 3/5
  73-D – 2

74. The first digit of the square root of 59043 is

  74-A 2
  74-B 3
  74-C 4
  74-D 5

75. A mixture of 200 pounds of coffee costing $1.06 and $1.26 a pound was sold for $1.15 a pound. If x is the number of pounds of $1.06 coffee in the mixture, how would you express the value of the $1.26 a pound coffee?

  75-A $1.26 – $1.06x
  75-B $1.26(200 – x)
  75-C $1.15(200) – $1.26x/$1.06x
  75-D $1.15($1.06x – 200)

76. The value of 27/8 x 24/9 ÷ 3/2 =

  76-A 6
  76-B 7 2/9
  76-C 8 1/4
  76-D 9 5/8

77. If the perimeter of an equilateral triangle is 6n-12, what is the length of the base?

  77-A 3(2n-4)
  77-B 2(3n-6)
  77-C 3n-6
  77-D 2n-4

78. Which one of the following is a polygon?

  78-A Circle
  78-B Ellipse
  78-C Star
  78-D Parabola

79. A man walks once around a regular hexagonal (six-sided) field. If he starts in the middle of a side and follows the contour of the field, he will make 6

  79-A 30° turns
  79-B 45° turns
  79-C 60° turns
  79-D 120° turns

80. The area of a rectangle 12 feet by 18 feet is equal to

  80-A 8 sq yds
  80-B 24 sq yds
  80-C 36 sq yds
  80-D 72 sq yds

81. Given the formulas d = rt and A = r + d/t, which formula below correctly expresses the value of A without using t?

    81-A   A = dr
    81-B   A = r + 2d/r
    81-C   A = 2r + d
    81-D   A = 2r

82. If a + 6 = 7, then a is equal to

    82-A   0
    82-B   1
    82-C   −1
    82-D   7/6

83. The distance in miles around a circular course with a radius of 35 miles is (use Pi = 22/7)

    83-A   156
    83-B   220
    83-C   440
    83-D   880

84. The expression "3 factorial" equals

    84-A   1/9
    84-B   1/6
    84-C   6
    84-D   9

85. If you multiply x + 3 by 2x + 5, how many x's will there be in the product?

    85-A   3
    85-B   6
    85-C   9
    85-D   11

86. Solve for x: $\frac{2x}{7} = 2x^2$

    86-A   1/7
    86-B   2/7
    86-C   2
    86-D   7

87. Solve the following equation for C

    $$A^2 = \frac{B^2}{C + D}$$

    87-A $C = \frac{B^2 - A^2D}{A^2B}$

    87-B $C = \frac{A^2 - D}{B^2}$

    87-C $C = \frac{A^2 + D}{B^2 - D}$

    87-D $C = \frac{B^2 - D}{A^2}$

88. The expression, −1 (3 −2), is equal to

    88-A   −3 + 2
    88-B   −3 − 2
    88-C   3 − 2
    88-D   3 + 2

89. The reciprocal of 5 is

    89-A   1.0
    89-B   0.5
    89-C   0.2
    89-D   0.1

90. What is the area, in square inches, of a circle whose radius measures

    7 inches? (Use $\frac{22}{7}$ for Pi)

    90-A   22
    90-B   44
    90-C   154
    90-D   616

STOP!

IF YOU FINISH THIS PART BEFORE THE TIME IS UP, CHECK OVER YOUR WORK ON THIS PART ONLY. DO NOT GO ON UNTIL YOU ARE TOLD TO DO SO.

PART 8

ELECTRONICS INFORMATION

TIME: 15 Minutes. 30 Questions.

This is a test of your knowledge of electrical, radio, and electronics information. You are to select the correct response from the choices given. Then mark the space on your answer form which has the same number and letter as your choice.

91. The most likely cause of a burned-out fuse in the primary circuit of a transformer in a rectifier is

   91-A grounding of the electrostatic shield.
   91-B an open circuit in a bleeder resistor.
   91-C an open circuit in the secondary. winding.
   91-D a short-circuited filter capacitor.

92. The primary coil of a power transformer has 100 turns and the secondary coil has 50 turns. The voltage across the secondary will be

   92-A four times that of the primary.
   92-B twice that of the primary.
   92-C half that of the primary.
   92-D one-fourth that of the primary.

93. The best electrical connection between two wires is obtained when

   93-A the insulations are melted together
   93-B all insulation is removed and the wires bound together with friction tape.
   93-C both are wound on a common binding post.
   93-D they are soldered together.

94. Excessive resistance in the primary circuit will lessen the output of the ignition coil and cause the

   94-A battery to short out and the generator to run down.
   94-B battery to short out and the plugs to wear out prematurely.
   94-C generator to run down and the timing mechanism to slow down.
   94-D engine to perform poorly and hard to start.

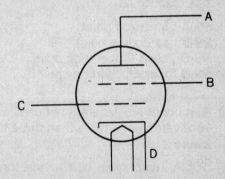

95. In the schematic vacuum tube illustrated, the cathode is element

   95-A A.
   95-B B.
   95-C C.
   95-D D.

96. The main reason for making wire stranded is

    96-A to make it easier to insulate.
    96-B so that the insulation will not come off.
    96-C to decrease its weight.
    96-D to make it more flexible.

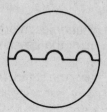

97. The oscilloscope image shown above represents

    97-A steady DC.
    97-B resistance in a resistor.
    97-C AC.
    97-D pulsating DC.

98. Voltage drop in a circuit is usually due to

    98-A inductance.
    98-B capacitance.
    98-C resistance.
    98-D conductance.

99. If an increase in grid voltage no longer produces an increase in plate current, the tube has reached its

    99-A inversion point.
    99-B saturation point.
    99-C class C operating point.
    99-D class A operating point.

100. Earphones are generally not used with radio receivers having more than three tubes because

    100-A earphones can handle only alternating current.
    100-B the amplification factor makes them unnecessary.
    100-C only one person may hear them at a time.
    100-D earphones are too delicate for normal use.

101. Of the non-metallic elements listed below, which one is the best conductor of electricity?

    101-A Mica.
    101-B Carbon.
    101-C Formica.
    101-D Hard rubber.

102. If an electric motor designed for use on AC is plugged into a DC source, what will probably happen?

    102-A Excessive heat will be produced.
    102-B It will operate the same as usual.
    102-C It will continue to operate, but will not get so warm.
    102-D It cannot be predicted what will happen.

103. Most electrical problems involving voltage, resistance, and current are solved by applying

    103-A Ohm's Law.
    103-B Watt's Law.
    103-C Coulomb's Law.
    103-D Kirchoff's Voltage and Current Laws.

104. If every time a washing machine is started the circuit breaker must be reset, the **best** solution would be to

    104-A oil the motor in the washer.
    104-B replace the circuit breaker.
    104-C tape the breaker switch closed.
    104-D repair the timing mechanism.

105. In most AC-DC radio circuits when one tube filament burns out, it will

    105-A cause the others to burn out
    105-B open the circuit and keep the others from operating.
    105-C cause the remaining ones to operate at higher current ratings.
    105-D cause the line voltage to drop.

106. The most stable type of radio oscillating circuit is the

    106-A   electron-coupled.
    106-B   crystal.
    106-C   heterodyne.
    106-D   colpitts.

107. The ampere is the unit of measurement of

    107-A   inductance.
    107-B   resistance
    107-C   voltage.
    107-D   current.

108. Hoping to make his car run faster, a "hot-rodder" decides to try changing the ignition mechanism. He finds all the components in good working order, so he decides to

    108-A   use a larger capacitor on the points.
    108-B   retard the ignition several degrees.
    108-C   put hotter spark plugs in the engine.
    108-D   check the ignition timing.

109. A mixer, in radio terminology, would function to

    109-A   jumble a carrier wave for security transmissions.
    109-B   couple the stages of two succeeding circuits.
    109-C   coordinate the triodes in a push-pull power amplifier circuit.
    109-D   combine the incoming and local oscillator frequencies.

110. Flux is used in the process of soldering together two conductors in order to

    110-A   provide a luster finish.
    110-B   prevent oxidation when the connection is heated.
    110-C   maintain the temperature of the soldering iron.
    110-D   prevent the connection from becoming overheated.

111. Which of the following devices converts heat energy directly into electrical energy?

    111-A   A piezoelectric crystal.
    111-B   A photoelectric cell.
    111-C   A steam driven generator.
    111-D   A thermocouple.

112. One use of a coaxial cable is to

    112-A   ground a signal.
    112-B   pass a signal from the set to the antenna of a mobile unit
    112-C   carry the signal from a ballast tube.
    112-D   carry grid signals in high altitude areas.

113. Which of the following has the **least** resistance?

    113-A   silver.
    113-B   aluminum.
    113-C   copper.
    113-D   iron.

114. A rectifier is used to convert

    114-A   alternating current into direct current.
    114-B   static current into direct current.
    114-C   direct current into alternating current.
    114-D   low frequency current into high frequency current.

115. The length of a radio transmitter antenna system is primarily determined by

    115-A   transmitter power.
    115-B   transmitter frequency.
    115-C   oscillator voltage.
    115-D   distance from receiving antenna.

116. Which one of the following may best be compared to electrical voltage?

    116-A   Tension.
    116-B   Resistance.
    116-C   Flow.
    116-D   Pressure.

117. The extent to which a radio receiver converts the signals received into sounds that
are undistorted is called

    117-A fidelity.
    117-B sensitivity.
    117-C selectivity.
    117-D resonance.

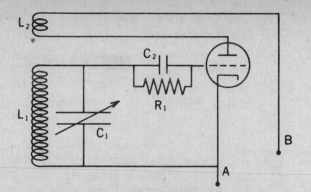

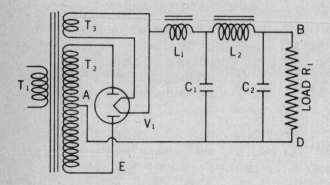

118. The tube in the figure above acts as a

    118-A voltage regulator.
    118-B voltage divider.
    118-C half-wave rectifier.
    118-D full-wave rectifier.

119. The oscillator in the circuit in the figure
shown above is known as a

    119-A tuned-grid oscillator.
    119-B tuned-plate oscillator.
    119-C electron-coupled oscillator.
    119-D resistance feedback.

120. The power supply in a vacuum tube equipped
auto radio differs from the power supply in an
AC home radio in that the former utilizes a

    120-A filter capacitor.
    120-B choke.
    120-C vibrator.
    120-D rectifier tube.

STOP!

**IF YOU FINISH THIS PART BEFORE THE TIME IS UP, CHECK OVER
YOUR WORK ON THIS PART ONLY. DO NOT GO ON UNTIL YOU ARE
TOLD TO DO SO.**

PART 9

MECHANICAL COMPREHENSION

TIME: 15 Minutes. 20 Questions.

This test has questions about mechanical and physical principles. Study the pictures and decide which answer is correct. Then mark the space on your separate answer form which has the same number and letter as your choice.

Here is a sample question.

Which bridge is the strongest?

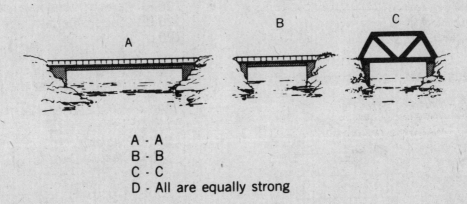

A - A
B - B
C - C
D - All are equally strong

The C answer is correct.

Your score on this test will be based on the number of questions you answer correctly. You should try to answer every question. Do not spend too much time on any one question.

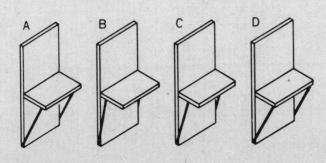

121. Which shelf could support the most weight?

121-A A.
121-B B.
121-C C.
121-D D.

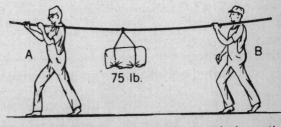

75 lb.

122. The weight is being carried entirely on the shoulders of the two men shown. Which man bears the most weight on his shoulder?

122-A A.
122-B B.
122-C Both men are carrying the same.
122-D It is impossible to tell.

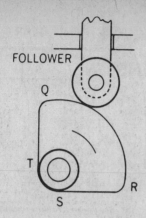

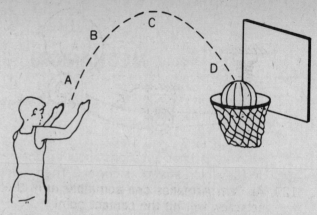

123. The follower is at its highest position between points

123-A Q and R.
123-B R and S.
123-C S and T.
123-D T and Q.

126. At which point was the basketball moving slowest?

126-A A.
126-B B.
126-C C.
126-D D.

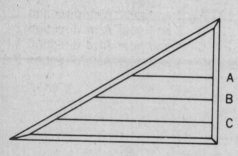

124. All of the wires are of the same substance, the same diameter, and under the same tension. Which will vibrate at the highest frequency?

124-A A.
124-B B.
124-C C.
124-D They will vibrate at equal frequency

125. A man in an elevator is carrying a heavy suitcase. The suitcase will feel heaviest to him when the elevator

125-A has not yet started moving.
125-B is gaining speed in descent.
125-C is maintaining a rapid steady speed of descent.
125-D is gaining speed in ascent.

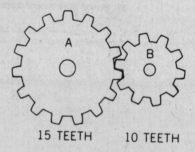

15 TEETH   10 TEETH

127. If gear A makes 14 revolutions, gear B will make

127-A 21.
127-B 17.
127-C 14.
127-D 9.

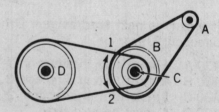

128. If pulley A is the driver and turns in direction 1, which pulley turns fastest?

128-A A.
128-B B.
128-C C.
128-D D.

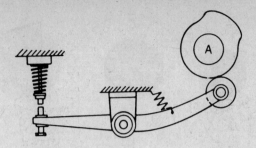

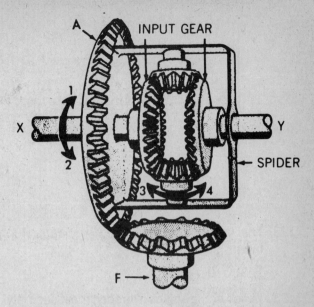

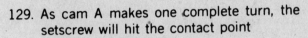

129. As cam A makes one complete turn, the setscrew will hit the contact point

    129-A Once.
    129-B Twice.
    129-C Three times.
    129-D Not at all.

131. If shaft X turns in direction 2 as shaft Y is held fixed, shaft F will turn in direction

    131-A 3 and gear A in direction 1.
    131-B 3 and gear A in direction 2.
    131-C 4 and gear A in direction 1.
    131-D 4 and gear A in direction 2.

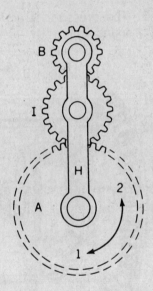

130. If arm H is held fixed as gear B turns in direction 2, gear

    130-A A must turn in direction 1.
    130-B A must turn in direction 2.
    130-C I must turn in direction 2.
    130-D A must be held fixed.

132. A 150-pound man jumps off a 600-pound raft to a point in the water 12 feet away. Theoretically, the raft would move

    132-A 12 feet in the same direction.
    132-B 6 feet in the same direction.
    132-C 3 feet in the opposite direction.
    132-D 1 foot in the opposite direction.

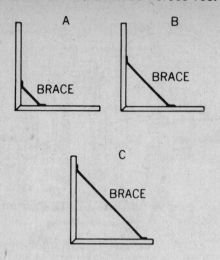

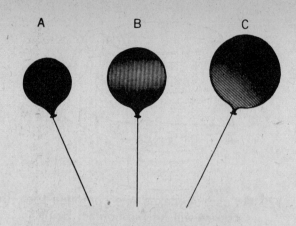

133. Which of the angles is braced most securely?

133-A   A.

133-B   B.

133-C   C.

133-D   All equally braced.

135. The amount of gas in the balloons is equal. The atmospheric pressure outside the balloons is highest on which balloon?

135-A   A.

135-B   B.

135-C   C.

135-D   The pressure is equal on all balloons.

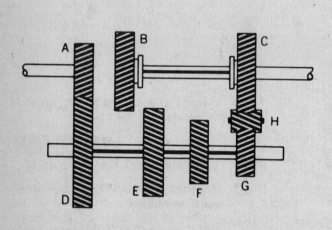

134. Gear B is intended to mesh with

134-A   gear A only.

134-B   gear D only.

134-C   gear E only.

134-D   all of the above gears.

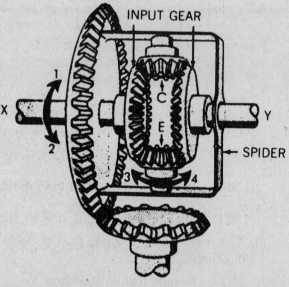

136. If shaft X turns in direction 1 and shaft Y is held fixed, gear C will turn in direction

136-A   3 and gear E in direction 3.

136-B   3 and gear E in direction 4.

136-C   4 and gear E in direction 3.

136-D   4 and gear E in direction 4.

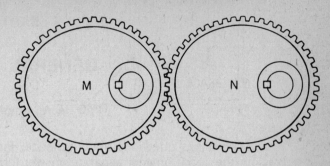

137. Liquid is being transferred from the barrel to the bucket by

137-A Suction in the hose.
137-B Fluid pressure in the hose.
137-C Air pressure on top of the liquid.
137-D Capillary action.

139. If gear N turns at a constant rpm, gear M turns at

139-A The same constant rpm as N.

139-B A faster constant rpm than N.

139-C A slower constant rpm than N.

139-D A variable rpm.

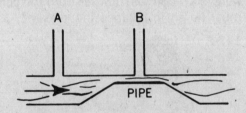

138. If water is pumped rapidly through the pipe in the direction shown by the arrow, it will

138-A Rise higher in tube A than in tube B.

138-B Rise higher in tube B than in tube A.

138-C Rise in tube A but not in tube B.

138-D Rise in tube B but not in tube A.

140. If gear M turns at a constant rpm, gear N turns at a number of rpm that

140-A Is constant and less than that of M.

140-B Is constant and the same as M.

140-C Reaches its maximum four times each revolution.

140-D Reaches its maximum eight times each revolution.

STOP!

IF YOU FINISH THIS PART BEFORE THE TIME IS UP, CHECK OVER YOUR WORK ON THIS PART ONLY. DO NOT GO ON UNTIL YOU ARE TOLD TO DO SO.

PART 10

GENERAL SCIENCE

TIME: 10 Minutes. 20 Questions.

This test has questions about science. Pick the best answer for each question, then blacken the space on your separate answer form which has the same number and letter as your choice.

141. Which of the following operates by suction?

    141-A A riveting hammer.
    141-B A balloon.
    141-C A vacuum cleaner.
    141-D An electric fan.

142. If a 33 1/3 rpm phonograph record is played at a speed of 45 rpm, it will

    142-A Sound lower-pitched.
    142-B Sound higher-pitched.
    142-C Give no sound.
    142-D Play louder.

143. The chief nutrient in lean meat is

    143-A Starch.
    143-B Protein.
    143-C Fat.
    143-D Carbohydrates.

144. Which one of the following metals is a liquid at room temperature?

    144-A Mercury.
    144-B Molybdenum.
    144-C Cobalt.
    144-D Magnesium.

145. The absence of any gravitational pull on an object is called

    145-A Weightlessness.
    145-B Mass.
    145-C Kinetic energy.
    145-D Force.

146. "Shooting stars" are

    146-A Exploding stars.
    146-B Cosmic rays.
    146-C Planetoids.
    146-D Meteors.

147. Two children are seated on a seesaw. The first child, seated 4 feet from the center, weighs 80 pounds. If the second child weighs 40 pounds, how far from the center must he sit to balance the seesaw?

    147-A 1 foot.
    147-B 2 feet.
    147-C 8 feet.
    147-D 16 feet.

148. A test for the presence of oxygen is that it

    148-A Turns limewater milky.
    148-B Turns litmus red.
    148-C Puts out a match.
    148-D Causes a glowing splinter to burst into flame.

149. An eclipse of the sun throws the shadow of the

    149-A Earth on the moon.
    149-B Moon on the earth.
    149-C Moon on the sun.
    149-D Earth on the sun.

150. Hearing an echo is most like seeing

    150-A Around the corner through a periscope.
    150-B Fine print under strong illumination.
    150-C Stars at night that are invisible in the daytime.
    150-D One's image in a mirror.

151. A thermometer which indicates the freezing point of water at zero degrees and the boiling point of water at 100 degrees is called the

151-A Centigrade thermometer..
151-B Fahrenheit thermometer.
151-C Reaumer thermometer.
151-D Kelvin thermometer.

152. Refraction of light affects the aim one should take when

152-A Shooting at a fish that has jumped out of the water.
152-B Spearing a fish in the water from the bank.
152-C Spearing a fish under water when one is swimming under water.
152-D Casting a fly on the surface of the water.

153. The primary reason designers seek to lower the center of gravity in automobiles is to

153-A Reduce wind resistance.
153-B Provide smoother riding.
153-C Increase stability.
153-D Reduce manufacturing costs.

154. Substances which hasten a chemical reaction without themselves undergoing change are called

154-A Buffers.
154-B Catalysts.
154-C Colloids.
154-D Reducers.

155. The change from ice to water is

155-A A chemical change.
155-B An elementary change.
155-C A physical change.
155-D A solid-state change.

156. The principle function of an air conditioner, aside from regulating heat, is to regulate the air's

156-A Speed of motion.
156-B Moisture content.
156-C Oxygen content.
156-D Density.

157. Lack of iodine is often related to which of the following diseases?

157-A Beriberi.
157-B Scurvy.
157-C Rickets.
157-D Goiter.

158. Why will a given quantity of steam always produce a more severe burn than that produced by the same quantity of boiling water?

158-A Steam always penetrates the epidermis.
158-B Steam causes the skin to contract and break.
158-C Steam always releases more heat per gram than water.
158-D Steam always covers more area of the skin.

159. A lead sinker weighs 54 grams in air, 23.8 grams in liquid A, and 28.6 grams in liquid B. From this information, what conclusions can be drawn concerning the densities of the two liquids?

159-A Liquid A has a greater density than liquid B.
159-B Both liquids are more dense than water.
159-C Both liquids are less dense than water.
159-D No conclusions can be drawn concerning the densities of the two liquids.

160. After adding a solute to a liquid, the freezing point of the liquid is

160-A Lowered.
160-B The same.
160-C Raised.
160-D Inverted.

PART 11

SHOP INFORMATION

TIME: 8 Minutes. 20 Questions.

This test has questions about shop practices and the use of tools. Pick the best answer for each question, then blacken the space on your separate answer form which has the same number and letter as your choice.

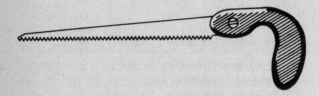

161. The saw shown above is used mainly to cut

161-A across the grain of wood.
161-B along the grain of wood.
161-C plywood.
161-D odd-shaped holes in wood.

162. Concrete is usually made by mixing

162-A only sand and water.
162-B only cement and water.
162-C lye, cement, and water.
162-D rock, sand, cement, and water.

163. The set of a saw is the

163-A angle at which the handle is set.
163-B amount of springiness of the blade.
163-C amount of sharpness of the teeth.
163-D distance the points stick out beyond the sides of the blade.

164. The principal reason for "tempering" or "drawing" steel is to

164-A reduce strength.
164-B reduce hardness.
164-C increase strength.
164-D increase maleability.

165. Sheet metal is dipped in sulphuric acid to

165-A clean it.
165-B soften it.
165-C harden it.
165-D prevent it from rusting.

166. The cut of a file refers to the

166-A shape of its handle.
166-B shape of its edge.
166-C kind of metal it is made of.
166-D kind of teeth it has.

167. In grinding a good point on a twist drill, it is necessary that

167-A the point be extremely sharp.
167-B both cutting edges have the same lip.
167-C a file be used for the entire cutting process.
167-D the final grinding be done by hand.

168. The tool used to locate a point directly below a ceiling hook is a

168-A a plumb bob.
168-B line level.
168-C transit.
168-D drop gauge.

169. The sawing of a piece of wood at a particular angle, for example 45 degrees, is accomplished by using a

169-A jointer.
169-B cant board.
169-C miter box.
169-D binder.

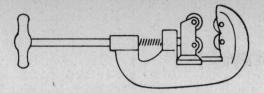

170. The tool above is a

    170-A   marking gauge.
    170-B   knurling tool.
    170-C   thread cutter.
    170-D   pipe cutter.

171. A high speed grinder operator will check the abrasive wheel before starting the machine because

    171-A   it must be wetted properly before use.
    171-B   if cracked or chipped, it could injure someone.
    171-C   a dry wheel will produce excessive sparks.
    171-D   previous work may have clogged the wheel.

172. When marking wood, an allowance of 1/16" to 1/8" should be made to allow for

    172-A   drying of the wood.
    172-B   absorption of water by wood.
    172-C   the width of the saw.
    172-D   knots in the wood.

173. A "pinch bar" is used for

    173-A   joining.
    173-B   leveling.
    173-C   prying.
    173-D   tightening.

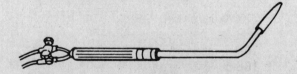

174. The tool shown above is used for

    174-A   pressure lubricating.
    174-B   welding steel plate.
    174-C   drilling small holes in tight places.
    174-D   holding small parts for heat treating.

175. The primary function of a power driven sabresaw is to

    175-A   cut angles.
    175-B   saw heavy wood stock.
    175-C   cut curves in flat wood.
    175-D   make perfectly straight cuts.

176. What tool is shown above?

    176-A   countersink.
    176-B   keyhole saw.
    176-C   hole saw.
    176-D   grinding wheel.

177. The tip of a soldering iron is usually made of

    177-A   iron
    177-B   steel
    177-C   lead
    177-D   copper

178. Which of the following is used with a miter box?

    178-A   back saw.
    178-B   keyhole saw.
    178-C   coping saw.
    178-D   compass saw.

179. The length of a six penny nail is about

    179-A   1 inch.
    179-B   2 inches.
    179-C   3 inches.
    179-D   4 inches.

180. High oil content or so-called "spar" varnish is used primarily for

    180-A   Finishing furniture.
    180-B   Obtaining a high-gloss finish.
    180-C   Finishing weather exposed surfaces.
    180-D   Finishing interior trim.

PART 12

AUTOMOTIVE INFORMATION

TIME: 10 Minutes. 20 Questions.

This test has questions about automobiles. Pick the best answer for each question, then blacken the space on your separate answer form which has the same number and letter as your choice.

Here is a sample question.

The most commonly used fuel for running automobile engines is

A - kerosene.
B - benzine.
C - crude oil.
D - gasoline.

Gasoline is the most commonly used fuel, so D is the correct answer.

Your score on this test will be based on the number of questions you answer correctly. You should try to answer every question. Do not spend too much time on any one question.

181. Which of the following devices prevents the generator/alternator from overcharging the battery in an automobile?
181-A Governor.
181-B Solenoid switch.
181-C Current regulator.
181-D Voltage regulator.

182. A torsion bar might be found in the
182-A Transmission.
182-B Distributor.
182-C Speedometer.
182-D Suspension.

183. A black gummy deposit in the end of the tail pipe of an automobile indicates that
183-A The automobile "burns" oil.
183-B There is probably a leak in the exhaust manifold.
183-C The timing is late.
183-D There are leaks in the exhaust valves.

184. What would be the most probable cause if an automobile has a weak spark at the plugs, "turns over" very slowly, and has dim headlights?

184-A Weak battery.
184-B Faulty condenser.
184-C Faulty ignition cable.
184-D Worn contact breaker points.

185. An automobile engine won't "turn over." If the battery charge is found to be normal, the next test would normally be for

185-A Defective starter motor.
185-B Short-circuited switches.
185-C Faulty battery cable connections.
185-D Defective generator.

186. The generator or alternator of an automobile engine is usually driven by the

    186-A   Camshaft.
    186-B   Flywheel.
    186-C   Fan belt.
    186-D   Cranking motor.

187. What source of trouble can be tested by removing a spark plug and holding a thumb over the spark plug hole while the engine is being cranked?

    187-A   Poor ignition.
    187-B   Low compression.
    187-C   High oil consumption.
    187-D   High fuel consumption.

188. If an automobile engine overheats while the radiator remains cold, the difficulty probably lies in

    188-A   Lack of engine oil.
    188-B   Stuck thermostat.
    188-C   Improper ignition timing.
    188-D   An overloaded engine.

189. It is best for an automobile's gas tank to be full or nearly-full to prevent

    189-A   gasoline from vaporizing in the fuel lines.
    189-B   moisture from condensing in the gas tank.
    189-C   drying out of the fuel pump.
    189-D   loss of vacuum in the vacuum line.

190. In troubleshooting the rear axle, an automobile is driven on a smooth road at 25 mph, and the accelerator is lightly pressed and released. If there is a "slapping" noise, the most probable trouble is

    190-A   a worn universal joint.
    190-B   an incorrect drive line angle.
    190-C   loose accelerator linkage.
    190-D   a bent transmission shaft.

191. An automobile handbrake is set tightly and the engine is idling at 30 mph road speed. If you shift into high gear, release the clutch, and the engine continues to run about the same, what would most likely need repair?

    191-A   clutch.
    191-B   throttle.
    191-C   high gear.
    191-D   carburetor.

192. The pistons of gasoline engines will sometimes increase in size so that they "stick" in the cylinder. This is often caused by

    192-A   low engine operating temperature.
    192-B   overheating of the engine.
    192-C   worn oil rings.
    192-D   worn compression rings.

193. If a 4-speed transmission makes noise when engaged in low gear, it will likely also make noise when in

    193-A   3rd gear.
    193-B   4th gear.
    193-C   reverse.
    193-D   neutral.

194. The letter "W" in the oil designation SAE 20-W means

    194-A   the oil was produced by a refinery in a western state.
    194-B   the oil is adapted for cold weather starting.
    194-C   the oil is water-soluble.
    194-D   it is a flushing oil.

195. What will happen if leaded gasoline is used in a car equipped with a catalytic converter

    195-A   intake valves will crack.
    195-B   catalytic converter will be damaged.
    195-C   engine will overheat.
    195-D   engine will begin backfiring.

196. Dual or multiple carburetors are used to obtain

    196-A a richer mixture of air and gasoline.
    196-B a more uniform distribution of fuel charge.
    196-C an overlapping of suction periods on one mixing tube.
    196-D flexibility of firing order.

197. If an automobile air conditioning system fails to cool, the first check to make is for

    197-A leaks in hoses.
    197-B malfunction of the compressor.
    197-C low oil level.
    197-D shortage of refrigerant.

198. If the air cleaner on an automobile engine becomes clogged, the effect on engine performance will be similar to that of a

    198-A partly closed choke valve.
    198-B vapor lock.
    198-C clogged fuel nozzle.
    198-D needle valve stuck in closed position.

199. Which of the following instruments can be used to adjust the air/fuel ratio, valve timing, and check for leaky head gaskets?

    199-A compression tester.
    199-B vacuum gauge.
    199-C timing light.
    199-D dwell meter.

200. In the operation of a gasoline engine, ignition coil failure is most often caused by

    200-A a low battery.
    200-B an overcharged battery.
    200-C burned coil terminal.
    200-D moisture entering coil case.

END OF EXAMINATION!

IF YOU FINISH BEFORE THE TIME IS UP, CHECK OVER YOUR WORK ON THIS PART ONLY. DO NOT GO BACK TO ANY PREVIOUS PART.

CORRECT ANSWERS FOR SPECIMEN ASVAB-5

(Please make every effort to answer the questions on your own before look-ing at these answers. You'll make faster progress by following this rule.)

PART 1—GENERAL INFORMATION

1.C	5.B	9.C	13.B	17.A
2.D	6.C	10.C	14.C	18.B
3.B	7.D	11.C	15.B	19.D
4.A	8.A	12.D	16.B	20.D

PART 2—NUMERICAL OPERATIONS

21.C	29.C	37.A	45.A	53.B	59.A	65.B
22.A	30.A	38.A	46.D	54.C	60.D	66.B
23.B	31.C	39.B	47.A	55.D	61.C	67.A
24.D	32.C	40.C	48.B	56.A	62.B	68.D
25.D	33.D	41.A	49.D	57.D	63.A	69.A
26.A	34.D	42.D	50.D	58.C	64.D	70.C
27.A	35.B	43.C	51.B			
28.C	36.D	44.B	52.D			

PART 3—ATTENTION TO DETAIL

71.13	76.14	81.15	86.11	91.13	96.12
72.12	77.15	82.15	87.13	92.15	97.15
73.12	78.14	83.13	88.13	93.13	98.15
74.11	79.12	84.15	89.12	94.14	99.11
75.13	80.14	85.14	90.15	95.12	100.11

PART 4—WORD KNOWLEDGE

1.C	6.B	11.D	16.D	21.A	26.B
2.C	7.D	12.A	17.C	22.C	27.D
3.B	8.D	13.A	18.A	23.D	28.A
4.D	9.D	14.C	19.A	24.A	29.A
5.A	10.D	15.B	20.A	25.C	30.A

PART 5—ARITHMETIC REASONING

31.C	35.C	39.B	43.C	47.C
32.A	36.A	40.A	44.B	48.B
33.D	37.D	41.C	45.D	49.C
34.B	38.A	42.B	46.B	50.C

PART 6—SPACE PERCEPTION

51.C	55.C	59.D	63.C	67.D
52.D	56.B	60.C	64.A	68.D
53.A	57.A	61.B	65.D	69.A
54.A	58.D	62.A	66.B	70.C

PART 7—MATHEMATICS KNOWLEDGE

71.B	75.B	79.C	83.B	87.D
72.D	76.A	80.B	84.C	88.A
73.B	77.D	81.D	85.D	89.C
74.A	78.C	82.B	86.A	90.C

PART 8—ELECTRONICS INFORMATION

91.D	96.D	101.B	106.B	111.D	116.D
92.C	97.D	102.A	107.D	112.B	117.A
93.D	98.C	103.A	108.D	113.A	118.D
94.D	99.B	104.B	109.D	114.A	119.A
95.D	100.B	105.B	110.B	115.B	120.C

PART 9—MECHANICAL COMPREHENSION

121.D	125.D	129.A	133.C	137.C
122.A	126.C	130.B	134.C	138.A
123.A	127.A	131.B	135.A	139.A
124.A	128.A	132.C	136.B	140.B

PART 10—GENERAL SCIENCE

141.C	145.A	149.B	153.C	157.D
142.B	146.D	150.D	154.B	158.C
143.B	147.C	151.A	155.C	159.A
144.A	148.D	152.B	156.B	160.A

PART 11—SHOP INFORMATION

161.D	165.A	169.C	173.C	177.D
162.D	166.D	170.D	174.B	178.A
163.D	167.B	171.B	175.C	179.B
164.C	168.A	172.C	176.C	180.C

PART 12—AUTOMOTIVE INFORMATION

181.D	185.C	189.B	193.C	197.D
182.D	186.C	190.A	194.B	198.A
183.A	187.B	191.A	195.B	199.B
184.A	188.B	192.B	196.B	200.D

SCORE SHEET—ASVAB 5

PART	NUMBER CORRECT		NUMBER OF QUESTIONS		
GENERAL INFORMATION	_____	÷ 15 =	_____	× 100 =	_____%
NUMERICAL OPERATIONS	_____	÷ 50 =	_____	× 100 =	_____%
ATTENTION TO DETAIL	_____	÷ 30 =	_____	× 100 =	_____%
WORD KNOWLEDGE	_____	÷ 30 =	_____	× 100 =	_____%
ARITHMETIC REASONING	_____	÷ 20 =	_____	× 100 =	_____%
SPACE PERCEPTION	_____	÷ 20 =	_____	× 100 =	_____%
MATHEMATICS KNOWLEDGE	_____	÷ 20 =	_____	× 100 =	_____%
ELECTRONICS INFORMATION	_____	÷ 30 =	_____	× 100 =	_____%
MECHANICAL COMPREHENSION	_____	÷ 20 =	_____	× 100 =	_____%
GENERAL SCIENCE	_____	÷ 20 =	_____	× 100 =	_____%
SHOP INFORMATION	_____	÷ 20 =	_____	× 100 =	_____%
AUTOMOTIVE INFORMATION	_____	÷ 20 =	_____	× 100 =	_____%
TOTAL	_____	÷ 295 =	_____	× 100 =	_____%

COMPARISON CHART

The parts of ASVAB-5 are not in the same order as the parts of the model exams. Skip around to fill in the blanks to compare your scores.

	Exam I	Exam II	Exam III	ASVAB 5
GENERAL SCIENCE	%	%	%	
ARITHMETIC REASONING	%	%	%	
WORD KNOWLEDGE	%	%	%	
PARAGRAPH COMPREHENSION	%	%	%	
NUMERICAL OPERATIONS	%	%	%	
CODING SPEED	%	%	%	
SPACE PERCEPTION	——	——	——	
AUTO & SHOP INFORMATION	%	%	%	
SHOP INFORMATION	——	——	——	
AUTOMOTIVE INFORMATION	——	——	——	
MATHEMATICS KNOWLEDGE	%	%	%	
MECHANICAL COMPREHENSION	%	%	%	
ELECTRONICS INFORMATION	%	%	%	
GENERAL INFORMATION	——	——	——	
TOTAL	%	%	%	